THE SIFFLER SYN

HOW TO SPEAK A FRENCH WITH ONLY 21 KILLER VERBS!

**A revolutionary approach
to speaking French
for beginners,
improvers and
experienced learners**

The only book you will ever need

Derek Davies

Published by Siffler Publications
Dedicated to perfecting your French

The Siffler Syndrome:
How to Speak Amazing French
With Only 21 Killer Verbs!

by
Derek Davies

Siffler Publications

To Karen and Bob, my target market.

ISBN 978-0-9931794-0-2

Printed by Short Run Press, Exeter.

Cover design by Richard Asplin

Acknowledgements

The list of people who have helped me in the preparation of this book is short but very sweet indeed: Geneviève Alves, Dr Mariette Ball, Jacqueline Mussotte, Valérie de Miler, Agnès and Thierry Pralong and Caroline Deayton, my executive assistant.

I am largely indebted to all those who lent their voices to the recording of all the conversations: Robert and Marie-Jo Castant, Bernard Culine, Monique and Geoffrey Grave, Jean-François and Maryse Guegan, Véronique Lambert, India Lebert, Philippe and Cécile Le Mée, Andre, Georgette and Annie Raynal, Lisa Sranquep, François Tur and Francine Valade.

The list of people who have fed my passion for France for over forty years is endless.

To my wife, goes a very special thank-you indeed. You organised the conversations effortlessly. How did you put up with me, Sue?

I am grateful to Éditions Gallimard for their kind permission to reproduce "Déjeuner du matin" by Jacques Prévert.

Foreward

Modern conventional wisdom has it that the **contextual** approach (at the baker's, at the dentist, at the airport etc…) is the best way to learn a language because it is likely to be more relevant. Perhaps. But the danger is that relevance consequently triumphs over rigour.

But languages are structured around **verbs** (and other parts of speech). Verbs are the beating heart of language; and where verbs in particular are concerned, the context matters very little indeed. If you want something – at the baker's, at the dentist's or at the airport, it does not really matter – you are likely to use one verb. That verb is "vouloir". "Je voudrais", I would like, you will use in all contexts. It is universal. Why? Because it allows you to express your needs, which are also universal. We all need to survive, to associate and to express ourselves. That is pretty much it.

So, in this book I adopt a **structural** approach, rather than a contextual approach. Yes, you will encounter many contexts on your journey through the book, particularly in Chapter Twenty-Four. But all the contexts serve merely to illustrate the structural role of the twenty-one most important verbs in the French language. A sound knowledge of the way these verbs are used by French people in daily conversation will bring you fluency in the language far more effectively and efficiently than learning all the vocabulary that would otherwise be necessary to handle the hundreds, if not thousands, of different contexts that you are likely to encounter throughout your French experience.

This is the rationale for this very original book.

Table of Contents

How to use this book

The book comprises an introductory chapter on French verbs in general, twenty-two verb chapters and a synoptic chapter putting all the verbs used into integrated context-related conversations. Each verb chapter is accompanied by self-assessment questions and answers.

It is not intended necessarily to be read cover-to-cover (though it can be). If you are a beginner you will probably read it **horizontally**, going through the **Basics** section of each verb first. When you feel you have mastered the basic level, you should go back to the first verb chapter and read it and every subsequent verb **vertically**, progressing through the other two levels, **Getting Better** and **Now You're Really Speaking French** for each verb in turn.

If you are already confident at basic French, you will simply progress from verb to verb in some sort of order, although you may well find the **Basics** section of each verb helpful for revision purposes.

The book comes with a CD containing all the conversations that come at the end of each verb chapter. Listen to them very carefully and very frequently.

I see it as a stand-alone work: you should need no other aid apart from a good grammar book. I recommend R. Hawkins and R. Towell, "French Grammar and Usage" (Hodder). But there are plenty of other good ones out there.

By all means consult other sources, the more the better. Once you feel confident enough, try dipping in to French newspapers and magazines. At first they will appear challenging, but you will soon get into them. I make no recommendations: it is a matter of taste and availability.

French films and music will help, too, of course, but, especially in the beginning, French-language films without sub-titles are difficult. French pop music is much easier; and "chanson", traditional French music as sung by Piaf, Brel and others is very clearly articulated indeed.

Finally, **go** to France – as often as possible. There is absolutely no substitute for putting into practice what you learn. And do not be fearful of making mistakes, the British disease. The French are very forgiving indeed!

If you already work or live in France, strive to give colour to your conversations using idiomatic expressions wherever appropriate. This book has more than enough for your needs. One day, perhaps quite soon, people will start to say, "vraiment, vous parlez bien le français, monsieur/madame." I cannot tell you how rewarding those few encouraging words sound. So, **bonne chance**!

Introduction

The Siffler Syndrome: How to Speak Amazing French
With Only 21 Killer Verbs!

If you are reading this book, my guess is that it's for one simple reason: **you want to speak better French**. And you want to speak better French for whatever reasons are relevant to you. Perhaps to go on holiday to a French-speaking country. Perhaps to take a French exam. Perhaps to spend some time working in France. Only you know.

But what I can guess is that you are approaching the task rather apprehensively. Maybe you feel that languages are not your bag (not even English, perhaps!) You may have learned some French at school and did not get on with it. Perhaps, if you are older, you feel that it is too late now to give it a go. Maybe you are being pressured at work by someone who believes you need better French – and this is discouraging you. Whatever your reason for feeling this way though, you want to learn it and improve. **That is the only thing that really matters**.

I know, because I, too, was once in your shoes and I know what it is like wearing them. Me? Well, I did not learn **any** French at school: Welsh and Latin were my foreign languages! It was not until I was 27 that I went to France for the first time. We were with some friends, my wife (then my girlfriend) and I and we drove to Spain in their car. Frankly, the holiday was more than a bit of a disaster: we did not like the part of Spain we had booked; and our two friends did nothing but quarrel. But the holiday was saved by the undisputed fact that a Brit, to go to Spain "en voiture" has to drive through **France** – there and back.

It was on theses two brief journeys through "la France profonde" (deep France, literally), that my wife and I fell in love with the country. On our return we vowed to learn some French, enough French so that at least we could return sometime soon and profit so much more from what the country clearly had to offer. **But how**?

Well, we started going to evening classes at our local school. Our teacher was a French national from Lille and a very good teacher, too. But, trying to learn the language once a week in an evening class of 20-odd other students from so many disparate backgrounds was very slow going indeed and, to put it mildly, deeply frustrating. So we agreed to go it alone, to develop our own learning techniques through the basic strategy of self-learning. We have done so ever since and continue to do so, incidentally. After all, you can never stop learning! Now we are both fluent French speakers and spend much of our time these days in the company of native French people.

Even so, it has not always been easy. Learning any foreign language is taxing, no matter what your background. But it is, at the same time, such a **rewarding** experience. If only we could have reached this level so much more **quickly**!

Well, now I realise that we could have done so and that **you certainly can** if you follow my method. Forty years of experience is too much to go to waste!

So what **is** my method? And how will it work for **you**?

In essence, the method stems from the fact, rarely appreciated, that French, like English, is cram-packed with hundreds of thousands of words, phrases and expressions that you never ever need to **know** – because you will never ever need to **use** them. For example, my excellent English-French dictionary has roughly 50,000 word headings and at least ten times as many words, phrases and expressions under each heading. But out of these 500,000+ words, my daily word need is the tiniest fraction of this total. Did you know that many people go through their whole life with a total vocabulary that rarely exceeds **5,000** words? Do the maths for yourself if you like, but I can tell you that this represents but **1%** of all the available words in my dictionary.

But that is not the end of the story. If 5,000 words are enough for life, what is one's daily word need? Well, that depends on the day of course and every day is different in some respect, so that some different words will be required most days. But that is not the important point. It is much more important to understand that far more words are words that are used every day and are **easily predictable**. After all, language is fundamentally the means by which regular social conventions are routinely expressed. All these conventions are determined, if not wholly at least in part, by the social contexts that shape our lives. To illustrate:

Most days, chances are, we meet people, some of them we know, some of them we do not know. But most encounters are likely to be with people we already know. So, after we meet them at school, say, or at work, our initial conversation is likely to be fairly perfunctory:

<u>Me</u>: "Hi Jack, how's it going?"

<u>Jack</u>: "Not bad mate but could be better. How about you?"

<u>Me</u>: "OK, thanks. How's the wife today? Her back still playing up a bit?"

<u>Jack</u>: "Afraid so. Never mind, that's how it is. See you at the pub tonight?"

<u>Me</u>: "Hope so, mate. See you later, bye!"

Of course, such a conversation, because it is between two people who know each other very well, only requires an English stripped to its bare essentials. But that does not matter. Jack's reason for speaking to me in this particular social context is both highly economic in its vocabulary and very predictable because such conversations occur on a **very frequent basis**.

And so it is when speaking French. With people you know well, similar conversations will also implicate very few but highly predictable words and phrases:

<u>Moi</u>: "Bonjour Stéphane, comment vas-tu?"

<u>Stéphane</u>: "Pas mal, mon vieux, et toi?"

<u>Moi</u>: "Ça va, mais ça pourrait être mieux. Ta femme, comment va-t-elle? Toujours mal au dos?"

<u>Stéphane</u>: "Malheurement. C'est la vie. Vas-tu au bar ce soir?"

<u>Moi</u>: "J'espère. À ce soir, alors. Salut!"

As this simple illustration demonstrates, meeting people in France always requires the use of the verb **aller**: depending on how well you know others, this may take the form "comment vas-tu", "comment ça va?", "comment va-t-elle?", "comment allez-vous? …" and so on; and often requires **aller** to express movement ("vas-tu au bar ce soir?") Indeed, if one were to count up how many times the verb **aller** was used in a day, it could easily be fifty times or more! Hardly surprising then, that anybody learning French must be very familiar with **aller**. It is a top priority verb.

And there is a very small group of other verbs that also occur and recur countless times in an average day. Amongst these are **être** (to be), **avoir** (to have) and **faire** (to do or to make). These three verbs in particular, but also all the others in my list of 21, occur so frequently in daily conversation that I call them the "killer" verbs. Learn these you **must**. Inside out.

But please do not come away from what I have said so far believing that only these 21 verbs matter and that these are the only 21 verbs you need to know! That would be crazy ("dingue")! Quite apart from anything else, my list reflects my own experience of learning French. Others, with a different experience might not agree with my list and would have produced a different looking one. Of course. But anybody else's list would only be partially different. Certainly more than a dozen of my verbs would appear in any list, simply because these verbs are undisputedly the most frequently used verbs in French. I am referring in particular, to verbs like **aller**, **avoir**, **faire** and **être**.

But if you are young, say, and learning French at school, other verbs you already know that are not in my list would be in yours. I am sure **apprendre** (to learn), **écrire** (to write) and, say, **jouer** (to play) would be amongst them. On the other hand, if you are older and working, verbs like **travailler** (to work) would certainly be on your list.

My point simply is this: because my list is culled from 40 years of learning experience it is, I hope, **representative** of the wide range of verbs out there. It contains regular and irregular verbs, reflexive and non-reflexive verbs and many more types, too. So my list is not only based on the wide range of such verbs, but also on their relevance in a wide array of contexts that are likely to be personally important to you.

So, what precisely is my method for learning French fast, well and convincingly? In essence, the method is **focus**. It selects from all those hundreds of thousands of words in the language and concentrates on the words, phrases and expressions, grammatical constructions and language that French people actually use very frequently, rather than on the language that is rarely, if ever, used by the average French citizen.

This focused approach is rooted in what I call **The Siffler Syndrome**. But what on earth do I mean by that?
Well, one day, not very long ago, I was flipping through a very well known verb book. It has been around for many years, has been through many re-editions and is widely recommended by French teachers everywhere. It is called "501 French Verbs". For no obvious reason, on this occasion I stopped on the verb **siffler**, to whistle. Now, the verbs in this book are presented in alphabetical order and (until the very latest edition) all 501 verbs are each allocated **one** page, regardless of each verb's relative importance!

Suddenly it occurred to me that as far as I could remember anyway, I had **never** used the verb **siffler** in conversation in my life – not once. Yet there it was in the book getting the same billing as the stars of the French verb galaxy, **avoir**, **être**, **faire**, **aller**… and the rest.

This struck me as frankly so plain dumb that I decided to count up all the verbs in the book that, to my knowledge and memory, I had never used in my life. To my astonishment, just over half of the verbs in the book I had never ever used, and many many more of the remainder were verbs I had used only once in a blue moon ("tous les trente-six du mois," literally every thirty-sixth day of the month). What on earth, I said to myself, was the point in learning now all those other **siffler** verbs that were not a top priority if any priority at all. I agree that if I were a football referee, a sports journalist or a traffic policeman, then **siffler** would be quite a useful verb to know. But I am **not**, so it **isn't**! In other words, we must ruthlessly distinguish between verbs you **must** know from verbs that are merely **nice to** know. And this principle, because it is a principle, applies to all components of language, not just verbs.

This principle of targeting and focus I learned when I worked in marketing. There, it was universally known as:

The 80 / 20 Rule

This "rule" (it is not a fixed rule but rather an approximation to what seems to happen most of the time) says, for example, that 80% of the profit comes from 20% of the customers; that 80% of the profit comes from 20% of the marketed products; that 80% of the complaints come from 20% of the customers… and so on. Of course, the ratio is not always precisely 80/20 and does not have to sum to 100%. For example, a similar principle has been known to economists for decades in the form of the Lorenz curve and the Gini Coefficient. These measure inequalities in the distribution of national income. To illustrate, in the US currently, 50% of the country's GNP (Gross National Product) goes to only 1% of the population. Such distributions are known to statisticians as "poisson" distributions.

What I have learned from this in my career both as an economist and as a marketer is that if I want to get better **quickly** in French, I have got to concentrate all my time, other resources and energy on what **really** matters, not what it would be nice to know. I need to focus on the 1% that in reality, accounts for most of the action.

So what does really matter most in language learning? Where **should** we focus?

One thing is clear. All languages, including French, are made up of what the grammar boys call "parts of speech". Both in French and English, these parts of speech include:

Nouns - ie **things** physical and abstract like chairs and pleasure

Pronouns - ie the words that take the place of a noun, words like **he**, **she** and **it**

Adjectives – ie words that describe nouns and pronouns such as "a **beautiful** sunset" or "she is **wise**"

Adverbs – ie words that describe adjectives, another adverb or a verb such as "Jack speaks **slowly**" or "Jack speaks **very slowly**"

Prepositions – the little words like **in**, **out**, **up**, **down**, **over**, **under** etc.

In truth, there are many more parts of speech in English **and** French and since this is not a grammar book (definitely not a grammar book!) but a book about how to communicate more effectively in French, I do not intend to bore you with or confuse you with them. But, because in my view there is one part of speech that stands head and shoulders above all others in its importance as a communication tool, **this book is entirely devoted to it**. This is of course, **the verb**.

The Verb

A famous Austrian-American author of some of the best books ever written on the subject of management, Peter Drucker, makes this brilliant distinction between work which is **efficient** and work which is **effective**. Efficient he says, is "doing things right". Effective is "doing the **right things**!" And that is my point – focus on learning **the right things**; the effective not merely the efficient. The efficiency of your French will come through repeatedly saying the right things, even if you are not always correct. For that is the problem with we Brits – we are so afraid of making mistakes that we never open our mouths! But French people, trust me, never mind when a Brit makes a mistake. Many of them make plenty themselves! But if it is clear to them that you are trying to speak their language, they will be flattered and hugely sympathetic to any errors you make and very encouraging, so that your confidence will grow with repetition, as will your efficiency, ie your fluency.

But, and this is very important indeed, although I am spotlighting verbs, that does not imply that I am neglecting other parts of speech. Indeed it is impossible to construct a sentence whose hero is the verb without employing other complementary bits of grammar. For example:

"I love dogs" ("J'adore les chiens"). Here we have the verb, love, (adorer), the personal pronoun, "I" (Je) and the object of the verb, dogs (chiens). In reality, of course, few sentences that we utter in French are likely to be this simple (I wish they were!) But the same principle applies. To give you one more example, before we move on to our first verb, **être** in Chapter Two:

"Everybody knows him. In fact, he is very well known". In French this translates as "Tout le monde le connaît. En fait, il est très bien connu". In this sentence, the verb is "connaît", the subject of the verb is "tout le monde", the object is "il", "bien" is the adverb and "connu" is the adjective. But note where "connu", the adjective, comes from. It comes from the verb to know, ie "connaître".

For this and a thousand other reasons, all parts of speech matter, **but verbs matter most**. This is where that 80/20 rule applies to verbs. Verbs should be where you focus. And what better to focus on than the **21 verbs that are most frequently used in French conversation most of the time**. Remember the Siffler Syndrome? That is why, I hope, you will plunge headlong into Chapter Two. **Être** awaits you! But first, some thoughts on verbs in general. Armed with some fairly simple grammar rules, **être, aller** and all my other "killer" verbs will make much more sense.

Pronunciation Guide

So many sounds in French – especially vowel sounds – are different from English, that the best way to start acquiring a good accent is to listen and imitate the speakers on the CD as often as possible. Yes, often they speak quickly and on the first hearing you may well struggle a bit occasionally. But persevere. Repetition is the key to familiarity. And do not be afraid of twisting your mouth into some unfamiliar shapes! In the early stages however, you may find the following brief guide a useful reference when working wih the book alone. But please bear in mind that in print, descriptions of sounds can only be approximate.

1. The final consonant in many French words is not pronounced at all

| banc | français | tout | regardez | les |
| tabac | vous | escargot | Paris | Londres |

In many verb tenses the third person plural ending …ent is not pronounced at all.

2. Vowels

a   is often similar to the Southern English 'a' sound in pat or cat:
Paris, Avignon, capitale, acteur

e   in many words is almost elided. The 'a' in English 'above' or the English article in a man and a woman are the same 'neutral sound as the French 'e':
le, petit, de Gaulle, Alain Delon

è / ê   are more similar to the English 'a' in dare:
père, mère, bière, infirmière, vous êtes, vêtement, honnête

é   is similar to, but crisper and shorter than, the 'ay' sound in English eighteen:
café, géographie, étudiant

i   is similar to the 'i' in police:
qui, il, ville, Maurice, police, vite, six, dix, cigarette

o   is similar to the 'o' in odd or holiday:
voleur, géographie, révolution
NB: 'O' at the end of the word is more similar to the Scottish 'o' in most or toast, ie pronounced with rounded lips. 'Eau' and 'au' are pronounced in the same way:
numéro, photo, château, bureau, au

u   is probably the most difficult sound to imitate for English speakers. Try rounding your lips as if whistling. Then place the tip of your toungue

	against the back of your bottom teeth and try to say 'dee'. The sound you make should be similar to the French word d<u>u</u>:
	d<u>u</u>, m<u>u</u>sique, <u>u</u>ne, revol<u>u</u>tion
eu	is like the 'u' sound in fur, but cut it short:
	d<u>eu</u>x, p<u>eu</u>, vi<u>eu</u>x
ou	is similar to the 'oo' sound in English food, but the lips are rounded more tightly:
	<u>où</u>, v<u>ou</u>drais, t<u>ou</u>t, v<u>ou</u>lez-v<u>ou</u>s, c<u>ou</u>turier
oi	this sound is similar to the 'wa' sound at the beginning of Southern English w<u>o</u>nder or the French word L<u>oi</u>re:
	au rev<u>oi</u>r, v<u>oi</u>x, tr<u>oi</u>s, p<u>oi</u>sson, b<u>oi</u>te, n<u>oi</u>r.

3. Nasals These are sounds in which a vowel is followed by an 'n' or 'm'.

en / an	Say the English word 'don' and you will see that the tip of the tongue touches the roof of your mouth at the end of the word. Now try saying the word again but stop your tongue touching the roof of your mouth at the last moment. The sound you make should be similar to the French <u>an</u> and <u>en</u> sounds:
	d<u>an</u>s, fr<u>an</u>çais, restaur<u>an</u>t, présid<u>en</u>t, Je<u>an</u>, Rou<u>en</u>, and… <u>en</u>semble
on	is similar to the <u>an</u>/<u>en</u> sounds but fuller and rounder, with lips slightly pursed. Try making the cavity of your mouth larger as you make this sound:
	b<u>on</u>, b<u>on</u>jour, Dij<u>on</u>, Avign<u>on</u>, tr<u>on</u>pette, attenti<u>on</u>, questi<u>on</u>
un	try saying 'sun' in the same way as 'don' above (ie preventing your tongue from touching the roof of your mouth) and you should make the <u>un</u> sound heard at the end of French words:
	<u>un</u>, Lebr<u>un</u>, auc<u>un</u>
in	same again only this time, try saying the word 'ban' in the same way:
	v<u>in</u>, Card<u>in</u>, <u>im</u>possible, <u>in</u>téressant, v<u>in</u>gt, pr<u>in</u>ce
	The same sound occurs in words ending –ien or –ain:
	b<u>ien</u>, music<u>ien</u>, paris<u>ien</u>, tr<u>ain</u>, p<u>ain</u>, terr<u>ain</u>. Exceptionally in the Midi, you will often hear vin, for example, pronounced veng.

4. Consonants A number of these are pronounced differently from the English equivalents:

c	before an '<u>e</u>' or '<u>i</u>' is like the 's' of sea and soap:
	mer<u>c</u>i, <u>c</u>'est, <u>c</u>igarette, <u>c</u>inq, <u>c</u>entime, <u>c</u>élibataire, Fran<u>c</u>e, Mauri<u>c</u>e, Alsa<u>c</u>e
c	before other letters is like the hard 'c' in English 'cat', 'cot', or 'cut':
	<u>C</u>alais, <u>C</u>ardin, <u>C</u>annes, Gis<u>c</u>ard, <u>c</u>afé, <u>c</u>arte, <u>c</u>outurier, a<u>c</u>teur
ç	is always pronounced like the soft 's' above:
	fran<u>ç</u>ais, gar<u>ç</u>on, <u>ç</u>a

ch	is like the 'sh' sound in 'shirt' or 'sugar': <u>Ch</u>arles de Gaulle, <u>Ch</u>artres, ar<u>ch</u>itecte, <u>ch</u>anteur, ri<u>ch</u>e
g	before an 'e' or 'i' is like the English 's' sound in plea<u>s</u>ure or mea<u>s</u>ure: <u>G</u>iscard, <u>g</u>endarme, <u>g</u>éographie
g	before other letters is like the hard 'g' in goat: de <u>G</u>aulle, <u>g</u>rand, ma<u>g</u>asin, <u>G</u>race Kelly
gn	an exception is the sound of 'g' followed by 'n'. This is pronounced rather like the 'ny' sound of English 'onion' or 'opinion': Champa<u>gn</u>e, Bourgo<u>gn</u>e, Avi<u>gn</u>on, Dordo<u>gn</u>e, campa<u>gn</u>e, monta<u>gn</u>e
j	is pronounced in the same way as the soft 'g' in gendarme above: <u>j</u>e, bon<u>j</u>our, Di<u>j</u>on, Beau<u>j</u>olais, <u>J</u>eanne d'Arc
th	is like the 't' in English 'tap' or 'tonic' or 'Thomas', but less staccato: <u>th</u>é, <u>th</u>éâtre, ca<u>th</u>édrale
qu	is always like the 'k' sound in 'kick' and <u>never</u> like the 'kw' sound in quick: <u>qu</u>'est-ce <u>qu</u>e c'est, <u>qu</u>i est-ce, <u>qu</u>estion, musi<u>qu</u>e
h	is not pronounced: <u>h</u>istoire, <u>h</u>ôtel, <u>h</u>ôpital, <u>h</u>ôtesse

5. Liaison The final consonant of a word is frequently not pronounced (see section 1). But if the word that follows in the sentence begins with a vowel or 'h', the final 'p', 't' or 's' of the preceding word is carried over (and the 's' is pronounced like 'z').

J'aime beaucoup but J'ai beacoup <u>a</u>imé

C'est le président *but* c'es<u>t un</u> acteur

Les femmes *but* le<u>s h</u>ommes

Chapter One
All You Need to Know About Verbs

Introduction

This chapter is about French verbs in general and in particular, what you really do need to know about my "killer" verbs etc. if only because there are other verbs out there that look like, even may be identical to, the twenty-one under the microscope in this book. In particular, we shall get a good working knowledge of:

1. What we mean by verbs.
2. Explain in a bit more depth why verbs are so important in language.
3. Demonstrate their role in conversation in relation to other parts of speech with which they are inextricably linked.
4. Distinguish between certain types of French verbs, notably:

    - The **regular** verbs following the "…er", "…ir" and "…re" patterns
    - Some of the **irregular** verbs (nearly three-quarters of our "killer" verbs are irregular)
    - **Reflexive** and **non-reflexive** verbs
    - Verbs that are either followed by the **preposition à or de** and those that are not **followed by any preposition at all**
    - **Compound** verbs that either have **avoir** or **être** as the auxiliary
    - **Figurative** verbs, particularly those that are frequently used in idiomatic expressions, sayings and proverbs.

5. How to make it easier to conjugate verbs using **on**.
6. Examine the **tenses** in which verbs tend to be used in day-to-day conversation, in particular:

    - The **present** tense
    - How to use the **future** tense – and how to avoid it
    - The four main **past** tenses ie the **imperfect** tense, the **perfect** tense, the **future-perfect** tense and the **pluperfect** tense
    - The present and past **conditional** tenses and…
    - The **present subjunctive** (ouch!) and…
    - The **imperative**.

Do note that I have given these tenses their English names, the ones we have inherited from Latin. The French have other names for some of these tenses, but I am not sure you need to know these yet!

Also, note that this brief account of the tenses involves only nine out of the fourteen that actually exist in French. Those that I have deliberately omitted are rarely used in speech, notably the three past subjunctives tenses and a tense called the simple past tense which, with one notable exception, is reserved uniquely for **written** French. This single exception is the expression "il fut un temps où" meaning "there was a time when". You will occasionally hear this in conversation. Clearly, this approach of mine to French tenses is much more focused than normal. Well, what else would you expect?!

1.   **So what are verbs?**
Verbs are words which indicate actions, events, states of mind… and so on and usually take different forms to show tense and agreement. Do not worry about this now. I will shortly show you what all that means. When they are expressed in the **infinitive**, eg in English, **to go**, **to have**, **to do**, etc, they correspond to the French verb forms **aller**, **avoir** and **faire** which are all examples of French verbs in the infinitive.

There is no equivalent in French of "to…" in English; in French it is the **ending** of the verb that signals it is a "to…" verb. Regular verbs in French (I will explain "regular" verbs later) all end either in "…er", "…ir" or "…re". From our list, **arriver** is a regular verb ending in "…er" as are **parler**, **passer** and **penser**. In my list there are no "…ir" and only one "re" regular verb, **rendre**, but examples outside my list include **finir** (to finish), an "…ir" verb and **tordre** (to twist) an "…re" verb. Other veb endings you will come across in my list are **irregular**; they include a**voir**, de**voir**, pou**voir**, sa**voir** and vou**loir**. Confusingly perhaps, some verbs, eg **aller**, look like regular verbs but are irregular.

2.   **But why are verbs so important to language?**
Well, one very influential "verbster", American Christopher Kendris, in "501 French Verbs", says, rightly, a "verb is where the action is" (literally **and** metaphorically!) In other words, it is the beating heart of every sentence we utter. In the sentence "the hunter killed the deer", the verb "killed" is in this case, at least, not only smack in the middle of the sentence, but much more importantly, if you were to take that verb out, you would not **have** a sentence and the result would be nonsense: "the hunter the deer!"

More than that though, what humans do, feel and think is the essence of what it means to be a human being. For inanimate objects, it is just the same; kettles boil, pens write, soap cleans… and so on. If these things did not do what they do, they would not **be** kettles, pens and soap.

No other parts of speech can lay claim to such attributes. For instance, I can construct grammatically correct sentences without nouns and adjectives: "I love you" has a verb (love), a subject pronoun (I) and an object pronoun (you). "Time flies" has a noun (time) and a verb (flies). There are no other parts of speech in this perfectly grammatical full English sentence; no adjective, no pronoun, no adverb, no preposition… etc. But all sentences **must** have a **verb**. Hence, **verbs matter most**.

3. **How do verbs fit into conversations where other parts of speech are present? How do they relate to other components of language?**
One thing is clear to me and, I hope, will become clear to you, too. It is quite difficult to answer my question without at least some of the basic grammar rules that, like cement that holds bricks together, give language its structure and hence its predictability. To illustrate, let us go back only a few sentences to my "time flies" example. I think everyone understands what this means, without any knowledge of grammatical rules. But can you make any sense at all of this sentence?:

"Time flies?; you cannot, they fly too fast". Does this make any sense to you? I would be surprised if it does. Why? Because I have deliberately changed the grammatical structure of the sentence. Our earlier rule said that "time" is a noun and "flies" is the verb. Not in this second sentence! Now "time" is the verb, to time, and "flies" is the noun, ie a group of flies. It is very difficult to measure how fast flies fly because they fly too fast!

This (silly?) example nonetheless hits this particular nail on the head. Yes, all of us can get by in a language by simply repeatedly using what we have learned parrot-fashion. But there comes a time when the mere repetition of rote learning, ie simply memorising words, phrases and expressions, will find you out. To illustrate:

When my wife and I first went on holiday together to France, I bought a French phrase book containing hundreds of very useful ways of making ourselves understood by French people. Some phrases I particularly remember learning by heart included:

- "Est-ce qu'il y a une banque par ici?" (Is there a bank nearby?)
- "Pour aller à Rouen, s'il vous plaît?" (How do I get to Rouen, please?) and
- "N'avez-vous rien de moins cher, s'il vous plaît?" (Don't you have anything cheaper, please?)

Of course, and you will have experienced this yourself, I am sure, the problem did not lie in posing **the question**; rather it was in understanding **the answer**! In part, this problem springs from not having an adequate vocabulary to understand the responses, but normally conversation can still make progress, if only through "franglais" (words borrowed from each other's languages, "le week-end", "les ros-bifs" etc) and body language, particularly from hands, shoulders and so on. By such improvisatory means, both parties can generally get their intended message across.

But that's not good enough. We want to do much better than that. More vocabulary will help, of course; but the old problem will still be there – particularly when we want to say something that is not exactly the same each time. For example, you have learned to use an expression with the verb in the first person singular – "Je voudrais aller au cinéma ce soir" (I would like to go to the cinema tonight) but you have not yet learned the expression "my friend and I would like to go the cinema tonight". To do this in accurate, convincing French you need the first-person **plural** of "je voudrais" (I would like). To do this you need to know your way around the verb **vouloir** (to want) to say, correctly, "Mon amie et moi, nous voudrions aller au cinéma ce soir". But you have not learned to say this parrot-fashion and so you are lost. You need to know, ideally, how to conjugate the conditional tense of **vouloir**. In short, you have to know the grammatical conventions that make the appropriate conjugation of this verb instantaneous. Only knowledge of the rules will allow that, not mere knowledge of phrases and expressions.

In practice (and I mean "practice" literally!) you should see language learning as a three-legged stool, "un tabouret à trois pieds":

The first leg of the stool is **words** and, other things being equal, the more words the better, obviously. However, not as many words as you might think. A highly acclaimed French professor of English at Cambridge University and the Harvard Business School, Enzo Mathews, has calculated that a good basic grasp of English can be had with only 900 words. If that is true for English, I am sure it is more or less true for French also.

The second leg of the stool is **usage**. The more you practice, the better you get. The better you get, the more confident you become. And the more confident you become, the more you will want to speak French.

The third leg of the stool is – guess what! – **grammar**. Yes, I know your eyes glaze over every time you hear the word, but, the fact is that sooner or later, grammar will come to your aid and it will help you economise on your vocabulary requirements. But what I am talking about here is nothing more than a good, basic knowledge of the **relevant** grammar. That is why much of this chapter only (I repeat that this is not a grammar book) is devoted to some basic grammar rules insofar as they influence our use of verbs and other appropriate parts of speech.

4. **There are many different types of French verb**
    We have already met the three groups of regular verbs in their infinitives – those ending in "…er", "…ir" and "…re" and we have noted that only six of our killer list are regular. Five of these are "…er" verbs and one, rendre, is a regular "…re" verb.

    With regard to irregular verbs, I cannot be very prescriptive, I'm afraid. They just don't fit easily into patterns (that is why they are called irregular verbs!). However, all our "killer" verbs are fully conjugated in all the relevant tenses at the beginning of each separate verb chapter – so I am not missing out on anything important. Promise!

    Reflexive verbs are very common in French. You can always spot the reflexive verb because it is always preceded by **se** in the infinitive form and by the appropriate reflexive pronoun when the verb is conjugated. These are **me**, **te**, **se**, **nous**, and **vous**. At first sight, you would say "but there are no reflexive verbs in your "killer" list because I cannot see any reflexive pronoun **se** preceding any of the verbs". True. However, in that list several exist in both non-reflexive and reflexive form. These are:

    *   aller and s'en aller*
    *   connaître and se connaître
    *   devoir and se devoir*
    *   dire and se dire
    *   faire and se faire
    *   mettre and se mettre
    *   parler and se parler*
    *   passer and se passer
    *   pouvoir and se pouvoir
    *   prendre and se prendre / s'en prendre*
    *   venir and s'en venir*
    *   vouloir and se vouloir.*

    Technically, the asterisked verbs are called **pronominal** verbs, but this is not a distinction that need worry you here. All you need to know is that they are conjugated in exactly the same way as normal reflexive verbs.

But what do we mean by reflexive verbs? Simple.

Parler means to talk; **se parler** means to talk to **oneself**. **Dire** means to say; **se dire** means to say to **oneself**. Not on the list but an important verb is **appeler**. **Appeler** means to call; **s'appeler** means to **call oneself**. To illustrate using appeler and s'appeler (not on my "killer" list but very important verbs nonetheless):

Appeler means to call, so: "**J'ai appelé** Christophe hier. Malheureusement, il n'était pas là". I called Christophe yesterday. Unfortunately, he was not in.

However, in its reflexive form, **s'appeler** means to call oneself. So:

Comment tu t'appelles? or **Comment vous vous appelez**?

Both sentences mean exactly the same; What is your name? ie, what do you call yourself? A complication arises from the fact, however, that social conventions and the conventions of the French language conspire to make it supposedly "de rigeur" to address someone you do not know at all well, or someone who is older or more senior to you using the **vous** form of the verb, whether it be reflexive or not. This is knows as **vouvoyer** ie to address someone using "vous" rather than "tu".

When my wife was having one-to-one French lessons with a native French speaker in London several years ago, her teacher insisted that my wife use the "vous" form of the verb on all occasions on the grounds that it would be "safer" – she would be much less likely to offend someone.

Our experience nowadays in particular, is that the young (particularly the young) but also middle aged people, are much more relaxed about this issue; frequently we meet new French people who, even on introduction, use the "tu" form of the verb (this is known as **tutoyer**) and insist that we do the same with them. (Incidentally, the former French President, Nicolas Sarkozy, constantly used the "tu" form with people he had never encountered before – although you might say: "and look what happened to him!")

One further complication: "vous" does not only mean the singular alternative to "tu", it also can mean you in the **plural**! (Ouch, again!)

Verbs and Prepositions

Many verbs in French are immediately followed by a **noun** or **another verb**. For example:

I would like to speak French – "J'aimerais parler **français**" Here français is a noun. Or "Véronique peut **lire** le russe" - Véronique can read Russian. Here **lire** (to read) is the following verb.

However, many other French verbs are immediately followed either by the preposition **à** or by the preposition **de** and then by a second verb in the infinitive. For example, in our "killer" list, three can be followed by **à** plus a verb:

- **arriver à** – meaning here to manage to… eg "**Je suis arrivé à finir** la vaisselle", I managed to do the washing up.
- **avoir à** – meaning here to have to… eg "**J'ai à travailler**", I have got some work to do.
- **(se) mettre à** – meaning here to begin to… eg "**Il s'est mis à manger** une pomme", He began to eat an apple.

But penser à – meaning here to think about or to focus one's attention on somebody or something… eg "**Je pense souvent à** Mireille; oui, **je pense souvent à** elle", I often think of Mireille; yes, I often think of her, shows **penser** followed by **à** plus a **noun**, Mireille.

With regard to the **de** verbs, only one in our list can be followed by **de** plus a verb and that is **parler de**, meaning to talk about. To illustrate, "**Elle a parlé d'**aller chez un médecin" ie, She talked about seeing a doctor.

However, **avoir** is frequently followed by **de** and an expression plus another verb:

- **avoir peur de faire**… eg "**Il a peur de voyager** en avion", He is afraid of flying.
- **avoir raison de faire**… eg "**Tu as raison de craindre** les ouragans aux Etats Unis", You are right to fear hurricanes in the United States.
- **avoir l'intention de faire**… eg "**J'ai l'intention de passer** une semaine dans les Alpes l'année prochaine", I plan to spend a week in the Alps next year.

Compound verbs with avoir and être

In English, when we want to speak about completed actions in the past, we use what we call the **perfect tense** which is "perfect" in the sense that the action is over and done with. This is in contrast to events in the past which were continuing when something else occurred, eg "It was raining when we left Manchester". Here we have the perfect tense "when we left" which is preceded by a continuing event, "it was raining". This so-called imperfect tense we shall examine later.

In English, the perfect tense can take two forms:

- "I have been to Italy" and
- "I went to Italy".

In French, however, there is only **one** way of expressing completed past actions. To do so, two components are required:

1. The **past participle** of the verb (the equivalent of "went" and "been")
2. The **auxiliary** verb (ie, the equivalent of "have" in my first English sentence example above).

Together these components form what the French call the "passé composé".

The past participle of regular verbs is formed by replacing the infinitive endings "…er", "…ir" and "…re" with "…é" for "…er" verbs, "…i" for "…ir" verbs and "…u" for "…re" verbs. To illustrate:

- parler becomes parl**é** (pronounced parl**ay**)
- finir becomes fin**i**
- rendre becomes rend**u**.

So, for all four remaining regular "…er" verbs in our "killer" list – **arriver**, **passer**, **payer** and **penser**:

- **arriver** becomes arriv**é** (pronounced arriv**ay**)
- **passer** becomes pass**é** (pronounced pass**ay**)
- **payer** becomes pay**é** (pronounced pay**ay**)
- **penser** becomes pens**é** (pronounced pens**ay**).

All the other verbs in our list are irregular and no rules to these and all other irregular verbs can be applied; you simply have to learn each one "au fur et à mesure", ie as you go along. These are the past participles of ou irregular "killer" verbs:

- aller   -   all**é**
- avoir   -   **eu**
- connaître   -   conn**u**
- devoir   -   dev**enu**
- dire   -   di**t**
- être   -   ét**é**
- faire   -   fai**t**
- mettre   -   m**is**
- partir   -   part**i**
- pouvoir   -   p**u**
- prendre   -   p**ris**
- savoir   -   s**u**
- venir   -   ven**u**
- vouloir   -   voul**u.**

With regard to the second component in compound verbs, the **auxiliary** verbs, the equivalent of "have" in "I have been ", one of two verbs will be required:

- **avoir** for the vast majority of French verbs
- **être** for so called "verbs of **movement**" eg **aller**, **arriver**, **partir** and **venir** in our "killer" list. The full list of each verb also includes **rester**, to stay!, **naitre**, to be born and **mourir**, to die. Well, I suppose there is some degree of movement with the last two!

There is one much larger group of verbs that also requires **être** in the auxiliary. These are the reflexive verbs I mentioned earlier.

So, how are avoir and être used in this auxiliary form?
The relevant present tenses of **avoir** and **être** are placed **before** the verb's past participle. These two verbs, conjugated in the present tense look like this:

Avoir conjugated in the present tense

- J'ai   -   I have
- tu as   -   you (singular) have
- il a   -   he has
- elle a   -   she has
- nous avons   -   we have
- vous avez   -   you (plural) have
- ils ont   -   they (masculine) have
- elles ont   -   they (feminine) have.

To illustrate from our "killer" list using **parler**:

J'ai parlé	nous avons parlé
tu as parlé	vous avez parlé
il a parlé	ils ont parlé
elle a parlé	elles ont parlé.

Être conjugated in the present tense

- Je suis   -   I am
- tu es   -   you (singular) are
- il est   -   he is
- elle est   -   she is
- nous sommes -   we are
- vous êtes   -   you (plural) are
- ils sont   -   they (masculine) are
- elles sont   -   they (feminine) are.

So how do these **être** auxiliaries work for one of the verbs on our "killer" list, **venir** (to come)?

Je suis venu(e)	nous sommes venu(e)s
tu es venu(e)	vous êtes venu(e)s
il est venu	ils sont venus
elle est venue	elles sont venues.

If you are really concentrating you will see that the past participle of venir, **venu**, **agrees** in **gender** and **number** with the **subject pronoun**. For example, if the subject pronoun is feminine, an "e" is added to the end of venu and if the subject pronoun is feminine and plural, to "venu" is added "e" and "s". This agreement between the subject pronoun and the past participle only occurs in the case of verbs that have **être** as the auxiliary verb. **Avoir** verbs (the majority of verbs in French, that is) do not agree.

However, as far as spoken French is concerned, you will not fear these changes to the past participle with **être**. They are only noticeable in written French. So don't worry about them at all.

Verbs used in figurative expressions

Much spoken and written French takes a **literal** form; the words you hear and see can be taken completely at face value and no other meaning can be inferred. To illustrate, first in English: "My sister and I ate a pizza last night". In French that is, "Ma soeur et moi avons mangé une pizza hier soir".

However, very often, particularly when we speak English or French some, if not much, of our conversation is **figurative**, ie words convey meaning other than the literal meaning. To illustrate:

"I've a frog in my throat", not literally of course, but everyone knows what I mean; I can't speak clearly because something is irritating my throat. The French, too, have a figurative expression for this problem; "J'ai un chat dans la gorge" ie I have a cat in my throat. (Incidentally it is quite amazing how many figurative expressions in both languages feature animals of one sort or another. Here are two more:

English:	"She's a silly **goose**".
French:	"C'est une petite **bécasse**", literally she's a little woodcock.

English:	"He's as sick as a **dog**".
French:	"Il est malade comme **un chien**, literally he's as sick as a dog).

Such expressions are often referred to as **idioms**; the words used do not immediately convey the meanings intended.

This idiomatic use of language is ever present in **proverbs**, many of which are widely used in conversational French. For example, in English, we say "better late than never". The French say "mieux vaut tard que jamais" . Note the verb used, though – **valoir**. This is not what is literally meant by **valoir**. Its normal meaning is "to be worth". So frequently are our "killer" verbs used in this way, that much of the following twenty-two chapters will be devoted to their use in figurative expressions.

5.   **Conjugating verbs using on**

So far we have seen certain verbs conjugated in the present tense; **avoir** and **être**, the auxiliary verbs required to form the perfect tense (I have gone or I went in English: Je suis allé(e) in French). To **conjugate** a verb means to show the **gender**, the **number** and the **tense** of the verb for each of the eight personal pronouns; **je**, **tu**, **il**, **elle**, **nous**, **vous**, **ils** and **elles**.

However, it is very common indeed in spoken French to find **on** substituted for the relevant personal pronoun. Then, only the third-person singular of the verb will be needed. **On** approximates to our use in English of the word **one**. To illustrate:

"**One** can see the sea from the top of this hill". There, one could mean "I can see the sea", "you (singular) can see the sea", "we can see the sea" and "you (plural) can see the sea…".

And so it is in French. For instance, in the sentence "**On** peut bien manger ici", ie "**One** can eat well here" can mean:

- "Je peux bien manger ici"
- "Tu peux bien manger ici"
- "Nous pouvons bien manger ici"
- "Vous pouvez bien manger ici" and at a push
- "Il/Elle, Ils/Elles, peut/peuvent bien manger ici".

The great benefit of this rather imprecise way of talking is precisely that – its imprecision! It allows for much more flexibility and only needs knowledge of the third-person singular of any verb. Not bad, eh?

So how can we use **on** to be so conveniently imprecise?

First, you can use **on** to refer to someone whose identity is not really known:

- "**On dit** que septembre est le meilleur mois sur la Côte d'Azur" ie People say that September is the best month on the Côte d'Azur.
- "**On m'a volé** ma voiture" ie "Someone has stolen my car".
- "Est-il vrai qu'**on peut** fumer dans cet endroit? " ie Is it true that **I/you** can smoke in this place?
- "**On pense** que ces gens-ci sont dangereux" ie We think that these people here are dangerous.

Alternatively, you can use it to express the collective **we** as in expressions such as **on y va**? ie "shall we go?" or **on se casse** ie "let's split".

This use of **on** to replace **nous** is very common indeed, in spoken French. It is so convenient that it can get over used.

6. **How the nine tenses are used**

The present tense is perhaps the most frequently used of all the French tenses. In English, we deploy it to say, for example, "I am going" or "I go". The second version often implies some degree of regularity as in "I go to Paris every year". French has no equivalent of this dual meaning. "I go" and "I am going" are both rendered by **Je vais**. The relative simplicity of this tense, combined with its ubiquity, means that this tense really has to be mastered for all the verbs you will ever use. More than that, though, is its flexibility; it can be used, as it can in English, both for expressing ideas in the future and the past as well as the present. In English, for example, we can say:

- "We are going to watch Manchester United on Saturday". Of course, "we are going" is the present tense of "to go", not the future, but it is used here to express intentions about the future, "on Saturday".

It is exactly the same in French; the present tense of French verbs can be deployed to talk about future actions or events. For example: "Je vais voir mon ami Jacques demain matin" ie I am going to see my friend Jacques tomorrow morning. But the present tense can also be used to talk about past events. Consider this:

- "So here I am in the middle of the road when, all of a sudden, this bloke on a bicycle comes out of nowhere and knocks me down". In such situations, the present tense is used to give a more vivid account of a past incident or series of incidents. Again, precisely the same use of the present tense to accentuate the importance of past events can also be used in French.

However, the future tense is often used to describe future events! Instead of saying "I am seeing her next week" we can say "I will see her next week". If there is a different nuance here it is the implication that "I will see her next week" is **emphatic** whereas "I am seeing her next week" is rather **vague** in tone. In French it is exactly the same; if you want to be adamant about the future event, you may well choose to use the future, rather than the present tense:

- "**Je la verrai** la semaine prochaine" ie I will see her next week. But in most other circumstances the present tense will work for you, even if the future event is a long way off:
- "Ma fille **va** au Canada l'année prochaine" ie My daughter is going to Canada next year.

The **imperfect** tense is normally used to describe actions or events:

- that were going on in the past at the same time as other actions eg:

    "Ma femme **regardait** la télé pendant que je **lisais** mon journal" ie My wife was watching the television whilst I was reading my newspaper.

- that were going on in the past when other actions occured eg:

    "Il **faisait** beau quand nous sommes partis de Paris" ie The weather was fine when we left Paris.

- that were going on regularly in the past eg:

    "Nous **allions** au cinéma tous les vendredis" ie We used to go to the cinema every Friday.

Alternatively, this tense can be used to express physical or mental conditions that applied in the past, eg:

- "Quand elle **était** jeune elle **était** très mince" ie When she was young she was very slim.
- "**J'étais** heureux quand ju **jouais** au foot le dimanche matin" ie I was very happy when I played football on Sunday mornings.

The **perfect** tense, as we have already noticed, is used to describe completed actions in the past:

- "**J'ai vu** ma cousine hier" ie I saw my cousin yesterday.

Nothing more need be said about this tense here but we will see plenty of it in the subsequent chapters.

The **future perfect** tense is used to describe an action or event which will happen in the future before another action in the future eg:

- By the time my mother gets back home, I will have left ie "Quand ma mère rentrera, **je serai parti**".

From this example alone you can see how the future perfect is formed; the past participle of the verb (here **parti**) is preceded by the auxiliary of **être** (because **partir** is a verb of movement, remember?) in the **future**, ie **serai**.

Alternatively, for verbs that take **avoir** in the auxiliary, **the appropriate future tense of avoir** is employed eg:

- By the time my mother prepares the meal, I will have finished my homework ie "Quand ma mère préparera le repas, **j'aurai fini** mes devoirs".

In these two examples please note that the main clause is in the **future** tense, not the **present** tense as it is in English, because **both** events will occur in the future. French is always more precise in such cases: it insists on what is called "la concordance des temps", the temporal agreement of tenses.

The **pluperfect** tenses is used to describe an event which occurred in the past prior to a past action eg:

- I realised that I had left my books in the library ie "Je me suis rendu compte que **j'avais laissé** mes livres à la bibliothèque".

Again, it is easy to see how the tense is formed; the past participle of a verb (here, **laissé**) is preceded by the appropriate form of **avoir** in the imperfect, **j'avais**.

Alternatively, for a verb that requires **être** in the auxiliary ie either verbs of movement or reflexive verbs, the tense is again formed by the verb's past participle and the appropriate form of **être** eg:

- I realised that I had left too late to catch my train ie "Je me suis rendu compte que **j'étais parti** trop tard pour attraper mon train".

The **present conditional** is used in exactly the same way in English and French to describe an action one **would** perform **if something were** to happen eg:

- **I would go** to Venice **if I had** the money ie "**J'irais** à Venise **si j'avais** l'argent".

But the tense is also frequently used to express a **conditional wish or desire**. Often the verb is an expression of politeness. For instance, instead of saying "I want" (which is a tad assertive) one can say "I would like", an altogether more pleasant way of saying that you want something, eg:

- "**Je voudrais** cette baguette-ci, s'il vous plaît" ie I would like this loaf of bread here, please. **Je voudrais** is an expression you are likely to hear and use yourself on innumerable occasions in France. It is the first-person singular conditional of **vouloir**, one of our very important "killer" verbs. If you like you can always say "j'aimerais" ("I would like"), but never say "je veux" ("I want") unless you feel a real need to be assertive when, for example, you wish to make a complaint ("faire une réclamation"):

"**Je veux** faire une réclamation" (with no s'il vous plaît!) is much more forceful than "**je voudrais** faire une réclamation".

Please turn to the relevant verb chapters for the formation of the present conditional.

The **past conditional** is used to express an action that you **would have** done **had something else been possible**:

- If I **had** known, I **would have** done it myself ie "Si **j'avais** su, **je l'aurais** fait moi-même".

In such **if** clauses, the past conditional takes the **past participle of the verb** and precedes it with the **present conditional** of **avoir** or **être**.

(Incidentally, can you see how many of these past tenses require knowledge of the verb's past participle? As we have already noted, the past participle of regular verbs is formed in the same way for each of the "…er", "…ir" and "…re" verbs. Unfortunately, by definition almost, irregular verbs follow no obvious consistent pattern and, therefore, have to be learned for each irregular verb. I know it is a chore but you will soon learn the past participles for each of our irregular "killer" verbs).

Now for the **present subjunctive**, a tense (technically a mood, but do not worry about that) which is very frequently used, especially in set expressions such as **il faut que**… ("it is necessary that…"). It contrasts very sharply with what is sometimes called the **indicative** mood (all the tenses so far encountered are in the indicative mood). This mood is the realm of **objective reality**: **I am**, **she went**, **I bought** etc. These are facts, if you wish. But the subjunctive mood (and, therefore, the present subjunctive) is very often used to convey all sorts of ideas that exist in the **subjective realm** of opinions, doubts, feelings and so on.

This ostensibly clear distinction between objective facts and subjective ideas is not generally at all clear to English speakers because nowadays the subjunctive is rarely, if ever, employed in English. Perhaps that is why English speaking students of French often have difficulties in using it in conversation. Indeed, they often have difficulties in getting to know it! But because so many of our verbs are irregular, I shall leave the formation of the subjunctive until each verb chapter is encountered. The really good news is that, like the future tense, there are several ways of avoiding this tricky little blighter! However, in conversation you ideally will want to identify it when it is used by French people although, again, you will often not know that a speaker is using the subjunctive because often it sounds (and spells) exactly the same as its indicative cousin.

Uses of the subjunctive

For the subjunctive to be used, the **subjects of the main clause and the subordinate clause must be different**. Yes, I know that is grammar jargon again, but some simple examples should clarify matters:

"**Je** veux (or je voudrais) que **tu** partes". Here, the subjects of the two clauses **je** and **tu** are different. Hence, the use of the present subjunctive of partir, **partes**. However, in the sentence "I want to leave" the two subjects are the same ie "I want that I leave" as it were, so that reads in French, **je veux partir**.

The subjunctive is formed after **que** and is often used to express wishes, fears, regrets and uncertainty. For example:

"**Je veux que tu viennes**" ie I want you to come.
"**J'ai peur que tu sois** très malade" ie I fear that you are very ill.
"**Je regrette que tu ne puisses** pas venir ce soir" ie I am sorry that you cannot come tonight.
"**Je doute que tout aille** bien chez lui" ie I am not sure that everything is all right with him.

However, there are so many more uses of the present subjunctive in French that I will discuss its application with regard to each of our "killer" verbs in the appropriate chapters.

Finally, some brief thoughts on the **imperative**, ie the **command** form of the verb. Here are some examples:

"Do not be afraid" ie **N'ayez pas peur**
"Be careful" ie **Soyez prudent**
"Know your verbs" ie **Sachez vos verbes**
"Let's eat" ie **Mangeons**
"Come on the Blues" ie **Allez les Bleus**
"Let's go there" ie **Allons-y**
"Go there" ie **Allez-y**
"Go away" ie **Va-t-en**.

You may have already noticed from this short list of examples that irregular verbs in particular make extensive use of the subjunctive to form the imperative (though I do not blame you if you have not!). So, again, we will examine its use when we meet our "killer" verbs in the following chapters.

<u>Conclusion</u>

And that's it! No more grammar rules. From now on it's the verbs **where the action is**! But I do want to impress on you the importance of grammar; that three legged stool will not stand up on only **two** legs. So, because, I repeat, this is not a grammar book – it is about the language as it is spoken by ordinary (and sometimes not so ordinary) folk and, given the fact that the French do not always speak good, accurate and compelling French themselves (any more than the Brits always speak good, accurate and compelling English!), I advise you to keep a good, basic grammar book by your side throughout our journey through the verbs. So, here we go! **Allons-y!**

Chapter Two
Être

Introduction

Être, to be in English, has a rightful place to be the most important verb in the French lexicon. Only **avoir** and **faire** can compete for this honour and it is simple to see why: as we have seen, it is the auxiliary verb in compound tenses; and it is used in hundreds, if not thousands of idiomatic expressions. But it is in its basic role, saying who and what people and things are, that it can be used and rattles up thousands more uses, At the other end of the language spectrum, it is used to describe the very essence of the human condition. Just check out Shakespeare's Hamlet if you are in any doubt: "**To be** or not **to be**, that is the question!" So, I will be giving it a lot of space in this verb book. But first, how is it conjugated in the tenses used in this book?

The Être Conjugations

Present Tense
Je suis	Nous sommes
Tu es	Vous êtes
Il est	Ils sont
Elle est	Elles sont

Future Tense
Je serai	Nous serons
Tu seras	Vous serez
Il sera	Ils seront
Elle sera	Elles seront

Imperfect Tense
J'étais	Nous étions
Tu étais	Vous étiez
Il était	Ils étaient
Elle était	Elles étaient

Perfect Tense
J'ai été	Nous avons été
Tu as été	Vous avez été
Il a été	Ils ont été
Elle a été	Elles ont été

Future Perfect Tense
J'aurai été	Nous aurons été
Tu auras été	Vous aurez été
Il aura été	Ils auront été
Elle aura été	Elles auront été

Pluperfect Tense
J'avais été	Nous avions été
Tu avais été	Vous aviez été
Il avais été	Ils avaient été
Elle avais été	Elles avaient été

Present Conditional Tense
Je serais	Nous serions
Tu serais	Vous seriez
Il serait	Ils seraient
Elle serait	Elles seraient

Past Conditional Tense
J'aurais été	Nous aurions été
Tu aurais été	Vous auriez été
Il aurait été	Ils auraient été
Elle aurait été	Elles auraient été

Present Subjunctive Tense
Je sois	Nous soyons
Tu sois	Vous soyez
Il soit	Ils soient
Elle soit	Elles soient

Imperative Tense
(Tu) Sois
(Nous) Soyons
(Vous) Soyez

Of course, you can learn all these forms of **être** "en bloc" and "par coeur"(by heart) if you wish but that's not, in my view, the best way to get the most out of the verb. My advice is to take a more pragmatic approach. Start by thinking how you would like to use the verb; identify the different ways you would like to say things and then dip into the verb tables provided here to help you get it right.

To illustrate, in the early days, especially on holiday, much of what you need to say is in the form of basic questions and what you need to understand are the responses. So you will use lots of the **vous** form of the verb and you will hear lots more **vous** in the responses you will get. Even more frequently, you will need to use **je** and **nous**, especially when you are saying who you are, where you come from, what you need and so on.

And much of this will be in the **present** tense, don't forget. It is only as you grow in confidence and knowledge will you "up the ante" with the imperfect and perfect tenses. Try to use as many of the set phrases and expressions as possible and try to use them as frequently as possible. Do not tire of constantly repeating the same words and phrases. Repetitive usage is a much more effective way of driving home the basic verb patterns than rote learning.

With these thoughts in mind, let's start with the basic uses of **être**.

Être: The Basics

Être is constantly used to say who is who and what is what, ie to describe people and things and to talk about yourself.

Use être to say who people are:

- **Qui est ce**?   **C'est** Johnny Halliday
- **Qui est-ce**?   **C'est** mon frère (my brother)
- **Qui est-ce**?   **C'est** Brad Pitt.

The question can also be put in reverse:

- **C'est qui ça**?   **C'est** David Cameron
- **C'est qui ça**?   **C'est** Madonna
- **C'est qui ça**?   **C'est** mon oncle (my uncle).

30

It can also be used in the negative:

- Non, **ce n'est pas** Madonna, c'est Marilyn Monroe
- Non, **ce n'est pas** David Cameron, c'est Nick Clegg
- Non, **ce n'est pas** mon oncle, c'est mon cousin (my cousin).

Negatives in French, we are told, are composed of **ne** and **pas**, **ne** and **plus**, **ne** and **jamais** etc: "Non, ce **n**'est **pas** le Pape".

In practice, at least in spoken French, the **ne** is very often omitted and you hear instead:

- Non, **c'est pas** ma mère (my mother)
- Non, **c'est pas** le président Obama.

Strictly speaking, the omission of the **ne** is a "grosse erreur" (a big mistake). In speech, however, the practice is so widespread that no-one bats an eyelid when **ne** is left out.

Just one point about "**c'est qui ça**?" before we move on to describing things.

Although I said, quite rightly, in our first chapter that a sentence is not a sentence **without a verb**, very often, French speakers will contract or shorten the phrase or sentence. (The French for "shorten", incidentally, is "abréger"). For example:

- C'est qui, ça? $\rightarrow$ **Qui ça**?
- C'est quand, ça? $\rightarrow$ **Quand ça**?
- C'est où, ça? $\rightarrow$ **Où ça**?
- C'est quoi, ça? $\rightarrow$ **Quoi ça**?

In these, and other similar expressions, the verb **c'est** is completely omitted. It is not correct but it is very frequently encountered.

Use être to say what things are:

- **Qu'est-ce que c'est que ça**?   **C'est** un stylo (a pen)
- **Qu'est-ce que c'est que ça**?   **C'est** une tondeuse (a lawnmower)
- **Qu'est-ce que c'est que ça**?   **C'est** un morceau de poulet (a piece of chicken).

However, this is a rather long-winded way of asking what something is. Very often instead, therefore, you will hear:

- **C'est quoi, ça**? **C'est** un rasoir (a razor)
- **C'est quoi, ça**? **C'est** une robe (a dress)
- **C'est quoi, ça**? **C'est** un verre à vin (a wine glass).

Être is also used to describe what people do for a job: **Qu'est-ce que vous faites dans la vie**?

> **Qu'est-ce que tu fais dans la vie**? Oh, **je suis expert comptable** (a chartered accountant).
>
> **Qu'est-ce que tu fais dans la vie**? Moi, **je suis étudiante** (student) – donc je ne fais rien! (therefore, nothing!)

Often when people describe other people's jobs, they use one of two forms:

> Lui? **Il est** chirugien (a surgeon).

But you might get the response: Lui, **c'est un** chirugien.

Please note the difference. If you use **Il est** there is no indefinite article before "chirugien" or whatever. However, if you use **c'est**, "c'est" is always followed by the indefinite article, **un** or **une**:

- Il est serveur (waiter)? Non, c'est **un** chef de cuisine (ie cook).
- Elle est vedette de cinéma (film star)? Non, c'est **une** journaliste (journalist).
- Il est éléctricien (electrician)? Non, c'est **un** plombier (plumber).

And **être** is very often used to describe what people and things look or taste like:

- Qu'est-ce quelle **est belle**! (How beautiful she is).
- **Il est grand**, lui (He is tall – "lui" is often added for emphasis).
- **Ils sont très charmants** (very charming).
- Ce frigidaire **est très vieux** (This fridge is very old).
- Ma voiture **est plus agée** même que mon frigidaire (My car is even older than my fridge).
- Ce café **est dégoutant** (This coffee is disgusting).

When is it appropriate to use c'est and il est?

Often you will hear French people using **c'est** and **il est** interchangeably as if there were no difference between the two. Unfortunately there is! Basically, **when être** is followed by anything other than an adjective, **ce** is the pronoun that you must use:

- **C'est** un plaisir (It's a pleasure) **not** Il est un plaisir
- **C'est** lui (It's him) **not** Il est lui
- **C'est** un hôtel **not** Il est un hôtel.

Finally on this, **c'est** versus **il est** issue, when **être** is followed only by an **adjective**, then **il est** is personal, whereas **c'est** is impersonal. For example:

- **Il est bête** (he is stupid), but **c'est bête** means things in general are stupid.

And of course, you can use **être** to talk about yourself using **adjectives** rather than **nouns** such as electrician, plumber, student etc.

> **Comment êtes-vous**? ie describe yourself:

- Moi? "**Je suis** jeune; **je suis** d'un certain âge" (a euphemism for getting on a bit!)
- Moi? "**Je suis** grande (tall); **je suis** petite" (small).
- Moi? "**Je suis** très heureux (happy) la plupart du temps" (most of the time).
- Moi? "**Je suis** fatigué (tired); **je suis** très énèrgique" (energetic).
- Moi? "**Je suis** crispée (on edge); **je suis** calme" (calm).
- Moi? "**Je suis** stressé" (stressed).

Et mon chef de service? (head of department) "Lui, **il est** con!" (stupid).

What about être in other tenses to talk about people and things?

So far we have only used the present tense to describe people and things but the past tenses and the future tense can also be employed in the same way. For instance:

- **Il était une fois** means "once upon a time," the standard opening to many a fairy story. Other examples include:
- "**C'était** un excellent dîner – un vrai régal" (It was an excellent dinner, a real treat).
- "La mer **était** agitée pendant notre traversée de la Manche" (The sea was rough during our channel crossing).
- "Le ciel **était** bleu toute la journée" (The sky was blue throughout the day).

Être is also frequently employed to talk about the future:

- "Ça **sera** formidable de voir Henri demain" (It will be great to see Henri tomorrow.)
- "Le concert samedi soir **sera** vachement chouette, je suis sûr" (The concert will be really super on Saturday night, I'm sure).

Être and the perfect tense

As we have seen, **être** is the verb used to form the auxiliary in this compound tense either when we use verbs of movement or when we use reflexive verbs. This is quite one of the most important and frequent uses of the verb. First, verbs of movement.

There are not too many verbs of movement in French, seventeen in all, but the ones that are there really have to be memorised. These are:

- aller (to go)
- arriver (to arrive)
- descendre (to descend)
- devenir (to become)
- entrer (to enter)
- monter (to go up)
- mourir (to die)
- naître (to be born)
- partir (to leave)
- passer (to pass by)
- rentrer (to return)
- rester (to remain)
- retourner (to go back)
- revenir (to come back)
- sortir (to go out)
- tomber (to fall)
- venir (to come).

However, when I said that there are 17 verbs of movement, I was not including all those verbs that share the verb with the immediate antecedent, **re**. For example:

- descendre – **re**descendre (to descend again)
- devenir – **re**devenir (to become again)
- partir – **re**partir (to leave again)
- passer – **re**passer (to pass by again; but please note that repasser can also mean to iron!)

- monter – **re**monter (to go up again)
- tomber – **re**tomber (to fall again).

These, as you might expect, also use **être** as the auxiliary verb.

And here are seventeen sentences, illustrating the use of **être** in the auxiliary for the verbs of movement above:

- "**Nous sommes allés** au musée hier" (We went to the museum yesterday).
- "Le train **est arrivé** à l'heure" (The train arrived on time).
- "**Je suis descendu** lentement" (I came down slowly).
- "Mon ami **est devenu** menuisier (My friend became a carpenter).
- "Quand je pense qu'il pleuvait quand **nous sommes partis** de Paris!" (When I think it was raining when we left Paris!).
- "Ma copine **est passée** mais tu n'étais pas là" (My girlfriend passed by but you were not in).
- "La pendule sonnait minuit quand **ils sont rentrés**" (The clock was striking midnight when they came home).
- "**Elle y est restée** toute l'année" (She stayed there all year).
- "**Elle est revenue** trop tard pour voir son petit fils" (She returned too late to see her grandson).
- "**Ils sont entrés** dans le magasin et ils ont réussi à déranger un cambrioleur" (They entered the shop and they succeeded in disturbing a burglar).
- "**Nous sommes montés** à vingt-deux heures" (We went up at 10pm).
- "Quand **il est mort** il avait cent ans" (When he died he was 100 years old).
- "Ma fille **est née** à la maison" (My daughter was born at home).
- "**Je suis partie** à huit heures et je suis revenue à midi" (I left at 8am and I came back at midday).
- "Il pleuvait quand **ils sont sortis**" (It was raining when they went out).
- "**Elle est tombée** malade pour la première fois quand elle avait dix-sept ans" (She fell ill for the first time when she was 17 years old).
- "Mes parents **sont venus** me voir à l'hôpital trois jours après mon accident" (My parents came to see me at the hospital three days after my accident).

Reflexive verbs

There are, literally, thousands of these but many of the basic reflexive verbs are about going to bed, getting up, dressed and washed etc. So **use être in the auxiliary to say**:
- "**Je me suis couché** parce que je me sentais malade" (I went to bed because I was feeling ill).

- "**Je me suis reveillé** de bonne heure parce que ma chambre était baignée de soleil" (I woke up early because my bedroom was bathed in sunshine).
- "**Je me suis endormi** après avoir lu un polar" (I fell asleep having read a detective novel).
- "**Je me suis levé** à huit heures et demie" (I got up at 8.30am).
- "**Je me suis lavé** et puis **je me suis brossé** les dents" (I washed and then I brushed my teeth).
- "Puis **je me suis rasé**. Ensuite **je me suis coiffé**" (Then I shaved. Next, I combed my hair).
- "**Je me suis habillé** et **je suis parti**" (I got dressed and then I left the house).

Summary

And for the moment, that is it! You will find many more basic words and expressions in the rest of the chapter but they will be incorporated into more advanced ways of expressing yourself. For now, if you made sense of what I have said so far – terrific! But do not expect that to happen on first reading. Keep on coming back to the basics to drive home the message ("enfoncer le clou" – a "clou" is a nail, by the way). You should now at least know:

- how to conjugate **être** in different tenses; to say what things are (what things are used for awaits in the **Servir** chapter later in the book)
- how to use **être** to say who people are and what they do for a living
- how to say what things are
- how to say what people and things look like
- how to use **c'est** and **il est**
- how to use **être** in tenses other than the present, notably the future, imperfect and perfect tenses
- how to use the auxiliary of **être** in the perfect (ie compound) tense with verbs of movement and reflexive verbs.
-

So we have made a good start. You are now "en route", on the road, so to speak. Let us now begin to pick up a bit of speed.

Getting Better

You can get better by acquiring a bigger, broader vocabulary of course. And I certainly do not want to discourage that: the more words you have, other things being equal, the better. But it is important to realise that things are not always equal. As you now realise, there is a disproportionately greater return from doing other things sometimes and that time is now.

Rapid improvement in your expressive powers will come, first of all at least, from digging deeper into that verb table we began the chapter with. With a bit of rummaging around you should be able to:

- say how you would be (or feel) if something else were to happen
- say how others would be (or feel) if you were to do something else
- go back in time (like the Time Lord, Doctor Who!) and say what would have happened if something else had happened and...
- start building a bank of useful phrases and expressions that will add colour to what you want to say.

So, how **would** you feel if, say, in a large supermarket ("une grande surface") the "caissière" (cashier), instead of giving you the change from a 10€ note that you had given her, gave you back the change from a 20€ note? Would you be pleased, irritated, honest, dishonest or what? In French:

"Si la caissière, au lieu de vous rendre la monnaie sur 10€ vous rend la monnaie sur 20€:

- **Seriez-vous** contente ou mécontente? (Would you be happy or unhappy?)
- **Seriez-vous** irritée? (Would you be irritated?)
- **Seriez-vous** honnête (Would you be honest?)
- **Seriez-vous** malhonnête?" (Would you be dishonest?)

Quelques réponses (some replies):

- "Oui, si cela m'arrivait (Yes, if that happened to me) **je serais** très contente" (I would be very happy).
- "Non, **je serais** très mécontente" (No, I would be very unhappy).
- "Oui, **je serais** très irritée, agacée même" (Yes, I would be very irritated, annoyed even).

- "Mais oui, bien sûr que **je serais** honnête" (But yes, of course, I would be honest).
- "J'ai honte de le dire, mais **je serais** malhonnête" (I am ashamed to say so but I would be dishonest).

Now imagine that your mother discovered that you had stolen ("voler", to steal) a packet of cigarettes from the corner shop. Would she be indifferent, mildly irritated, annoyed or furious? In French:

"Imagine que ta mère a découvert que tu avais volé un paquet de cigarettes du commerçant de coin. Serait-elle indifférente, un peu irritée, agacée ou furieuse?"

Quelques réponses

- "Non, **elle ne serait pas** indifférente" (No, she would not be indifferent).
- "**Elle serait** plus qu'un peu irritée" (She would be more than a bit irritated).
- "**Elle pourrait être** agacée" (She could be annoyed).
- "Mais je pense qu'**elle serait** furieuse" (But I think that she would be furious).

So, to express how you or someone else would feel if something else were to happen, you need the **present conditional** of **être**: "I would be", "she would be" etc.

However, there need not be an **if** clause present to say how you would feel etc, for example:

- "**Je serais** contente de voir la Tour Eiffel, cet après-midi" (I would be happy (if I were) to see the Eiffel Tower this afternoon). Here, "if I were" is implied, but not stated.
- "**Ça serait** un très grand plaisir de dîner chez vous la semaine prochaine" (It would be a great pleasure (if I were) to have dinner at your place next week).
- "**Seriez-vous** heureux de m'accompagner au match demain après-midi?" (Would you be happy (if you were) to come with me to the match tomorrow afternoon?)

Another way of expressing the **if** clause is to employ the verb **devoir** (one of our "killer" verbs) in the **imperfect tense plus an infinitive**. Here is an example:

- "Si je **devais faire** le même rôle stéréotypé de sex-symbol jusqu'à la fin de mes jours, cela **serait** complètement ridicule" (If I were to play the same sex-symbol role to the end of my days, that would be completely ridiculous).

Now for some time travel!

How would you have felt if something else had happened? Already, you can see, perhaps, that although we are once more going to meet the conditional tense, this time it's the **past conditional** that we will have to use, not the present conditional. So:

Je serais… now becomes **J'aurais été**…

You can also see that the past conditional has two components (ie it is a compound verb):

- the past participle of **être**, **été**
- the auxiliary verb **avoir** in the present conditional, **j'aurais**, **tu aurais**, **il aurait**, **elle aurait**, **nous aurions** etc.

So let's begin with a few sentences in English that illustrate these constructions in action:

- "If I had my mac, I would not have got wet."
- "You would never have come to the party if I had not invited you."
- "They would never have stayed at that hotel if they had realised how expensive it was."

Let's now try some similar sentences, this time in French:

- "Si **j'avais su** qu'il allait me donner un cadeau, **j'aurais été** très embarrassée" (If I had known that he was going to give me a present, I would have been very embarrassed).
- "S'il **y avait eu** des élections à ce moment-là, ça **aurait été** la fin du gouvernement" (If elections had taken place at that time, that would have been the end of the government).
- "Si Jacques **m'avait donné** son parapluie, je **n'aurais pas été** si mouillé" (If Jacques had given me his umbrella, I would not have been so wet).

Yes, I do agree that these sentences using the conditional tenses – present and past - with **if** clauses are a bit complicated, indeed difficult, at first. But, because you will not be using them very frequently, you can go easy a bit on learning them. But they will only stick with practice. One thing is certain, if you **were** to use them, only very occasionally, French people **would** now be saying to you: "Vraiment tu parles / vous parlez bien le français!" (Really, you speak very good French)!

But armed with just a few colourful phrases sprinkled around your conversation ("éparpillées un peu partout!") you will win over a lot more French admirers! Let's just have a look at some of the simplest **colloquial**, **idiomatic** and **figurative** expressions that are likely to get this result.

How to express pleasure

C'est un vrai régal – it's a real treat
C'est pas mal – it's not bad
C'est génial – it's super. This word is used a lot
C'est super – it's great
C'est vachement chouette – it's really great
C'est sensas, c'est impec, c'est le pied, c'est dément, c'est nickel, c'est nickel chrome – all mean that something is **great**.

How to express indifference

There are far fewer expressions in this category, perhaps because the French are rarely indifferent about anything! However, three in particular I have always found very useful are:

Ça m'est égal – It is all the same to me. But it is useful because you can always change the **pronoun**, eg:

- Ça **lui** est égal – It is all the same to him / her
- Ça **nous** est égal – It is all the same to us
- Ça **leur** est égal – It is all the same to them.
-

The second expression is:

Çe n'est pas la peine – Do not bother, it's ok.

The third is:

C'est kif-kif (or **c'est du kif**). This is much more colloquial and corresponds to the English expression, "it makes no odds".

Saying that something/someone is not great

Ce n'est pas terrible – literally something is not too awful. In truth, it **means the exact opposite!** "Pas terrible" means terrible! This is a very common expression.

C'est moche/plutôt moche – something is ugly. Again, a very common expression.

C'est du bidon – something is a load of codswallop or rubbish.

Ce n'est pas le Pérou – it's nothing great, nothing to write home about.

C'est de la camelote – another way of saying something is rubbish, junk, tat etc or of very poor quality.

C'est du vol – something is daylight robbery.

C'est dégueulasse – something is disgusting and it is often used to describe food and drink, although it has wider meanings than that.

C'est de l'arnarque – something is a rip off.

C'est donné – something is cheap but not cheap and nasty.

C'est du toc – something is fake.

C'est une vraie galère – it's hell.

C'est pas une partie de plaisir – something is no pleasure.

C'est un bled – something or somewhere is a god-forsaken hole.

C'est de l'hébreu pour moi – it is "double dutch" to me. (Every country seems to have an expression that suggests linguistic bafflement. It always seems to be **what others perceive to be a difficult language** eg Greek or Chinese.)

How to express problems and difficulties

Ce n'est pas vraiment mon truc / machin / bidule – it's not my thing.

Ce n'est pas rien – it's not nothing.

C'est la bouteille à l'encre – it is as clear as mud.

Ce n'est pas de la tarte – it is no easy job.

C'est un travail de Romain – there is a long and difficult task ahead.

Ce n'est pas évident – not obvious how something should be done.

C'est la fin des haricots – that is the last straw.

C'est le comble – that is the limit.

C'est du boulot – something is hard work, another very frequently encountered expression.

Ce n'est pas moi qui fais la pluie et le beau temps – I'm not the boss around here.

How to express how easy somethings are to do

C'est simple comme bonjour – it could not be easier.

Ce n'est pas la mer à boire – it's not the sea to drink. It conveys the idea that you do not see any problems; that something is not a big deal.

C'est cousu de fil blanc – it is perfectly predictable.

C'est dans la poche – it is in the bag.
C'est le cadet de mes soucis – that is the least of my worries.
C'est du tout cuit – something is a cinch.
C'est fait – it's done.
C'est dans mes cordes or **c'est mon rayon** – something is up my street.

You will have noticed, I'm sure, that all the examples of colloquial and idiomatic speech at this intermediary level of knowledge, ie **Getting Better**, begin with **c'est** (or **ce n'est pas**): these are perhaps the easiest to get to grips with; and this is where this chapter began. With **c'est**. But a lot of colloquial and idiomatic French is a tad more difficult to acquire and use. For this reason, I have reserved suitable expressions for the next level, **Now You Are Really Speaking French**.

But you may feel that you have already been overwhelmed with so much figurative language. Well, yes, there are quite a lot of useful expressions here but, again, you really do not need to plunge into some headlong rush for fluency in this register. Just a few words and phrases here and there will be enough to impress your French-speaking audience and convince them that you are making great strides in what is, by common consent, a pretty scary language. So, onwards and upwards! In Welsh, that was the motto of my primary school. I have never forgotten it!

Now You Are Really Speaking French!

It should not be much of a jump to the third level of competence and conviction; already you should feel very comfortable in the company of **être**, the killer of "killer" verbs. Two things you could (dare I say should) do to get to be really convincing with your use of **être** are:

- get to know your way around the **subjunctive**
- get to be even more confident and ambitious when you use **figurative expressions** ie idiomatic and colloquial French.

So here we go.

The Subjunctive

I have already had a few words to say on the subjunctive in **Chapter One** but here we are going to step up a notch or two. In the hope that the conjugation of **être** in the present subjunctive holds no fear for your (see again the verb table at the beginning of this chapter) we can move on and look at the deployment of the verb/mood; and we shall obviously set out plenty of examples of it in use.

The subjunctive is widely used to express wishes and hopes for the future. As we have already seen, if there is only one verb subject in the sentence, **the infinitive** will follow the verb expressing the wish. For example:

- "Je veux (or je voudrais) **partir** à Paris" ie I want (or more politely, I would like) to leave for Paris.

However, if there are two people in the sentence, **the subjunctive** tense is required:

- "Je veux (voudrais) **que tu partes** à Paris" ie I want (I would like) you to leave for Paris.

You can also use **aimer** to express the same wish in the same way:

- "**J'aimerais que tu partes** à Paris" ie I would like you to leave for Paris.

Many more expressions formed in this way are followed by the subjunctive tense – and I shall list several of them very shortly. But since the hero of this chapter is **être**, not **partir** (that comes later in this book), let us specify how **être** is implicated. Here are some examples:

- "Je veux que **tu sois** contente" – I want you to be happy.
- "Nous voudrions que **vous soyez** polis" – We would like you to be polite.
- "Ils aimeraient qu'**elles soient** heureuses" – They would like them to be happy.

Other verbs expressing the general notion of wishes and desires also follow this pattern, but notably **not espérer**, to hope. This is a common error made by those learning the subjunctive for the first time.

Other feelings in this subjective realm also require the subjunctive, including **préférer**, for example:

- "Mon père **préfère que tu sois** proche pendant cette période difficile" ie My father would prefer you to be close during this difficult period.

Another use of the subjunctive occurs when you want to say that people or things are special in some way or another (even if they do not exist!):

- "Je cherche quelqu'un **qui soit plutôt autoritaire**" ie I am looking for someone who is rather authoritarian.

The subjunctive also follows the verbs **penser** and **croire**, **but only when they are questions**:

- "**Pensez-vous** que le prix du boeuf **soit** bon marché en France?" ie Do you think that beef is cheap in France?
- "**Croyez-vous** que ce **soit** vrai?" ie Do you believe that this is true?

Another use of the subjunctive occurs after **qui** or **que** when you want to talk about things or people that are **superlative** in some way or another, ie the best, the nicest, the fastest… and so on:

- "Il est l'homme **le plus beau qui ne soit** jamais venu dans cette maison" ie He is the most handsome man that has ever come to this house.

But perhaps the most frequent use of the subjunctive in French follows the verbs of necessity, notably **falloir** ("to want", "to have to"). The expression **il faut que** you will hear many times in a day, I suspect. Tenses other than this present tense use of **falloir** which also occur fairly often include:

- **il faudra que** – you/someone else will have to…
- **il fallait que** – it used to be necessary for…
- **il a fallu que** – it was necessary for…

Here are just a few examples of "il faut que" followed by the subjunctive:

- "Il faut que **vous soyez** présent à la cérémonie" – You have to be at the ceremony.
- "Il faut qu'**elles soient** bien habillées pour la présentation demain matin"– They really must be well dressed for the presentation tomorrow morning.
- "Il faut que tous les détails **soient** corrects" – All the details must be correct.

For now, that is enough on the use of the subjunctive and how it affects **être**. But we shall return to this topic throughout many of the remaining chapters, both to illustrate other uses of the subjunctive and its significance for all our other "killer" verbs.

Familiar or informal French featuring être

Often much French that might be considered idiomatic, colloquial or even down right vulgar or rude is more properly thought of as merely informal or familiar French – the sort of French that is heard constantly in conversation that fails to raise the hackles of all but the most "collet monté" (straight-laced) French people.

At this third level of French, many of the differences between informal, familiar, colloquial, idiomatic and even argotic French (ie slang) are so fine that it largely depends on the social context; **who** is speaking to **whom**, **when**, **where**, **how** and **why**. In my experience, much depends upon how well you know someone. I confess that I have some French friends (good ones, I hasten to add) with whom my conversations are very familiar indeed! But it is always wise to avoid all but the least offensive slang.

But that is the same in English. Social conventions largely determine the extent of say, bawdiness, in conversation. Perhaps at an English football match, for example, a group of English friends might use words you would never hear in a public meeting. But if a Frenchman joined a group of English football enthusiasts for the first time and started using some of the most vulgar English words, they would be surprised and quite possibly offended. So a degree of discretion is always a good idea when a conversation takes place between people with different cultures and languages. With this cautionary thought in the background, let us examine many more words, phrases and expressions using **être**, whose meanings might just depend on circumstances. In what follows, I therefore make no attempt to classify them according to degrees of familiarity, nor do I try to group them thematically. They are presented randomly – so that you have to work a bit!

C'est de la blague or **c'est une blague** – something is intended as a joke. A more conventional way of expressing this idea is **Je plaisante** – this is very frequently used.
C'est coton – something is difficult.
C'est drôlement coton – it is awfully hard.
C'est super – exactly what it says.
Ce n'est pas fameux – something is not very good.
Ce n'est pas vrai – use this with your voice rising in disbelief, even astonishment. For further emphasis, preface it with **ça alors**!, which means "strewth!" or in my view, even better, **ah bon**?, again with the voice implying more than a gram of disbelief. I cannot tell you how many times a day I will say **ah bon**? It is **such** a useful little expression.
C'est un drôle de numéro – can mean that someone is a funny (ha! ha!) sort of bloke; but it can also mean that he is a funny (peculiar) sort of bloke. So be careful there.
C'est la poisse (or **quelle poisse**) – is a rather vulgar way of saying "what bad luck!"
C'est la vie! – "That's life!" It is often used to convey a certain sense of powerlessness (a very common French sentiment, incidentally!)

There are two words in French in particular that are used to suggest the notion that something is not working at all or that something is buggered, to give you a sense of the English alternative! They are:

- **foutu** and…
- **fichu**.

Of the two, the former is generally considered the more vulgar. So you can say:

- "Cet aspirateur (vacuum cleaner) **est foutu**", or
- "Ce tuyau (hosepipe) **est fichu**".
- Alternatively, **c'est mort** (dead).

But with these two words, we are entering a potential minefield. I recommend a good dictionary of French slang, definitely written by a "frog!"

C'est de la rigolade – is one expression with two meanings. It means either, it's nothing to be taken seriously or it's very easy to do.

C'est une sale histoire – means that something is a sordid business. If, however, you want to say to someone that you have got a dirty story to tell, then **une histoire cochonne** is the appropriate phrase!

Ce n'est pas sorcier – means that something is simple enough.

C'est du tonnerre – means that something is terrific.

Again, you will have noticed that all these expressions begin with **C'est** or **Ce n'est pas** on the grounds that, for the most part anyway, they are relatively short, sharp and easy to memorise. But I am now going to give you some expressions that begin with **être** itself, rather than **c'est**. Many of these are longer expressions and many have taken on a proverbial role. Again, with no particular effort on my part to classify them in any way, we have:

Être au bout du rouleau – to be at the end of one's tether; to have had more than enough.

Être une vraie girouette – to be someone who changes with the weather ("une girouette" is a weather vane).

Être au four et au moulin – to be in two places at the same time ("four" is an oven and "moulin" is a mill).

Être complètement allumé – (lit up like a lightbulb) means to be crazy.

Être habillé comme l'as de pique – the ace of spades. This means to be dressed in a weird assortment of clothes. (Incidentally, the familiar word for clothes is "fringues". You will hear this word a lot).

Être branché – (switched on) means to be in the know.

Être timbré – (stamped) means to be nuts.

Être sur le retour – means to be getting on a bit; perhaps over the top.

Être près de ses sous – (a "sou" is a vey small coin, hence the expression "je n'ai pas un sou, ie I have not got a penny) means to be tight with one's money. ("Radin" is a good single word for mean with money).

Être pantouflard – is to be **a man** who likes to stay at home (the reference here is to les pantouffles, ie slippers).

Être pot-au-feu – has the same meaning but this time with a culinary reference point and relates to **a woman**. **Être soupe au lait** has the same meaning.

Être gonflé – means to be brave. **Se dégonfler** means to chicken out.

Être chocolat – to be had; to be conned: "me voilà chocolat!" – I've been had/done!

Être au trente-sixième dessous – to be at a very low ebb. It is amazing how many times the number 36 crops up in French idioms! Remember "tous les trente-six du mois" in the earlier chapter?

Être dans la purée – to be hard up. (Incidentally, "une purée" in French is only ever mashed potato. So, if you want to buy, say, some tomato purée, you have got to ask for "sauce à la tomate concentrée").

Être à l'aise dans ses baskets – (this word is a classic piece of franglais as it translates as "trainers" in English) means to be comfortable in one's own skin ie **être bien dans sa peau**.

Être du coin – means to be from around the neighbourhood.

Être chaud chaud – (no, I am not unintentionally repeating myself!) means to be really keen on whatever.

Être plein à craquer – means to be full to bursting and is very often used to describe restaurants, bars, public places and so on. Alternatives include:

Être bourré, **être plein comme un oeuf** or **être truffé de** all mean to be stuffed full. They are not polite and if , in a restaurant, you want to say that you have had plenty to eat, say: "J'ai bien mangé, merci."

Être au parfum – means to be in the know.
N'être jamais sorti de son trou - means never to have left one's own backyard.
Ne pas être dans son assiette - means to feel under the weather.

Être dans les vapes – means to be out for the count (from drink or drugs).

Ne pas être né d'hier – means not to have been born yesterday.

Être aux anges – means to be in seventh heaven.

Ne pas être gâté – means to be out of luck.

Être en fonds – to be in funds.

Être fauché – to be broke, is a popular expression. (Incidentally, if you want to say that something is popular, "populaire" can be used. But this word also means working class, so it is the context that fixes its meaning).

Être à la hauteur – means to be on form.

Être de mauvais poil – means to be in a foul temper.

Être soupe-au-lait – means to be touchy.

Être crevé(e) - or **Être claqué(e)** – to be tired. This is a classic example of expressions which are distinctly familiar rather than vulgar.

Être sur les dents – means to be under pressure.

Être le dindon (turkey) **de la farce** (stuffing) – means to be taken for a ride.

Être la cinquième roue du carrosse – means to feel like a spare part (and that is the polite translation!)

Être à côté de la plaque – means to be clueless.

Être tiré à quatre épingles – means to be all dressed up.

Être long comme un jour sans-pain – means to be endless.

Être cul et chemise – means to be as thick as thieves. The word "cul" is pronounced without the "l", ie "cu". It is one of those words which has more than one meaning. We know it in the English (but really French) expression "cul-de-sac", ie a road with no exit. But it also means, and this is putting it very politely, bottom or bum in English. To appreciate its full meaning, you have got to go a bit further!

Être dans de beaux draps (sheets) - means to be in a right mess.

Être dans le pétrin – (mess) means literally to be in a fine mess.

Être à la bourre – means to be late.

Être sur la paille – means to be penniless.

Être un pince-sans-rire – means to have a deadpan sense of humour.

Être à poil – means to be naked and is generally considered to be vulgar.

Être au poil – (careful!) means to be great, perfect even.

Être casse – pieds – means to be a real pest and is very frequently encountered, often in phrases such as "il me casse les pieds", he gets on my nerves.

Être culotté – means to have a nerve or be cheeky.

Être gris, être parti, être rond, all convey the general idea of being seriously inebriated (will pissed do?!)

Être vanné – means to be dead tired.

Être sur la même longeur d'onde means to be on the same wavelength.

Some other useful expressions using être

There are some useful expressions relating to time, for instance:

Être en avance – to be early
Être à l'heure – to be on time
Être en retard – to be late. Here is a mini-conversation using these expressions:

Jeanne	"Je suis désolée, Mariette. J'espérais être au moins à l'heure, même un peu en avance, mais mon train était un peu retardé, voilà pourquoi j'ai quinze minutes de retard. Et je sais que tu as tellement de choses à faire avant de pouvoir partir."
Mariette	"T'en fais pas, Jeanne, il n'y a pas d'urgence. Je ne suis pas pressée. J'ai commandé notre taxi pour midi. Ça nous donnera une bonne demi-heure pour arriver au restaurant."

Here are two more useful expressions:

Où en est… This expression is used to convey the current state or position of something, eg:

- "**Où en est** la France de nos jours?" meaning what is the position or state of France, nowadays? Ask this question at the moment and you may well get some very candid replies. "La France est franchement dans la merde", for example?
  "Merde", of course, is every French person's favourite swear word ("juron" or "mot de Cambronne") and time was when it was considered a very vulgar word. But times change (when in France!) and these days some ostensibly proper people let it slip from time to time. But again, if you are not sure, refrain from using it. Slightly lower in the vulgarity stakes:

Il faut qu'elle **se démerde** means she (ie France) has got to pull her finger out.

Other uses of **où en est** include:

Où en est le cinéma français de nos jours? – What is the current state of French cinema?

Où en sommes-nous dans ce livre? – Where are we in this book?

My second useful expression, used to describe somebody who "could not be more… (whatever)", in other words, very typical indeed, is **on ne peut plus**, as in:

- "Vous voyez Pierre là-bas? **Il est on ne peut plus** français" – You see Pierre over there? He could not be more French (if he tried!)

Conclusion

Être is perhaps the most important verb in French, simply because it is used to describe the most fundamental of life's characteristics – **being** ie **existence**. To be able to say who you are, who someone else is and so on is about as basic as any language gets. But **être** can do much more that that: in particular we can use it to talk about our feelings. And we also saw that **être** is a very important verb in idiomatic speech. For all these reasons (and more) **être** is **the must learn** verb.

And that should be enough for now. You have got plenty to get on with the verb **être**. Before we leave this verb, here are two real, live conversations which feature our "serial killer" verb, **être**.

Être: Conversation One

Here, our interviewer, Annie, stops people in the streets of Paris. She shows them photos of famous people and asks the passers-by to identify them:

Annie:	Voici une photo, c'est qui?
Une femme:	C'est Carla Bruni.
Annie:	Et là c'est qui?
Femme:	C'est Charlie Chaplin, "Charlot."
Annie:	Bravo! Et qui c'est, Charlot?
Femme:	C'est un acteur comique de cinéma.
Annie:	Il est français?
Femme:	Non, il est anglais je crois.
Annie:	Et là, c'est qui?
Femme:	C'est Salvador Dali, n'est-ce pas?
Annie:	Oui, mais c'est qui, Salvador Dali?
Femme:	C'est un peintre.
Annie:	Français?
Femme:	Non. Je pense qu'il est espagnol.
Annie:	Et là, qui c'est?
Femme:	Je ne sais pas.
Annie:	C'est une princesse… et c'est une actrice aussi.
Femme:	Ah, oui, je la connais, c'est Grace Kelly!
Annie:	Oui. Et là, qui c'est?
Femme:	C'est Nicolas Sarkozy, bien-sûr!
Annie:	Et ce personnage-ci?
Femme:	Ça, c'est le nouveau président de la République, monsieur François Hollande.
Annie:	Et là, c'est qui?
Femme:	Encore une fois, je ne sais pas.
Annie:	Merci beaucoup, madame.

Etre: Conversation Two

Annie meets a young girl, Laurence, in the perfume department of a Paris department store.

Annie:	Comment t'appelles-tu?
Laurence:	Je m'appelle Laurence.
Annie:	Qu'est-ce tu veux faire dans la vie, Laurence?
Laurence:	Je voudrais être inspecteur de police.
Annie:	Et tes parents, que pensent-ils de cette idée?
Laurence:	Ils sont d'accord.
Annie:	Ils veulent que tu sois inspecteur de police?
Laurence:	Disons qu'ils ne sont pas contre.
Annie:	Et si tu étais mariée, est-ce que tu penses que ton mari serait obligé d'être aussi inspecteur de police?
Laurence:	Pas du tout. Je suis pour une certaine liberté dans le couple, de ne pas être trop dépendant, l'un de l'autre.
Annie:	Penses-tu que ce ne soit pas incompatible que ton mari appartienne à une autre catégorie sociale?
Laurence:	Non, pas forcément.
Annie:	Ça ne te dérangerait pas qu'il soit garçon de café, qu'il boive, qu'il soit joueur?
Laurence:	C'est sûr que je ne veux pas qu'il boive, qu'il se drogue et...
Annie:	Et tu ne voudrais pas un homme qui soit autoritaire ou plutôt timide même?
Laurence:	Autoritaire, non, parce que moi, je suis déjà autoritaire, donc je pense que ça ne marcherait pas. Timide? Non plus.
Annie:	Nickel et merci bien, Laurence.
Laurence:	Je t'en prie.

Some words you might not yet know

• incompatible -	incompatible
• appartenir à -	to belong to
• pas forcément -	not necessarily
• boire -	to drink
• jouer -	to play
• déranger -	to disturb someone
• un garçon de café -	a waiter (in a coffee bar)
• se droguer -	to take drugs
• autoritaire -	authoritarian
• marcher -	to work
• je vous en prie -	you're welcome

Être: Exercises

Fill in the blank spaces:

1.   Qui est-ce? (   ) le Prince Charles.

2.   Non, (   ) John Lennon, c'est Ringo Starr.

Here is the answer, what is the question?

3.   C'est une voiture (   ).

4.   Elle est infirmière (   ).

You are in a café. The coffee is disgusting:

5.   Monsieur, ce café (   ) dégoutouant.

Now you are complaining about the wine glass, which is much too small:

6.   Monsieur, ce verre à vin, (   ) trop petit.

You are describing your best friend to someone else:

7.   Mon ami (   ) jeune.

8.   Mon amie (   ) grande; elle est petite.

You are hoping to see your best friend(s) tomorrow:

9.   Ça ( ) formidable de voir Hélène demain.

10.   Jean-Claude dit qu'ils (   ) dans le café demain à onze heures.

Unfortunately, they did not turn up:

11.   Je suis arrivé à onze heures mais ils (   ) venus.

12.   Elles (   ) montées se coucher très tôt ce soir.

13.   Je (   ) couché parce que je me sentais fatigué.

14. Il ( ) brossé les dents, puis il ( ) parti.

15. Si cela m'arrivait je ( ) très irrité.

16. Si je devais me lever à cinq heures, ça ( ) complètement ridicule.

17. Si j'avais su qu'elle allait me donner son manteau de fourrure, j'( ) très embarrassée.

18. Merci pour le dîner hier soir, ( ) un vrai régal.

19. Ma mère veut qu'elles ( ) contentes avec leur chambre.

20. Mon frère ne pense pas que la clé ( ) dans le placard.

21. Il faut que vous ( ) présent quand il arrivera.

Être: Answers

1. C'est
2. ce n'est pas
3. Qu'est-ce que c'est que ça?
4. Qu'est-ce quelle fait dans la vie?
5. est
6. c'est
7. est
8. n'est pas
9. sera (or serait)
10. seront
11. ne sont pas
12. sont
13. me suis
14. s'est, est
15. serais
16. serait
17. aurai été
18. c'était
19. soient
20. soit
21. soyez

Chapter Three
Avoir

Introduction

If **être** is the **king** "killer" verb, then **avoir**, to have, is the killer **queen**, if you like the **Lady Macbeth** of our verb list! And for several good reasons.

First, as we have already seen, **avoir** is the auxiliary verb used in compound tenses wherever it is **not être**. Therefore, thousands of **regular** verbs have **avoir** in the auxiliary; and many, many more **irregular** verbs also have **avoir**. In our list, these irregular verbs all use **avoir**:

- avoir (yes, I know that sounds odd but don't we say in English, "I have had?")
- connaître
- passer (in some uses)
- devoir
- dire
- être
- faire
- mettre
- pouvoir
- prendre
- savoir
- servir
- vouloir.

Second, **avoir** is a mainstay in familiar, colloquial, idiomatic and argotic language, just as is **être**.

Third, it is used in many frequently used fixed expressions ("expressions figées"), notable amongst them being **il y a**, meaning, there is or there are and…

Fourth, because in its most **literal** form, to have, in other words **to possess**, is at the core of our beliefs and, therefore, language, in all western societies (and others, too).

So, let's being by conjugating avoir.

The Avoir Conjugations

Present Tense

J'ai	Nous avons
Tu as	Vous avez
Ils a	Ils ont
Elle a	Elles ont

Future Tense

J' aurai	Nous aurons
Tu auras	Vous aurez
Il aura	Ils auront
Elle aura	Elles auront

Imperfect Tense

J'avais	Nous avions
Tu avais	Vous aviez
Il avait	Ils avaient
Elle avait	Elles avaient

Perfect Tense

J'ai eu	Nous avons eu
Tu as eu	Vous avez eu
Il a eu	Ils ont eu
Elle a eu	Elles ont eu

Future Perfect Tense

J'aurai eu	Nous aurons eu
Tu auras eu	Vous aurez eu
Il aura eu	Ils auront eu
Elle aura eu	Elles auront eu

Pluperfect Tense

J'avais eu	Nous avions eu
Tu avais eu	Vous aviez eu
Il avait eu	Ils avaient eu
Elle avait eu	Elles avaient eu

Present Conditional Tense

J'aurais	Nous aurions
Tu aurais	Vous auriez
Il aurait	Ils auraient
Elle aurait	Elles auraient

Past Conditional Tense

J'aurais eu	Nous aurions eu
Tu aurais eu	Vous auriez eu
Il aurait eu	Ils auraient eu
Elle aurait eu	Elles auraient eu

Present Subjunctive Tense

J'aie	Nous ayons
Tu aies	Vous ayez
Il ait	Ils aient
Elle ait	Elles aient

Imperative

Aie
Ayons
Ayez

So, armed with the knowledge of how to conjugate **avoir**, let us begin with some basic ways of using this very **versatile** verb.

Avoir: The Basics

The **basic** meaning of **avoir** is, quite literally, to have, ie to possess. So:

- "**J'ai** de la monnaie dans ma poche" ie I have some change in my pocket. Please note that "monnaie" does **not** translate as "money". The correct word for money is "l'argent"(m).
- "Est-ce que **tu as** un tire-bouchon? Je voudrais ouvrir cette bouteille de vin" ie Do you have a corkscrew? I want to open this bottle of wine. (Incidentally, if you want to open a bottle of beer, you will need "un décapsuleur"; and

if you want a thing ("machin") that does both jobs, then you will need "un limonadier").

- "**Avez-vous** un stylo? Je crois que j'ai perdu le mien" ie Do you have a pen? I think that I have lost mine.

And of course, **avoir** works in exactly the same way in tenses other than the present:

- "Dans le temps, nos gosses **avaient** une grande tente dans le jardin" ie In the past, our kids used to have a large tent in the garden.
- "Je pense que j'irai à Londres demain. **Il y a** une petite boutique qui **a** beaucoup de baskets américaines en stock" ie I think that I will go to London tomorrow. There is a small shop which has lots of American trainers in stock.

Very often too, you can use **avoir** to say that you "possess" all sorts of non-physical things – like a cold in the head!

- "Maman, je me sens mal. Je crois que j'ai un rhume." If it is something worse, it could be "la grippe" ie the flu, or
- "Papa, **j'ai eu** une bonne note pour mon devoir de chimie à l'école aujourd'hui" ie Dad, I got a good grade for my chemistry homework at school today.

So, use **avoir** when you want to say that you have something, be it physical or intangible. In fact, as you will see later in this chapter, **avoir** is extensively used to describe intangibles, for example, feelings, difficulties, opportunities. Just a few examples here and then we will move on. First:

- "Qu'est-ce qu'**il y a** François?" (or "Qu'est-ce que **tu as**, François?) **Tu as** mauvaise mine" ie What is the matter, Francois? You do not look too well.

My second example is when you want to say that you are fed up. There are several ways in French of expressing this. Amongst them are:

- **J'en ai marre** – I am fed up.
- **J'en ai ras la casquette** – I am up to here with it, pointing to your forehead. This is the expression often used in south-west France.
- **J'en ai assez** – I have had enough, and…
- **J'en ai ras le bol**.

An expression to use when you think you have "got" somebody ie when you think you have fooled them is:
- **Je t'ai eu**! – I got you!

Avoir is extensively used to describe people. We saw in the **Être** chapter that this verb, too, can be used for this purpose: "il est grand"; "elle est petite" and so on. So if you are describing someone to somebody, you might say:

- "Elle **a** des yeux bleus et les cheveux blonds". That is to say, she has blue eyes and blond hair. Please note that "hair" in French is always in the plural. If you want to talk about a single hair, then the word is "poil".

You can also use **avoir** to describe the shape and dimensions of things:

- "Je voudrais une table qui **ait** (subjunctive) cette forme-là, s'il vous plaît" ie I would like a table shaped like that, please.

Il y a can mean "there is" or "there are" and is just about one of the most frequently heard expressions in French. So here are just a few of the enormous number of examples that abound in the language:

- "**Il y a** pas mal de beurre dans le frigo" means that there is quite a lot of butter in the fridge. Note here the use of "pas mal" instead of beaucoup. Beginners in French tend to over-use beaucoup for lack of any good alternatives: "pas mal" makes an excellent change. Note, also "frigo" for fridge. If you want to say it is in the freezer, you need "congélateur" (m).
- "**Il y a** un bar Irlandais à deux pas de chez nous. L'ambiance y est fantastique" means that there is an Irish bar very close to us. The atmosphere there (it is the "y" in the sentence that tells you it is "there") is fantastic.
- "**Il n'y a** plus de rouge, mais il nous reste du blanc" means that there is no more red (wine) left, but we still have some white.

We spoke in an earlier chapter about the omission of **ne** in expressions of negation. **Il y a** is also a very frequent victim of this habit. Very often in spoken French, **il** is omitted and what you get then is '**y a**…. Once more, the young in particular favour this expression. But it is not correct. I advise you to stick to the full expression, **il y a**, unless you are in very relaxed company.

But perhaps confusingly, **il y a** can also mean "ago" in time clauses. For example:

- "Je l'ai vu **il y a** trois mois" – I saw him three months ago.
- "Mon fils est parti **il y a** deux jours" – My son left two days ago.
- "C'était **il y a** trois ans que nous sommes allés au Mexique – It was three years ago that we went to Mexico.

Avoir is always used to express age when it is a question of ("il s'agit de") a specific age:

- "**J'ai** trente-deux ans" – I am thirty two years old. But
- "**J'aurai** trente-trois ans le 30 septembre" – I will be thirty-three years old on the 30th of September.

You also need **avoir** when you want to say that you are hot or cold:

- "Oui, **j'ai** froid. Pourriez-vous fermer la porte s'il vous plaît?" – Yes, I am cold. Could you close the door, please?
- "Je crois qu'**elles avaient** chaud. Voilà pourquoi elles sont sorties pour quelques minutes" – I believe they were (feeling) hot. That is why they went out for a wee while.

(Incidentally, if you want to say that **something** is hot or cold, you need **être**:

- "**Ce four est chaud**!" ie This oven is hot!
- "**La voiture est froide**. C'est pour ça qu'elle ne veut pas démarrer" ie The car is cold. That is why it does not want to start.

Also, use **avoi**r when you want to say that you are hungry (or thirsty, ie "soif"):

- "Maman, **j'ai** tellement faim. Pourrais-tu me donner quelque chose à grignoter, s'il te plaît?" – Mummy, I am so hungry. Could you give me something to snack on, please?

And if you want to **describe the weather**; is it hot or cold?, you need **faire**:

- "Qu'est-ce qu'**il fait** chaud cet après-midi! Je voudrais aller à la piscine" ie How hot it is this afternoon! I would like to go to the swimming pool. We will study **faire** in much more depth to talk about the weather in the **Faire** chapter).

To be honest, we could go on and on with these different basic illustrations of **avoir** in action. But we will leave it there for now. In any case, many of the uses of **avoir** that I consider appropriate at the intermediate level, **Getting Better**, are also highly accessible to fairly inexperienced French speakers. It is a "pick-n-mix" really.

Summary

Quite the most important use of **avoir** is in expressing possession – whether it be physical or intangible possession. But it is incredibly important, too, in describing the shape and size of objects; and in describing age. But it also figures in expressing other personal characteristics – whether you feel cold or hot and whether you feel hungry or thirsty. For all these reasons – and many more – **avoir** is truly a "killer" verb at this basic level.

Getting Better

As with **être** that we saw in the **Être** chapter, **avoir** can also be used very effectively in some other past tenses and in the conditional tenses. Because we went through some of these, particularly the conditional in **if** clauses, it should be enough here to reprise a little the use of these tenses and then to move on to lots of examples of **avoir** in use in these tenses.

The present conditional we use quite simply to say that, for example, we would like something or somebody, and provided that there is no second person or thing, the **infinitive** can follow the verb, as in:

- "**Je voudrais voir** mon père aujourd'hui" ie I would like to see my father today.

Alternatively, verbs like **vouloir** and **aimer** can be followed by a **noun**, as in:

- "**Je voudrais du pain**, s'il te plaît" ie I would like some bread please.

Using **avoir**, we might say, for example:

- " **J'aurais** bien pris plus de pain mais, franchement, **j'ai** déjà bien mangé" ie I would have had some more bread but frankly, I am already quite full. (Incidentally, as we noted in the **Être** chapter, whilst we Brits do not consider it rude in company to say that we are "full", the French would not consider it polite if instead, you said that you were "plein" or "truffé": as we noted earlier, "Merci, mais j'ai bien mangé" is the prudent phrase to adopt in such cases. Of course, French slang is full of very impolite ways of expressing this idea, but I do not intend to pursue them here!)

In **if** clauses, either in the present or past conditional, **avoir** works exactly like **être**. For instance:

- "**Nous aurions** un deuxième lit dans cette chambre s'il **y avait** de la place" ie We would have a second bed in this bedroom if there were room.

And using the past conditional:

- "**J'aurais** encore pris du vin s'il **y avait eu** un bon rouge à boire" ie I would have had more wine if there had been a good red to drink.

Avoir and the subjunctive

The present subjunctive of **avoir** can be used in countless ways to express the feelings of wishing, hoping, desiring etc:

- "**Nous voudrions** que tu **aies** ton parapluie ce matin: il va pleuvoir" ie We would like you to have your umbrella this morning: it is going to rain.

To express necessity:

- "**Il faut** absolument **que vous ayez** un congé bientôt. **Vous avez l'air** bien fatigué" ie You absolutely must have some time off soon. You look very tired.

In this example, you will have noticed the expression **avoir l'air**, to seem or to appear. This is just one example of the use of **avoir** in the set expressions that now follow. The list of such expressions is not exhaustive – but it will give you a good feel for the use of **avoir**, particularly in idiomatic expressions.

Avoir in some very common idioms

Instead of saying **il faut que…** and, therefore, employing the subjunctive, you can often say that you need something or someone. To talk about your (or someone else's) needs, use **avoir besoin de**. For example:

- "**J'ai besoin de** chaussures: cette paire-ci est vraiment usée" ie I need some shoes: this pair is really worn.
- "**Tu as besoin de** sommeil. Tu as trop bossé aujourd'hui" ie You need more sleep. You worked too hard today. (Incidentally, "bosser" is a familiar word for to work. It is widely used and is not generally considered impolite).
- "**Elles ont besoin de** vitamine C. Toutes les deux éternuent" ie They need some vitamin C. They are both sneezing. (Incidentally, when somebody sneezes in your company, it is normal to say "à tes/vos souhaits!" and is the equivalent of "bless you!" in English).

If you want to say that you feel like something or doing something, you can use **avoir envie de**… For instance:

- "**J'ai envie d'**aller dans un restaurant indien, ce soir" – I feel like going to an Indian restaurant this evening.

- "**Il avait envie de** faire la grasse matinée mais son oncle passait à neuf heures" – He had wanted to stay on in bed but his uncle was passing by at nine o'clock. The expression "faire la grasse matinee" - literally to do the fat morning – is a common colloquialism. We will see lots like it later, in the **Faire** chapter, particularly.
- "**Ils auront envie de** manger des Saint Jacques ce soir mais je leur ai dit qu'elles sont trop chères en ce moment" – They will want to eat Saint Jacques (delicious scallops) tonight but I told them that they are too expensive at the moment.

If you ever need to see a French doctor you will need to explain your symptoms. Here, use **avoir**, followed by your problem:

- "**J'ai mal au dos** et ça me fait vraiment mal" – I have a pain in the back and it really hurts. Should you ever want to say that someone is a "pain in the neck", you will need a completely different expression, "casser les pieds!"

If you want to say that you have got a headache, you need **J'ai mal à la tête.**

If your mother needs to explain to the doctor that you have a pain in the knee, she will need to say **Il/elle a mal au genou.**

And if you have got more than one symptom, you will need the plural of **mal**, which is **maux.**

If you would like to tell someone that you have just received some good news, then you can say:

- "**J'ai reçu une bonne nouvelle**". Notice though, that "some good news" is in the singular; "une bonne nouvelle". If you want to talk about some bad news, then it is "une mauvaise nouvelle". And if, because of the bad news, you want to say that you feel down, you can say:
- "**J'ai le cafard**". ("Un cafard", incidentally, is a cock-roach!)

If you want to say to someone that you have got an appointment for this or that, you can say:

- "**J'ai rendez-vous** avec quelqu'un". Alternatively you can say "J'ai **un** rendez-vous avec quelqu'un". And if you want suddenly to have your haircut (or whatever), look for a sign outside or in the shop window saying "sans RDV" ie without an appointment. (RDV signifies "rendez-vous").

If you want to say in conversation that you think someone else could be right or wrong over something, say:

- "Oui **tu as raison**, c'est bien le vingt octobre aujourd'hui" – Yes, you are right, it is indeed October 20th today.

  If you think someone is wrong, you can say:

- "Non, **vous avez tort**, monsieur, le président de la France n'est pas Marine le Pen – elle dirige le Front national" – No, you are wrong, monsieur, Marine le Pen is not the French President – she is leader of the National Front, (a right-wing, some say **extreme** right-wing, French political party).

Avoir and meanings other than to have

To have in some way or another is a very important meaning of **avoir**. However, **avoir** is one of those verbs that has lots of meanings of which physical or intangible possession is only one. Here are some other ways in which the verb can be deployed:

Avoir can be used to express location, ie where something is. To illustrate:

- "Pour aller à la gare, s'il vous plaît?" ie How do I get to the station, please? "Ah, **vous avez la gare** tout près, madame – première route à gauche" – Yes, the station is really quite close, madam, just on the right. Often when the French want to say that something is somewhere they will use **se trouver** or even **se situer**:
  "La gare **se trouve/se situe** à côté de la station-service".

Avoir can also be used to say that you want to get something, in a library ("une bibliotheque"), for example:

- "Pourriez-vous **avoir** ce livre, s'il vous plaît?" ie Could you get this book, please? (Incidentally – and Brits get confused with this one – a "bibliothèque" is a library; if you want a book shop, you will need to ask for "une librairie". I know, confusing, isn't it!)

Avoir can also mean to receive someone at your home, for example:

- "J'aime **avoir des amis**" means that you like having friends around.

To express difficulties or problems that you are experiencing you can use **avoir du mal à**…:

- "**J'ai du mal à** réparer la télé. Elle est foutue, peut-être" ie I am having difficulty fixing the television. Perhaps it is buggered. (Some care is needed with "foutu"!)

On the other hand, you may be having problems understanding how something works:

- "**J'ai du mal à comprendre** comment marche ce bidule", means that I am having problems understanding how this thing works. (Incidentally, the French have three very common ways of talking about a "thing" or a "thingamajig". They are all pretty interchangeable – and you have met all three of them in the course of the book to date, "truc", "machin" and "bidule").

Finally, at least for now, you can use **avoir** to say to somebody, you're welcome when they have thanked you for doing something for them:

- **Il n'y a pas de quoi,** monsieur, c'était un plaisir.

But there are two other ways of saying exactly the same:
Je vous en prie – This is a very common expression, as is **de rien**.

Please understand that French people on the whole are very polite in this regard and will almost unfailingly say "you're welcome" after you have thanked them for whatever. Do try to reciprocate with one of these three respectful phrases.

Now You Are Really Speaking French!

With **avoir**, the step up to this third level is not difficult. There are no more tenses to worry about; and the grammar is not likely to bother you either. For the most part, it is a question of familiarising yourself with slightly more complex uses of the basics – and of studying some less often used but none the less important idiomatic applications of the verb.

Building on the basics: il y a

We saw earlier that **il y a** can mean "there is" or "there are". Many other expressions can be built around **il y a**:

Il y en and **il n'y en a pas**
Il y en a means there is or there are some, for example:

Est-ce qu'il y a du pain? - Is there some bread?
Est-ce qu'il y en a? - Is there some **of it**? Here, **en** replaced du.
Oui, **il y en a** – Yes, there is some **of it**.
Non, **il n'y en a pas** – No, there is not any **of it**.

Il n'y a pas que ça means "And not only that….."
Il n'y a pas le feu means, as the expression suggests, "take it easy, where's the fire?"

Il y a de l'eau dans le gaz again as the expression implies, means that things are not necessarily going too smoothly. Imagine boiling water dropping on to a gas flame on the cooker.

Il n'y a pas photo says literally, "there is no photo" but means that there is no question about it. The allusion is to a photo-finish at a race course.

Il n'y a pas de quoi – You have already met earlier in this chapter. But you can add a **verb in the infinitive** at the end of this expression and you have something entirely different. For example:

- "Il n'y a pas de quoi **rire**!" – There is nothing to **laugh** about.
- "Il n'y a pas de quoi **pleurer**" – There is nothing to **cry** about.
- "Il n'y a pas de quoi **s'inquièter**" – There is nothing to **worry** about.

69

- "Il n'y a pas de quoi **avoir peur**" – There is nothing to **fear**.
- "**N'ayez pas peur**" means don't be too frightened and is an expression you will hear frequently.
- "Il n'y a pas de quoi **écrire**" – There is nothing to **write with**. I have often had to use this expression at hotel receptions where there is no pen provided for signing in.
- "Il n'y a pas de quoi **manger**" – There is nothing to eat.

Vous n'avez que – "You only have to". **Avoir** is often used to say that you only have to do something. For example:

- "**Vous n'avez qu' à** faire l'appoint et la caissière sera très contente" – You only have to give the checkout lady the right money and she will be very happy. "Je peux vous faire l'appoint, madame" means that I can give you the precise amount of money, madam.
- "**Vous n'avez qu' à** regarder à votre droite, madame, et vous pourrez voir la Tour Eiffel" – You only have to look to your right, madam, and you will be able to see the Eiffel Tower.
- "**Tu n'as qu' à** ranger tes jouets et puis nous pourrons sortir" – You only have to tidy and put away your toys and then we can go out.

N'en avoir que can be used to say that someone will be (gone for)… For example:

- "**Je n'en ai que** pour quelques instants" – I will only be a few moments.
- "**Il n'en a que** pour deux minutes" – He will only be gone for two minutes.

N'avoir pas à... means "to have nothing to…." For example:

- "**Vous n'avez** vraiment **pas à** vous faire des soucis à ce propos, monsieur" – You really have nothing to worry about on that score, sir.

Avoir que… means "to have nothing but…" For example:

- "**On n'a eu que** des emmerdements" – We have had nothing but damned trouble.
- "**Je n'ai eu que** des ennuis avec" is a slightly more polite way of expressing the same idea. But notice the absence of the impersonal pronoun "it" after "avec". Other examples include:

    Je suis pour – I am for (it)
    Je suis sorti sans – I went out without (it).

Some other idiomatic expressions using avoir

There are literally hundreds of **avoir** idioms that we have not covered, but here are some that you should find useful:

Avoir la trouille – to be scared eg:

- "Rien que d'y penser et **j'ai la trouille**" – Just thinking about it and I am scared.

Avoir le trac – to have butterflies in the stomach eg:

- "**J'avais le trac** pendant les répétitions mais en fin de compte, tout s'est bien passé" - I had butterflies in my stomach during the rehearsals but in the end, everything turned out well.

N'avoir rien à voir avec - to have nothing in common with eg:

- "J'ai vu "Titanic" l'autre jour, mais ce film-ci **n'avait rien à voir avec** tous les autres films avec Leonardo di Caprio que j'ai vus" - I saw Titanic the other day but this film has nothing in common with all the other films with Leonardo de Caprio that I have seen. Often you will hear people say **Ça n'a rien à voir avec**… as if to say that it has nothing to do with (whatever).

J'en ai rien à foutre – I don't give a damn (there's that "foutre" verb again!)

Avoir le temps – to have time to… For example:

- "**Vous avez largement le temps**. Le train part dans deux heures" – You have plenty of time. The train leaves in two hours. (Incidentally, try not to confuse **dans** et **en**. If I say, "Je le ferai **en** une heure" that means that it will take me an hour to do whatever. However, if I say "Je te verrai **dans** une heure" that means that I will see you in an hour's time. Often on a train, you will hear someone saying, for example "nous arrivons à Marseille **dans quelques instants**" ie we will be arriving in Marseille **in a few moments**).

Avoir l'habitude – to be in the habit of. For example:

- "**Je n'ai pas l'habitude** qu'on me fasse (subjunctive) du chantage" – I am not in the habit of being blackmailed.

Avoir le droit – to have the right to… Often this is a legal right. For example:

- "Il paraît que les propriétaires **ont le droit** de majorer les loyers comme bon leur semble" - It appears that property owners have the right to increase rents as they see fit.
- "Je crois que tout le monde **a le droit** d'entrer dans un bar et de demander un verre d'eau du robinet sans rien payer" - I believe that every one has the right to go into a bar and ask for a glass of tap-water without paying (for it). A very similar expression **avoir droit à** means to be entitled to.

I referred earlier to the good-mannered French. **Avoir du savoir-vivre** means to have good manners. And **avoir du savoir-faire** means to have tact.

Avoir hâte de faire quelque chose means to be anxious to do something, or even to be looking forward to doing something. If you are looking forward to seeing someone you can say "J'attends de te voir avec impatience".

And we have already seen **avoir faim** and **avoir soif**, to be hungry and to be thirsty. We can use the same idiomatic construction to say **avoir sommeil**, to feel drowsy and **avoir l'impression** – to be under the impression that… For example:

- "**J'ai l'impression** d'avoir fait pas mal de navets récemment" - I am under the impression that I have made quite a few second-rate films recently ("un navet" is literally a turnip!)

If you want to say that you intend doing something you can say **J'ai l'intention de faire quelque chose**. For example:

- "**J'ai l'intention d'acheter** la robe rose que j'ai vue hier" - I intend buying the pink dress that I saw yesterday.

If you feel you have got an occasion to wear that pink dress, you can use **avoir l'occasion de**….. For example:

- "**J'aurai l'occasion de** porter cette robe rose quand nous sortirons dîner avec Jean-Luc et Maxime le mois pochain" - I will have the occasion to wear this pink dress when we go out to dinner with Jean-Luc and Maxime next month.

Avoir tendance à faire quelque chose means to tend to do something. For example:

- "Mon mari **à tendance à manger** des choux de Bruxelles à Noel" - My husband tends to eat brussel sprouts at Christmas. (Incidentally, in a ladies dress shop, say, you might hear the sales-lady, "la vendeuse," saying,

"Madame, la jupe vous va et c'est vraiment très tendance en ce moment" ie Madam, the skirt really suits you and it is all the rage at the moment).

Of course, such sales-people often have what we call "the gift of the gab" in English. In French, this translates as **avoir la langue bien pendue**, literally to have a well-hung tongue!

Avoir beau is a very curious expression. You will find it in sentences such as these:

- "**J'ai beau** dire, il m'ignore" – Whatever I say, he ignores me
- "**J'ai beau** faire, j'ai l'impression que c'est jamais vaut l'effort - Whatever I do, I get the impression that it is never worth the effort.

In other words, **avoir beau** means to do something in vain.

Avoir du mal à… means to have difficulty doing something. French people can often be heard complaining about rising prices and the cost of living in France, claiming that they can no longer afford this or that:

- "**Oh là là!, j'ai du mal à** joindre les deux bouts" - I am having problems making ends meet.

Avoir de la chance means to be lucky. For example, you might pass a fisherman on a riverbank and say "Avez-vous eu de la chance?" or even "De la chance?" ie have you had any luck? More colloquially, even pejoratively, you might say of somebody who seems to be forever lucky, "quel veinard!", what a lucky/jammy so and so!

As I pointed out in the **Être** chapter, lots of French idioms make reference to the animal kingdom in one way or another. Those using **avoir** include:

Avoir mangé du lion – this suggests that you have the energy of a lion, to be incredibly energetic.

Avoir l'air d'une poule qui a trouvé un couteau means literally, that you look like a hen that has found a knife, meaning to look puzzled, baffled even.

Another hen idiom using **avoir** is the well-known French proverb **Quand les poules auront des dents!** ("when hens get teeth") which is their equivalent of our "when pigs will fly!" (Incidentally, une **poule** is a hen whereas un **poulet** is a chicken. Putting aside the biology for a moment, be very careful in supermarkets; sometimes "poules" are sold as if they were "poulets" and you have to read carefully the small print. If you make a mistake and buy a "poule" you will soon know it; "poules" on sale are old birds whose egg-laying life is over. They are best boiled and for at least three hours. They are good for stock and their flesh eventually gets tender enough to eat. But, if you want to prepare and offer to your guests the classic French dish, "poule au pot", boil a chicken (or "a coq"). It will cook in not much over an hour – and will be a lot more enjoyable to eat!)

And sticking for a moment to the subject of hens, **avoir la chair de poule** means to **have** goose-pimples. If you want to say that something **gives** you goose-pimples, use **donner:** "ça me **donne** la chair de poule".

Avoir une araignée (spider) au plafond means to be a bit crazy, if you like, to have a screw loose.

Here are two cat idioms:

Avoir d'autres chats à fouetter (to whip) means to have other fish to fry.
Il n'y a pas de quoi fouetter un chat means that it is nothing really to make a fuss about.
And don't forget "J'ai un **chat** dans la gorge", ie I have a **frog** in my throat.

Idioms that make reference to parts of the body include:

Avoir le coeur sur la main means to be kind enough even to give the shirt off one's back.
Avoir un poil dans la main means to be lazy or to be work-shy. The reference here is to a single hair growing in the palm of the hand, so lazy is its owner.
Avoir le bras long means to have influence in high places.
Avoir bon dos means to take the blame for something.
Avoir un oeil au beurre noir means to have a black eye.
Avoir un couteau sous la gorge means to have a gun held to one's head and is often used in a business context to suggest that the bank is holding a gun to the head of its customers, for example.
Avoir un coeur d'artichaut (an artichoke) means to fall in love with everyone you meet.
Avoir une dent contre quelqu'un means to hold a grudge against someone. Note here the gender of dent: **une** dent. Many people expect that "tooth" is masculine because it does not have an **e** at the end. Again, on the subject of teeth:
Avoir les dents longues means that someone with "long teeth" is likely to be very ambitious. Alternatively, you can use **avoir les dents qui rayent le parquet** - to scrape or scratch the wooden floor.
N'avoir pas froid aux yeux is to be adventurous.

Avoir deux pieds dans le même sabot ("un sabot" is a clog) means to relax and simply wait for things to happen.

Avoir l'estomac dans les talons is literally to have your stomach in your heels. Its idiomatic meaning is to be starving. If you want to make your hunger even stronger, you might say "**je meurs** de faim" - I am starving **to death**.

(Incidentally, one other thought on the subject of **mourir**, the verb "to die". Many otherwise well-educated French have problems in conjugating this verb. Everyone knows "il/elle est mort(e)", he/she died. But in other tenses they are often lost. With some friends recently, I challenged people around the table to give me the French for "he was dying". Nobody knew the answer except me! But then I had already looked it up in my dictionary before arriving! My motto is "be prepared!"

But my experience is that the French – at least the ones I know – love playing word games; they take great pride in their language and they take it very seriously. If you really want to win their admiration, show them that you know some words, phrases or expressions that they don't. They are unlikely to consider you a "smarty pants" but rather an English person who also takes an interest in their language. Such people are quite rare!)

Avoir la dalle also means to starve. Dalle can mean throat but it also means a paving stone.

Avoir la gueule de bois literally means to have a wooden mouth but it is a very informal way of saying that you are badly hungover. The word "gueule" features in quite a lot of idiomatic, even argotic French. If somebody should say to you "ta gueule!" for example, it really is time to stop showing how clever you are; "ta gueule" means "shut up!"

And **finally**, on the subject of body parts, (there are many more examples incidentally):

Ne pas avoir la langue dans sa poche means not to be lost for words.

And **finally** on the subject of **idiomatic expressions using avoir**, here are some "odds and sods":

Avoir des lettres means to be well read.

Avoir du plomb dans l'aile means to have lead in the wing. I strongly suspect that this is a hunting allusion, referring to a bird that has been shot in the wing. The idiomatic meaning of this expression is to be in pretty bad shape or in a bad way. It need not necessarily be physical problems by the way. You could be talking about personal problems.

Avoir les jetons means to be shaking with fear, though do not ask me why! A jeton is a token, the sort of thing you might put in the supermarket trolley, for example.

Avoir du pain sur la planche is much more obvious. It means to have lots to do, plenty on your plate, so to speak.

Avoir du bol means to be lucky. "Bol" in this context at least, means one's bottom. "Fesses" is the more polite word and "cul", as we have noted elsewhere, is decidedly vulgar!

And finally:

Avoir de la bouteille literally to have bottle, suggests that this might be a reference to personal courage. In English we say that someone has bottle eg is courageous. Here, however, it means to be getting on a bit. I suspect that this might be a reference to a well-aged bottle of wine. Well, you know the French!

Conclusion

Yes, that's it! Another hugely important verb under your belt. With **avoir**, you should be able to:

- conjugate **avoir** in all the important tenses
- talk about things and qualities that you and others possess; the basic job of **avoir**
- use **il y a** to talk about what **is** and what **are** – and to use **il y a** to talk about events in the past
- use **avoir** to talk about people and things in other tenses, particularly the future, the conditional and the imperfect
- employ the subjunctive of **avoir** whenever necessary
- use **avoir** to mean things other than just **to have**
- employ **avoir** in a very wide range of colloquial and idiomatic expressions – to give your conversations life, colour and authenticity.

But before we move on to our next big "killer" verb, **faire** (to do or to make), here are a couple of conversations that use **avoir** quite frequently so that you can put at least some of your newly-acquired knowledge into context.

Avoir: Conversation One

Annie is in the marché d'Aligre, a very cosmopolitan market in the 12th arrondissement of Paris. She stops a lady who has obviously been shopping there:

Annie: Excusez-moi de vous déranger, madame, est-ce que vous avez quelques minutes pour répondre à mes questions?

La dame: Je suis un peu pressée, madame, mais quand même...

Annie: C'est gentil, madame. D'abord, qu'est-ce que vous avez dans votre sac, les produits que vous avez achetés au marché ce matin?

La dame: Tout à fait. J'ai acheté des pommes de terre, des oignons, des carrottes, des navets, un rutabaga, des poireaux, des haricots verts... ah, oui, et j'ai acheté aussi quelques abricots. C'est tout, je crois.

Annie: Tout est très sain, bon pour la santé. Bravo! Et dites-moi, madame, ça fait longtemps que vous habitez ce quartier?

La dame: Ah oui. Je suis tombée par hasard sur ce quartier il y a quarante ans et ça m'a tellement plu que j'ai décidé de rester.

Annie: J'espère que cette question ne vous gêne pas, madame, mais quel âge avez-vous, approximativement?

La dame: Au contraire, madame, j'ai quatre-vingts ans en ce moment et j'aurai quatre-vingt-un ans la semaine prochaine.

Annie: Félicitations, madame! Mais il fait froid ce matin et vous devez avoir froid. Merci pour vos réponses.

La dame: Il n'y a pas de quoi, madame. Au revoir.

Annie: Au revoir, madame.

Avoir: Conversation Two

Maryse is not feeling well. In fact, she has been "off colour" for several days so she decided to telephone a local doctor.

Maryse:	(on the telephone) Bonjour, madame, je voudrais prendre rendez-vous avec le Docteur Lancré. Est-ce que vous avez une place dans son agenda pour cet après-midi?
Réceptionniste:	Oui, madame, je peux vous donner rendez-vous à seize heures trente. Ça vous va?
Maryse:	Oui, ça me convient parfaitement.
Réceptionniste	Bon. Quel nom, madame?
Maryse:	Madame Reynal.
Réceptionniste:	Madame Reynal. C'est noté.
Maryse:	Merci bien, madame.
Réceptionniste:	Il n'y a pas de quoi. À seize heures trente, alors.
Maryse:	Oui, et merci bien d'avoir trouvé un rendez-vous aussi rapidement. Au revoir.
Réceptionniste:	Au revoir, madame.

A few hours later at the doctor's:

Docteur Lancré:	Bonjour Madame Reynal. Que puis-je faire pour vous aujourd'hui?
Maryse:	Je ne sais pas pourquoi, mais ça fait quelques jours maintenant que je me sens mal.
Docteur Lancré:	D'accord. Décrivez-moi vos symptômes .
Maryse:	D'accord, j'ai du mal à dormir, puis j'ai mal à la tête. Et ensuite j'éternue beaucoup. Et je crois que j'ai de la fièvre. Je suis enrhumée, peut-être?
Docteur Lancré:	D'accord. Il faut que je vous examine.

Two minutes later:

Docteur Lancré:	Oui, je crois que vous avez raison Madame Reynal. Vous avez de la fièvre. Pour ça je vais vous donner ce médicament. Mais je crois aussi que vous avez besoin de sommeil. Pour ça je vais vous donner ce médicament -ci. Et si vous avez besoin de faire la grasse matinée… mais bien sûr. Mais à votre place, avec vos symptômes, moi, j'aurais déjà acheté de la vitamine C. Regardez, je l'écris sur votre ordonnance. Ça vous va?
Maryse:	Oui, ça va. Et merci infiniment Docteur Lancré.

Docteur Lancré:		Il n'y a pas de quoi, Madame Reynal. Prenez tous les médicaments que je vous ai donnés.
Maryse:		Ça va sans dire, Docteur. Au revoir.
Docteur Lancré:		Au revoir Madame Reynal.

Some words you might not yet know

- répondre - to reply to
- quand même - all the same
- gentil - kind
- d'abord - first of all
- tout à fait - absolutely
- un rutabaga - a swede
- un poireau - a leek
- sain(e) - healthy
- la santé - health
- Bravo! - Well done!
- ça fait longtemps? - is it a long time?
- tomber - to fall
- par hasard - by chance
- tellement - so much
- gêner - to embarrass someone
- approximativement - approximately
- Félicitations! - Congratulations!
- convenir - to suit
- trouver - to find
- que puis – je faire? - what can I do?
- se sentir - to feel
- d'accord - OK
- raconter - to tell
- puis - then
- ensuite - next
- avoir de la fièvre - to have a temperature
- être enrhumé(e) - to have a cold
- donner - to give
- un médicament - a medicine
- regarder - to look
- une ordonnance - a prescription
- merci infiniment - thanks a million
- ça va sans dire - that goes without saying

Avoir: Exercises

Fill in the blank spaces:

1.   Je voudrais ouvrir cette boîte. Est-ce que vous (   ) un ouvre-boîte?

2.   Dans le temps nous (   ) un bac-à-sable dans le jardin.

3.   Je vais à Liverpool demain. (   ) un magasin où je peux acheter des patins à roulettes pour mon fils.

4.   J'(   ) assez. Je vais sortir.

5.   Il (   ) les yeux verts et les cheveux boucles.

6.   (   ) plus de bière mais il nous reste du vin blanc.

7.   Quel âge (   ) tu? J'(   ) quinze ans.

8.   Maman j'(   ) faim. Est-ce qu'il (   ) du fromage au frigo?

9.   Nous (   ) un lave – vaisselle dans la cuisine s'il y avait de la place.

10.   Vous (   ) l'air triste. Tu devrais lire cette lettre.

11.   Mon fils m'a dit qu'il (   ) envie de voir son copain, Christophe cet aprèm mais il ne sera pas là.

12.   Docteur, ma fille (   ) mal au genou. Pouvez-vous l'examiner s'il vous plaît?

13.   J'(   ) rendez-vous à onze heures mais la coiffeuse était malade, paraît-il.

14.   Oui, tu (   ) raison. C'est bien le trente juillet aujourd'hui.

15.   Vous (   ) un arrêt de bus à cent mètres d'ici, monsieur.

16.   Il m'a dit qu'il était polonais mais j'(   ) du mal à comprendre son accent.

17.   C'est gentil, merci bien. (   ) de quoi, madame.

18.　(　　　　) avoir peur madame. De nos jours les avions ne sont pas dangereux.

19.　J'(　　　　) le trac quand j'ai commencé à parler mais après quelques minutes je me sentais mieux.

20.　Au début, j'(　　　　) du mal à lire le français mais maintenant je (　　　　) aucun problème avec.

21.　Je ne peux pas te voir cet aprèm. J'(　　　　) du pain sur la planche.

Avoir: Exercises

1. avez
2. avions
3. Il y a
4. en ai
5. a
6. Il n'y a
7. as, ai
8. ai, y a
9. aurions
10. avez
11. avait
12. a
13. avais
14. as
15. avez
16. avais
17. Il n'y a pas
18. Il n'y a pas de quoi
19. avais
20. avais
21. ai, n'ai

Chapter Four
Faire

Introduction

Our third serial killer verb, **faire**, means to do or to make; and this basic role alone is enough to justify its position as a top four French verb. Almost nothing is more fundamental to language than notions of **doing** and **making**. And although it is not also an auxiliary verb like **être** and **avoir**, it is so important in conversational and idiomatic expressions, particularly those related to the weather, that it gets star billing in our "killer" list. So, let's begin by conjugating it in the nine tenses that matter most.

The Faire Conjugations

Present Tense

Je fais	Nous faisons
Tu fais	Vous faites
Il fait	Ils font
Elle fait	Elles font

Future Tense

Je ferai	Nous ferons
Tu feras	Vous ferez
Il fera	Ils feront
Elle fera	Elles feront

Imperfect Tense

Je faisais	Nous faisions
Tu faisais	Vous faisiez
Il faisait	Ils faisaient
Elle faisait	Elles faisaient

Perfect Tense

J'ai fait	Nous avons fait
Tu as fait	Vous avez fait
Il a fait	Ils ont fait
Elle a fait	Elles ont fait

Future Perfect Tense

J'aurai fait	Nous aurons fait
Tu auras fait	Vous aurez fait
Il aura fait	Ils auront fait
Elle aura fait	Elles auront fait

Pluperfect Tense

J'avais fait	Nous avions fait
Tu avais fait	Vous aviez fait
Il avait fait	Ils avaient fait
Elle avait fait	Elles avaient fait

Present Conditional Tense

Je ferais	Nous ferions
Tu ferais	Vous feriez
Il ferait	Ils feraient
Elle ferait	Elles feraient

Past Conditional Tense

J'aurais fait	Nous aurions fait
Tu aurais fait	Vous auriez fait
Il aurait fait	Ils auraient fait
Elle aurait fait	Elles auraient fait

Present Subjunctive Tense

Je fasse	Nous fassions
Tu fasses	Vous fassiez
Il fasse	Ils fassent
Elle fasse	Elles fassent

Imperative

Fais
Faisons
Faites

The only comment I want to make here is about the **pronunciation** of faire in some of theses conjugations. In the **imperfect tense** throughout, from **je faisais** to **elles faisaient**, the **fais** part of the word **sounds** as if it is spelt "feu" as in the noun "feu" (m), meaning fire. And in the present conditional, too, from **je ferais** to **elles feraient**, it **sounds** as though the conjugation is said **je feurais**, **tu feurais**… **elles feuraient**. And don't forget either, that in the third-person plural of **faire** (and **être**, **avoir** and all those other verbs whose third-person plurals end in "..aient"), the last two letters, "..nt") are **not pronounced at all**. So, armed with these points of pronunciation, let's move on and see how **faire** is actually used in French.

Faire: The Basics

The simplest use of **faire** is to say what people and things **do**, **used to do** or **will do**. Here are some good examples of **faire** employed in this way:

- "Ma mère **fait** la vaisselle elle-même parce qu'elle n'a pas de lave-vaisselle" ie My mother does the washing up herself because she does not have a dish washer.
- "Normalement, je **fais** mes devoirs aussitôt que je rentre" ie Normally I do my homework as soon as I come home.
- "Pour la plupart du temps, ma soeur **fait** ses courses en ville" ie For the most part, my sister does her shopping in town.
- "Qu'est-ce que tu **fais** en ce moment?" ie What are you doing at the moment? Perhaps the answer is nothing!: **Je ne fais rien**. And you might get the reply: **Ça ne fait rien** ie That does not matter. This is a very useful and frequently encountered expression.

Faire le ménage means to do the housework. For example:

- "Dans le temps, les bonnes **faisaient** le ménage; de nos jours c'est nous!" ie In the old days, maids did the housework; nowadays it is us!

Faire les valises means to pack the suitcases. **Charger** is to load and can also be used here.

Faire son lit means to make one's bed. For example:

- "Mon fils **fait son** lit tous les matins avant de sortir" ie My son makes his bed every morning before going out.

84

Faire un appel (téléphonique) means to make a phonecall, although more often these days you will hear the expression, **passer** or **donner un coup de fil** instead. For example:

- "**Donne-moi un coup de fil** aussitôt que tu arrives, chérie" ie Give me a call as soon as you arrive, darling.

Faire du pain means to bake bread.

These are all examples in the **present** tense, of course, but you can also use **faire** for **future** events, for example:

- "**Je le ferai** quand j'aurai un moment" ie I will do it when I have a moment. Notice here that the two clauses both have their verbs **faire** and **avoir** in the future tense. Of course, as you know, you can always avoid this future construction using **aller** instead of **faire** in the future:
  "**Je vais** le **faire** quand j'aurai un moment" ie I am going to do it when I have a moment.

And for past events, for example:

- "Quand nous habitions à la campagne, **nous faisions** une promenade quand **il faisait** beau" ie When we used to live in the country, we used to go for a walk when we had fine weather.

The subject of walking is quite a complex one – and it merits some comments here, I feel, simply because there are several ways of speaking about walking. For example, if you want to talk simply about walking, ie the action of walking, **marcher**, to walk, is the correct word to use. For example:

- "Ma fille à commencé à **marcher** quand elle avait dix-huit mois" ie My daughter began walking when she was 18 months old.

However, if you want to talk about walking as, say, a sport or a pastime, then **faire de la marche** is the correct expression to use:

- "**Faire de la marche** vous fait du bien; c'est excellent pour la santé" ie (Regular) walking does you good; it is excellent for your health.

However, **faire une promenade**, to go for a walk, is much more specific:

- "S'il ne pleuvait pas on pourrait **faire une promenade** le long de l'esplanade" ie If it were not raining, we could go for a walk along the promenade. Note that "promenade" is a noun, ie a walk. But if, for example, you wanted to take your dog for a walk, you need the verb **promener**. It is all a bit complicated, I agree, but you will never go far wrong if you use **faire** instead of **promener** or whatever. You will always be understood.

Although **faire** often refers to what **people** do, it can also be used to say what **things** do. For example:

- "J'ai des pucerons sur mes rosiers. Ce pesticide, **fera-t-il** l'affaire?" ie This pesticide here, will it do the job? I've got greenfly on my rose bushes.

Faire in place of other verbs

Faire can also be employed very broadly in the sense of to do, to replace other verbs which also suggest doing-verbs like **jouer**, to play sport, or to play musical instruments, **parcourir** to travel or cover the ground, **mesurer** to measure, **peser** to weigh, **coûter** to cost… and so on. So here are examples of **faire** used in this broader sense of to do:

Question: "Qu'est-ce que **tu fais de ton temps libre**?". What do you do with your spare time?:

- "J'aime **faire du ski**" – I like skiing.
- "J'aime **faire du foot**" – I like playing football.
- "Moi, j'aime **faire du rugby**" – Me, I like playing rugby.
- "J'aime **faire de la natation**" – I like swimming.
- "J'aime **faire de la voile**" – I like sailing.
- "J'aime **faire de la boxe**" – I like boxing. Note the **gender** of this noun. I suspect most of us would **expect** it to be **masculine**.

And what about musical instruments?:

- "Oui, j'aime **faire de la guitare électronique**" – Yes, I like playing the electric guitar.
- "Oui, j'aime **faire du piano**" – Yes, I like playing the piano.
- "Oui, j'aime **faire du violon**" – Yes, I like playing the violin.
- "Non, je déteste la musique: **je ne fais rien**" – No, I hate music: I don't play anything.

To talk about how much ground you have covered on some activity or other, you can also use **faire**:

Question: "Combien de kilomètres **as-tu parcouru** cet après-midi?". How many kilometres have you covered this afternoon?:

- "**J'ai fait** cinq kilomètres en tout: j'en ai fait deux en marchant et j'en ai fais trois en courant" – I did five kilometres in total: two of them walking and I did three of them running. Two points to note here:

First, note how "en" is used to say "of them"

Note also the use of the present participle "courant" for "running. To this point, I have said nothing about the present participle, only about the past participle when it is used in compound verbs. In fact, all verbs have present participles (for "courir", to run, it is "courant" ie running). However this is not a grammar book and I see little or no need here to discuss the present participle. Sufficient to say that this part of speech is frequently used to describe how people do things. For example, consider this English sentence: "She ran across the road". Simple enough in English, but not quite so simple in French, for the French have no verb for the English phrasal verb, "to run across". So to translate my English sentence into French, you have got to say:

- "Elle a **traversé** la route **en courant**" ie She **crossed** the road **running**! Enough said!

To talk about the dimensions of things, **faire** can often replace **être**. For example, we could say: how wide is this table?

Question: "Quelle **est** la largeur de cette table?:

- "Cette table-ci **fait** un mètre de large" – This table is one metre wide.

To talk about the weight of something:

Question: "Ce potiron, combien de kilos **pèse-t-il**? How heavy is this pumpkin?:

- "Ce potiron – là, **ça fait** deux kilos, grosso modo" – That pumpkin there weighs two kilos, more or less.
- "Ce gigot d'agneau **fait** un kilo soixante, madame" – This leg of lamb weighs one kilo and six hundred grams, madam.

And **faire** can be used to talk about how much something costs:

Question: "**Ça coute** combien, cette robe noire? How much does this black dress cost?:

- "Cette robe-ci **fait** cent euros, madame" – This dress costs 100 euros madam.

And **faire** can also be used instead of other verbs – **chercher** to look for, **vendre** to sell, **avoir** to have, **ressembler** to look like, **sentir** to feel **physically** and many, many more. Once again, here are some examples of how **faire** can be used instead of these verbs above:

- "J'ai **fait** tous les placards mais je n'ai pas réussi à trouver mon pull" ie I searched in all the cupboards, but I did not manage to find my pullover.
- "On **fait** les sous-vêtements ici" means either that we stock or sell underwear here.
- "Cet hôtel **fait** aussi restaurant" means that this hotel also has a restaurant.
- "Mon fils, lui, il veut **faire** médecin" means my son wants to be a doctor.
- "Ça **fait** un peu années trente avec ses vieilles affiches et le ventilateur au plafond" means it looks a bit thirties-ish with its old posters and the ceiling fan.
- "Ça **fait** très branché en ce moment, mais dans quelques années, qui sait?" means it looks very trendy at the moment, but in a few years, who knows?
- "Le thé à quinze heures: ça **fait** tellement anglais!" means Tea at three o'clock: that feels so typically English!

And **faire** can also replace to kill, as in this very commonly heard proverb:

- "J'ai **fait** d'une pierre deux coups" – I killed two birds with one stone.

Now in this section of the chapter, here are some examples of **faire** used in its basic sense of **to make**:

- "**J'ai fait un blanc-mangé** hier avec le lait qui restait dans le frigo" ie I made a blancmange yesterday with the milk that was still in the fridge.

(Incidentally, if you want to talk abut **making food**, ie cooking, you have quite a few alternatives:

Faire cuire also means to cook, as does **faire la cuisine**.

But you can express the same general notion of cooking without using **faire** at all:

Cuisiner also means to cook, as does **préparer** in some cases.

The precise choice of phrase depends on the precise meaning of "cook". You will see **faire cuire** used in recipes, for example:

- "**Faites cuire** le rôti de boeuf pendant au moins une heure" – Roast the beef for at least one hour.

Faire la cuisine, however, means to do the cooking in a more general sense, for example:

- "Mon mari **fait la cuisine** tous les dimanches" – My husband does the cooking every Sunday).

Faire followed by another verb in the infinitive

In all but one of these examples, we have seen **faire** followed by a noun. **Faire cuire** is an important exception because in this construction, **faire** is followed by another verb in the infinitive, **cuire**. Now, this use of faire is very common indeed, so here are some other examples of this so-called **faire faire** use of the verb:

- **Faire penser à quelque chose** means to be reminded of something or somebody, eg "La façade de la cathédrale, est-ce qu'**elle vous fait penser à quelque chose**?" ie Does the front of the cathedral remind you of something?
-
- **Faire rigoler quelqu'un** means to make someone laugh, eg "L'acteur comique a commencé à me **faire rigoler** dès le lever du rideau" ie The comedian began to make me laugh from the moment the curtain went up.

(Incidentally, here is an example of what is called a "faux ami", literally a false friend, that is a word or phrase that does not mean what you would take it to mean. If you want to talk about actors and actresses, the correct words are "comédien" and "comedienne". But what we call a comedian is, in French, "un acteur comique").

Faire sourire means to make somebody smile, **faire pleurer** means to make somebody cry and **faire rire** means to make someone laugh.

Faire manger means to make someone eat, eg:
- "Ma mère me **faisait manger** des épinards dans ma jeunesse" ie My mother made me eat spinach in my youth.

Faire dormir means to send someone to sleep, eg:
- "Ce genre de musique me **fait dormir**" ie This sort of music makes me want to sleep.

Faire venir means to get someone to come, as in:
- "J'ai essayé de **faire venir** mon mari à ma classe de yoga mais il trouve que c'est du bidon" ie I tried to get my husband to come to my yoga class but he thinks it is a load of old rubbish.

From this last and several other examples, you can see that the **faire faire** construction can be used to express ideas about getting or having things done. These next examples should really make this clear:

- "**Nous avons fait construire** une belle maison au bord de la mer" ie We have had a beautiful home built by the seaside.
- "Malgré le fait que "Le Parrain" soit sorti il y a quelques années, **ça fait toujours courir les foules**" ie Despite the fact that The Godfather film appeared several years ago, it is still pulling in the crowds.

Faire entrer quelque chose dans la tête de quelqu'un means to get something in to someone's head. For example:

- "Quelque fois les hommes sont vraiment bêtes. J'ai beau dire, je trouve impossible de **faire entrer dans la tête de mon mari** que le yoga n'a rien à voir avec la religion" ie Sometimes men are really stupid. No matter what I say, I find it impossible to get it into my husband's head that yoga has nothing to do with religion.

Summary

And that will do for the moment. We shall return to the many basic uses of **faire** in the sections of the chapter that follow, where we will describe some slightly more advanced uses of **faire**. But before moving on, let us reprise what you have already learned. You now know how to:

- conjugate **faire** in the nine tenses
- use **faire** to talk about what people and things do in the present, past and future tenses
- use **faire** in place of many other verbs to talk about having, being, going, playing, walking, running, cooking, measuring, weighing, costing and even killing!

- use **faire** with a following verb in the infinitive to get people and things to get done.

I reckon that is a good start with **faire** – like **être** and **avoir**, one of the three "serial killer" verbs we have met so far. So onwards and upwards!

Getting Better

I hope by now that you are fairly comfortable with our verbs in **if** clauses and the conditional tense. We have already seen how **être** and **avoir** function in these situations and **faire** is no different. So you should be able to plug in the appropriate form of **faire** using the verb tables provided at the beginning of this chapter. However, I do think that we can spend more time here on **faire** in the subjunctive and in the imperative. These you will encounter very frequently. First, the subjunctive.

Faire and the subjunctive

Already you have met the use of the subjunctive with expressions related to wishes, desires and so on – what I earlier called the subjective realm. But the subjunctive can be employed in the objective realm, too. Perhaps the most important of these is the expressions of necessity. The main three are:

> **Il faut que**
> **Il est nécessaire que** and...
> **Il est indispensable que**.

Of these, the first – **il faut que** – is quite the most common. For example:

- "**Il faut que tu fasses** tes devoirs ce soir, Stéphane" ie You must do your homework this evening, Stéphane.
- "Mon père m'a dit hier soir: Laurence, **il faut absolument que tu fasses** le bac S" ie My father said to me last night: Laurence you absolutely must do the S bac.

(Incidentally, the bac is short for the "baccalauréat", the exam that marks the end of studies at the French lycées. It is rather like A Levels in Britain, although many feel that it is much tougher. It is the jumping-off point for university in France. There are in fact many different types of bac, all with letters. These letters indicate the nature of the specialisation. The S bac is strongly oriented towards maths and the physical sciences).

- "Mon chef d'atelier m'a dit: **Il faut que vous fassiez gaffe** parce qu'il m'a vu de ses propres yeux en train de boire de l'alcool dans l'atelier – ce qui est tout à fait inadmissible" ie My foreman told me that I must be very careful:

he saw me with his own eyes drinking alcohol in the workshop – which is completely forbidden. **Faire gaffe** is a familiar way of saying to be careful, ie "soyez prudent". This leads us naturally on to the use of **faire** in the imperative.

Faire and the imperative

To this point in the book I have said very little about the imperative, in other words the command form, of which there are three in general terms:

> **Be**… (singular)
> **Let us be**… (first-person plural) and
> **Be**… (plural).

You can see from the verb table at the beginning of the chapter for **Faire** that this means:

- **fais**   -   you do (singular)
- **faisons**   -   let us do
- **faites**   -   you do (plural).

Some examples will illustrate:

- "**Fais** de ton mieux, Sébastian: je sais que c'est difficile" ie Do your best, Sebastian: I know that it is difficult.
- "**Faisons** la promenade ensemble, mes amis" ie Let us do the walk together, my friends.
- "**Faites** commes chez-vous" ie Make yourself at home.
- (Incidentally, this is a very frequently encountered expression when guests arrive at your home. And should they bring you a gift, no matter how small, it is polite to say "Il ne fallait pas!" – it really was not necessary or "you shouldn't have!" And on this subject of giving something to the host and hostess when you arrive, many of the etiquette books tell you not to take wine: the suggestion is that you do not think that the host's wine will be good enough! This is, frankly, sheer nonsense! Our experience is that French friends always bring a bottle of wine to our dinner parties; and very often, too, to casual drinks "autour d'un verre" as one of our recent guests so charmingly put it. Wine, at least a good-ish one, is always very well received. Wine is destined for the host, of course: the hostess normally receives flowers).

Faire and some other verb forms

Faire can often be used to express ideas about someone's past or one's future. For example:

- "Qu'est-ce que **tu as fait** de ta vie, Henri?" ie What have you done with your life, Henri? Or
- "**Je ne sais pas quoi faire** de mon temps libre dans l'avenir" means I don't know what I will do with my spare time in the future. Notice **quoi** cropping up again. We last saw it in the **Avoir** chapter: **il n'y a pas de quoi écrire**, remember? **Quoi** is a tricky little word to use, but it is so useful and flexible. Stick with it!

These are both examples of **faire de**… But **faire** can also be used in the **faire que** construction. This means "to do nothing but…" For example:

- "**Il ne fait que** se plaindre" ie He does nothing but complain. Se **plaindre** is to complain but "plaindre" has some other meanings.
- "**Elle ne fait que** bavarder" ie She does nothing but chat. Yes, I know blokes can chat too!
- "**Je ne fais que** dire la vérité" ie I am only speaking the truth, or…
- "**Je ne faisais que** passer" ie I was only passing by.

And there is also the construction: **N'avoir que faire**… as in:

- "**Ils n'ont que faire** de vos conseils" in other words, they don't need your advice.

And if you want to say that you have not seen someone for a long time, say:

- "Cela **fait** très longtemps **que je ne t'ai pas vu**" ie It's a long time since I last saw you.

And in a similar vein:

- "**Ça fait** trois ans qu'il est parti" ie That is three years (now) since he left.
- **Ça fait que**… means "that means that…" For example:
- "**Ça fait que** nous devons partir" ie That means that we should/must leave and…
- "**Ça fait qu**'il est arrivé en retard" ie That means that he arrived late.

Note also:

- "Qu'est-ce que **ça fait**?" ie "What's it to you?"
- "On ne **me la fait pas** à moi!" ie "I wasn't born yesterday!" (Can you remember how to say exactly the same thing using **être**?)

Faire plus a noun / other word plus à

Faire features heavily in constructions of this type. Here are some examples:

Faire mal à quelqu'un means to hurt someone physically, whereas:
Faire de la peine à quelqu'un means to hurt somebody emotionally.

Faire part de quelque chose à quelqu'un means to inform somebody about something.

Faire peur à quelqu'un means to frighten someone, whereas:
Faire plaisir à quelqu'un means to give pleasure to someone.
Faire ses amitiés à quelqu'un means to give one's regards to someone:

- **"Fais mes amitiés à** Georgette la prochaine fois que tu la croises", in other words: Give my regards to Georgette the next time that you see her. The verb "croiser" can be used in the context of seeing or meeting somebody. "Se croiser" can mean to come across each other in the street, for example, or in a lift.

The weather is set "faire"!

There is nothing more guaranteed to kick-start a conversation than the weather! And we Brits are weather world champions! The French, in my experience, are not quite so obsessed with climatic conditions; nonetheless, it is a pretty sure-fire way of getting things going, more particularly in the country.

Our French house is in the depths of rural south-west France – and virtually our only near neighbours live in the farm immediately opposite. Almost every day, once our shutters are open, we get going:

Moi: Comment vas-tu ce matin, André?
André: Pas mal, et toi, Derek?
Moi: Pas mal, André, malgré ce sale temps.
André: Oui, qu'est-ce qu'**il fait mauvais** ce matin. Mais selon la météo (the

weather forecast) **il fera beau** cet après-midi, heureusement pour moi, parce qu'il faut que je ramasse le foin (I must gather in the hay) aussitôt que possible – quand **il fait sec**, bien sûr.

You have seen in this mini conversation the word for the weather "le temps" ("temps" can also mean "time", incidentally) and a couple of uses of **faire** to help describe it. In fact, **faire** as in **il fait**, is the standard way of describing general weather conditions – although there are some other constructions in use, as we will see in a moment. So: **Quel temps fait-il**?

Aujourd'hui:

- **il fait beau**   -   it is a lovely day
- **il fait mauvais**   -   it is an awful day
- **il fait du soleil**   -   it is sunny
- **il fait chaud**   -   it is hot
- **il fait lourd**   -   it is heavy (oppressive)
- **il fait sec**   -   it is dry
- **il fait humide**   -   it is humid
- **il fait du brouillard** -   it is foggy
- **il fait de l'orage**   -   it is stormy
- **il fait trente degrés** -   it is thirty degrees.

However, you may have noticed some gaps. How, for example, do you say: "it is raining"? For expressions of this sort you need the appropriate verb for to rain or whatever. Although **faire** is **not** used in the following expressions, I am giving you them for the sake of completeness. The so-called "impersonal" verbs (they are impersonal in the sense that they only exist in the **il** form) generally provide much greater precision when describing the weather:

- it is raining   -   il pleut (pleuvoir)
- it is snowing   -   il neige (neiger)
- it is hailing   -   il grêle (grêler)
- it is thundery   -   il tonne (from tonnérre, thunder)
- it is windy   -   il vente (venter)
- it is drizzling   -   il bruine (bruiner).

But as you might expect, given that we are speaking about the weather, the subject is replete with frequently heard idiomatic expressions, some of which border on the rude! So here are some weather idioms:

il pleut à seaux means it is bucketing it down ("un seau" is a bucket).

il pleut des cordes or **il pleut des hallebardes** (these are spears). Both expressions mean "it is raining cats and dogs!"

il pleut à grosses gouttes means it is raining heavily and if you want, perhaps, the most graphic idiom for raining, how about:

il pleut comme vache qui pisse! ie it is raining like a cow pissing!

il tombe de la flotte means it is pouring down.

If it is just a bit nippy you can say **il fait frisquet ce matin**.

If it is cold, you can say **il fait un froid de canard** (a duck).

In truly foul weather, you might say **il fait un temps de chien** (or **cochon**) - there is **faire** again!

Finally, in this **Getting Better** part of the chapter, here are a few more uses of **faire**. They are all quite frequently heard:

Faire ses commissions can mean to do one's shopping, to run errands, to pass on messages or, incidentally, to go to the toilet! You will hear this said very frequently.

Should someone ask you how something specific is going, you might use **faire des progrès**. For example:

- "Le mur qu'on est en train de faire construire – **on fait des progrès**" ie The wall that we are in the process of having built is making (good) progress. Note that it is "des" progrès not "du" progrès.

If you want to say that you are doing something deliberately or on purpose, the expression you need is **faire exprès**, for example:

- "J'ai laissé le rôti de boeuf au four une heure de plus que conseillé. Mais nous aimons notre viande bien cuite. Donc, **je l'ai fait exprès**". ie I left the roast beef in the oven an hour longer than advised. But we like our meat well cooked. So I did it on purpose.

Faire face à quelqu'un / quelque chose means to face up to somebody or something.

Faire la connaissance de quelqu'un means to meet someone for the first time. On some occasions, you might be introduced to someone and wish to say something along the lines of "Hello! It's a pleasure to meet you" and you could say rather formally:

- "Je suis enchanté(e) de **faire votre connaissance**" or more simply "Enchanté(e) de **faire votre connaissance**".

If you really did want to lay it on a bit thick, so to speak, you might say "je suis ravi(e) de **faire votre connaissance**".

However, if all this is a bit too much for you, you can always say quite simply "Bonjour monsieur, bonjour madame!"
Quite frankly these days, the French are much more relaxed than they used to be, particularly in the countryside in my experience. However, if you really want to show your respect for someone, particularly for elderly people who might be much more traditional or conservative, then the formal approach works well.

Faire la sourde oreille means to turn a deaf ear to, not because someone is deaf necessarily, but rather because someone chooses not to hear what someone has got to say.

Finally in this section, an expression which I find myself using on almost a daily basis:

"**Faites-vous la queue, madame**?" Are you in the queue, madam?
Particularly in the country, for French people, shopping is an important means of social contact; and people use their supermarket sometimes rather like we use the pub, to chat, dare I say, even to gossip! Both "bavarder" and "papoter" can be used in this context but these words are not in the slightest bit pejorative. There are other words altogether for malicious gossip.

One final thought on queuing. We Brits are famed for our patience in queues although it is not always merited these days, I fear, and the French, according to national stereotype, are supposed to be infamous for their lack of patience. Well if you want to give the lie to that "canard" just have a look outside almost any Parisien cinema, in particular on a Sunday evening. French people love the cinema (they call it "le septième art" – the seventh artform) and are frequently encountered queuing very patiently on a Sunday night, many people's favourite night for going to the cinema.

So, there we are! Lots of progress made. Just a little bit more and you will be sitting on top of that **faire** mountain, lord (or lady!) of all that you survey (I hope!)

Now You Are Really Speaking French!

And what does it take to breathe that clear **faire** air?! Two things, I feel:

First, get to grips with **faire** in its reflexive forms and then learn how to add even more colour to your conversations using some of the more advanced idiomatic expressions. For this verb has more even than any other of our "serial killer" verbs.

Reflexive faire

As we have already seen, **faire** is used to talk about doing things:

- "**J'ai fait la vaisselle** hier soir" – I did the washing up last night and…

also to get things done:

- "**J'ai fait faire la vaisselle à mon fils hier soir**" – I got my son to do the washing up last night. On a rather more historical note…
- "Catherine de Medicis **a fait venir** ses cuisiniers italiens au château de Fontainebleau en 1533" – Catherine de Medicis (the wife of King Henry II) got her Italian chefs to come to the French King's château at Fontainebleau (outside Paris) in 1533.

Here is a very important cultural aside: yes, we all know that France has an unrivalled reputation for its cuisine, but did you know that at court before 1533, French chefs really were not up to much? That is why when Louis married Catherine, an Italian, so disgusted was she with what his court had to offer, that she brought her Italian chefs over to raise French standards more than somewhat. The culinary jewel in her crown was her pastry chefs, who laid the foundations for subsequent French pâtisserie excellence. But try telling this to the French!

But back to **faire**. In the last two examples, somebody is getting somebody else to do whatever. But, if you want to say, so to speak, that you got, or want to get, **yourself** to do something, you need the reflexive form of **faire**. Remember some of my getting out of bed examples in the **Être** chapter?

"**Je me suis** levé, **je me suis** lavé, **je me suis** rasé…" and so on. So instead of saying:

"Je fais la cuisine" – I cook (for whoever), you can say:
"Je **me** fais la cuisine" – I cook for myself.

In fact, there are countless illustrations of this construction in action, so here are some of the more common ones:

- "**Je me suis fait** beaucoup d'amis" – I made lots of friends (for myself).
- "Ce fromage / vin **se fait** bien" – This cheese/wine is maturing nicely.
- " Il **s'est fait** tout seul" – He is a self- made man.
- "Les choses finissent toujours par **se faire**" – Things always get done in the end.
- "**Ça se fait** – d'offrir les fleurs à un homme?" - Is it the done thing to offer a man flowers?
- "Les jupes longues **se font** beaucoup cette année" – Long skirts are all the rage this year.
- "Il pourrait **se faire** qu'il pleuve (subjunctive) – It could rain, and…
- "**Comment ça se fait que**…?" – How come that…? This is a particularly useful expression and can be used in all sorts of situations. For example:

  "**Comment ça se fait que** la voiture est tombée en panne?" – How come that the car has broken down?
  "**Comment ça se fait que** Paris ne te manque pas?" – How come that you are not missing Paris?
  "**Comment ça se fait qu'**ils sont partis avant la fin du film?" – How come they left before the end of the film?

- "**Il se faisait tard** quand nous sommes arrivés à l'hôtel" – It was getting late when we arrived at the hotel.
- "Parce que nous sortons ce soir, **il faut que je me fasse** (subjunctive) belle, chéri" – Because we are going out tonight I must make myself look beautiful, darling.
- "**Il se fait** plus bête qu'il n'est" – He makes himself out to be more stupid than he really is.
- "**Il se faisait** apporter son journal tous les matins" – He had his paper brought to him every morning.
- "Je vais chez mon coiffeur **me faire couper les cheveux**" – I am going to my hairdresser to get my hair cut.
- "**Tu m'as fait** renverser mon thé" – You made me spill my tea.
- "Il ne peut pas **se faire** au climat" – He cannot get used to the climate.
- "**On s'est fait** un restaurant" – We went to a restaurant.

Whilst there really are lots more examples like this out there, I feel you have got enough here to get really used to this particular reflexive construction. So, let's move on a bit and have a look at some of the more familiar ways that **faire** can be used in conversation.

The familiar use of faire

I said earlier that I would eschew the use of slang in the book because the precise meaning of a word or phrase will so often depend on the context. However, very often you will find in French that the same word might be quite acceptable used in one context and frankly rather vulgar in another. With this warning in mind, here are some familiar uses of faire that can, even do, have potentially stronger associations! Again, I have made no particular effort to organise them in any way:

Se faire quelqu'un can mean to pick-up someone, although the more usual word for to pick up is "draguer". Somebody who does the picking-up is known as a "dragueur".

Savoir y faire (not "savoir-faire") means to be very competent, to "know one's onions".

La faire à quelqu'un means to trick or to fool somebody, hence...

- "**On ne me la fait pas**" – "You can't pull the wool over my eyes".

Être fait comme un rat perhaps surprisingly does **not** mean to be "as p****d as a rat, but means either to be cornered, trapped or even to be arrested by the police.

Faut le faire can mean simply "nice going" or "well done".
(Incidentally, if you do want to congratulate somebody by saying "Well done!", then you need "Bravo!". If you translate well done literally as "bien fait", you will actually be saying "serves you right!") However, **faut le faire** is often employed ironically, such as "Tu me téléphones à une heure de matin? **Faut le faire!**" This translates as "You telephone me at one-o-clock in the morning? Nice one!" And more or less the same sentiment is conveyed by the expression:

Ça commence à bien faire, that is to say "I have had enough of this".

Faire ses besoins ("un besoin" is literally a need) could be a reference to your dog doing his business in the street:

- "**Il ne fait que ses besoins**" – He is only doing his business. On this subject, time was when the streets of Paris in particular were foul with dogs' "saloperies". However, these days it seems, possibly because of the heavy fines that can be imposed on dog owners, Paris streets are much cleaner, "Dieu merci!" Thank God!

Ça le fait quite simply means that something looks good or does the trick.

Ça le fait pas means that something is not up to scratch.

Se faire cinq mille balles par jour used to mean to earn five thousand francs per day. Then, in pre-euro days of francs, une balle was a thousand francs. Although France went over to the Euro in the year 2000, this word is still used, particularly in country areas and amongst older citizens.

Il faut se le faire means that someone is a real pain in the …

S'en faire means to worry. I use this expression a lot!:

- "**T'en fais pas**!" in other words, relax, chill out, take it easy, do not worry!

The idiomatic and proverbial uses of faire

Faire, like **être** and **avoir**, seems to crop up in countless idiomatic expressions. So here again, are examples of the many that abound, beginning (appropriately given my last example above) with expressions of worry:

Se faire du mouron (this word has strong botanical associations). For example:

- "Arrête de **te faire du mouron** pour lui" – Stop worrying about him. Other similar expressions include:

Se faire de la bile, pronounced "beel", but actually exactly the same word as our bile, in other words, what we can get in our stomach.

Se faire des cheveux, not to be confused with cheveaux, ie horses!

Still on a worrying theme:

Faire son deuil de quelque chose means to give something up for lost, your wallet, for example ("deuil" means mourning, incidentally).

Ne pas faire dans le détail however is the worrying antidote: do not worry about the finer points!

Faire un dessin / croquis (a drawing or a sketch) means to spell something out to make oneself understood.

Faire un malheur, literally unhappiness, sounds very negative indeed. But surprisingly, it means quite the opposite. Rather like "pas terrible", (do you remember?) which means terrible, **faire un malheur** means to be a terrific success:

- "Les vignerons du Beaujolais (the region of Beaujolais) **ont fait un malheur** un peu partout avec leur Beaujolais nouveau." That is to say, the wine growers of the Beaujolais region have had a huge success pretty much everywhere with their Beaujolais nouveau.

Ça fait deux simply means "and that makes two of us" who do not understand something, technology, for example.

Faire du plat à quelqu'un means to chat somebody up, closely related to pick somebody up, but with a slightly different nuance.

Se faire virer means to get expelled from school. Perhaps because:

Tu as fait l'école buissonnière, literally you have done school in a bush ie you have skipped school or played truant. When I was a boy in Wales, we would talk of "mitching" school, but I have never heard it since.

Of course, some children, even their parents sometimes, could not care less. There are several ways of expressing this sentiment, and you have already met a couple, "je m'en fous" for example. A more polite way of saying this, apart from the three I have already given you elsewhere, "ça m'est égal", "ce n'est pas la peine" and "c'est kif-kif" is:

Ça ne me fait ni chaud, ni froid and means literally that it does not make me hot **or** cold. It might do, though, if someone:

Se faire tirer l'oreille ie gives you a good telling off. Mind you, some school kids in particular these days, might act a bit crafty, ie:

Faire une réponse de Normand which means to reply like a Norman. Normans are typically regarded by the French from other regions as crafty, often it seems because they appear reluctant to commit themselves to a "yes" or a "no" (neither hot nor cold, it seems). For such prevarication there is a very impressive French verb: "tergiverser".

Faire quelque chose les doigts dans le nez literally means to do something with your fingers in your nose. It actually means to do things so easily that you could do them with your eyes closed.

There are lots of ways of saying "get lost!" in French, most of them unrepeatable here. The colloquial but quite polite expressions are:

Se faire la malle and
Se faire la paire.

Faire un créneau has strong motoring associations, meaning to find a gap to park the car. (The French are masters of this devilish art, incidentally). Continuing the motoring theme:

Faire une queue (there are four consecutive vowels in this word!) **de poisson** (fish) **à quelqu'un** means to carve somebody up on the road. And "Poisson d'avril!" by the way, means April Fool!

Faire le saut (jump) means to take the plunge – and if you are ever crazy enough to drive around the Arc de Triomphe in Paris, you will certainly need to take the plunge. There, it is the survival of the fittest!

Now, here is something that we say in English **very** regularly, whenever we want to suggest doing something with someone – "How's about….?" In French there is a particular construction:

Si on faisait (or whatever)…? ie How's about doing this or going there etc…? The construction always begins with **si on** and is always followed by the appropriate **verb in the third-person singular of the imperfect tense**, for example:

- "**Si on faisait** une maquette de la Tour Eiffel? – How about making a model of the Eiffel Tower? or
- "**Si on allait** en Espagne cette année?" – How about going to Spain this year? or
- "**Si on regardait** la télé ce soir?" – How about watching telly tonight?

Now here is something that the French say and do a lot:

Faire le pont literally means to make the bridge. We all know how much the French love their food and wine. Perhaps less well known is their passion for leisure. They have more Bank Holidays ("jours férriés") than we do; and their long summer holiday is sacrosanct - generally four weeks taken in one block, normally between July 14th, Bastille Day and August 15th, Assumption Day. Then, of course, there is the obligatory week in February, "pour faire du ski", not to mention the 35 hour week that most (not all) French workers are statutorily bound by.

But all that is never enough! "Donc, **ils font le pont**," normally by taking one or more of their Bank Holiday days when they occur, say on a Thursday, Monday or Tuesday and perhaps tacking on a day of holiday here or there so that they can go off somewhere, typically to the mountains or to the sea or to their "résidence secondaire", their second home. "Profitez-en!" as the French like to say!

And here is another stereotypical French national sport – refusing to pay parking fines!:

Faire sauter une contravention means to avoid paying a parking fine. How do they get away with is so easily and so regularly? Someone, somewhere has influence and most French people know who and where such people are. Remember the expression in the **Avoir** chapter – "avoir le bras long", to know somebody in high places who has influence?

Now here is some advice if you are driving in France:

Faire l'âne pour avoir du son literally means to play the donkey to get the bran. In practice, it is a rather old-fashioned phrase to pretend ("faire semblant", remember?) that you do not know or do not understand how things work in France – like the language, for instance. Time was when this technique worked well. I remember the first time I was breathalysed in France (yes, it's happened more than once!). I pretended that I did not understand because I did not speak French, and it worked! But that was many years ago – and I really do not recommend that strategy these days. Nowadays, French police are very stony-hearted: they have heard it all before and are ruthless in their interpretation of French traffic laws. The drink limit is lower in France that in Britain (one small glass of wine could see you over that limit). So, if you have got any sense, do not drink anything if you are planning to drive. And if you do, be particularly diligent on Saturday and Sunday afternoons – the "gendarmes" are everywhere!

We have already met a couple of expressions for "to be had", but here is a particularly idiomatic one:

Se faire rouler dans la farine literally means to get rolled in the flour, but even this meaning makes things pretty clear! In the big cities such as Paris, Marseille and the like, it is particularly easy to be had, more so if you look like a tourist. For Brits arriving by Eurostar to Paris, be careful ("faites gaffe", remember?), stations like the Gare du Nord and Chatelet, a metro station, are particularly shady places. If you plan to use the Paris Metro, try to buy your tickets in advance.

Finally, here is another word of warning. Do not:

Faire un chèque en bois literally to make out a wooden (we call it a "rubber") cheque, ie, a cheque that will "bounce", so to speak. And do note that unlike Britain, where we are so obsessed with all these pieces of plastic we carry around in our wallets and having virtually given up using cheques, French country dwellers love their cheques and are surprisingly reluctant to "flash the plastic", particularly in supermarkets. If, like me, you can be a wee bit impatient, control yourself, when, say, an elderly man or woman seems to be taking an age to fill out that cheque (even though the process is semi-automatic these days). Sometimes you just need to be a bit philosophical in France – "c'est la vie!"

Here are even more idiomatic uses of **faire** to keep you busy! Again, there is no particular structure to them:

Faire l'autruche – to bury one's head in the sand.
Faire table rase – to make a clean sweep.
Faire le calcul – to add up.
Faire le forcing – to lay it on hard.
Faire interdiction à quelqu'un de faire quelque chose – to ban someone from doing something.
Faire revivre quelque chose – to bring something to life.
Faire des ravages – to create havoc.
Faire démarrer quelque chose – to get something off the ground.
Faire tout son possible – to do everything possible.
Faire grief à quelqu'un de quelque chose – to hold something against someone.
Faire acte d'autorité – to put one's foot down.
(Se) faire rembourser de quelque chose – to get re-imbursed for something.
Faire pression sur – to put pressure on.
Faire intervenir quelqu'un – to bring someone in.
Faire le plein – to fill up (the car).
(Se) faire chier – to be bored out of one's mind.
Faire passer un message – to get a message across.
Faire de la pub pour – to advertise.
Faire l'avocat de quelqu'un – to speak up for somebody.

Faire salle comble – to play to a packed house.
Faire fausse route – to bark up the wrong tree.
Faire recette – to be a success.
Que faire? – what to do? ·
Ne savoir que faire – not to know what to do.
Faire ses preuves – to prove oneself.
Faire le poids – to measure up.
Faire des pieds et des mains – to make a great effort to do something.
Faire peau neuve – to turn over a new leaf.
Faire les cents pas – to pace up and down.
Faire des affaires en or – to make a mint of money.
Faire machine arrière – to back track.
Faire la lumière sur quelque chose – to clarify something.
Faire la loi – to lay down the law.
Faire l'impossible pour faire quelque chose – to make every effort to do something.
(Se) faire l'apôtre de – to become the spokesperson for.
(Se) faire hacher pour quelqu'un – to do anything for someone.
Faire les frais de quelque chose – to bear the brunt of something.
Faire contre mauvaise fortune bon coeur – to put a brave face on things.
Faire feu de tous bois – to make use of all available means.
Faire chorus avec quelqu'un – to agree with someone.
Faire du chemin – to make progress.
Faire boule de neige – to snowball.
Ne faire qu'une bouchée de – to make short work of something…

…and now, a proverb:

Une hirondelle ne fait pas le printemps – One swallow does not make a summer.

Last, here is an expression which will almost certainly draw gasps of admiration and approval, should you use it. No other phrase that I could give you will work as well in the conviction stakes! So here it is:

Faire avancer le schmilblick means to progress something or other. It is almost always used in the **negative**:

- "**Ça ne fait pas avancer le schmilblick**" ie That is not going to get us very far. The word **schmilblick**, meaning "thingamy", first appeared in the French language in 1949 and was later parodied hilariously by Colluche, a French comedian, in a very famous TV sketch. Every French person I have ever met over 40 years old remembers the sketch – and, therefore, knows the expression. So use it, whenever the opportunity arises!

Conclusion

Well, once more, I suspect, "ça suffit!", that is enough! You have plenty to get your teeth into with **faire** for this is the longest chapter in the book. But that should come as no surprise. No verb is more versatile than **faire**, because it can be used instead of so many other French verbs, particularly if you do not know or cannot remember the ideal verb. **Faire** will always get yourself understood. Even if you use it incorrectly, French people will forgive you. They are very understanding people! And **faire** is used in far more idiomatic expressions than any other verb.

So, now you have three of my big four "serial killer" verbs under your belt. Let us move on to the fourth, **aller**. Indeed, "allons-y!" But not before we have had a look at some conversations that showcase the verb **faire**.

Faire: Conversation One

Georgette is in the streets of Paris and she is stopping people to ask them about their past-times, ("leurs passes-temps").

Georgette:	Excusez-moi, jeune homme, je fais de la recherche pour un client sur les passes-temps des Français (et Françaises bien sûr – ça va sans dire!) Avez-vous un moment, s'il vous plait?
Jeune homme:	Mais bien sûr, madame. Ça me ferait plaisir. Allez-y!
Georgette:	Bon. D'abord une question de sport. Evidemment vous êtes encore jeune. Que faites-vous comme sport?
Jeune homme:	Bon, j'aime presque tous les sports, mais j'aime beaucoup le rugby.
Georgette:	Est-ce que cela veut dire que vous faites du rugby?
Jeune homme:	Oui, je fais du rugby tous les week-ends. Faire du rugby me plaît énormément. À vrai dire, c'est plutôt une obsession. qu'une distraction. Quand même je peux trouver le temps pour d'autres sports.
Georgette:	Ah, bon? Lesquels?
Jeune homme:	J'aime faire de la natation.
Georgette:	Excellent. Et, dites-moi, est-ce que vous êtes musicien?
Jeune homme:	Ah, oui, la musique me plaît énormément. Quand j'étais gosse je faisais aussi de la guitare accoustique mais de nos jours je préfère faire du piano.
Georgette:	Et c'est tout?
Jeune homme:	Oui, ça suffit je crois!
Georgette:	Merci bien jeune homme.
Jeune homme:	Il n'y a pas de quoi, madame. Au revoir.
Georgette:	Merci infiniment. Au revoir.

Faire: Conversation Two

This time, Corinne is in one of her favourite Paris restaurants and has just had a splendid lunch which included a delicious "jarret de veau" (a knuckle of veal). The service over and all but Corinne having left the restaurant, she asks her waiter if the chef would be kind enough to explain precisely how he prepared the dish. A few minutes later the chef / proprietor comes out of the kitchen still wearing his toque, (the chef's tall hat) and sits down at her table.

Corinne: Merci d'être sorti de votre cuisine. Pourriez-vous m'expliquer comment vous faites pour réussir votre jarret?

Chef: Bien sûr madame. Pour réussir ce plat il faut d'abord acheter les meilleurs ingredients: un beau jarret de veau de 800 grammes environ, 60 grammes de beurre doux, deux gousses d'ail en chemise, trois tomates bien mûres, du sel et du poivre. Et pour les légumes, 250 grammes de carrottes nouvelles, 500 grammes de pomme de terre nouvelles, 30 grammes de beurre doux, un peu d'huile d'olive, sel et poivre.

Corinne: Et avec tous ces ingrédients, qu'est-ce que vous faites?

Chef: Pour commencer, faites fondre le beurre dans une cocotte. Sur une planche, salez et poivrez le jarret puis posez-le dans le beurre bien chaud, en évitant que le beurre noircisse. Faites dorer le jarret avec les deux gousses d'ail sur toutes ses faces pour, mettons, quinze minutes à peu près. Puis couvrez et faites mijoter le jarret pendant 45 minutes à feu moyen, tout on retournant la viande de temps à l'autre.

Corinne: Et puis?

Chef: Puis, passez les tomates à l'eau bouillante, épluchez-les, coupez-les en quarts et ajoutez-les dans la cocotte. Épluchez les carrottes et les pommes de terre, rincez-les puis enveloppez-les dans un torchon.

Corinne: Et les légumes, qu'est-ce que vous faites avec?

Chef: Les légumes? Bon. Dans une deuxième cocotte, faites fondre le beurre et l'huile. Dès que la matière grasse est chaude, mettez les carottes coupées en bâtonnets et les pommes de terre coupées en deux, puis ajoutez du sel et du poivre.

Puis, dès que les légumes commencent à revenir, faites-les sauter et laissez cuire à feu moyen pendant 20 minutes grosso modo. Si le jus s'évapore trop, ajoutez une louche d'eau chaude.

Corinne: Et c'est tout?

Chef: Oui, plus au moins. Une fois la cuisson terminée, découpez le jarret sur une planche. Servez-le bien chaud avec la sauce dans la cocotte. C'est simple comme bonjour!

Corinne: Pour vous, oui – mais pour moi...

Chef:	Ne vous en faites pas, madame. Je suis sûr que le vôtre sera aussi bon que le mien.
Corinne:	Vous êtes très gentil, monsieur.
Chef:	Il n'y a pas de quoi, madame. Régalez-vous. Bon appétit!
Corinne:	Merci mille fois, monsieur, et au revoir.
Chef:	À très bientôt j'espère!
Corinne:	Oui. À bientôt.

Some words you might not yet know

- la recherche - research
- évidemment - obviously
- encore - still
- cela veut dire que - that means that
- à vrai dire - to tell the truth
- une distraction - a relaxation
- lesquels(m) - which ones
- Quand j'étais gosse - when I was a kid
- guitare(f) accoustique - acoustic guitar
- être sorti - to have come out of
- réussir - to make a success of
- beurre (m) doux - unsalted butter
- une gousse d'ail en chemise- a clove of garlic with its skin
- une cocotte - a casserole dish
- éviter - to avoid
- noircir - to blacken
- faire dorer - to brown
- mettons (from mettre) - for say
- à peu près - more or less
- couvrir - to cover
- mijoter - to simmer
- à feu moyen - on a medium heat
- la viande - meat
- de temps à autre - from time to time
- passer - to pass
- l'eau (f) bouillante - boiling water
- éplucher - to peel
- ajouter - to add
- rincer - to rinse
- envelopper - to wrap up
- un torchon - a tea towel
- un légume - a vegetable
- faire fondre- to melt
- dès que - as soon as
- la matière grasse - fat
- un bâton - a stick
- faire revenir - to turn colour
- s'évaporer - to evaporate
- la louche - ladle
- plus ou moins - more or less
- terminer - to finish
- le / la vôtre - yours
- le / la mien/mienne - mine
- régaler - to treat
- bon appétit! - enjoy your food!

Faire: Exercises

Fill in the blank spaces:

1.   Qu'est-ce que tu (   ) en ce moment? Je voudrais sortir.

2.   Dans le temps, je (   ) le ménage. Maintenant, j'(   ) une femme de ménage.

3.   Je le (   ) quand j'aurai un moment.

4.   Voudriez-vous (   ) une promenade demain?

5.   Si j'achète ce produit-ci, (   ) l'affaire?

6.   Quand j'ai un moment, j'aime (   ) du piano.

7.   Combien de kilomètres ont-il (   ) ce matin?

8.   Ce rutabaga-ci, ça (   ) un kilo à peu près.

9.   Mon fils, il veut (   ) chauffeur de taxi.

10.   Tu as acheté ce canapé chez Laura Ashley? Ça (   ) tellement anglais!

11.   J'ai (   ) cuire mon rôti de porc pendant deux heures. C'était délicieux!

12.   Est-ce que cela vous (   ) penser à quelque chose?

13.   J'ai beau dire, je trouve impossible de (   ) entrer dans la tête de mon fils qu'il devrait passer moins de temps devant la télé.

14.   Il faut que vous (   ) gaffe, monsieur. Vous êtes trop proche du bord de la rivière.

15.   (   ) de ton mieux, chérie. Franchement je crois que la tondeuse est foutue.

16.   Il ( ) beau aujourd'hui mais il ne (   ) beau demain, paraît-il.

17.   Le jardin est presque fini. J'ai (   ) beaucoup des progrès hier.

18.   (   )-vous la queue, madame? Ne vous en ( ) pas. Je ne suis pas pressé.

19.   Je me suis (   ) beaucoup d'amis au lycée. J'y étais très content.

20.   Comment ça (   ) que votre machine à coudre est tombée en panne?
       Elle est presque toute neuve!

21.   Je ne peux pas (   ) un créneau. Il y a trop de voitures dans cette rue-ci.

Faire: Answers

1. fais
2. faisais, ai
3. ferai
4. faire
5. fera-t-il
6. faire
7. fait
8. fait
9. faire
10. fait
11. fait
12. fait
13. faire
14. fassiez
15. Fais
16. fait, fera pas
17. fait
18. Faites, faites
19. fait
20. se fait
21. faire

Chapter Five
Aller

Introduction

Aller, to go, is a bit different from our three other "serial killer" verbs, particularly **faire**, in that it has relatively few uses beyond its basic role in describing movement. Unlike **être** and **avoir**, which are employed as auxiliary verbs in compound tenses and **faire** which has literally thousands of idiomatic uses, **aller** is in the "serial killer" category for one very simple reason – its **frequency** of occurrence. You will hear no verb more times in an average day than **aller**, simply because it is used to ask people how they **are**, how they are **going**. For this reason alone, you need to be very familiar with this verb. However, there are other uses of **aller**: it can be used instead of some other verbs; and you will often find its reflexive cousin, **s'en aller** used in conversation, too. So, let us move on, beginning, as always, with its conjugations.

The Aller Conjugations

Present Tense

Je vais	Nous allons
Tu vas	Vous allez
Il va	Ils vont
Elle va	Elles vont

Future Tense

J'irai	Nous irons
Tu iras	Vous irez
Il ira	Ils iront
Elle ira	Elles iront

Imperfect Tense

J'allais	Nous allions
Tu allais	Vous alliez
Il allait	Ils allaient
Elle allait	Elles allaient

Perfect Tense

Je suis allé(e)	Nous sommes allé(e)s
Tu es allé(e)	Vous etes allé(e)s
Il est allé	Ils sont allés
Elle est allée	Elles sont allées

Future Perfect Tense

Je serai allé(e)	Nous serons allé(e)s
Tu seras allé(e)	Vous serez allé(e)s
Il sera allé	Ils seront allés
Elle sera allée	Elles serons allées

Pluperfect Tense

J'étais allé(e)	Nous étions allé(e)s
Tu étais allé(e)	Vous étiez allé(e)s
Il était allé	Ils étaient allés
Elle était allée	Elles étaient allées

Present Conditional Tense		**Past Conditional Tense**	
J'irais	Nous irions	Je serais allé(e)	Nous serions allé(e)s
Tu irais	Vous iriez	Tu serais allé(e)	Vous seriez allé(e)s
Il irait	Ils iraient	Il serait allé	Ils seraient allés
Elle irait	Elles iraient	Elle serait allée	Elles seraient allées

Present Subjunctive Tense		**Imperative**
J'aille	Nous allions	Va
Tu ailles	Vous alliez	Allons
Il aille	Ils aillent	Allez
Elle aille	Elles aillent	

Aller: The Basics

As you know **aller** is to go. Now in English, **to go** is one of the most versatile verbs in our language. In French it is fairly versatile too. As I have said, its basic role is to describe where, when and how you can go somewhere:

- "Où **allez-vous** aujourd'hui? Aujourd'hui **je vais** à Lyon" ie Where are you going today? Today I am going to Lyon.
- "Et où **êtes-vous allez** hier? Hier **je suis allé** à Avignon" ie Where did you go yesterday? Yesterday I went to Avignon.
- "Et la semaine prochaine? Vous avez l'intention **d'aller** où? La semaine prochaine, j'ai l'intention **d'aller** en Angleterre" ie And next week? Where do you intend going? Next week I intend going to England.

So use aller to say where you are going, where you went and where you intend going.

But you can also use it to describe **how** you will get there:

- "**Allez-vous** à Bordeaux en train? Non, **j'y vais** en voiture" ie Are you going to Bordeaux by train? No, I am going there by car.
- "**Êtes-vous allé** à Rouen en train? Non, **j'y suis allé** en avion" ie Did you go to Rouen by train? No, I went there by plane.
- "**Irez-vous** à l'opéra en taxi? Non, **j'y irai** en bus" ie Will you go to the opera by taxi? No, I will go there by bus.

Two points are really worth noting in these examples:

First, **aller** is followed by the preposition **à** in each of the three questions: **à** Bordeaux, **à** Rouen and **à** l'opéra. If **aller** is to be followed by a **noun**, then the preposition **à** is required. I will return to this point very shortly.

Second, each form of transport – plane, taxi and bus, is preceded by **en**. This is true with **most forms of transport**:

> **en vélo** by bicycle
> **en car** (careful here! "car" means **coach**!)
> **en camion** by lorry… and so on
> Though do note that if you are **walking**, it's **à** pied.

You can also use **aller** with **time** clauses:

- "**J'y vais à midi**" ie I am going there at midday.
- "**J'y suis allé à minuit**" ie I went there at midnight.
- "J'avais l'intention **d'y aller hier**" ie I intended going there yesterday.

If you **want** to go somewhere, but do not know **how** to get there, use the construction **pour aller à?** eg:

- "**Pour aller** au Syndicat d'Initiative s'il vous plaît?" ie How do I get to the Tourist Information Office, please?
- "**Pour aller** au Mans, s'il vous plaît?" ie How do I get to Le Mans, please? Do notice in this example that Le Mans becomes **au** Mans when you want to get to it. It is exactly the same with all place-names beginning with **Le**:

> **au** Havre means to **Le** Havre
> **au** Baux means to **Le** Baux
> **au** Bugue means to **Le** Bugue.

But when you **pose** the **pour aller** question, do not automatically expect a reply using **aller**. People **might** use **aller**:

- "Oui, **pour aller** au Bugue **vous allez** tout droit pendant dix kilomètres" – Yes, to get to Le Bugue you go straight on for 10 kilometres. However, it is more likely that the response will be more **precise** and employ verbs **other** than **aller**. Consider this mini-conversation:

Moi:	Excusez-moi, madame, mais **pour aller** à Lyon, s'il vous plaît?
La dame:	Êtes-vous en voiture, monsieur?
Moi:	Oui, je suis en voiture.

La dame:	Eh bien, vous **continuez** jusqu'à la place, ensuite vous **prenez** le troisième boulevard à droite. Puis, vous **continuez** jusqu'au feu rouge… (the traffic lights)
Moi:	Oui.
La dame:	Au feu rouge vous **verrez** des panneaux pour Lyon. Vous y allez par l'autoroute à péage?
Moi:	Oui.
La dame:	Alors, vous **prenez** la deuxième route à gauche et vous **suivez** la direction de Beaune. Après, c'est tout droit. Bonne route, monsieur!
Moi:	Merci bien, madame.
La dame:	Je vous en prie, monsieur.

This example has **continuer, prendre, voir** and **suivre**. Others you might expect to hear include:

monter to climb or to go up
descendre to go down
traverser to cross
tourner to turn.

Often, your interlocutor will not bother with the **vous** at all – then you will get your answer in what sounds like the verb's imperative form, ie the equivalent of **turn, cross, climb** etc.

Aller – other prepositions and other verbs

We saw just now that **aller** is often followed by the preposition **à**, thus meaning "to go to". But think about **aller**'s English equivalent for a moment. I said that in English, to go is a very versatile verb, if only because "to go" can be followed by any number of different prepositions to express very different meanings. In English, we can go:

Up, down, in, out, to, from, under, over, past, through… and so on. When any of these prepositions immediately follows a verb in English, it is known as a **phrasal** verb. And English is **replete** with **phrasal verbs**. The verb **to hold**, for example: one can hold on, hold off, hold up, hold down… etc.

Phrasal verbs exist in French, too, but in very general terms, they are not **quite** so ubiquitous. Very often, as you have just seen with **pour aller à** the French will use **another verb altogether** in place of **aller**: **continuer, traverser** and **prendre** etc. Consider these very obvious examples:

To go forward. The French are highly likely to use **avancer**.
To go backward. Here, **reculer** is likely to be used.

And so it is likely to be with many **verbs of movement**. To illustrate:

- to go off - **partir**
- to go up - **monter**
- to go down - **descendre**
- to go in - **(r)entrer**
- to go out - **sortir**.

But verbs other than those of movement can also replace **aller**:

- to go about - **rouler**
- to go across - **traverser**
- to go after - **suivre**
- to go ahead - **passer (en tête)**
- to go by - **passer**
  … and many more.

So what about **aller** and prepositions other than **à** to go **to**? Well, earlier in the book we met the notion of **going to the doctor**, remember? There, I used the expression **chez** le medécin, meaning to **go to** the doctor. In fact, **chez**, a preposition, can be used to express going to pretty much anybody:

aller **chez le dentiste**
aller **chez le/la coiffeur(se)**
aller **chez le boucher**
aller **chez un(e) ami(e)**… and so on.

Other prepositions that are commonly employed after **aller** include:
Aller en – to go by a mode of transport, to go to a country, even to go into town.
Aller sur – to go to: "Je vais **sur** Paris", I'm going to Paris.
Aller vers – to go in the direction of, to go towards.
Aller (jusqu')à – also means to go to.
Aller dans – to go down… and so on.

In many other cases, **aller** can be followed **by another verb without a preposition**. For example:

- "Je **vais jouer** au rugby cet aprèm" – I am going to play rugby this afternoon. Young people in particular often shorten "après-midi" to "aprèm".
- "Je **vais faire** l'ascension de la montagne" – I am going to climb the mountain.
- "Je **vais avancer**: la voiture derrière moi a très peu de place" – I am going to go forward: the car behind me has very little space.

Sometimes, however, the English reader can be puzzled by **aller** and another verb in the infinitive **elsewhere in the sentence**. Consider these examples:

- "Je suis allé chez le garagiste **acheter** une nouvelle voiture".
- "Je vais dans mon bureau **chercher** un stylo".

Do you feel that there is anything **missing** from these two French sentences? Well, perhaps you have noticed the absence of "for" or "in order to" in both sentences:

> I went to the garage (in order) to buy a new car. But there is no "pour" (in order to) in this sentence.
> I went into my study (in order) to look for a pen. It is exactly the same – no "pour".
> The explanation lies partially in the fact that because the second verb is in the **infinitive**, which always means "to…", "pour" is not necessary. However, in verbs other than those of movement, "pour" is usually employed. For example:

- "Pourriez-vous me donner un euro **pour** acheter une baguette, s'il vous plaît?" ie Could you give me a euro to buy a loaf of bread, please?

Aller as a noun

For the moment that is enough, I feel, on the subject of **aller** and movement, except to add that **aller** can sometimes be a **noun**, as you will find out for yourself at the "guichet" (ticket office) of a railway station, for example. If you ask for a ticket, "un billet" for, say, Paris, you are likely to be asked:

- "Désirez-vous un **aller-simple** ou un **aller-retour**, monsieur?" ie Do you want a single or return, sir?

However, perhaps the most important reason for the daily use of aller in conversation is its role in asking and saying how you and other people are or feel.

- "Comment **allez-vous**?" – How **are** you?
- "Comment **vas-tu**?" – How **are** you?, using the informal **tu** in place of **vous**.

So when someone asks you how you are, you have a range of replies, the most obvious of which are:

- "**Ça va** bien" – I am fine.
- "**Ça va** mal" – Things are not going well.

Sometimes you feel somewhere in the middle:

- "Pas mal" – Not bad.

Sometimes the question is slightly more impersonal:

- "Comment **ça va**?" And your response might be:
- "**Ça va** mieux maintenant"- Things are getting better now.

The question can also be used to ask how things are going **somewhere**:

- "Comment ça va **à l'école**?" – How are things going at school?
- "Comment ça va **au bureau**?" – How are things going at the office?

And in the business context, you can ask how someone's **business** is going:

- "Comment vont **les affaires** en ce moment?" – How is business at the moment? Note here that business in the general sense is always in the plural: **les affaires**. In the singular **l'affaire** has several different meanings.

And should you go to the **hairdressers** for a shampoo and cut, the shampooist will almost certainly ask:

- "La température, **ça va**?" – Is the water temperature ok?

Aller and exclamations

We have just seen that **ça va** in its interrogative form means "how is it going?" but this expression is also used in an exclamative fashion. Here are some of the most useful of these:

- **Ça va!** – this is not a question; it is an exclamation and means "that's enough!":

  "Tes bêtises, **ça va** comme ça!" – Your stupidity, I've really had enough of it!

- **Allons** or **allons-y** or **allez** or **allez-y** all mean pretty much the same thing, as does **vas-y** ie "come on, let's go" and so on. Often at national sporting events, the crowd will shout **Allez les Bleus!**, a reference to the blue shirts worn by their sporting heroes. Then there is:

- **Allons-donc!** which is used to exclaim disbelief as in "come off it!"
- **Allons bon!** can be used to say "oh dear!" But be careful with the next one:
- **Va donc!** which means "you idiot!"

Summary

In its basic form **aller** is a very important and even more frequently heard verb than any other. Use aller to:

- ask for or give directions
- talk about different ways of getting to your destination
- ask how other people are or feel and to tell others how you yourself are or feel
- say "come on, let's go" and other similar ideas.

Getting Better

In fact, if you have battled your way fairly successfully through the basics of **aller**, you are already pretty good. But to build on your knowledge you should also be aware of **other verbs** that **aller** can substitute for. You should also be familiar with **aller** in the present subjunctive, and finally in this section you should familiarise yourself with **aller**'s very close relative, **s'en aller**, the pronominal form of the verb.

Aller and other verbs

In the last chapter, we saw just how many other verbs **faire** can replace. **Aller** can stand instead for far fewer. There are only **five** you need to know:

Mener - to lead to. For example, "Cette route-ci doit **mener** à la forêt" ie This road must lead into the forest.

S'étendre – to stretch to. For example, "Les champs-là **s'étendent** à la vallée d'en face" ie Those fields stretch as far as the valley opposite.

Durer – to last. For example: "Les fleurs devraient **durer** jusqu'à la fin de la semaine" ie The flowers should last to the end of the week.

> In each of these three cases **aller** can be used instead:
> In sentence 1, **aller** can replace **mener**.
> In sentence 2, **vont** can replace **s'étendent**.
> In sentence 3, **aller** can replace **durer**.

Marcher/fonctionner – to work in the sense of to function. So, instead of saying: "Ça va **marcher** maintenant" one can say "Ça va **aller**, maintenant" ie That is going to work now or **ça ira** – that will work.

My fifth example is a little different. Should you and your partner go, for example, into a dress shop and the lady in question tries on, say, a coat ("un manteau") which you think particularly suits her, you can say:

- "Ce manteau te **va** rudement bien" ie This coat really suits you.

You can also use the same verb to describe things that seem to go really well **together**:

- "Cette table **ira** parfaitement **avec** les chaises au fond du magasin" – This table will go perfectly with the chairs at the back of the shop.

In these examples, **aller** is employed instead of **convenir**.

Aller and the subjunctive

We looked at asking for directions earlier in the chapter: **pour aller à**…? If you wanted to be a bit more emphatic about what you need to do to get to wherever, you could say:

- "**Qu'est-ce qu'il faut que je fasse** pour arriver à Aix-en-Provence, s'il vous plaît?" ie "What do I need to do to get to (say) Aix-en-Provence, please?

This time, the reply might be:

- "Pour aller en voiture à Aix-en-Provence, monsieur, d'abord **il faut que vous alliez** à Lyon par la N7, puis il faut que vous preniez l'autoroute à Aix. C'est indiqué à Lyon".
  To get to Aix-en-Provence by car, first of all you must take the N7 to Lyon then you must take the autoroute to Aix. It is shown at Lyon.

(Incidentally, N roads are "Routes Nationales", roads similar to our A roads in Britain. These days many of them are excellent dual carriageways and often avoid busy town centres. They are, of course, toll-free. Other roads you can use include D roads, departmental roads and C roads, communal roads. These are generally very quiet indeed and, over relatively short distances, can be almost as quick as N roads).

Other expressions featuring **aller** in the **subjunctive** are those you would by now expect plus a few more that you are not yet familiar with. For example, the subjunctive is implicated in phrases expressing ideas about **aiming** at something. For example:

> **pour que**
> **de telle sorte que**
> **de sorte que**...
> all mean **so that** (as does **de manière à ce que**).

To illustrate:

- "Allez-y en voiture **pour que**
  de telle sorte que vous **y alliez** plus vite".
  de sorte que
  ie Go there by car so that you go more quickly.

S'en aller

This pronominal verb is used basically in the sense of **to go** but more in the sense of **to be off**: "Alright, I'm off now – see you tonight" ie "D'accord, **je m'en vais** - à ce soir". Other examples:

- "Les gosses? Ils **s'en vont** bientôt" ie The kids? They are off soon.
- "**Ils s'en vont** à Paris demain" ie They are off to Paris tomorrow.

S'en aller can also be used in place of **to retire** ("prendre sa retraite"):

- "**Il s'en est allé** l'an dernier. Je ne sais pas où il est maintenant" ie He retired last year. I do not know where he is now.

It can also be employed to talk about the **money that you or someone else spends**:

- "Mon fils, oh là là! Tout son argent **s'en va** en cigarettes!" ie My son, oh dear! All his money goes on cigarettes.

You can even use it to talk about **getting dirty marks out of your washing**!:

- "T'en fais pas - ça **s'en ira** au lavage" ie Don't worry, that will come out in the wash.

Of course, one can be off, sadly, in an altogether more permanent form, for **s'en aller** can also be used euphemistically to say that someone has died:

- "Elle avait quatre-vingt-neuf ans quand finalement **elle s'en est allée**" ie She was eighty-nine years of age when, finally, she passed away.

Now You Are Really Speaking French!

Aller's **basic** role is easily its most important, but **aller** also figures in some useful idiomatic expressions. For example:

Ça va sans dire – it goes without saying.
Il (ça) va de soi which means pretty much the same thing.
Allez savoir! means who knows?
Y aller mollo means to tread carefully.
Y aller de sa petite larme means to have a bit of a cry.
Ne pas y aller avec le dos de la cuillère (the back of a spoon) means to lay it on a bit thick, as does "en rajouter", which you have already met.
Aller dans le décor means to go off the road and hit something.
Aller à pince(s) means to "leg it".
Aller au charbon (coal) means to knuckle down to some hard work.
Ne pas y aller de main morte means not to pull your punches.
Allez au diable! literally means go to the devil or to go to hell!

Getting a bit higher in the familiar stakes is:

Où tu vas? meaning "are you off your head?"
Va te faire cuire un oeuf! meaning "go and get stuffed!".

And virtually (but not quite) at the top of the vulgarity list is:

Va te faire foutre! meaning "bugger off!"

Other expressions featuring **aller** include:

Aller comme un gant (a glove) means that something suits perfectly.

Aller vite en besogne means to hurry things along.

Aller tout seul means to be plain sailing.

And, whilst "un aller-retour" is, as you know, a return ticket to somewhere, "un aller **et** retour" is a slap in the face, first with the palm of the hand, then with the back of the hand (get it?!)

Finally some **proverbs** featuring **aller** (there are not a lot in the language):

Tant va la cruche à l'eau qu'à la fin elle se casse, literally, so often does the pitcher go to the water that it finally breaks means "enough is enough".

Qui craint le danger ne doit pas aller en mer, literally, if you fear danger do not go to sea means "if you cannot stand the heat, get out of the kitchen".

Qui va à la chasse perd sa place means that if you step out of the line, you will lose your place.

Conclusion

Aller is the fourth of our "killer" verbs and the last of our four "serial killer" verbs. Armed with a good working knowledge of these, you should already be feeling fairly confident about your French – and the progress that you have made. There now follow seventeen more "killer" verbs (and one for luck!) but I have deliberately **not** organised them in any order of importance. Some **may** generally be more important than others, but as I emphasised in an earlier chapter, much depends on the situations you find yourself in. All I can say is that each verb builds, at least to some extent, on its predecessors, as the conversations at the end of this chapter should make clear. Whilst much will be new to you, much will also be very familiar. That is how it should be.

Aller: Conversation One

Maryse has gone to the 19th arrondissement in Paris to see Anna, a good friend from their days at school together. Maryse rings the doorbell and Anna opens the door.

Anna:	Bonsoir, Maryse, comment vas-tu? Ça va?
Maryse:	Oui, ça va. Et toi?
Anna:	Oui, tout va bien. Mais quel plaisir de te revoir! Ça fait longtemps que...
Maryse:	Ça fait au moins trois mois.
Anna:	Que le temps passe vite! Bon. Donne-moi ton manteau et fais comme chez toi – à côté de moi sur le canapé, peut-être, Sinon...
Maryse:	Non. Le canapé me va parfaitement, merci.
Anna:	De rien. Mais avant de m'installer, que désires-tu, une boisson fraîche, une boisson chaude ou quelque chose de plus fort!? J'ai un bon vin blanc dans le frigo et j'ai un excellent rouge sur le bahut.
Maryse:	Tu as l'embarras du choix! Je crois que je vais prendre un petit verre de blanc, Anna – et toi, qu'est-ce que tu prends?
Anna:	Comme toi, je prends du blanc.

A minute or two later, Anna returns from the kitchen with the drinks:

Bon, santé, Maryse. Tchin-tchin!

Maryse:	Tchin-tchin!
Anna:	À propos, Maryse, j'adore ta robe décolletée. Ça te va, vraiment bien. Et la couleur est belle. Où est-ce que tu l'as achetée, à "A La Mode" peut-être?
Maryse:	Pas cette fois, non. Je suis allée Rue du Faubourg Saint Antoine où j'ai trouvé une toute petite boutique pleine à craquer de belles choses – et aux prix très raisonnables, massacrés même.
Anna:	Tu dois me donner l'adresse, Maryse. Il faut que j'y aille! Mais parlons d'autres choses. Quoi de neuf? Es-tu partie en vacances cet été? La dernière fois que nous nous sommes rencontrées, tu parlais d'aller en Grèce, non?
Maryse:	Si. Mais j'ai été trop occupée cet été. Mais j'ai l'intention d'aller quelque part au mois d'octobre quand j'aurai deux semaines de congé. Et toi?
Anna:	Moi aussi – nulle part. Mais j'ai une idée, Maryse. Dis-moi ce que tu en penses. J'ai une semaine de vacances au mois d'octobre, aussi. Si on allait quelque part ensemble? La dernière fois que nous

	sommes parties ensemble, nous avons passé un bon moment, tu te souviens?!
Maryse:	Oui, bien-sûr. Et quelle excellente idée. Mais, où partir? Si on allait en Corse? Je n'y suis jamais allée et on-dit que c'est une île d'une grande beauté – où ils parlent français, bien-sûr!
Anna:	L'idée est fort tentante, Maryse. Je vais chercher quelques prospectus demain. Nous pourrons choisir quelque chose ce week-end, peut-être.
Maryse:	Oui, je repasserai samedi matin si cela te convient?
Anna:	Oui, et à propos de ta robe nous pourrions...

They continue talking well into the night!

<u>Aller: Conversation Two</u>

It is just a few days before Christmas and Francine has gone to the Gare d'Austerlitz, hopefully to interview some people who are leaving Paris for their Christmas holidays. She meets a young couple who are waiting for their train to be made ready for departure.

<u>Francine:</u>	Excusez-moi mais j'espère que vous avez le temps de répondre à quelques questions que je voudrais vous poser?
<u>Jeune fille:</u>	Pas trop, j'espère! Mais oui, nous avons trente minutes à peu près avant le départ de notre train. Allez-y!
<u>Francine:</u>	Merci bien, c'est gentil. D'abord, où allez-vous ce matin, dans le Midi peut-être?
<u>Jeune homme:</u>	Oui. En fait, nous allons à Menton.
<u>Francine:</u>	Oui, sur la Côte d'Azur, ça va sans dire! Mais Menton est très proche de la frontière italienne, n'est-ce pas?
<u>Jeune homme:</u>	Tout à fait. En effet, la maison familiale de ma copine, Valérie, ne se situe qu'à deux pas de la frontière dont vous parlez.
<u>Jeune fille:</u>	Oui, Philippe a raison. Nous sommes à dix kilomètres de l'Italie.
<u>Francine:</u>	Et vous allez voir votre famille, j'imagine.
<u>Jeune fille:</u>	Nous allons passer quelques jours chez mon père. Malheureusement, ma mère s'en est allée l'an dernier et mon papa est tout seul.
<u>Francine:</u>	Il sera très heureux de vous voir, alors.
<u>Jeune homme:</u>	Oui, j'en suis sûr. Hélas, Noël ne rime pas toujours avec bonheur. Donc, il faut y aller mollo. Sa femme lui manque terriblement. Ce dont il a besoin, c'est d'être dorloté.
<u>Francine:</u>	Naturellement. Et après la fête de Noël vous repartez sur Paris, peut-être?
<u>Jeune fille:</u>	Non, après Noël nous allons passer quelques jours chez les parents de Philippe.
<u>Francine:</u>	Et où ça?
<u>Jeune homme:</u>	Pas loin de Menton, à Nice où je suis né.
<u>Francine:</u>	Bon. Nice est belle, n'est-ce pas?
<u>Jeune homme:</u>	Hors saison, oui. Mais l'été ce n'est pas très calme. Trop de touristes.
<u>Francine:</u>	Oui. Et après? Où allez-vous?
<u>Jeune homme:</u>	Après dix jours de vacances, c'est difficile d'aller au charbon, mais il le faut. Le train-train quotidien, vous savez.
<u>Francine:</u>	Oui, je le connais aussi. Mais regardez, votre train est presque prêt à partir. Allez-y! Et merci bien.

| Jeune fille: | Je vous en prie, madame. Au revoir. |
| Francine: | Au revoir. Et bonnes fêtes! |

Some words you might not yet know

- revoir - to see again
- fais comme chez toi - make yourself at home
- un canapé - a sofa
- s'installer - to sit down
- un bahut - a sideboard
- l'embarras (m) du choix - so much to choose from
- à propos - by the way
- une robe décolletée - a dress with a low neckline
- une boutique - a small shop
- prix (m) massacrés - knock-down prices
- quoi de neuf? - what is new?
- occupé(e) - busy
- quelque part - somewhere
- nulle part - nowhere
- fou (folle) - mad/crazy
- tentant(e) - tempting
- un prospectus - a brochure
- le Midi - the South of France
- la frontière - the border
- tout à fait - exactly
- en effet - indeed
- la maison familiale - the family home
- une copine - a girlfriend
- dont - of which/about which
- dorloté(e) - pampered
- hélas - unfortunately
- rimer - to go with
- le bonheur - happiness
- hors saison - out of season
- le train-train quotidien - the daily grind
- bonnes fêtes! - happy holidays!

Aller: Exercises

1.   Choose one of the three words in the bracket and put it in the space below
        (va, allons, vont):
        Mon fils (   ) à Paris ce week-end.

2.   Do the same with one of these three word (allait, irais, irons):
        Nous (   ) à Newcastle ce week-end prochain s'il fera beau.

3.   Do the same with one of these three words (ailles, allez, iraient):
        Il faut que tu (   ) à l'ecole.

4.   Fill in the blank space:
        J'y suis (   ) en voiture. J''étais très contente.

5.   Do the same with this sentence:
        Il voudrait y (   ) en avion mais c'était trop cher.

6.   You want to go to the butchers. Choose one of these three expressions in
        brackets and write in the space below (aller à, aller chez, aller en):
        Je veux (   ) le boucher ce matin. Je voudrais de la viande pour mon
        diner.

7.   Fill in the blank space:
        Je (   ) jouer au tennis cet après-midi.

8.   Again, fill in the blank space, choosing one of the three bracketed words
        (allait, allez, allons):
        Comment (   ) vous? Tout va bien, j'espère.

9.   Translate this sentence into French:
        How is business at the moment?

10.   Now translate this sentence into French:
        Is the water temperature ok?

11.   Translate this sentence into French:
       This dress really suits you madam.

12.   Fill in the gap below:
       Pour (   ) à Rouen, s'il vous plaît?

13.   Fill in the gap:
       Il avait quatre-vingt-deux ans quand il (   ) allé.
       Translate into French the underlined part of the following sentence:
       It goes without saying that property is very expensive in London nowadays.

14.   Do the same with this sentence:
       You have had it easy all summer, son, but now you must knuckle down to
       some hard work.

15.   Fill in the missing word:
       Qui craint le danger ne doit pas (   ) en mer.

16.   Do the same with this sentence:
       St Tropez est magnifique. Il faut que tu y (   ).

17.   Translate the underlined part of the following sentence into French:
       How about going to Venice this year, darling?

18.   Fill in the blank space:
       Elle n'est jamais (   ) à New York.

19.   Again, complete the blank space:
       Il faut y (   ) mollo.

20.   Translate into English the underlined part of this sentence:
       Je sais que vous n'avez pas aimé son attitude, mais n'y allez pas avec le dos
       de la cuillère.

21.   Fill in the blank space:
       Arrête de dire des bêtises et (   ) te faire cuire un oeuf!

Aller: Answers

1. va
2. irons
3. ailles
4. allée
5. aller
6. aller dez
7. vais
8. allez
9. Comment vont les affaires en ce moment?
10. La température de l'eau, ça va?
11. Cette robe vous va rudement bien, madame
12. aller
13. s'en est
14. aller au charbon
15. aller
16. ailles
17. Si on allait
18. allée
19. aller
20. Do not exaggerate too much, do not lay it on too thick
21. va

Chapter Six
Vouloir

Introduction

Vouloir, like **aller,** is a verb that deserves its place at the high table because it occurs so frequently in every day speech. For example, it is well-nigh impossible to do any shopping for anything at all without using **vouloir**, even if you say **je veux** rather than **je voudrais**, its much more polite equivalent. But **vouloir**, basically meaning, to want, has several other uses; and it can also be used in its pronominal form, **se vouloir**. For these reasons alone it is a very important French verb. We should get to know it. So first, let's conjugate it.

The Vouloir Conjugations

Present Tense
Je veux	Nous voulons
Tu veux	Vous voulez
Il veut	Ils veulent
Elle veut	Elles veulent

Future Tense
Je voudrai	Nous voudrons
Tu voudras	Vous voudrez
Il voudra	Ils voudront
Elle voudra	Elles voudront

Imperfect Tense
Je voulais	Nous voulions
Tu voulais	Vous vouliez
Il voulait	Ils voulaient
Elle voulait	Elles voulaient

Perfect Tense
J'ai voulu	Nous avons voulu
Tu as voulu	Vous avez voulu
Il a voulu	Ils ont voulu
Elle a voulu	Elles ont voulu

Future Perfect Tense
J'aurai voulu	Nous aurons voulu
Tu auras voulu	Vous aurez voulu
Il aura voulu	Ils auront voulu
Elle aura voulu	Elles auront voulu

Pluperfect Tense
J'avais voulu	Nous avions voulu
Tu avais voulu	Vous aviez voulu
Il avait voulu	Ils avaient voulu
Elle avait voulu	Elles avaient voulu

Present Conditional Tense
Je voudrais	Nous voudrions
Tu voudrais	Vous voudriez
Il voudrait	Ils voudraient
Elle voudrait	Elles voudraient

Past Conditional Tense
J'aurais voulu	Nous aurions voulu
Tu aurais voulu	Vous auriez voulu
Il aurait voulu	Ils auraient voulu
Elle aurait voulu	Elles auraient voulu

Present Subjunctive Tense
Je veuille	Nous voulions
Tu veuilles	Vous vouliez
Il veuille	Ils veuillent
Elle veuille	Elles veuillent

Imperative
Veuille
Veuillons
Veuillez

Vouloir: The Basics

The basic meaning of **vouloir** is **to want** – normally to want something or to want someone to **do** something for someone. In its simplest form, you will probably use **vouloir** to ask somebody to provide you with something. For example, you want to send some postcards home. For that, apart from the postcards themselves of course, you will need some stamps, "des timbres". So you go to the nearest Post Office, "La Poste" to buy some:

- "Bonjour, madame, **je voudrais** des timbres pour ces cartes postales destinées à l'Angleterre, s'il vous plaît" ie Good morning, madam, I would like some stamps for these postcards going to England, please.

    "Vous en avez combien, monsieur?" ie How many of them do you have, sir?

    "Au total, j'en ai six" ie In total, I have got six (of them).

    "D'accord, six timbres pour l'Angleterre ça fait 3.60€, monsieur" ie OK, six stamps for England, that's 3.60€ please.

You then decide to pop into the nearest "Maison de la Presse" (newsagent) to see if you can find today's edition of your favourite English newspaper:

- "Bonjour, madame, est-ce que les journaux anglais se vendent ici? **Je voudrais** The Daily Mail" ie Hello madame, do you sell English newspapers here? I would like a copy of The Daily Mail.

    "Désolée, monsieur, nous ne vendons que les journaux français ici" ie Sorry, sir, but we only sell French newspapers here.

(Incidentally, English daily newspapers are surprisingly hard to find in many parts of France, and if you are lucky enough to find one that you actually want to buy, chances are that at best it is yesterday's and at worst, last week's. This is perhaps understandably so in **rural** France, but you would expect Paris to be a lot better. I am afraid not. We live in the 11th arrondisement, a highly multi-cultural district of Paris; but even here, English reading material is conspicuous by its absence. Should I want today's copy of my favourite English newspaper, I will probably have to go to the Gare du Lyon or even to the Gare du Nord, the railway station where British travellers to Paris arrive. All the more reason, therefore, to start reading French newspapers – anyway, they are cheaper!)

And now, because it is that time of day, you decide to stop off at a local café for a cup of delicious French coffee:

> Serveuse: "Bonjour, monsieur, que désirez-vous?" - Hello, sir, what would you like?
>
> Vous: "**Je voudrais** un grand crème, s'il vous plaît" – I would like a large coffee with milk, please.
>
> Serveuse: "Bien sûr, monsieur – un grand crème. J'arrive tout de suite" – Of course, sir, a large milky coffee. I will be with you in a minute.

(Here is another "incidentally!" Yes, you **can** ask for a **café au lait**. Most English people probably do. But asking for **un crème** or **un grand crème** makes you sound more convincing. **Un crème** is short for **un café crème**: it rarely comes with cream; normally it is made with milk. But it should be delicious nonetheless – but do not count on it!)

From these three examples, you can see that **if you want to buy something**, stamps, newspapers, coffee… or whatever, you will need to say:

- "**Je voudrais**… s'il vous plaît".

This very useful expression indeed is not new to you; you met it in an earlier chapter. So you already know that this is the polite way of asking for something you want or need. You can say "Je veux…" but it is less polite and more assertive. It is fine if you want to make a complaint; otherwise it does not usually get the best results! And if it is results that you are after, smile broadly as you say "Je voudrais…" You will be amazed how popular you suddenly are!

Getting somebody to do something for you

More often that not, **Je voudrais** is followed by a noun: timbres, journal, café etc. Sometimes, however, it is not something that you want but rather **someone to do something for you**. Clearly, this introduces a second subject into the sentence and this (hopefully!) you will remember, requires the second verb in the subjunctive, not the conditional or the imperfect. For example:

- "I would like you to put my suitcase on the conveyor belt, please. I have a painful back". "**Je voudrais que vous mettiez/posiez** ma valise sur le tapis roulant, s'il vous plaît. J'ai mal au dos". In this example, **mettre**, to put, is one of our "killer verbs" so you can look it up in the relevant verb table.

Or perhaps at that café just now, you would like the waiter to clear the remains of the previous customers' coffees on the table you are sitting at:

- "Bonjour, monsieur, avant de commander quelque chose, **je voudrais que vous débarrassiez** la table s'il vous plaît. "Debarrasser" means to clear (the table, in this case).

Or you need a taxi to the station, so you say to the taxi-driver ("le chauffeur de taxi"):

- "Bonjour, monsieur, **je voudrais que vous m'emmeniez** à la gare, s'il vous plaît" ie Hello. I would like you to take me to the station, please.

In this last sentence, you will notice that **emmener** is the verb used for **to take**. It is one of what I like to consider, a **family** of four French verbs:

- **emmener** - to take away (**someone**)
- **amener** - to bring (**someone**)
- **emporter** - to take away (**something**)
- **apporter** - to bring (**something**)

The first two relate to **people**, the second two relate to **things**. Do try to remember this important distinction. You would be amazed how many French people **do not** remember it!

Vouloir and other tenses

Je voudrais, **nous voudrions** etc. are all in the **conditional** tense, of course. It should be fairly obvious to you now though that it can be coupled with the imperfect tense with **si** clauses. For example:

- "**S'il** devait arrêter de fumer, **je voudrais** lui acheter un nouveau complet" ie If he were to stop smoking, I would like to buy him a new suit.

But **vouloir**, like all our other "killer" verbs, can be used in all our other tenses. To illustrate:

- "**Elle voulait** m'acheter un nouveau costume mais le modèle que **j'ai voulu** était trop cher" ie She wanted (imperfect) to buy me a new suit but the one I wanted (perfect) was too expensive, or
- "**Elle aurait voulu** venir chez nous pour Noël mais les routes étaient trop dangereuses à cause de la neige" ie She would have wanted (past conditional) to come to us for Christmas but the roads were too dangerous because of the snow.

Summary

The basic role of **vouloir** is to express your wishes or desires and is most frequently encountered in the conditional tense for the sake of politeness. But as we will see in the next section, it has other uses, too, and can be used in place of several other French verbs.

Getting Better

You can tighten your grip on **vouloir** by understanding some of the other ways that this verb can be deployed. For the most part, however, these are nuances rather than radically different meanings for **vouloir**.

First, **vouloir** is used, largely in **written** French, particularly still in letters, in what the French themselves call "formules de politesse", literally formulaic and rather verbose ways of beginning and ending letters. I am not concerned with these here, but there is one formulaic expression that you will **hear** from time to time ("de temps en temps"):

- "**Si vous voulez bien me suivre**" ie Come this way.

Second, **vouloir** can be used in place of **essayer**, to try. For example:

- "**Il a voulu** dormir mais la rue était trop bruyante" ie He tried to sleep but the street was too noisy.

Third, it can be used instead of **demander**, to ask, where prices are involved. For example:

- "**Il en voulait** 5,000€" ie He was asking 5,000€ for it.

Fourth, it can be used instead of **s'y attendre**, to expect, in sentences such as:

- "Eh bien, que **voulez-vous**?" ie Well, what do you expect?
- "Que **voulez-vous** qu'on y fasse?" ie What do you expect me to do about it?

  Or again, with a real sense of helplessness:

- "Que **veux-tu**, c'est comme ça, on y peut rien" ie What do you expect, that's how it is, I/we can't do anything. In this example, notice the absence of a French word for **do** in the phrase "on y peux rien". This is a very common construction in French.

Fifth, instead of **apparaît**re, to appear. For example:

- "La voiture **ne veut pas** démarrer" ie The car doesn't appear to want to start.

- "Le feu **ne veut pas** prendre" ie The fire doesn't appear to want to catch.

Sixth, in this sentence **vouloir** is used instead of **aller**, in English, "going to…"

- "Si vous me dites que ce sont des chênes là-bas, **je veux** bien vous croire" ie If you tell me that those are oak trees over there, I really am going to believe you.

Seventh, it can be used instead of **ordonner,** to command:

- "**Veuillez** quitter l'immeuble immédiatement: il y a un incendie au sous-sol" ie Please leave the building immediately: there is a fire in the basement.

Note here that I have written **au** sous-sol rather than **dans** le-sous sol, which you might expect to be the correct way to render "in". In fact, there is a subtle but important difference between "au" and "dans". The former is the appropriate preposition when talking of something that is **temporary**; the latter applies when something is considered to be **permanent**. So:

- "Il y a un congélateur **dans** la cave" ie There is a freezer in the basement. But:
- "Jean-Louis est descendu **à** la cave chercher une bouteille de vin" ie Jean-Louis went down into the basement to get a bottle of wine.

Much less formally **vouloir** can be used by a frustrated parent:

- "**Veux-tu** bien arrêter!" ie Please stop it!

Eighth, it can be used in place of **affirmer**, to claim. For example:

- "L'Existentialisme est une philosophie qui **veut** que nous soyons tous condamnés à la liberté" ie Existentialism is a philosophy which claims that we are all condemned to freedom.

Ninth, **vouloir** can be used in place of **avoir besoin de** as in this example:

- "Les rosiers **veulent** un sol riche en fumier" ie Rose bushes require soil which is rich in manure.

Finally, there is one other very important use of **vouloir** – when it is coupled with **dire** in the expression **vouloir dire** which means to **mean** or **signify**. For example:

- "Quand le soleil se couche et que le ciel est rouge, est-ce-que cela **veut dire** que le lendemain sera beau?" ie When the sun goes down and the sky is red, does that mean that the following day will be fine, or
- "On a loupé le dernier bus. Ça **veut dire** qu'il faut prendre un taxi" ie We have missed the last bus. That means that we will have to take a taxi, or
- "**Il en veut** 2,000€. Cela **veut dire** que c'est trop cher pour moi" ie He is asking 2,000€ for it. That means that it is too expensive for me.

Now You Are Really Speaking French!

There is not much more you need to know about **vouloir**. It remains simply to see how **vouloir** is used with prepositions, to take account of the verb in its very limited pronominal form and to note some idiomatic uses of the verb.

Vouloir and some prepositions

Vouloir can also be coupled with certain prepositions, notably **en**, but also **de** and **sans**. For example:

- **Il en veut** means he wants to win:
  "L'équipe d'Angleterre **en veut** demain" means that the English team is raring to go and out to win tomorrow.

There are also the constructions **en vouloir à quelqu'un** and **en vouloir à quelque chose**. For example:

- "Les deux soeurs **s'en veulent à mort**" means that the two sisters hate each other. **En vouloir à quelqu'un** means to bear a grudge.
- Here is another example:
- "**Je leur en veux** d'avoir abandonné mon projet" ie I hold it against them for having jettisoned my project.

In this next example it is **something** rather than **someone**, that is the object:

- "Il s'est marié avec Nathalie parce qu'il **en voulait à** son argent" ie He married Nathalie because he was after her money.
- "Il **en voulait à sa réputation** après le procès" ie He wanted to ruin his/her reputation after the trial.

The expression **sans le vouloir** can be used to describe something that happens inadvertently. For example:

- "Si j'ai dit quelque chose que tu as trouvé offensant, c'était **sans le vouloir**" ie If I said something that you found offensive, it was unintentional.

144

Pronominal vouloir

Se vouloir can be used in the sense of something being supposed to be (or do) whatever. Here is an example:

- "Le quotidien britannique, The Independent, **se veut** objectif" ie The British daily newspaper, The Independent, sees itself as objective.
- "Le croquis **se veut** authentique, mais je crois que c'est la copie d'un Picasso" ie The sketch is supposed to be authentic but I think that it is a copy of a Picasso.

Idiomatic vouloir

In fact, **vouloir** figures in very few colloquial or idiomatic expressions. But here are some expressions that you are likely to hear from time to time:

Vouloir c'est pouvoir means "where there is a will there is a way".
Quand on veut on peut means exactly the same.
Qui veut la fin veut les moyens means "the end justifies the means".
Vouloir le beurre et l'argent du beurre is the equivalent of our expression to "have your cake and eat it".

Conclusion

I have devoted relatively little space to **vouloir**, largely because its applications in spoken French are fairly limited. However, it is definitely one of our "killer" verbs because you will hear and use it daily:

- to say I/We would like ie **Je voudrais/Nous voudrions**
- in the command form **Veuillez** meaning "Please do" something or other.

Together with the other applications I have listed in this chapter, means that **vouloir** is a must learn verb.

Post-script: Although I am not suggesting that you try to avoid vouloir in conversation – why should you? – two other ways of rendering **Je voudrais** etc… are on the table:

Aimer, to like or to love. Whilst this verb has connotations well beyond **wanting** something or someone, you can say, for example:

- "**J'aimerais** ces chaussures-là" ie I would like those shoes there.

You can also use **avoir envie de**… in much the same way:

- "**J'ai envie d**'aller en ville: les soldes commencent aujourd'hui" ie I would like to go into town: the sales begin today.

Finally, as always, here are a couple of conversations that illustrate **vouloir** in action.

Vouloir: Conversation One

The bi-annual sales have just begun and Maryse is in the Boulevard Haussemann, home of two of Paris' most famous department stores (grands magasins) – Printemps and Galleries Lafayette. (Unfortunately for her!) she is accompanied by her husband, François, whose needs are, by common consent, greater than hers. At the moment they are in the mens' clothes department (rayon habillement) at Printemps.

Maryse:	Tout d'abord, tu as besoin d'un nouveau costume, François. Après les fêtes de fin d'année tu as un peu grossi. Tu as besoin d'un complet d'une taille au dessus.
François:	C'est vrai ce que tu dis. D'accord. J'aime celui-ci: la couleur est belle. Je vais l'essayer. Monsieur, s'il vous plaît. Je voudrais essayer ce costume-ci, s'il vous plaît. Est-ce que vous avez une cabine d'essayage?
Vendeur:	Mais oui, bien sûr, monsieur. C'est là-bas.
François:	Merci, monsieur.

A few minutes later:

François:	Qu'est-ce que tu en penses, chérie?
Maryse:	C'est pas mal, François, pas mal du tout. La couleur te va. Et c'est la bonne taille.
François:	Oui, mais c'est un peu froissé, n'est-ce pas?
Maryse:	Mais, ça c'est le look du moment, François – c'est très tendance!
Vendeur:	Oui, madame a raison, monsieur. On se les arrache cette année.
François:	D'accord. Je le prends. Et je voudrais aussi une belle chemise qui ira avec. Qu'est-ce que vous pouvez me montrer, monsieur?
Vendeur:	Mais bien sûr, monsieur - et peut-être des chaussures et une cravate? Tout sur ce niveau est soldé: sur les chaussures il y a un rabais de trente pour cent et sur les cravates il y a un rabais de cinquante pour cent – une affaire, eh?
Maryse:	Oui. Mais, dépêche toi, François. Le temps passe et je voudrais aller au rayon mode – il y a des robes à des prix massacrés. Dites-moi, monsieur, est-ce qu'il y a un escalator sur cet étage au rez-de-chaussée?
Vendeur:	Oui, madame. Si vous voulez bien me suivre: l'escalator est un peu caché au fond du magasin.
Maryse:	C'est gentil, monsieur. Viens, François, je suis sûre que tu voulais que j'achète une jolie robe pour notre soirée de la semaine prochaine!
François:	Mais, bien-sûr, chérie, bien-sûr, je te suis.......

Vouloir: Conversation Two

François bought a garden strimmer (une débroussailleuse) from a garden centre a few weeks ago but he has had nothing but trouble with it. He decides, therefore, to take it back to see what can be done about it.

François: Bonjour, monsieur. Je viens d'acheter cette débroussailleuse et...

Vendeur: Oui, monsieur, je me souviens de vous. Je vous ai montré quelques modèles et vous avez choisi le modèle haut-de-gamme. J'espère que tout va bien avec... Je ne voudrais pas que vous soyez mécontent.

François: Franchement je ne suis pas du tout content. Je n'ai eu que des ennuis avec. J'ai payé cher ce machin. La première fois que j'ai voulu la mettre en marche, elle ne voulait pas démarrer. Puis je me suis rendu compte que je n'avais pas rempli le réservoir jusqu'au bon niveau, et...

Vendeur: Et puis...?

François: Oui, ça démarre maintenant mais…

Vendeur: Alors si ça marche, que voulez-vous qu'on y fasse? Il faut toujours lire le mode d'emploi avant d'utiliser n'importe quoi, monsieur.

François: Mais, c'est pas pour ça que je viens faire une réclamation, monsieur. J'ai eu d'autres problèmes avec.

Vendeur: Ah bon? Par exemple?

François: Les lames en plastique – les trucs qui coupent l'herbe, vous savez, n'arrêtent pas de tomber… et c'est une marque allemande, n'est-ce pas? Là-bas les fabricants se veulent les meilleurs.

Vendeur: Attendez un instant, monsieur, s'il vous plaît. Si vous me dites que les lames n'arrêtent pas de tomber, je veux bien vous croire. Mais, je suis certain qu'il y a une solution facile à ce problème. Évidemment vous voulez que je vous la fasse réparer mais avant de la passer à notre atelier, laissez-moi la regarder.

A few seconds later:

        Mais oui, c'est simple comme bonjour! Il manque une vis dans les lames, c'est tout. Regardez.

François: Oui, vous avez raison, monsieur.

Vendeur: Bon, voici mon tournevis et une vis de la bonne taille. Ça devrait faire l'affaire. Voila, ça tient maintenant. Quand on veut on peut!

François: Tout à fait.

Vendeur: Et vous pouvez bien croire que si nous vous avons vendu quelque chose que vous avez trouvé irritant au début, c'était sans le vouloir,

	monsieur. Tout est bien qui finit bien, n'est-ce pas!
<u>François:</u>	Pas encore parce que je veux un produit pour mes rosiers! Ils veulent un sol riche en engrais, paraît-il.
<u>Vendeur:</u>	Incontestablement. Et voici le bon produit, monsieur. Mais n'oublions pas qu'il faut lire le mode d'emploi très attentivement, d'accord!
<u>François:</u>	D'accord!

At this point, a voice comes over the loudspeaker (le haut-parleur):
"Veuillez terminer vous achats. Le magasin va fermer dans cinq minutes."

<u>François:</u>	Oh là, là! Je m'en vais. Je crois que ma voiture est mal garée sur le parking. Mais je voudrais vous remercier pour votre aide et pour votre compréhension, monsieur. Au revoir.
<u>Vendeur:</u>	De rien. Au revoir. À la prochaine fois!

Some words you might not yet know

- tout d'abord - first of all
- un costume - a suit
- les fêtes de fin d'année - the end of year celebrations
- grossir - to put on weight
- une cabine d'essayage - a changing room
- la bonne taille - the right size
- froissé(e) - crumpled
- tendance - trendy
- s'arracher - to fight over
- une chemise - a shirt
- les chaussures (f) - shoes
- une cravate - a tie
- un rabais - a discount
- une affaire - a bargain
- se dépêcher - to hurry up
- un escalator - an escalator
- le rez-de-chaussée - the ground floor
- caché(e) - hidden
- se souvenir de - to remember
- montrer - to show
- mécontent(e) - unhappy
- haut-de-gamme - top of the range
- franchement - frankly
- les ennuis - problems
- mettre q.ch.en marche - to start
- se rendre compte - to realise
- remplir - to fill
- le réservoir - the tank
- le mode d'emploi - the usage instructions
- les lames(m) - blades
- une marque allemande - a German brand
- évidemment - obviously
- réparer - to repair
- l'atelier (m) - the workshop
- une vis - a screw
- un tournevis - a screwdriver
- tenir - to hold
- l'engrais (m) - fertiliser
- incontestablement - without doubt
- être mal garé(e) sur le parking - to be badly parked
- la compréhension - understanding
- à la prochaine fois - until the next time

Vouloir: Exercises

1.   Choose one of the three words in the bracket and put it in the sentence below (voulons, voudront, voudrait):
      Ma femme (   ) un grand crème et un croissant, s'il vous plait.

2.   Fill in the blank space:
      Je ne (   ) pas cette patisserie-ci: c'est trop cher.

3.   Again, fill in the blank space:
      Mon mari (   ) que vous mettiez mes valises sur le tapis roulant.

4.   (   ) débarrasser la toute, sil vous plaît?

5.   Do the same with this sentence:
      Si j'arrêtais de fumer, il (   ) m'acheter une nouvelle robe.

6.   And here:
      Il ne vous aime pas. Mais que (   ) vous?

7.   And here:
      Si vous (   ) bien me suivre, madame.

8.   And again here:
      (   ) quitter l'immeuble immédiatement. Le magasin ferme dans cinq minutes.

9.   Le magasin est sur le point de fermer, monsieur. Cela (   ) que vous n'avez pas de temps pour acheter cette complet.

10.   On a loupé le dernier train. Cela (   ) qu'il faut prendre un taxi.

11.   Translate this sentence into French:
      The French team is raring to go: they want to win tomorrow.

12.   Fill in the blank space below:
      Les deux frères (   ) à mort.

13. Do the same here:
    Elle s'est mariée avec Nathan parce qu'elle (   ) à son argent.

14. And here:
    Le diamant (   ) authentique mais le bijoutier n'est pas du tout certain.

15. Translate this sentence into French:
    Where there is a will, there is a way.

16. And this one:
    The end justifies the means.

17. And this one:
    My wife would like to try on these shoes, please.

18. Fill in the blank space:
    Je ne (   ) pas que vous soyez mécontent.

19. And here:
    Si vous me dites que ce sont des jonquilles là-bas, je (   ) bien vous croire.

20. And here:
    Je (   ) qu'il ne soit pas autoritaire.

21. And finally, here:
    Si j'ai dit quelque chose que vous avez trouvé offensant, madame, c'était sans le (   ).

Vouloir: Answers

1.   voudrait (or veut)
2.   veux
3.   veut
4.   veuillez
5.   voudrait
6.   voulez
7.   voulez
8.   veuillez
9.   veut dire
10.   veut dire
11.   L'équipe française en veut demain
12.   s'en veulent
13.   en voulait
14.   se veut
15.   Vouloir, c'est pouvoir **or** Quand en veut, on peut
16.   Qui veut la fin veut les moyens
17.   Ma femme voudrait essayer ces chaussures s'il vous plaît
18.   veux / voudrais
19.   veux
20.   veux / voudrais
21.   vouloir.

Chapter Seven
Devoir

Introduction

We met the **noun** "devoirs" in a previous chapter: there it meant homework. And perhaps you can see the link with the **verb devoir**, because school homework is something one is expected, even **obligated** to do. That is what **devoir** is widely used to express – ideas about obligation, in other words, **having** to do things. "Must" is an English word that readily springs to mind in such situations: "I really must do my homework tonight".

But **devoir** has other connotations in French, the most important of which is **to owe**, often to owe money, but other things, too – favours, for example. So we will also examine this basic role of **devoir** in our first section.

And do not forget we have already met one of **devoir**'s important applications in the **Être** chapter: "**Si je devais** faire le même rôle stéréotypé de sex-symbol jusqu'à la fin de mes jours, cela serait complètement ridicule". Here. **devoir** in the imperfect tense is used to express the idea if one **were** to do something or other. But, like all our verbs to date, **devoir** has several other meanings which we will explore.

And it is also a pronominal verb, there being several applications of **se devoir**. Naturally, we will also consider these.

One final point by way of introduction: **devoir**'s idiomatic usage is very limited indeed. However, all the other uses described above render it a must learn verb. It is another true "killer".

So, let's begin, as always, by conjugating **devoir**.

The Devoir Conjugations

Present Tense

Je dois	Nous devons
Tu dois	Vous devez
Il doit	Ils doivent
Elle doit	Elles doivent

Future Tense

Je devrai	Nous devrons
Tu devras	Vous devrez
Il devra	Ils devront
Elle devra	Elles devront

Imperfect Tense

Je devais	Nous devions
Tu devais	Vous deviez
Il devait	Ils devaient
Elle devait	Elles devaient

Perfect Tense

J'ai dû	Nous avons dû
Tu as dû	Vous avez dû
Il a dû	Ils ont dû
Elle a dû	Elles ont dû

Future Perfect Tense

J'aurai dû	Nous aurons dû
Tu auras dû	Vous aurez dû
Il aura dû	Ils auront dû
Elle aura dû	Elles auront dû

Pluperfect Tense

J'avais dû	Nous avions dû
Tu avais dû	Vous aviez dû
Il avait dû	Ils avaient dû
Elle avait dû	Elles avaient dû

Present Conditional Tense

Je devrais	Nous devrions
Tu devrais	Vous devriez
Il devrait	Ils devraient
Elle devrait	Elles devraient

Past Conditional Tense

J'aurais dû	Nous aurions dû
Tu aurais dû	Vous auriez dû
Il aurait dû	Ils auraient dû
Elle aurait dû	Elles auraient dû

Present Subjunctive Tense

Je doive	Nous devions
Tu doives	Vous deviez
Il doive	Ils doivent
Elle doive	Elles doivent

Imperative

Dois
Devons
Devez

Devoir: The Basics

The most important basic function of **devoir** is to express ideas that lie within a continuum from **obligation** to **necessity** – in other words, from things one **should** do, to things one really **must** do. To illustrate, first in English:

- "I really have got to get my sister a birthday present. There will be all hell let loose if I don't". Here, there is a real sense of **obligation** underpinning the requirement to buy the present.

This second sentence implies more urgency, however:

- "She absolutely must catch the last bus tonight. She does not have the money for a taxi". Here, it is **imperative** that she catches the last bus.

In these two examples above, it is easy to see that English can express these nuances very flexibly: "should", "have to" and "must" offer a range of expressive possibilities. In French, most of these nuances are captured by **devoir** although, as we have seen in the **Être** chapter, you can use constructions like **il faut que** to express necessity. At **this** end of the spectrum, **devoir** and **falloir** are virtually interchangeable.

So let's have a look at some examples in French, this time, of **devoir** in action:

At the **obligation** end of the spectrum, use devoir to suggest what someone else might reasonably be supposed to do or to say, ie what someone should do or ought to do. Very often in these circumstances, **devoir** will be used in the **conditional** tense: like **je veux** and **je voudrais** (remember?), **tu devrais** is altogether more gentle on the ear than **tu dois**. So:

- "Monette, tu **devrais** porter une écharpe aujourd'hui. Il fait rudement froid dehors ce matin" ie Monette, you should wear a scarf today. It is really cold outside this morning. Again, this time using the **past** conditional:
- "Ils **auraient dû** rentrer à dix-huit heures. J'espère que tout va bien" ie They should have come home at six o'clock. I hope that everything is alright.

In English, though, we might want to say that they are **bound** to be back by six o'clock ie it is highly probable that they will be back at this time. Now the sentence might read:

- "Ils **doivent** rentrer à dix-huit heures". (Incidentally, note the use of the 24hr clock here. This is **very** common in French – and I will have more to say on this subject in a later chapter, **Venir**).

Devoir is often used in this probabilistic sense of "should". Here is another example:

- "**Il devait être** onze heures quand elle est descendue de l'avion" ie It must have been eleven o'clock when she got off the plane.

In this example, to express "it must have been", I could have written **il a dû être** ie the **perfect** tense of **devoir**. **Il devait être** is clearly the **imperfect** tense of **devoir**. However, whilst the perfect tense can express notions of certainty, so too can the imperfect.

Again, note too the **flexibility** of the English word "must". Here it does not imply necessity, rather probability. The French use **devoir** to express these subtleties. However, we are now straying from the strict world of obligation; and when we talk about possibilities or probabilities we can easily find ourselves in a world of hypotheses. In other words, we **wonder**:

- "Paris **doit** être calme au mois d'août – tout le monde a quitté la capitale, j'imagine" ie Paris must be quiet in August – everyone has left the capital, I imagine.
  Here we are expressing supposition. We may even be guessing. Or again:

- "La table n'est pas trop grande. **Ça devrait** rentrer dans le coffre de la voiture si nous sortons le sac-au-dos" ie The table is not too big. There should be room in the car boot if we take out the ruck-sack.

In this last example, we are using **devoir** to speculate about what might be feasible ("faisable"). Here is another example:

- "**Si on devait** acheter un beau poulet et plusieurs légumes, on pourrait préparer une poule-au-pot pour demain, belle-maman" ie If we were to buy a nice chicken and some vegetables, we could make "poule-au-pot" for tomorrow, mother-in-law.

In these last two examples, you will see the now familiar combination of the imperfect and conditional tenses with the **if** clause. I referred to this use of **devoir** in the Introduction: if I/we/they etc **were to**… do something or other… This is a very common way of employing **devoir** and is quite far removed from its use in expressing obligation or even necessity.

The **second** basic role for devoir is to say or ask how much someone **owes** somebody. So, at the bar, having supped up and ready to leave, you will naturally want to say: "How much do I owe you?" This translates as:

- "Combien **je vous dois**, monsieur?"

This literally translates as: How much I owe you, monsieur? Straight away, you will notice the missing word **do**. How much **do** I owe you? But this way of posing the question is one of three possible ways of asking a question in French:

1.   **Invert** the verb – "Avez-vous des croissants?"
2.   Add **est-ce-que** – "Est-ce-que vous avez des croissants?"
3.   Make a **statement** with the pitch of your voice **rising at the end of the sentence** – "Vous avez des croissants?"

Questions taking this form merely solicit yes/no answers, of course. But interrogative words such as **combien**, **comment**, **pourquoi** and so on can also normally be accommodated within these constructions:

1.   "**Combien** de croissants avez-vous?"
2.   "**Combien** de croissants est-ce que vous avez?"
3.   "Vous avez **combien** de croissants?"

I suspect that some French people cannot be bothered with the rigmarole of inversion (it can get quite tricky in complex sentences) and opt, often, for the easier third route. Hence, **Combien je vous dois**? My advice, particularly in the early days of grappling with questions in French, is to make life easy for yourself and go for the third route, too. As you get more accomplished, you can start to experiment with the

157

other forms of question. But always remember the K.I.S.S. formula: **K**eep **I**t **S**imple, **S**tupid!

One further thought on the subject of financial debt: "Surtout, souvenez-vous que si vous devez 100 livres à la banque vous avez un problème; mais si vous lui devez un million de livres, c'est elle qui a un problème!" (Get it?) Above all, remember that if you owe the bank £100 you have a problem; but if you owe them £1 million then it is they who have a problem!

Sometimes though, the debt is not monetary. One can be indebted to somebody for something they may have done for you – or said on your behalf. Again, we will use **devoir**. To illustrate:

- "C'est à mes parents que **je dois** ma réussite en tant que médecin" ie I owe my success as a doctor to my parents. Or…
- "C'est aux scientifiques qu'**on doit** cette découverte extraordinaire" ie It is to the scientists that we owe this extraordinary discovery.

And if you want to ask **questions** about your indebtedness, even if it is only a trivial debt of gratitude, you might, for example, say:

- "À qui **devons-nous** cette charmante soirée?" ie Whom do we have to thank for this charming evening? And on a much more serious, even profound, level:
- "Les enfants, **doivent-ils** le respect à leurs parents sans se poser de questions?" ie Should children respect their parents without question?

Summary

Frankly, I think that is more than enough of **devoir** at the basic level. In summary, use **devoir**:

- to express in French English words such as "should", "must" and "absolutely have to do" ie from obligation to necessity
- when you want to talk about the possibility or probability of something being done or happening
- when you want to speculate or imagine something
- to talk about owing someone money or someone owing you money
- when you feel you owe someone gratitude for something they may have done for you.

Getting Better

Perhaps surprisingly, there is not a lot more to know about **devoir**, even at this intermediate level. The main refinement to your knowledge comes in the form of **pronominal devoir**, that is to say **se devoir**, which has **four** useful applications.

Pronominal devoir

Very often in the case of pronominal and reflexive verbs, the reflexive pronoun **se** suggest some degree of reciprocity. Although you have not yet encountered the verb **s'entendre**, to get on with (someone), it is a very good verb to know how to use **and** it illustrates the point I want to make:

- "**Ils s'entendent bien**" means that they get on **well with each other**.

So it is with the **first** of **se devoir**'s uses:

- "**Ils se doivent** la vérité" means **They owe it to each other** to tell the truth.

Second, in the same vein, a husband and wife have a duty (I would like to think!) to be faithful to each other:

- "Les époux **se doivent** fidelité".

In these first two applications of **se devoir** the verb is followed, in these cases at least, by **abstract nouns**, "la vérité" and "la fidélité". But in the **third** application, often you will hear the verb followed by a **preposition**, either **à** or **de**. To illustrate:

- "Elle croit qu'elle **se doit à** son frère cadet de l'aider à ses devoirs, parce qu'il l'aide avec sa musique" ie She believes that she owes it to her younger brother to help him with his homework, because he helps her with her music.

In this example of **se devoir** in use, **someone** owes it to **someone else** to do **something**. But the verb can also be used in the sense of **someone** feeling an obligation to **something**, as in this illustration:

159

- "Je **me dois à** mon entreprise de travailler les week-ends, si nécessaire, parce que je considère que je suis bien payé pour ce que je fais" ie I owe it to my company to work week-ends when necessary because I reckon that I am well paid for what I do.

Se devoir can also be followed by the preposition **de**. For example:

- "L'entreprise croit qu'elle **se doit de** plonger ses clients dans l'extase!" This translates as The company believes that it has a duty to its customers to send them into raptures!

I agree that sounds just a bit o.t.t ("dépasser la mesure") but leading marketing practitioners now believe that it is no longer enough to **satisfy** customers. To retain their loyalty in the face of intense competition, you must transport them into raptures of delight! If very few British firms achieve this heady objective, my experience is that even fewer French companies manage it. But then I am not a woman: my wife would doubtless argue that LVMH (Louis Vuitton Moët et Hennessy) and L'Oréal, have that effect on her every time she goes into their stores on the mythical Champs Élysées!

In this example above you will note that **se devoir de** is followed by a **verb** in the **infinitive**. Here is another example:

- "Si notre nouveau logiciel se veut un succès commercial il **se doit d'être** facile à utiliser" ie If our new software is going to be a commercial success, it has to be easy to use.

My **fourth** and final example of **se devoir** in use is a little different in that the expression **comme il se doit** conveys the idea of someone's expectations being met. For example:

- "**Comme il se doit** en pareil cas, quand mon nouvel aspirateur est tombé en panne, le vendeur était tout à fait d'accord de l'échanger contre un autre" ie As you would expect in such cases, when my new vacuum cleaner broke down, the salesman was perfectly happy to exchange it for another one.

Now You Are Really Speaking French!

Quite honestly, there is very little more you need to know about **devoir** and **se devoir**, if only because you are now in this verb's driving seat, so to speak. (Incidentally, so to speak translates as "pour ainsi dire" – and you will often hear this said. However, you can convey exactly the same meaning simply by tacking "quoi" on the end of your sentences. To illustrate:

- "J'ai très peu d'experience, quoi" ie I have very little experience, so to speak.
- "Il est con, quoi" ie He is stupid, so to speak.
- "Où allez-vous habillé comme l'as de pique, quoi?" ie Where are you going dressed up like the ace of spades, so to speak. To be dressed thus means to wear an assortment of different clothes that really do not match, remember?).

The **idiomatic** use of **se devoir** is very limited indeed. Here is the only genuine idiom that comes to mind:

- **Devoir une fière chandelle à quelqu'un** means to be terribly indebted to someone.

Conclusion

Devoir is a "killer" verb because it is frequently encountered in daily conversation. It is more likely to be heard when people talk about how much they **owe** and how much they are **owed**. You can easily say **combien je vous dois**? several times a day. But its role in expressing what should be, ought to be or needs to be done, is also hugely significant and again features very regularly in daily conversation. So, as for all our "killer" verbs, get to know it!

Devoir: Conversation One

Maryjo and Robert are giving an informal buffet party "autour d'un verre", the following evening, so Maryjo has gone out shopping to buy many of the things she will need. Luckily for her, there is a wonderful pâtisserie just around the corner from her flat, so she makes that her first port of call.

Maryjo:	Bonjour, madame. Comment-allez-vous?
Serveuse:	Ça va bien, madame, et vous?
Maryjo:	Pas mal du tout.
Serveuse:	Et que désirez-vous?
Maryjo:	J'ai l'embarras du choix. Je crois que je devrais commencer avec des trucs salés plutôt que sucrés. Ces tartelettes-ci, elles sont bonnes?
Serveuse:	Délicieuses, madame. Combien en voulez-vous?
Maryjo:	Nous devrions être dix, je pense. Alors, donnez m'en vingt, s'il vous plaît?
Serveuse:	Et avec ça?
Maryjo:	Les petites tartelettes aux framboises ont l'air délicieuses, aussi. J'en voudrais une douzaine s'il vous plaît.
Serveuse:	Désirez-vous autre chose, madame?
Maryjo:	Vos flans sont très raisonnables à un euro cinquante la pièce. J'en prends une douzaine aussi.
Serveuse:	Mais bien-sûr, madame. C'est tout?
Maryjo:	Pour l'instant, oui. Mais je repasserai demain chercher mes pains. Donc, combien je vous dois, madame?
Serveuse:	Vous me devez soixante-quinze euros et vingt centimes, madame. Mais oublions la ferraille!
Maryjo:	C'est gentil, madame. Ça veut dire que je peux vous faire l'appoint, madame. Voilà: soixante-quinze euros. Merci bien, madame.
Serveuse:	C'est moi, madame. À demain, alors
Maryjo:	Oui, à demain, madame. Au revoir.

A half an hour passes and Maryjo is almost finished. She now only has to visit her local boucherie-charcuterie.

Serveur:	Bonjour, madame, que puis-je faire pour vous aujourd'hui? Encore un gigot peut-être? J'espère que celui que je vous ai vendu l'autre jour était bon?
Maryjo:	C'était plus que bon; c'était fabuleux, monsieur!
Serveur:	Une bonne nouvelle. Alors, cette fois-ci, qu'est-ce que vous désirez?

<u>Maryjo:</u>	J'ai invité quelques amis pour demain soir et je crois que je devrais leur offrir une bonne sélection de charcuterie. Qu'est-ce que vous me conseillez?
<u>Serveur:</u>	J'avais déjà préparé une excellente sélection pour une cliente qui vient de me téléphoner, disant qu'elle devait annuler la commande parce que son mari vient d'avoir une crise cardiaque. C'est donc à vous si vous la voulez.
<u>Maryjo::</u>	Le pauvre! Oui, en principe, mais je devrais la regarder, je crois.
<u>Serveur:</u>	Ça va sans dire, madame. La voici.
<u>Maryjo::</u>	Ah, oui, c'est parfait. Je la prends. Alors, combien, je vous dois, monsieur?
<u>Serveur:</u>	Attendez un instant que je fasse le calcul. Oui, ça fait trente trois euros cinquante, madame.
<u>Maryjo::</u>	(under her breath) Merde! (and out loud) Mince! J'aurais dû garder ma petite monnaie mais j'ai tout donné au sans abri dehors. Voici quarante euros, monsieur.
<u>Serveur:</u>	Merci bien, madame. Ça veut dire que je vous rends six euros cinquante. Voilà.
<u>Maryjo::</u>	Merci, monsieur.
<u>Serveur:</u>	De rien, madame. Et amusez-vous bien demain soir! Au revoir
<u>Maryjo::</u>	Au revoir, monsieur.

Devoir: Conversation Two

The Christmas and New Year festivities now over, it is time for the obligatory attempts to discard some of that all too easily accumulated weight. Corinne has decided "de faire d'une pierre deux coups" (to kill two birds with one stone, remember?) and attend her local Paris weight-loss class, both to lose some weight and to interview some slimmers for her client. To her surprise, she finds quite a few **men** there! One of them is quite happy to be interviewed.

Corinne:	Ça me fait plaisir de vous voir ce soir, monsieur. On a tendance à supposer que ce n'est que les femmes qui se présentent à ces classes.
Homme:	Peut-être. Mais de nos jours certains hommes croient qu'ils devraient essayer de maintenir leur poids, vous savez.
Corinne:	Voulez-vous dire qu'ils se doivent à eux-mêmes de rester sains?
Homme:	Oui dans une certaine mesure. Mais ils se doivent aussi à leurs familles, à leurs épouses et à leurs enfants – même à leurs employeurs. A la boîte où, moi, je travaille, mon patron donne l'exemple: il mange d'une façon saine, il boit très peu d'alcool et il continue de faire du sport même à son âge. Il ne doit peser que quatre-vingts kilos et il est aussi grand que moi. En ce moment, je pèse quatre-vingt-quinze kilos!
Corinne:	Oh là, là! Qu'est-ce que vous devez faire, alors, si vous voulez maigrir?
Homme:	Je sais que je devrais boire moins de vin – le rouge est mon faible – ce que je fais en ce moment. Ça fait déjà deux semaines que je suis "sec", quoi!
Corinne:	Bravo, monsieur. Et quoi d'autre?
Homme:	Je mange moins de tout: mes portions sont très réduites, et je sais que je dois prendre moins de féculents. J'ai donc réduit ma consommation de pommes de terre, de pâte et de riz et j'ai augmenté ma consommation de fruits et légumes.
Corinne:	Et ça marche?
Homme:	Mais bien sûr que ça marche! J'ai déjà perdu trois kilos – pas mal en trois semaines, hein?
Corinne:	Félicitations, monsieur. Et est-ce que vous avez modifié votre programme physique?
Homme:	Bof! Je n'aurais jamais dû arrêter de jouer au foot il y a plusieurs années. Malheureusement, je me suis cassé la jambe et depuis je n'ai eu que des ennuis avec.
Corinne:	C'est dommage. De toute façon, vous faites des progrès, monsieur. Félicitations encore une fois.
Homme:	Vous êtes très aimable, madame. Mais si je devais continuer

	longtemps avec ce programme, je pourrais perdre trop de poids. Ma femme m'a donné un avertissement à ce sujet: "Perds un maximum de cinq kilos", elle m'a dit. Elle m'aime un peu potelé, vous savez!
<u>Corinne:</u>	Je comprends, monsieur. Mais regardez l'heure. Je dois m'en aller. Mon mari aura faim! Merci bien, monsieur, et bonne chance avec le régime que vous suivez.
<u>Homme:</u>	Il n'y a pas de quoi, madame. Au revoir.

Some words you might not yet know

- "autour d'un verre" - (literally) around a glass of something alcoholic
- une pâtisserie - a cake shop **and** a cake
- trucs (m) salés - savoury things
- trucs sucrés - sweet things
- les framboises (f) - raspberries
- une douzaine - a dozen
- un flan - (usually) a slice of custard tart
- la pièce - each one
- pour l'instant - for the moment
- oublier - to forget
- la ferraille - the metallic change
- c'est à moi - it's my pleasure / it's for me…
- une boucherie-charcuterie - a shop that sells both raw meat and cured pork products
- un gigot (d'agneau) - a leg of lamb
- annuler - to cancel
- une commande - an order
- souffrir - to suffer
- une crise cardiaque - a heart attack
- le / la pauvre! - poor thing!
- un calcul - a calculation
- mince! - drat/blast it!
- garder - to keep
- la petite monnaie - small change
- les sans abri - homeless people
- s'amuser - to enjoy oneself
- supposer - to assume
- se présenter - to present oneself
- dans une certaine mesure - to some extent
- une boîte - a company
- le patron - the boss
- donner l'exemple - to set an example
- manger d'une façon saine - to eat in a healthy way
- maigrir - to lose weight
- un faible - a weakness
- quoi d'autre? - what else?
- les féculents (m) - starchy foods
- la pâte - pasta
- ça marche? - that works?
- modifier - to modify
- se casser la jambe - to break a leg
- c'est dommage - its a shame
- de toute façon - all the same
- aimable - kind
- potelé(e) - chubby
- un régime - a diet
- suivre un régime - to be on a diet

166

Devoir: Exercises

1. Choose between the alternatives in the brackets for the space in the sentence
    below (devons, dois, doit):
    Mon frère m'a dit qu'il (   ) acheter une nouvelle voiture cette année.

2. Now do the same (devait, doivent, devras):
    Ils (   ) se lever de bonne heure demain.

3. And again (devez, dire, doit):
    Londres (   ) être chère de nos jours.

4. Once more (devait, devrez, aurions dû):
    Si on (   ) faire cuire le même plat tous les soirs, ça serait vraiment
    barbant.

5. Translate the underlined part of the English sentence below into French:
    It must have been eleven o'clock when my train arrived in Budapest.

6. Do the same with this sentence:
    If we were to spend Friday night in Paris, we could see a film on the Champs
    Élysées.

7. Fill in the blank space:
    Combien je vous (   ), madame?

8. Do the same with this sentence:
    Vous me (   ) cent euros. J'espère que vous pourrez régler cette dette
    bientôt.

9. Translate the underlined part of this English sentence into French:
    I should have gone to Madrid this week. Unfortunately my partner was ill.

10. Do the same with this English sentence:
    Whom do we have to thank for this charming evening?

11. Choose between the following three alternatives to complete the sentence below (se doivent, auraient dû, ont dû):
Ils se fâchent beaucoup et je ne suis pas sûr qu'ils sont toujours fidèles, mais ils (   ) fidélité quand meme.

12. Complete this sentence, filling in the blank space:
Comme (   ) en pareil cas, quand son ordinateur est tombé en panne, je l'ai réparé pour lui.

13. Fill in the blank space:
Je (   ) une fière chandelle à mon père.

14. Je crois qu'il (   ) perdre au moins dix kilos. Franchement il est obèse. Fill in the missing word.

15. Avant d'acheter ce gros pavé, je crois que je (   ) le regarder. Fill in the missing word.

Devoir: Answers

1. doit
2. doivent
3. doit
4. devait
5. Il devait être
6. Si on devait
7. dois
8. devez
9. J'aurais dû aller
10. À qui devons-nous
11. se doivent
12. il se doit
13. dois
14. devrait
15. devrais

Chapter Eight
Pouvoir

Introduction

In many ways **pouvoir** resembles **devoir**, the subject of the preceding chapter. It occupies much common ground with **devoir**, particularly when it is used to express uncertainty, hypothesis and conjecture. Its core basic meaning is to **be able to** do something or other but often when it is used to render the English equivalent "can" and "may", doubts and uncertainty can be expressed. And as sometimes simply to be polite in English we might choose **could** over **can**, echoing **je voudrais** and **je veux** in Chapter Six, **pouvoir** can be used in this way, too.

In its pronominal form, **se pouvoir**, the verb can imply even stronger degrees of doubt, yet at the other end of the spectrum, the expressions **n'y pouvoir rien** is clear and emphatic: nothing can be done about it. In the expression **n'en pouvoir plus** and its variants, ideas very different indeed from its core meaning can be expressed. And there are a few idiomatic expressions that feature **pouvoir**, too.

So, for all these reasons, **pouvoir** is a very important French verb. This is how it is conjugated:

The Pouvoir Conjugations

Present Tense

		Future Tense	
Je peux	Nous pouvons	Je pourrai	Nous pourrons
Tu peux	Vous pouvez	Tu pourras	Vous pourrez
Il peut	Ils peuvent	Il pourra	Ils pourront
Elle peut	Elles peuvent	Elle pourra	Elles pourront

Imperfect Tense

		Perfect Tense	
Je pouvais	Nous pouvions	J'ai pu	Nous avons pu
Tu pouvais	Vous pouviez	Tu as pu	Vous avez pu
Il pouvait	Ils pouvaient	Il a pu	Ils ont pu
Elle pouvait	Elles pouvaient	Elle a pu	Elles ont pu

Future Perfect Tense

		Pluperfect Tense	
J'aurai pu	Nous aurons pu	J'avais pu	Nous avions pu
Tu auras pu	Vous aurez pu	Tu avais pu	Vous aviez pu
Il aura pu	Ils auront pu	Il avait pu	Ils avaient pu
Elle aura pu	Elles auront pu	Elle avait pu	Elles avaient pu

Present Conditional Tense

		Past Conditional Tense	
Je pourrais	Nous pourrions	J'aurais pu	Nous aurions pu
Tu pourrais	Vous pourriez	Tu aurais pu	Vous auriez pu
Il pourrait	Ils pourraient	Il aurait pu	Ils auraient pu
Elle pourrait	Elles pourraient	Elle aurait pu	Elles auraient pu

Present Subjunctive Tense

Je puisse	Nous puissions
Tu puisses	Vous puissez
Il puisse	Ils puissent
Elle puisse	Elles puissent

Imperative
Does not exist

Pouvoir: The Basics

Pouvoir's basic meaning is to be able to, to "can", so to speak in English. So, use **pouvoir** for example when you want instructions or information about something. To reprise the construction "pour aller à?" that we met in the **Aller** chapter, imagine you are at the railway station in Deauville, in Normandy and you need to get to Rouen, also in Normandy, for a meeting. So you go to the "guichet" to seek information about ("se renseigner sur") the times of the trains ("les horaires des trains") to Rouen:

Vous: Pouvez-vous me donner les renseignements pour aller à Rouen, s'il vous plaît? ie Can you give me information about trains to Rouen, please? Note that you might have said "Pourriez-vous…" It would have been more polite, but in your anxiety to get to your destination, you have forgotten your manners!

L'employé: Désirez-vous y aller aujourd'hui, madame? (You do not need me to translate this for you!)

Vous: Oui, cet après-midi en fait (This neither!)

Lui: Alors, vous pourriez prendre le train qui arrive dans vingt minutes. Mais c'est pas direct. Pour un train direct pour Rouen vous devez attendre le train en provenance de Nantes qui arrive à quinze heures trente. ("En provenance de…" means coming from).

Vous: Et pourriez-vous me dire combien de temps dure le trajet, s'il vous plaît?

Lui: Le trajet dure une heure cinq, madame.

Vous: Bon. Et pouvez-vous me donner le prix du billet, s'il vous plaît?

Lui: Mais certainement. Vous voyagez en première ou en deuxième classe, madame?

<u>Vous:</u>	Ah, deuxième classe, moi.
<u>Lui:</u>	Vous prenez un aller-simple ou un aller-retour?
<u>Vous:</u>	Un aller-simple. Et est-ce que je peux prendre le billet ici, s'il vous plaît?
<u>Lui:</u>	Bien sûr, madame.
<u>Vous:</u>	Pouvez-vous me donner le prix du billet, monsieur?
<u>Lui:</u>	Oui, madame. Ça vous fait quatorze euros cinquante.
<u>Vous:</u>	Voici quinze euros, monsieur.
<u>Lui:</u>	Merci, madame. Voilà, votre billet, madame.
<u>Vous:</u>	Merci, et au revoir.
<u>Lui:</u>	Attendez, madame, je vais vous rendre la monnaie. Voilà.
<u>Vous:</u>	Merci beaucoup, monsieur. Au revoir.

This unusually long example shows how **pouvoir** can be used to ask what is possible. Notice the **infinitives** that follow in this example:

- "Pouvez-vous me **donner**…"
- "Vous pourriez **prendre**…"
- "Pourriez-vous me **dire**…"

And if you wanted to be **shown**, you could say:

- "Pourriez-vous m'**indiquer**..?" or
- "Pourriez-vous me **montrer**..?" and so on.

So you can see how useful **pouvoir** is when you want someone to help you in one way or another.

But what if you want to ask someone whether **you** can do something or not? A very common way of saying "Can I?" is:

Puis-je?

Normally when you **invert** a verb **in the first person singular** to **pose a question** it is a straight-forward affair. So:

Je dois becomes **Dois-je**? ie I must, becomes Must I? Following the rule set by this example, "Je peux" **should** become "Peux-je?" Instead, it becomes **Puis-je**? and the two words are pronounced as if there were no hyphen: **Puisje**? Of course, if you prefer to formulate the question using **est-ce que**…, you can. Now it is as you would expect:

- "**Est-ce que je peux** prendre un billet ici, s'il vous plait?"

But my example showed **pouvoir** in use both in the present and the conditional tenses. It is more usual to hear **pouvez-vous**? than **voulez-vous**? I suspect, but it is generally prudent to use the **conditional** of **pouvoir**: it is more likely to get you what you want.

Pouvoir is widely used in other tenses, too, of course: the future, the imperfect and the perfect tenses, for example. **J'ai pu** translates as I have been able to do something or other and **Je n'ai pas pu** as I haven't been able to… More often though, it is **pouvoir** in the **imperfect** that you will hear: "**Je ne pouvais pas** venir hier parce que j'avais une fièvre" ie I could not come yesterday because I had a temperature. But the difference between **je n'ai pas pu** and **je ne pouvais pas** is very fine indeed. Doubtless the grammar boys can tell you what the difference is but in conversation, the two tenses are often used interchangeably.

But one past tense where **pouvoir** has a very clear and distinctive role is the **past conditional** tense to express the notion **I could have** done something or other. For example:

- "If I had known that your car had broken down, **I could have repaired it myself**" ie
- "Si j'avais su que ta voiture était tombée en panne, **j'aurais pu la réparer moi-même**".

You will also find **pouvoir** employed in the subjunctive tense. You will know already that this tense is used to express ideas of necessity – **il faut que**… in particular. So:

- "**Il faut que vous puissiez** conduire une voiture de nos jours" ie You have to be able to drive a car these days.

The subjunctive, as you know, is also needed after expressions conveying the idea of aiming at something:

- "Tu dois te rendre au bureau ce matin **pour que tu puisses** trouver le dossier dont tu as besoin" ie You must go to the office this morning **so that you can** find the dossier that you need.

But there are other roles for the subjunctive which, to date, I have not described. For example, use the subjunctive after negative expressions such as **je ne pense pas que**, **je ne crois pas que** and **je ne trouve pas que**. To illustrate:

- "**Je ne pense pas qu'ils puissent** venir ce soir" ie I do not think that they can come tonight, or
- "**Je ne crois pas qu'elle puisse** jouer du piano" ie I do not believe (or think) that she can play the piano, or
- "**Je ne trouve pas que l'aspirateur puisse** vraiment nettoyer la moquette" ie I do not find that the vacuum-cleaner can really clean the carpet. (Incidentally, there are two words here that can easily be confused: une **moquette** is a **fitted** carpet; un **tapis** is a **rug**).

The subjunctive is also employed to convey ideas of "whichever", "whoever" and "whatever". So **pouvoir** can be used in the **first** of these:

- "**De tous les côtés qu'on puisse** le regarder" ie Whichever way you look at it.

The subjunctive is also needed sometimes to say **although**. Two expressions for this word are **malgré que** and **bien que**. So:

- "**Malgré que je puisse** réparer les vélos, je ne peux pas réparer les appareils électroménager" ie Although I can repair bicycles, I cannot repair household appliances. Note here that the second **pouvoir** verb is **not** in the subjunctive.
- "**Bien qu'ils puissent** partir en vacances cette année, je ne crois pas qu'ils puissent partir avant la fin d'été" ie Although they can go on holiday this year, I do not believe that they can leave before the end of the summer.

Note also the use of the subjunctive with **pouvoir** in this expression:

- **C'est le moins qu'on puisse dire!** which loosely translates as "And that is putting it mildly!"

These examples do not end the subjunctive story. Far from it: it can run and run! However this is enough for now, I suspect. Anyway, several other verbs to come illustrate well other uses of the subjunctive. So hang on to your hat!

Summary

Use **pouvoir** to:

- ask someone if you can do something or other
- ask someone if they can do something or other
- express ideas in tenses other than the present, notably the present and past conditional, where you or someone else could do x or y, often with **si** in **if** clauses
- express ideas about necessity using the subjunctive
- express doubt, in sentences using the negatives of penser, croire and trouver, about your (or someone else's) capability to do x or y – again using the subjunctive of **pouvoir**.

Getting Better

So, how can you build on the excellent base established in the **Basics** section? Well, first, you should know how to use **pouvoir** in the **negative** to say that you (or someone else) cannot do anything about something or other. Second, you should become familiar with the **pronominal** form of the verb, **se pouvoir**. This construction is very useful because it allows you to be a bit more subtle, a bit more nuanced, with regard to what might only just be possible. That should do it at this level, I feel.

Pouvoir in the negative

The single expression to describe helplessness in particular is:

> **N'y pouvoir rien**. For example:

- "Je suis désolé, monsieur, **mais je n'y peux rien**. Cette débroussailleuse est foutue. Jetez-la aux ordures" ie I am sorry sir, but there is nothing I can do (about it). This garden strimmer is finished. Throw it in the dustbin.

There are two noteworthy points in this example:

First, notice how **emphatic** it is. There is **nothing** he can do about it. End of story.

Second, and not for the first time, note the absence of a **second verb**. In English, we say "I cannot **do** anything about it". Therefore, you would expect that to translate as "je n'y peux rien **faire**". But in French, **pouvoir** is not always followed by a verb although you can say, for example:

- "**Je ne peux rien faire** pour vous".

Pronominal pouvoir

Se pouvoir offers the opportunity to be much les emphatic – to be more nuanced. **Se pouvoir** is generally employed when you want to say that something may be, might be or could be possible:

Ça se peut ie That is possible. Perhaps. Maybe. So:

- Do you think that it is going to snow tomorrow? It might: "Croyez-vous qu'il va neiger demain? **Ça se pourrait bien**".

Alternatively, you might get the reply:

- "**Ça ne se peut pas**" ie That is not possible.

Often you will find that **se pouvoir** is followed by the subjunctive, as in this example:

- "**Il se peut qu'**elle **sorte** ce soir" ie She could well go out tonight. Or
- "**Il se pourrait que** le gouvernement **perde** sa majorité aux prochaines élections" ie The government might well lose its majority at the next election.

With these examples we are clearly entering the realm of conjecture and hypotheses for which **se pouvoir**, like **devoir** in the last chapter, is well suited.

But, as you will see in the next level, **pouvoir** can also be used in several other constructions to express ideas which are very different from those we have encountered to this point. Before we move up to this third level, one point needs to be made here. Although pouvoir can be used instead of several other verbs, there is one verb in particular that can – and often does – **supplant pouvoir**. That verb is **savoir**. For example:

- "Est-ce que tu **sais** nager?" Literally, this translates as Do you **know** how to swim? But the much better translation is "Can you swim?" This construction can be applied to many activities other than swimming – many other sports, just for starters.

This use of **savoir** in place of **pouvoir** is particularly evident in the conditional and perfect tenses. To illustrate:

- "Il **saurait** convaincre tout ceux qui en doutent" ie He would know how to convince everyone who doubts it. And again:
- "Je n'**ai** pas **su** la convaincre" ie I was not able to convince her.

Now You Are Really Speaking French!

To reach this level there are certain constructions using pouvoir that you really ought to know. In fact, you already know one of them! Remember this in the **Être** chapter?:

- "Vous voyez Pierre là-bas? Il est **on ne peut plus** français" ie You see Pierre over there? He could not be more French (if he tried).

Another example which illustrates this construction in use is:

- "Elle a été **on ne peut plus** aimable" ie She could not have been kinder.

A variant on this expression is **on ne peut mieux**. For example:

- "Il la connaît **on ne peut mieux**" ie No-one knows her better than he does.

Three other set expressions also should be learned:

N'en pouvoir plus
N'en pouvoir plus de followed by a **noun**
N'en pouvoir plus de followed by a **verb** in the infinitive.

N'en pouvoir plus conveys a variety of ways of saying "I have had it! I'm up to here!" Remember **j'en ai marre** and **j'en ai ras la casquette** in the **Avoir** chapter? It can also mean that you are "knackered", worn out, exhausted. And it can even be used to suggest that someone is really rather proud of himself – "up" himself, even. So here are some examples of this construction in use:

To suggest that you are **exhausted**, for example:

- "**Je n'en peux plus**" But this phrase can also be used to say that you are "up to here" that you simply cannot go on any longer, that you cannot stand something any longer… and so on.

You can also use **n'en pouvoir plus** to suggest that something rather than someone is **fichu** or **foutu**. For example:

- "Mon portable (mobile) **n'en peut plus**" ie My mobile phone has had it.

But note also this use of **n'en pouvoir plus**:

- "Regardez-le dans sa décapotable. **Il n'en peut plus!**" ie Look at him in his convertible car. He is as proud as a peacock!

N'en pouvoir plus de (followed by a **noun**) – a couple of examples can illustrate this construction:

- "**Il n'en pouvait plus** de **peur**" - He was terrified
- "**Elles n'en pouvaient plus** de ses **grossièretés**" – They could not take anymore of his foul language.

N'en pouvoir plus de (followed by a **verb**). Here, again, are a couple of examples which illustrate this construction in action:

- "**Je n'en peux plus d'attendre**" – I am fed up with waiting
- "**Je n'en pouvais plus de rire**" – I laughed so much it hurt.

Idiomatic pouvoir

Like **devoir** in the last chapter, **pouvoir** has very few idiomatic uses. Here are just three that you are likely to hear, however:

- "**Avant qu'on puisse dire "ouf"**, il était derrière moi" ie Before you could say "Jack Robinson", he was behind me. If you are not familiar with the "Jack Robinson" allusion, the phrase translates as "Before I knew it…"

Sometimes when a group of people are talking and you simply cannot get a word in edgeways, so to speak, the following expression is useful:

- **Je ne peux pas en placer une**.

Finally, perhaps when someone has asked you to do them a favour and you steadfastly refuse, you can say:

- "**Tu peux toujours courir!**" Literally, You can always run, meaning "not a chance!", even "on your bike!"

Conclusion

Once again, we have tucked yet another "killer" verb under our belt. As you have seen, **pouvoir** is a versatile verb, cropping up very often in conversation. It can be used not merely to say that you want someone to do something for you (can you..?) or that you wonder if you, yourself, can do something (**puis-je**?) for someone, but it can also be used in the pronominal form to express degrees of possibility (**il se peut que**…) It is also used in fixed expressions such as **on ne peut plus**; and it does have some limited idiomatic uses. We also noted that on occasions, **pouvoir** can be replaced by **savoir** when you want to ask someone whether they can, say, swim. All that remains now, therefore, as always, is to study some conversations that employ this verb.

Pouvoir: Conversation One

Corinne and Thierry have decided that this year they should take a well-deserved holiday. But where? There are many places, both in France and abroad that they would like to see – but because they cannot make their minds up, they have decided to draw up a list ("dresser une liste") of the relevant criteria that their chosen destination must meet.

Corinne:	Alors, Thierry, où partir? Nous avons l'embarras du choix, évidemment, mais quel pays peut satisfaire à toutes nos exigences? Moi, je suis tenté par l'Israël. Nous n'y sommes jamais allés et tu sais que j'ai une cousine à Tel-Aviv. Nous pourrions passer quelques jours chez-elle, j'en suis sûre, et elle pourrait nous montrer les sites religieux. Elle m'a dit souvent que nous serions toujours les bienvenus là-bas.
Thierry:	Tu as raison, Corinne, et il y a tellement de choses qu'on pourrait y faire. Tu pourrais te baigner dans la mer et, moi, je pourrais faire du ski nautique, par exemple.
Corinne:	Oui, mais il y a un problème, Thierry.
Thierry:	Quoi ça?
Corinne:	Nous ne savons pas parler l'Hébreu!
Thierry:	T'en fais pas, Corinne. Ils parlent anglais, n'est-ce pas?
Corinne:	Pour la plupart je crois que oui. Mais nous ne pouvons pas parler anglais non plus, Thierry!
Thierry:	Attends, Corinne. Nous avons appris quelques mots quand nous étions à Londres chez mon frère l'an dernier. Je peux dire "bye bye!"

Corinne:	Tu rigoles ou quoi! Non, Thierry, si nous devions voyager à l'étranger, il serait prudent d'aller dans un pays francophone. Je veux qu'on puisse communiquer avec les indiens!
Thierry:	Si on allait au Canada, alors – à Québec ou à Montréal?
Corinne:	L'idée est fort tentante, Thierry, mais les Québecois – j'ai du mal à comprendre leur accent. Même le vocubulaire est différent.
Thierry:	Peut-être que nous devrions rester en France, alors!
Corinne:	Quelle excellente idée, Thierry! Moi, j'adore la France et il y a tellement de régions françaises où je ne suis jamais allée. La Bretagne, par exemple et la Haute Savoie et...
Thierry:	Ou la Corse, Corinne. On dit que c'est une île d'une grande beauté et il fait chaud là-bas.
Corinne:	Oui. Vivement les vacances!

Pouvoir: Conversation Two

Corinne and Thierry have arrived in Corsica for a two week summer holiday. But the weather has not been good since their arrival. They are not happy bunnies!

Thierry:	À proprement parler, Corinne, nous ne devrions pas nous impatienter. Ça ne fait que deux jours depuis notre arrivée en Corse, et il n'a plu que la moitié du temps!
Corinne:	Oui, mais…
Thierry:	Mais rien, Corinne! Nous aurions pu connaître le même temps si nous étions allés sur la Côte d'Azur. Et je n'y peux rien, Corinne. C'est pas moi qui fais la pluie et le beau temps. Je ne suis pas le grand manitou, tu sais. Et il se pourrait que le ciel se dégage pendant l'après-midi. Je peux voir déjà quelques belles éclaircies.
Corinne:	Tu as raison, Thierry. Je sais que je suis trop impatiente. Bon. En supposant qu'il fera beau plus tard, que faire?
Thierry:	Je ne crois pas que tu puisses te baigner, Corinne – la mer est encore trop agitée; et il va de soi que je ne peux pas faire de ski nautique – pour la même raison.
Corinne:	Je suis d'accord, Thierry, mais si on faisait l'ascension de la montagne derrière notre hôtel? Ça nous ferait du bien.
Thierry:	Oui, ça se peut. Si on allait à Ajaccio? On dit que c'est une ville on ne peut plus française, tu sais.
Corinne:	Ah bon? Je ne suis pas sûre, Thierry. Tu te souviens du type assis à côté de toi dans l'avion? Il t'a dit qu'il était allé à Ajaccio une fois et il n'en pouvait plus de peur dans les petites rues. Il trouvait qu'il avait vu pas mal de gars à l'aspect fuyant. Et apparement il ne se passe jamais une semaine sans qu'il y ait un meurtre dans les rues. Rien que d'y penser j'ai la trouille!
Thierry:	Mais tu n'as vraiment pas à te faire de soucis à ce propos, Corinne! Je suis d'accord, si on s'éloigne des rues principales, oui, c'est plus dangereux, bien sûr. Mais si tu ne me lâches pas, il n'y aura pas de problème. T'en fais pas, chérie.
Corinne:	Mais je ne peux pas te lâcher d'une semelle pendant toutes les vacances, Thierry!
Thierry:	Tout à fait, Corinne. Mais si on devait aller à Ajaccio cet aprèm et si on faisait gaffe, bien sûr, nous pourrions faire d'une pierre deux coups, tu sais.
Corinne:	Vraiment?
Thierry:	Mais oui, Corinne. Tu pourrais faire du lèche-vitrines et, moi, je pourrais acheter un imper. Cette pluie pourrait continuer toutes les vacances, tu sais!

Corinne:	Thierry, tu sais ce que tu peux faire?	
Thierry:	Quoi?	
Corinne:	Va te faire cuire un oeuf! Espèce de phallocrate!	

Some words you might not yet know

• un pays -	a country
• les exigences (f) -	demands
• une cousine -	a cousin
• les sites (m) religieux -	the religious sites
• le bienvenu -	the welcome
• le ski nautique -	water skiing
• l'Hébreu (m) -	the Hebrew language
• rigoler -	to laugh/to joke
• prudent -	sensible
• la Bretagne -	Brittany
• la Haute Savoie -	the most northerly department in the French Alps
• vivement les vacances! -	roll on the holidays!
• à proprement parler -	strictly speaking
• s'impatienter -	to become impatient
• le grand manitou -	the big boss
• se dégager -	to clear
• de belles éclaircies -	bright periods
• en supposant que -	assuming that
• se baigner -	to bathe
• agité(e) -	rough
• se souvenir de -	to remember
• le type -	the chap
• à l'aspect fuyant -	shifty-looking
• un meurtre -	a murder
• s'éloigner de -	to stray from
• lâcher -	to let go/release
• la semelle -	the sole of a shoe
• faire du lèche-vitrines -	to go window shopping
• un imper(méable) -	a raincoat
• espèce de…! -	you…!
• un phallocrate -	a male chauvinist pig (m.c.p.)

Pouvoir: Exercises

1. Complete the blank spaces:
   (   ) –vous me passer la confiture, s'il vous plaît? There are two possible answers.

2. Il aurait (   ) me passer le beurre si…

3. Nous (   ) y aller tout de suite si vous voulez. Two answers are possible.

4. Autant que je (   ) dire…

5. Que (   ) – je faire pour vous, monsieur?

6. Je ne (   ) pas venir hier parce que j'étais enrhumé.

7. Je ne pense pas qu'elle (   ) nous accompager à Paris aujourd'hui.

8. De tous les côtés qu'on (   ) le regarder, son idée est dingue.

9. C'est dingue? C'est le moins qu'on (   ) dire.

10. Je suis désolé, jeune homme mais je ne (   ) rien faire pour toi.

11. Translate the underlined part of this English sentence into French:
    Do you think that it will rain this afternoon? <u>No, that is not possible.</u>

12. Do the same with this sentence:
    <u>He might well have to</u> pay a charge / fine for his traffic offence.

13. And with this one:
    I saw Andrew yesterday. <u>He could not be more English</u> if he tried.

14. Again with this one:
    Look at him with his new girlfriend. <u>He is as proud as a peacock.</u>

15. And this one:
    <u>She could not take any more</u> of his rudeness.

Pouvoir: Answers

1. Pouvez, pourriez
2. pu
3. pouvons, pourrions
4. puisse
5. puis
6. pouvais
7. puisse
8. puisse
9. puisse
10. peux
11. Ça ne se peut pas
12. Il se pourrait qu'il
13. on ne peut plus anglais
14. Il n'en peut plus
15. Elle n'en pouvait plus

Chapter Nine
Passer

Introduction

Passer is the French verb that most reminds me of that famous British wood-stain product: "it does exactly what it says on the tin"! For **passer** means exactly that – **to pass**. That is not to say that this is the end of the story. Far from it. In English, to pass can mean a multitude of things. In its phrasal verb guise one can pass up, pass down, pass over, pass under, pass to, pass from, pass through, pass around… and so on. In French it is the same because the basic meaning of **passer** will take on different characteristics in different contexts. To illustrate, if you phone an organisation asking to be put through to someone or other, the receptionist will almost certainly say: "**Je vous passe**, madame". At the dinner table you might well say to someone: "**Passez-moi** le sel s'il vous plaît". Because there are so many such contexts, I plan to spend quite a lot of time with you on these basic uses of **passer** and on one or two grammatical complications that arise in using it.

But at the higher levels, **passer** can also replace quite a few other verbs – so we will examine these, too.

And **passer** also has several very important applications in its pronominal form, **se passer**.

Finally, it is frequently encountered in idiomatic speech – so, naturally, we will look at some of these as well. So let's get on, first with the conjugation of **passer**.

The Passer Conjugations

Present Tense

Je passe	Nous passons
Tu passes	Vous passez
Il passe	Ils passent
Elle passe	Elles passent

Future Tense

Je passerai	Nous passerons
Tu passeras	Vous passerez
Il passera	Ils passeront
Elle passera	Elles passeront

Imperfect Tense

Je passais	Nous passions
Tu passais	Vous passiez
Il passait	Ils passaient
Elle passait	Elles passaient

Perfect Tense

J'ai passé	Nous avons passé
Tu as passé	Vous avez passé
Il a passé	Ils ont passé
Elle a passé	Elles ont passé

Future Perfect Tense

J'aurai passé	Nous aurons passé
Tu auras passé	Vous aurez passé
Il aura passé	Ils auront passé
Elle aura passé	Elles auront passé

Pluperfect Tense

J'avais passé	Nous avions passé
Tu avais passé	Vous aviez passé
Il avait passé	Ils avaient passé
Elle avait passé	Elles avaient passé

Present Conditional Tense

Je passerais	Nous passerions
Tu passerais	Vous passeriez
Il passerait	Ils passeraient
Elle passerait	Elles passeraient

Past Conditional Tense

J'aurais passé	Nous aurions passé
Tu aurais passé	Vous auriez passé
Il aurait passé	Ils auraient passé
Elle aurait passé	Elles auraient passé

Present Subjunctive Tense

Je passe	Nous passions
Tu passes	Vous passiez
Il passe	Ils passent
Elle passe	Elles passent

Imperative

Passe
Passons
Passez

Passer: The Basics

Because **passer** means to pass, use it to ask people to pass you this or that. As always, you can do this fairly brusquely as in "pass me the salt, please" or rather more politely as in "would you mind passing me the salt, please?" So:

- "**Passez-moi** le sel, s'il vous plaît"
- "**Voudriez-vous me passer** le sel, s'il vous plaît?"

This second version is obviously more polite and perhaps a little more formal – but that is wholly appropriate in company that you do not know very well and where the "vous" rather than the "tu" form of address is in use. On the other hand, with people you know well, it is much more likely that you will say "**passe-moi** le sel", particularly when you use the person's name.

- "**Passe-moi** le sel, **Jean-Claude**, s'il te plaît".

These are cultural and social sensitivities though, rather than any fundamental change in the use of the verb. On the football pitch, say, no such sensitivities are likely to be catered for:

- "**Passe-moi** le ballon – vite!?"

(Incidentally, in English we make no distinction between the different types of balls used in different sports: a golf ball is just that – a ball; and a rugby ball is a ball, too. Not so in French. In sports using big balls – if you will pardon the expression! – like football, basketball and so on, they are **ballons**, whereas in sports where the balls are relatively small, such as tennis, for example, they are **balles**. Crazy, eh!)

In the examples of the salt and the ball, obviously someone is passing something to someone else. Here are some more examples:

- "Pouvez-vous **passer le pain**, s'il vous plaît?" ie Can you pass the bread around, please?
- "Elle ne veut pas me **passer le journal**" ie She does not want me to have the newspaper.
- "Ils vont **passer la moutarde** aussitôt qu'ils auront fini avec" ie They are going to pass around the mustard as soon as they have finished with it.

In summary, all these examples use **passer** in the sense of passing something to someone. The important point to grasp here is that in all three cases, **passer** is followed by **a direct object**. We shall see shortly why this is so important.

In grammar jargon, verbs which are followed by an **object** are called **transitive** verbs. They are to be distinguished from intransitive verbs, ie ones that **do not take an object**.

Passing a place

But **passer** can also be used to describe someone passing a place. For example:

- "Pour arriver à l'épicerie, vous devez tout d'abord **passer le supermarché**" ie To get to the grocer's shop you must first pass by the supermarket.

Passing somewhere

But passer can also describe someone passing somewhere. Here is an example:

- "Je descends en ville bientôt: je peux facilement **passer au pressing** si tu veux" ie I am going down into town shortly. I can easily drop in to the drycleaners if you like.

However, and this is very important to understand, this last example shows **passer** followed immediately by a **preposition**, not a **noun**. The implications of this will become clear in the following section.

Passer and prepositions

Very often, as we have just noted, **passer** can be followed by a **preposition** rather than by a noun. Here are examples of **ten** different prepositions with **passer**:

- "La Dordogne **passe à** Bergerac" ie The river Dordogne goes **through** Bergerac.
- "La A89 **passe à** Périgueux" ie The A89 (autoroute) goes **through** Périgueux.
- "Je **passe par** Paris pour aller à Calais" ie I go **through** Paris to get to Calais.
- "Si **je passe par** la boulangerie, je peux te déposer" ie If I go past the baker's shop, I can drop you off.
- "Heureusement, les petits poissons **passent au travers** des filets" ie Fortunately, the small fish slip through the net.
- "Le soir mon mari **passe dans** la rue avec notre petite-fille" ie In the evenings my husband walks down the street with our grand-daughter.

  (Incidentally, "le" before a noun implying time – soir, matin, juillet etc… - indicates **regularity**. So here "**le** soir" means **in the evenings**, not "the evening").

- "Tous les matins **ils passent devant** la mairie pour arriver à l'usine" ie Every morning they go past the town-hall to get to the factory.

  Note here that in contrast to **le soir** above, **tous** les matins means **every** morning **without fail**. Regularly does not mean **quite** that.

- "Puis-je **passer devant** toi pour te montrer l'église située dans la vallée?" ie Can I go ahead of you to show you the church in the valley?
- "La voie ferrée **passe le long du** fleuve jusququ'à Bordeaux" ie The railway runs alongside the river right down to Bordeaeux.

  (Incidentally, there is an important difference in French between **un fleuve** and **une rivière**: un fleuve is a river that runs out to the **sea**; une rivière on the other hand does **not** lead into the sea. So the Seine – pronounced "Senne" not "Sayne" – is **un fleuve** but, say, la Marne, which flows into the Seine, is, therefore, **une rivière**. One further complication: some French rivers are **masculine** whilst others are **feminine**. So the Seine, despite being

189

un fleuve is known as **La** Seine! And in the Loire valley there are **two** rivers: the famous one which passes through the great towns in the valley such as Orléans, Tours and Châtres is **La Loire**; but another smaller, much less famous river that runs close-by is **Le Loir**. And you wonder why French can be so infuriatingly difficult!)

- "**Je passe sur** la lettre que vous m'avez envoyée" ie I am going to pass over (ie ignore) the letter that you sent me.
- "Il m'a dit qu'elle veut bien **passer sur** mes fautes de frappe" ie He told me that she is prepared to ignore my typing errors.
- "Un courant d'air **passe sous** la porte" ie A draught is coming in from under the door.
- "Un petit ruisseau **passe sous** le pont" ie A small stream flows under the bridge.
- "Mes études **passent avant** mes activités sportives" ie My studies come before my sporting activities.
- "Moi, j'ai voulu acheter un canapé-lit mais ma femme m'a dit qu'à son avis l'utilité d'un lit **passe après** son confort" ie I wanted to buy a sofa-bed but my wife said to me that, in her opinion, the usefulness of a bed is less important than its comfort.

Passer and other tenses

Because **passer** is a regular verb and is, therefore, conjugated like all regular "... er" verbs, several tenses other than the present should pose no obvious problems for you. I am talking here about the **future** tense, the **imperfect** tense, the **present conditional** tense and the **subjunctive**. However, in all **compound** tenses there are complications arising from the fact that **passer** can be followed by a direct object, an indirect object, by other parts of speech including other verbs in the infinitive – or nothing at all!

Why is this a problem? Simply because in compound tenses either **avoir** or **être** will be the auxiliary verb. With verbs having **avoir** as the auxiliary there is no problem that need worry you. However, with **être**, there is. Let me illustrate using **monter**, to go up. Now you already know that **monter**, like **passer**, is a verb of movement and, therefore, has **être** as its auxiliary verb. So, for example using **monter**, we can say:

"Je **suis** monté" ie I went up.

However, if I want to say "I went **upstairs** (or **up the stairs**), I must now say:

"J'**ai** monté l'escalier".

Why? Because l'escalier is a **direct** object immediately following **monter** and, therefore, takes **avoir** in the auxiliary.

And it is exactly the same with **descendre**, to come down. If you simply wanted to say "I came down" then it is "Je **suis** descendu". However, if you wanted to say "I brought the dirty sheets down" you will have to say "**J'ai** descendu les draps sales". Again, we have a direct object in the sentence, hence **avoir**.

So, if you wanted to say "he passed me the ball" then it is "il **m'a passé le ballon**" because "ball" is **passer's direct** object. Here, the verb is being used **transitively**. And it is exactly the same when you use **dépasser** in the sense of **passing someone** in the street:

"Elle les **a dépassés** hier dans la rue" ie She passed them yesterday in the street. (Incidentally, you may have spotted the "s" at the end. This is because when **avoir** is the auxiliary of any verb, if the **direct object** comes **before** the verb then the verb has to agree with the direct object in number and gender. So here, **them**, ie **les** is a **direct** object. Hence the verb must **agree**: **les**, masculine plural, means that "dépass**és**" is the correct past participle. However, there is no change in pronunciation, only in spelling: in conversation you will not hear any difference at all).

However, when **passer** or **dépassér** is followed by **a preposition**, as in our examples earlier in the chapter, **être** rather than **avoir** is the correct auxiliary verb because now the object of the verb is followed by an **indirect** object. To illustrate:

- "Je **suis** passé **par** Paris pour aller à Calais"
- "Heureusement, les petits poissons **sont** passés **au travers** des filets"
- "Un courant d'air **est** passé **sous** la porte".

And when **passer** means to **pass by**, drop in etc. it is exactly the same:

- "Je **suis** passé hier, mais tu n'étais pas là". In this example, there is no object at all, be it direct or indirect.

Summary

You should already be able to see how versatile **passer** is. Use it:

- to ask someone to pass you something or other
- to talk about passing a place or a person
- to talk about going into somewhere

- to talk about roads, railways, rivers and so on going under, over, in, out, around etc, objects and places
- in compound tenses with both **avoir** and **être** in the auxiliary
- to talk about passing by and dropping in to see someone.

And that is definitely enough for now. Used in the present tense, you should have no problems at all with this verb. I agree, it is a bit trickier in compound tenses and some thought is necessary. But with practice, you will soon get the hang of it.

Getting Better

Passer often combines with other verbs in the infinitive to open up new meanings. Notable are **prendre**, **chercher** and **faire**. We shall examine these.

Often **passer** is used in lieu of other verbs to express meanings other than those that we have documented to date. We shall have a look at some of these, too.

Then, as in English, there is **passer** with time clauses.

And there is also, what to our ears, is the rather strange business of **passer** and examinations.

All these applications of **passer** are opportunities to build on the knowledge you have already acquired.

Passer with prendre and chercher

Passer with **prendre** and **chercher** can be used to talk about **fetching**, **collecting** or **picking up** people and things. To illustrate:

- "Mes deux amis **passent me prendre/chercher** tous les samedis que notre équipe joue à domicile" ie My two friends come to fetch me every Saturday when our team plays at home (To play away from home, incidentally, is "jouer à l'extérieur").
- "Je dois **passer prendre/chercher** mes bûches dans ma remorque toutes les deux semaines"ie I have to collect my logs in my trailer every two weeks.
- "Je **passerai te prendre/chercher** comme prévu avant de partir pour le week-end" ie I shall collect you as arranged before leaving for the week-end.

As you can see in the examples, **prendre** and **chercher** are completely interchangeable.

Passer with faire in the infinitive

Faire passer is often used in the context of food and drink to express the idea of getting something down, ie swallowing. To illustrate:

- "Mon dîner **ne passe pas**. Je dois prendre un cachet pour le **faire passer**" ie My dinner will not go down. I will have to take a tablet to get it down.

But you will also encounter this use of **faire passer**:

- "**Elle a fait passer Marianne** avant les autres" ie She let Marianne go first. Here, **faire passer quelqu'un** means to allow someone to…

Passer in lieu of other verbs

Passer can be used instead of **devenir** to mean to become. Here is an example:

- "Dans le temps il était comptable mais après dix ans dans l'enterprise **il est passé PDG**" ie Formerly he was an accountant but after ten years with the company he became Managing Director. The initials PDG signify **P**resident **D**irecteur **G**énéral.

The verb can also be used in place of **être montré** ie to be showing. Here is an example you will hear very frequently:

- "Est-ce que le film **passe** en salle cette semaine?" ie Is the film showing in cinemas this week?
- "Le film **passe** à quelle heure, s'il vous plaît?" ie What time is the film on, please?

Passer is also used for radio and television:

- "À quelle heure l'émission **passe-t-elle** à la télé, s'il vous plaît?" ie What time is the programme showing on the television, please?

Passer is also a verb that can be used to describe mislaying or losing sight of something or someone:

- "Je ne sais pas où **sont passées** mes lunettes" ie I do not know where I have left my glasses.
- "Où **étais-tu** donc **passé**?" ie Where on earth were you?

Then there is **passer** in place of **disparaître** in several contexts. For example, as in English when we talk of someone having "passed away", **passer**, too, can mean to die. Other examples include to pass over or wear off, as in a pain, for example:

- "La douleur **passe** maintenant" ie The pain is wearing off now.

Or one can talk of weather passing over or dying down:

- "L'orage était très fort, mais ça **passe**, Dieu merci" ie The storm was very strong, but it is dying down, thank God.

Passer can also be used to describe crossing something, like a river, for example:

- "Malgré la puissance du courant, il a réussi à **passer** la rivière à la nage" ie Despite the strong current, he managed to swim across the river. In this case **franchir** is the verb being replaced.

In English we would talk about sitting or taking a driving test, for example. In French one might say:

- "Je viens de **passer** mon permis de conduire" ie I have just taken my driving test. Note that here **passer** means to **take**, not to **pass**, your driving test.

And here is the one that sounds strange to our ears:

- "Je viens de **passer** mon examen d'anglais" ie I have just **taken** (or sat) my English exam. If you want to say that you have **passed** that exam, you can say:

- **"J'ai passé** mon examen d'anglais **avec succès"** or more usually
- **"J'ai réussi** mon examen d'anglais".

Passer can also replace **utiliser**, to spend:

- "Elles ont **passé** le week-end à Edimbourg" ie They spent the week-end in Edinburgh.

To be honest, I could list many more uses of **passer**, so many are there. But you have got enough examples here to demonstrate just how useful **passer** is in such contexts.

Passer with time clauses

"Que le temps **passe** vite!" ie How time flies! is perhaps the best and simplest illustration of **passer** with time clauses. But it can also mean to spend time, say, doing things, for example:

- "Mon frère **passait** beaucoup de temps dans sa cabane à bois avant son accident" ie My brother used to spend lots of time in his woodshed before his accident.
- "Mon fils **passe** très peu de temps avec son chien" ie My son spends very little time with his dog.
- "Cette année nous allons **passer** deux semaines à Berlin" ie This year we are going to spend two weeks in Berlin.

So to build on your basic knowledge of passer, you should familiarise yourself with **passer**:

- used in conjunction with other verbs, notably **chercher**, **prendre** and **faire**
- used in lieu of many other verbs, notably those relating to success in exams and other tests
- used with time clauses, notably those that describe how fast time flies.

Now You Are Really Speaking French!

Quite the most important progress you can make at this level is to become acquainted with **passer** in its **pronominal** form ie **se passer**. Here we have **se passer** itself, then **se passer de** plus a **noun** and finally **se passer de** with a **verb in the infinitive**.

In the **non**-pronominal form it is useful to be familiar with **passer pour**, with **y passer** and with **laisser passer**.

Finally we will have a look at **passer** in its **idiomatic** role.

Pronominal passer

Perhaps the most useful of **se passer**'s applications lies in describing or asking what is, was or will **happen**:

- "Qu'est-ce qu'il **se passe**?" - What is happening?
- "Qu'est-ce qui **s'est passé**?" - What happened?
- "Qu'est-ce qu'il **se passera**? - What will happen?

Closely related is the notion of things **going well (or badly)**. For example:

- "Tout **s'est** bien **passé**, j'espère?" ie Everything went well, I hope?
- "Les vacances **se sont** bien **passées**?" ie Did your holidays go well?

Let's hope that the answer isn't:

- "Elles **se sont** mal **passées**" ie They did not go well at all, more particularly, if say, the plane was hijacked!:
- "Il ne **se passe** jamais une semaine sans qu'il y ait (subjunctive) un détournement" ie Never a week goes by without a hijacking.

Or perhaps it was the rain that spoilt the holiday:

- "Il ne **s'est pas passé** un seul jour sans qu'il ne pleuve" (subjunctive) ie Never a day went by without it raining.

Se passer could also be used on holiday to say that you applied plenty of sun cream:

- "**Je me suis passé** pas mal de crème solaire sur le visage" ie I put plenty of sun cream on my face. Note here that it is **le visage** not **mon visage**. The notion of **my** face is captured by the indirect object pronoun **me**. So it is with many other uses of this construction. For example, if you want to say that you broke your nose on holiday (heaven forbid!) you would need to say "Je **me** suis cassé **le** nez".

In the heat on holiday you might often have to wipe your forehead with a towel or a tissue (**un Kleenex**, in French!):

- "**Je me suis passé** une serviette sur le front".

And after all that cream and perspiration you needed to rinse your hands!:

- "J'étais obligé de **me passer** les mains sous l'eau".

And if you and your partner were playing with a football, say, on the beach:

- "**Nous nous passions** le ballon sur la plage".

We met that idea of passing a ball in the **Basics** section but there it was a case of someone passing the ball to **him**. But in the **pronominal** use of the verb we are talking about passing the ball **to each other**. This act of reciprocity requires **se passer**, to pass to each other.

Finally on holiday, I am sure that you will have allowed yourselves a few indulgences ("fantaisies"):

- "Mais oui, en vacances il faut bien **se passer quelques** fantaisies!" Yes, "une fantaisie" can mean a fantasy, but here it simply means a treat, an extravagance, an indulgence – or even a **whim**:
- "**Elle lui passe toutes ses fantaisies**" ie She gives in to his every whim.

Se passer de, plus a noun

This construction means "to do without". So, for example:

- "Je peux **me passer de tes conseils**" ie I can do without your advice.

Se passer de, plus a verb in the infinitive

Again, it broadly means "to do without". For example:

- "Le match **passe** à la télé ce soir, chérie. Franchement, **je me passerai** bien d'aller chez les Martin" ie Darling, the match is on the television this evening. Frankly, I could do without going to see the Martins.

A tiny grammatical note here: French surnames in the **plural** never have a plural "s" on the end as they do in English – unless, of course, the name already has an "s", eg Duclos.

But if you both stayed in and he wanted to smoke, you might say:

- "Je serais vraiment contente si tu pourrais **te passer de fumer**, chérie!" ie I would be really happy if you could manage not to smoke, darling!

Se faire passer means "to pass oneself off" as something or someone. For instance:

- "A l'entretien **il s'est fait passer** pour un ingénieur expérimenté" ie At the interview he passed himself off as an experienced engineer.
- Note the "faux ami" here: "experimenté" means experienced. It has nothing to do with ("rien à voir avec") experiments!

Passer pour

Passer pour means exactly what it says on the tin! To pass for... something or someone, so:

- "Vous savez, vous pourriez **passer pour un Français**!" ie You know, you could pass for a Frenchman!

Y passer

The **y** in this construction means "it" or "on it":

- "The garage: I spent a fortune on it" – Le garage, toute une fortune **y est passée**
- "Si tu continues à conduire d'une façon aussi dangereuse, tout le monde **va y passer**!" ie If you carry on driving in such a dangerous way we have all had it!

And for the would-be film star contemplating the casting couch:

- "Si elle veut devenir vedette de cinéma, il faudra bien qu'elle **y passe**!" ie If she really wants to become a film star, she will have to sleep with the director!

Laisser passer

This construction means to overlook or let pass something or other. To illustrate:

- "On ne peut pas **laisser passer** ce manquement grave au règlement comme si de rien n'était" ie We cannot overlook this serious breach of the rules, as if nothing had happened.

Idiomatic passer

Thankfully, perhaps, there are relatively few idiomatic expressions involving **passer**. Here are the ones you are most likely to encounter in your travels:

Passer sous le nez de quelqu'un means to miss an opportunity.

Faire passer un mauvais quart d'heure à quelqu'un literally meaning to make someone go through a tough quarter of an hour, means to give somebody a bad time.

Faire passer le goût du pain à quelqu'un can mean either to wipe the smile off someone's face or the much more sinister, "to bump someone off!"

Passer un savon à quelqu'un (to pass a bar of soap to someone) also means to give someone a bad time. To illustrate:

- "Mon fils est rentré à minuit hier soir. Quand il est arrivé, je lui **ai passé un savon**", meaning, My son got home at midnight last night. When he arrived, I gave him a right old ear full!

Ça passe comme une lettre à la poste means It was so simple it could not have been easier. And finally, here is my favourite:

Passer devant Monsieur le Maire means…. to get married!

When the French get married they are legally required to have a civil ceremony at the **Mairie**, the equivalent if you like, of our town hall or city hall. The service is performed by the **Maire**, the equivalent in some ways only of our Mayor. In fact he (or she) has much more power than a British Mayor, whose duties are largely ceremonial. **Monsieur le Maire** in contrast, heads up and has administrative responsibility for the **commune**, of which there are some 35,000 in France. Most of these are quite small (ours in the Dordogne only has about 3,000 inhabitants) but some are enormous. As I write, Anne Hidalgo is the Maire de Paris and has huge power some would say. But all **Maires** are state employed and are empowered to perform marriages, which take place in the "salle de marriages". They are also required to keep an accurate register of births, marriages and deaths. (Incidentally, I do not want you to think Madame Hidalgo personally marries everyone in Paris! France's capital and many other large cities like Lyon for example, are divided up into districts called **arrondissements**. Paris has 20 of these – and each one, too, has a **Maire**. Even here, of course, the marriage ceremony is subcontracted to one of his or her "adjutants").

Many French people also have a second, religious ceremony in a church (or whatever). French brides often wear very extravagant looking wedding dresses and often – frankly – resemble meringues! But, as one French expression has it: "**Des goûts et des couleurs (on ne discute pas")**!: There is no accounting for taste! And if you want to say that "it takes all sorts to make a world", you would say "**Tous les goûts sont dans la nature.**"

Conclusion

Passer is a very important verb in French. It has so many different applications that it should not surprise you to know that it is in regular daily use. So really get to know it. The only difficulty posed by **passer** arises because it is both transitive and intransitive. It therefore can take a direct object, an indirect object – or no object at all. None of this matters, other than in compound tenses with **avoir** and **être**. However, it allows me to say either, say "**passe-moi la moutarde, s'il te plaît**" or say "**je suis passé hier**". All the other uses of **passer** are mere icing on the cake, or "la cerise sur le gâteau". So, good luck with it!

Passer: Conversation One

Maryse is at home one morning when she gets a telephone call from her friend, Anna. Clearly Anna is in a state of anxiety:

Anna: Bonjour, Maryse, je suis désolée de te déranger mais j'ai un problème. J'espère que tu peux m'aider.

Maryse: Entendu, Anna, mais qu'est-ce qu'il y a? Qu'est-ce qui s'est passé? Rien de sérieux, j'espère.

Anna: Assez sérieux, oui. Hier soir, après le boulot, je suis tombée en descendant du train – et je me suis cassée le bras droit. Je suis allée immédiatement à l'hôpital et maintenant j'ai le bras dans le plâtre. Pourrais-tu passer cet après-midi?

Maryse: Mais oui, bien-sûr. Je passerai vers seize heures. Ça va?

Anna: Ça va. C'est gentil.

Maryse: Et je pourrais passer à la pharmacie, Anna. As-tu besoin de quelque chose?

Anna: Oui, tu pourrais m'acheter quelques analgésiques, Maryse. Ça me fait mal, tu sais.

Maryse: Pauvre de toi! Je passerai aussitôt que possible. À tout à l'heure.

A few hours later...

Anna: Que je suis contente de te voir, Maryse! T'as les comprimés?

Maryse: Oui, les voici.

Anna: Merci bien, Maryse. Passe-moi le verre d'eau sur la table, tu seras un ange.

Maryse: Bien sûr. Voici l'eau. Mais dis-moi, Anna, qu'est-ce qui s'est passé au juste? Comment ça ce fait que tu es tombée en descendant du train?

Anna: Mince! Qu'est-ce que j'ai été bête! Histoire d'être la première à descendre du train à Chatelet, j'ai trébuché sur les pieds d'un mec assis sur un strapontin à côté de la porte.

Maryse: Quelle poisse!. Mais ça peut se passer, aux heures de pointe dans le métro. C'était pas ta faute, Anna. Et si cela veut dire que tu dois prendre quelques semaines de congé maladie, tant mieux. Peut-être que nous pourrions passer une semaine de vacances ensemble! Si on allait en...

Anna: Maryse, tu es incorrigible! Mais cette fois-ci…

They continue talking well into the night – again!

Passer: Conversation Two

A couple of weeks have passed by since Anna broke her arm and Maryse decides to phone her to find out how she is getting on.

Maryse:	Bonjour, Anna. Comment vas-tu? Tu es allée à l'hôpital ce matin pour ton premier bilan de santé, n'est-ce pas?
Anna:	Oui.
Maryse:	Tout s'est bien passé, j'espère?
Anna:	Oui merci. La radio a montré que l'os est en bonne voie de guérison mais le toubib m'a dit que le plâtre doit rester au moins trois semaines de plus. Et je ne peux pas retourner au boulot jusqu'à ce que tout se passe bien. Pas mal, hein!
Maryse:	Bravo, Anna! Mais tu dois continuer de bien manger, Anna. Un régime sain est important. Et pas de malbouffe, tu sais! Dis-moi, est-ce que tu es libre demain à midi?
Anna:	Oui, mais qu'est-ce qu'il se passe?
Maryse:	Pas grand-chose, mais on se téléphone demain matin et on se fait une bouffe? Ça te convient?
Anna:	Pourquoi pas. Ça serait chouette. À demain matin alors. Au revoir.

The following morning Maryse calls again:

Maryse:	Ça va, Anna?
Anna:	Oui, ça va pour midi?
Maryse:	Oui, je connais un tout petit resto assez près de chez toi qui est très raisonnable.
Anna:	C'est pas un boui-boui j'espère, Maryse.
Maryse:	Quoi, tu me prends pour une radine?! Non, ce resto se trouve Rue Talbot. Tu connais le coin. Les petits restos pullulent là-bas.
Anna:	D'accord. Tu passerais me chercher?
Maryse:	Entendu. Mettons à midi pile ça va?!
Anna:	Parfait. À toute à l'heure.

It is now 12 o'clock and Maryse has arrived at Anna's apartment:

Maryse:	D'accord? Allons-y!

Five minutes later and they have arrived at the restaurant:

Anna:	Oh là, là! C'est plein à craquer!
Maryse:	C'est plutôt bon signe.

A waiter approaches them:

> Ah, bonjour, monsieur. Nous sommes deux. Est-ce que vous avez une table dehors, s'il vous plaît?

Serveur:	Oui, une table dehors vient de se libérer. Suivez-moi. La voici. Nos formules déjeuner sont sur l'ardoise à côté.
Maryse:	Merci, monsieur.

Maryse and Anna choose from the slate and five minutes later their starters arrive. They are half-way through when a man at the next table lights up a cigarette:

Anna:	(To the man): Excusez-moi, monsieur mais nous serions vraiment contentes si vous pouviez vous passer de fumer pendant quelques instants. Je sais que vous avez le droit de fumer dehors mais votre fumée passe par notre table et, franchement, c'est pas très agréable.
L'homme:	Excusez-moi, madame, je ne me suis pas rendu compte. Regardez, je l'écrase. Et bon appétit!
Maryse:	Merci bien, monsieur. C'est gentil.

The meal now over, the waiter returns:

Serveur:	Ça a été?
Maryse:	Délicieux, monsieur.
Serveur:	Bon. Et désirez-vous autre chose, mesdames?
Maryse:	Tu prends un café, Anna?
Anna:	Non, merci.
Maryse:	Moi non plus. Je voudrais l'addition, s'il vous plait.
Serveur:	Bien sûr, madame. Je reviens dans quelques instants.

Five minutes later he returns with the bill:

> Voici votre addition, madame.

Maryse:	(To Anna): C'est pas exactement une note salée. Quand même ça peut passer sur la note de frais. Le client pour qui je travaille en ce moment est très compréhensif et il laisse passer mes prodigalités de temps en temps! D'accord, allons-y et si tu n'est pas trop pressée, Anna, nous pourrions toujours passer à la boutique où j'ai acheté la robe décolletée que tu as admirée récemment.
Anna:	Pourquoi pas. Au point où en est, autant faire les choses jusqu'au bout!

Some words you might not yet know

• aider -	to help
• entendu -	of course/understood
• rien de sérieux -	nothing serious
• le boulot (fam) -	work
• tomber -	to fall
• un bras -	an arm
• le plâtre -	plaster
• les analgésiques(m) -	pain killers
• pauvre de toi! -	poor you!
• les comprimés (m) -	tablets
• tu seras un ange -	be an angel
• au juste -	exactly
• histoire de -	just to
• trébucher -	to trip
• assis -	seated
• un strapontin -	a folding seat
• aux heures de pointe -	in the rush hour
• congé(m) maladie -	sick leave
• incorrigible -	incorrigible
• un bilan de santé -	a health check-up
• la radio (graphie) -	an x-ray
• être en bonne voie de guérison -	to be well on the road to recovery
• un toubib (fam) -	a doctor
• la malbouffe -	junk food
• se faire une bouffe -	to have a bite to eat
• un resto (fam) -	a restaurant
• un boui-boui (fam) -	a grubby little restaurant
• un(e) radin(e) -	a cheapskate
• pulluler -	to swarm
• c'est plutôt bon signe -	it's rather a good sign
• dehors -	outside
• se libérer -	to become available
• les formules (f) déjuner -	the fixed-price lunch menus
• l'ardoise(f) -	the slate/the board
• écraser (une cigarette) -	to stub out
• l'addition(f) -	the bill
• une note salée -	a stiff bill
• la note de frais -	the expense account
• compréhensif(ve) -	understanding
• les prodigalités (f) -	extravagances
• (au point où en est), autant faire les choses jusqu'au bout -	in for a penny, in for a pound

Passer: Exercises

1.   Complete the blank spaces:
        Je (   ) vous voir demain matin.

2.   Je suis (   ) hier, mais tu n'étais pas là.

3.   (   )-moi le pain s'il vous plaît.

4.   J'aurais pu (   ) hier mais…

5.   (   ) devant moi. Vous êtes plus petite que moi.

6.   Si j'avais eu le temps je (   ) passé.

        Translate into French the underlined parts of these English sentences:

7.   The river Seine <u>goes through</u> Paris.

8.   Fortunately the small fish <u>slip through the net.</u>

9.   If <u>I go past</u> the bank, I can drop you off.

10.   Every evening my sister <u>goes past</u> the Post Office.

        Complete the blank spaces in the following sentences:

11.   Il m'a dit qu'il veut bien laisser (   ) mes erreurs d'orthographe.

12.   Je (   ) vous chercher avant de rendre visite à ma tante.

13.   La viande que je viens de manger ne (   ) pas. Je dois prendre un cachet pour la faire ( ).

14. Qu'est-ce qu'il se (   ). Êtes-vous malade?

15. Vos vacances se sont bien (   )?

16. Je me suis (   ) pas mal de crème solaire sur le visage.

17. Nous nous (   ) le ballon dans le jardin quand je suis tombée dans les fleurs.

18. Je me (   ) bien d'aller au cinéma ce soir. Le président Hollande (   ) à la télé.

19. Vous pourriez (   ) pour un Français.

20. Je suis tellement contente, Angélique, Pascal et moi allons (   ) devant Monsieur le Maire l'année prochaine!

21. Malheureusement, ça m'a (   ) sous le nez.

Passer: Answers

1. passerai
2. passé(e)
3. Passez
4. passer
5. Passez
6. serais
7. passe à
8. passent à travers
9. je passe par
10. passe devant
11. passer
12. passerai
13. passe, passer
14. passe
15. passées
16. passé(e)
17. passions
18. passerai, passe
19. passer
20. passer
21. passé

Chapter Ten
Parler

Introduction

"**Parlez-vous anglais, madame**?" "**Parlez-vous espagnol, monsieur**?" "**Parlez-vous gallois, jeune homme**?" "**Parlez-vous français, jeune fille**?" How many times, I wonder, have you heard some variant or other of the "**parlez-vous…?**" question? Chances are, many times. Of course. Because **parler**, to speak or to talk, is as about as basic as a French verb can possibly get.

But **parler** is much more than just a basic verb. In the French sentence "**Je parle français**", parler is employed transitively, and is immediately followed by a direct object, in this case **français**. But it can also be followed by an **indirect** object when, for example, the verb is followed by the preposition **a**, by the preposition **de** by the prepositions **pour** and **contre** or by some other part of speech, notably adverbs in sentences such as "parlez **haut**, s'il vous plaît".

Then of course there is **se parler**, to talk to oneself and to talk to each other.

Finally **parler** is used in several idiomatic expressions, too, including proverbs. So, once more, we have got plenty to get on with! Let's start with its conjugations.

The Parler Conjugations

Present Tense

Je parle	Nous parlons
Tu parles	Vous parlez
Il parle	Ils parlent
Elle parle	Elles parlent

Future Tense

Je parlerai	Nous parlerons
Tu parleras	Vous parlerez
Il parlera	Ils parleront
Elle parlera	Elles parleront

Imperfect Tense

Je parlais	Nous parlions
Tu parlais	Vous parliez
Il parlait	Ils parlaient
Elle parlait	Elles parlaient

Perfect Tense

J'ai parlé	Nous avons parlé
Tu as parlé	Vous avez parlé
Il a parlé	Ils ont parlé
Elle a parlé	Elles ont parlé

Future Perfect Tense

J'aurai parlé	Nous aurons parlé
Tu auras parlé	Vous aurez parlé
Il aura parlé	Ils auront parlé
Elle aura parlé	Elles auront parlé

Pluperfect Tense

J'avais parlé	Nous avions parlé
Tu avais parlé	Vous aviez parlé
Il avait parlé	Ils avaient parlé
Elle avait parlé	Elles avaient parlé

Present Conditional Tense		**Past Conditional Tense**	
Je parlerais	Nous parlerions	J'aurais parlé	Nous aurions parlé
Tu parlerais	Vous parleriez	Tu aurais parlé	Vous auriez parlé
Il parlerait	Ils parleraient	Il aurait parlé	Ils auraient parlé
Elle parlerait	Elles parleraient	Elle aurait parlé	Elles auraient parlé

Present Subjunctive Tense		**Imperative**
Je parle	Nous parlions	Parle
Tu parles	Vous parliez	Parlons
Il parle	Ils parlent	Parlez
Elle parle	Elles parlent	

Parler: The Basics

Use **parler** either to say that you speak a language or to ask someone else whether they speak a particular language. So:

- "Je **parle** français quand je suis en France" ie I speak French when I am in France.
- Note that **français** is written with a lower-case f whereas we tend to use the upper-case F. Of course, it does not matter at all in **spoken** French but will matter should you want to write it.
- "Ma soeur **parle** français **et** espagnol. En effet, elle est bilingue" ie My sister speaks French **and** Spanish. Indeed, she is bilingual.
- Note here that anyone claiming to be bilingual must be equally comfortable in each of the two languages. In reality, this is a demanding requirement. Unless you have lived and/or worked in a country, perhaps for a very long time, it is unlikely that you will be bilingual. It is much more prudent to claim fluency. I shall return to this issue a little later in this section.
- **"Parlez-vous** italien, jeune homme?"

Of course, you already know very well now that you can pose such questions in other ways:

- "Est-ce que **vous parlez** italien, jeune homme?" or quite simply,
- "**Vous parlez** italien, jeune homme?"

So far, so good, I hope. However, if you were to look up the French word for Italian in a French dictionary, you would find it expressed as **l'italien**; and were it French you looked up, this would be shown as **le français**… and so on. Of course. These are nouns like any others and they are all preceded by the definite article **le** or **la** in the case of feminine nouns. But in the sentence:

Je parle français there is no definite article, I agree. However, were you to say in English "I speak French well" you would have to translate this as:

- "Je parle **bien le français**". Note here that with the insertion of, in this case, the adverb bien, "français" now becomes "le français". In fact the insertion of other parts of speech can also have this effect. So, you need a grammatical rule to help you here (yes, I know – eyes glazing over again!) Here it is, in two parts:

1. Use the definite article with all languages where they are the **subject** of a verb. For example: "**Le français est** facile à apprendre" (I wish!)

2. Use the definite article if it is the **object of any verb other than parler**. To illustrate: "Je **comprends l'**italien" ie I **understand** Italian. Here the verb is not parler, but comprendre. Hence the definite article is required.

It follows from these two related rules that if the verb **is** parler and the direct object is any language, the definite article is **not** required. So:

- "**Je parle portugais**": I speak Portuguese

Before leaving this little complication (for good, I would like to think!), let us briefly return to the issue of bilingualism and fluency that I raised earlier in this section. Suppose now you wanted to say: "My sister speaks fluent French and Spanish", you would need to say:

- "Ma soeur parle couramment le français et l'espagnol". And if she spoke only French fluently it would be exactly the same:
- "Ma soeur parle couramment le français".

Parler without an object

To this point, we have considered **parler** in its transitive role to speak a language. But parler can also be employed intransitively, without an object at all. Take this example to illustrate:

- "Mon fils a commencé à **parler à dix-huit mois**" ie My son began speaking at 18 months. Or this example:

211

- **"Parlez plus doucement**, s'il vous plaît" ie Speak more quietly, please. Or this one:
- **"Parle pour toi!**" ie Speak for yourself!

In an earlier chapter we talked about using sign language to communicate. This translates as **parler par gestes**, as in this example:

- "Chaque fois que nous nous rencontrons, je dois lui **parler par gestes**" ie Each time that we meet, I have to use sign language.

And if you meet someone who wants to talk business, he or she is likely to say:

- **"Parlons affaires"**. Indeed, **parlons** anything: **parlons bouffe**, for example (let's talk about grub); or **parlons politique** (let's talk politics); or **parlons sport** (let's talk sport) etc.

Summary

Use **parler** in its basic role:

- to say that you can (or cannot) speak any languages; and to ask others if they can speak any languages.
- to talk about how well you speak this or that language.
- (And do not forget that when you want to say how well you speak a language, the **definite article** must precede the language).
- Also use **parler** in its intransitive role in a wide range of different applications, for instance, to say that somebody should speak more quietly (or more loudly, of course).

Getting Better

Very often **parler** is used in conjunction with a **following preposition**. Quite the most important are **parler à**, to speak **to** someone and **parler de**, to speak **about** someone or something. So we will look at these in a bit of detail.

We will also examine **parler pour** and **parler contre**, by the way.

Then there is **entendre parler** which means to hear about (hear speak of, literally). We will also study this construction in this second-level section.

Parler à

As I have just said, use **parler à**, either transitively to speak to someone or intransitively as in the expression **parler à haute voix**, to speak in a loud voice. First, **parler à** someone:

- "Histoire d'être gentil, **j'ai parlé à** Anna, hier soir. Elle était très contente d'avoir fait ôter son plâtre" ie Just to be kind, I spoke to Anna last night. She was very happy to have had her plaster removed. Or…
- "Il faut que **je lui parle** de nouveau: j'ai oublié de lui dire que je ne passerai pas demain parce que les cheminots font grève" ie I must speak to him (her) again: I forgot to tell him (her) that I cannot drop by tomorrow because the railwaymen are on strike.

I hope you can see what has happened in the French sentence above. Because the verb is parler **à**, **lui** represents **him** or **her**. You could say: **Je parle à lui** or **Je parle à elle** but it is much better French to say: **Je lui parle**.

Parler de

As you know, **parler de** means to talk about something or someone. To illustrate:

- "J'ai croisé Angélique dans la rue l'autre jour et **nous avons parlé de** choses et d'autres" ie I bumped into Angélique in the street the other day and we talked about this and that.

An alternative way of talking about this and that is to say:

- "Nous avons parlé de la pluie et du beau temps" in other words, the weather.

Please note that when talking about things, phrases introduced by **de** can be replaced by the pronoun **en**. To illustrate, instead of saying that we talked about the weather ("**de** la pluie et **du** beau temps" in this last example) we might say:

- "Nous **en** avons parlé" ie We talked about **it**. Or instead of saying "Nous parlions de l'émision à la télé hier soir" ie We were talking about the broadcast on the television last night, we might say:
- "Nous **en** parlions" ie We were talking about **it**.

Talking about people, here is an illustration:

- "J'assistais au match samedi dernier et j'ai vu ce que je considère le meilleur footballeur que j'aie jamais vu: **je parle**, bien sûr, **de** Gaston Lefèvre" ie I was at the match last Saturday and I saw whom I reckon to be the greatest footballer I have ever seen: I am speaking, of course, about Gaston Lefèvre.

Here is another example:

- "**J'ai parlé d**'elle à son prof. Elle est nulle en math, paraît-il. D'autre part, sa géo est excellente" ie I spoke to her teacher about her. It seems that she is useless at maths. On the other hand, her geography is excellent.

And if on meeting someone, you wanted to say "Oh, I have heard a lot about you!" you would say:

- "**On m'a beaucoup parlé de vous**!"

Parler de is also used when you want to talk about doing something. For example:

- "**Nous parlions d'aller** à New York ce mois-ci mais tous les vols sont archipleins en ce moment" ie We were talking about going to New York this month but all the flights are chock-a-block at the moment.
  Note here the use of the suffix **archi**. It means "enormously" or "tremendously" and can be used to preface many adjectives. For example, if you wanted to say that you find French tremendously difficult, you could say: "Le français? C'est archidifficile!"

And **parler de** can also be employed when you want to talk about memories coming back to you. For example:

- "Cette vieille voiture-ci **me parle de** ma jeunesse quand nous vivions aux

Etats-Unis" ie This old car reminds me of my youth when we lived in the United States.

- "Tout dans cette maison **parle de** toi" ie Everything in this house reminds me of you.

I hope you can see that this construction used in this way is another way of saying **faire penser à** that we encountered in the **Faire** chapter.

Parler pour et parler contre quelqu'un

The two other prepostions that can be used after **parler** are **pour** and **contre**, for and against someone. To illustrate:

- "Au dernier moment, Jean-Luc ne pouvait pas adresser la parole à notre public. Donc, **j'ai parlé pour** lui" ie At the last moment, Jean-Luc could not speak to our audience. So I spoke for him.
- "**Je ne parlerais jamais contre** notre députée: je la trouve archicourageuse" ie I would never speak against our MP. She is tremendously courageous.

Entendre parler

- "Je n'ai jamais **entendu parler** de lui. Est-il bien connu en tant que comédien?" I have never heard of him. Is he a well-known actor?

This example illustrates the use of **entendre parler**, to hear of or hear about someone or something. Here is another example;

- "**J'ai** vaguement **entendu parler** du nouveau resto Rue Gilbert Bécaud. Si on y allait bientôt?" ie I have vaguely heard of the new restaurant in the Rue Gilbert Bécaud. How about going there soon?
- "Est-ce que **vous avez** jamais **entendu parler** de PROM? En anglais ça veut dire: Programmable Read Only Memory. Je ne sais pas comment ça se dit en français!" ie Have you ever heard of PROM? In English that stands for: Programmable Read Only Memory. I do not know what it is called in French!

I think we will stop here. I have said enough to demonstrate the importance of **parler**, particularly when it is used in conjunction with the prepositions **a**, **de**, **pour** and **contre**. Let us now move on and see where else **parler** can take us.

Now You Are Really Speaking French!

Parler has very limited reflexive/pronominal applications but, **se parler**, to talk to oneself is something all of us do from time to time! But it is also used in the context of people talking to **each other**. So we will examine it.

Then there are lots of colloquial uses of **parler** such as **ne m'en parlez pas**! – "you are telling me!" So we will have a look at some of these, too.

Finally, there are several idiomatic uses of parler, including some proverbial phrases.

After all of this you should have **le don de la parole**, the gift of the gab!

Se parler

In the first instance, this means to talk to oneself:

- "Quand je suis tout seul, **je me parle** souvent, mais je ne voudrais pas que mes amis me prennent pour un imbécile!" ie When I am alone I often talk to myself, but I would not like my friends to take me for an idiot!

Secondly, **se parler** can be used when people are talking to each other;

- "**Elles se sont parlées** toute la soirée. C'était épouvantable. Elles ont vraiment gâté le match qui passait à la télé! ie They talked amongst themselves all evening. It was dreadful. They really ruined the match on the television!

Colloquial parler

Parler is used in many colloquial expressions. Here are some very familiar uses of the verb:

Tu parles (Charles)! – this means (and take your pick here):
You're telling me!
You bet!
Too bloody right!

You must be joking!
You have got to be kidding!

Parles d'un… – choose between:
What a …!
Talk about…!
I have never seen a… like it!

Tu parles d'un culot – means what a bloody cheek!
Tu parles si c'est marant – means, ironically, "what a laugh!"

But here is my personal favourite! Have you ever seen Martin Scorsese's 1976 film, "Taxi Driver"? Well, in it Robert de Niro plays the character Travis Bickle, a highly unstable taxi driver who, in the film's most famous scene, is looking at himself in the mirror, brandishing a revolver and repeatedly saying: "You talkin' to me? You talkin' to me?" In the French version, this translated as:

"Tu parles à moi? Tu parles à moi?" This is a classic example of "lost in translation", I feel!

The scene provides frightening evidence of his degeneration – and his words have entered cinematic and linguistic legend. To take the example one step further:

"On **ne parlait que** de lui" ie He was (Hollywood's) talk of the town.

Stretching the example even further:

"**Ils en ont parlé** pendant des heures et des heures" ie They went on and on about it.

In the **Avoir** chapter, we met the expression **vous n'avez que**…, you only have to/ you have only to… Insert **parler** and you have:

Vous n'avez qu' à parler ie You only have to say the word.

And here again in the example I gave you in the introduction:

Ne m'en parlez pas! ie "You're telling me!"
Vous parlez! also means "You're telling me!"

In a similar vein:

N'en parlons plus! means "Let's drop the subject"

Tu peux parler! means "You can talk!"
Tu parles si ça nous aide! means "A fat lot of good, that is!"
C'est parler à un mur means "It is like talking to a brick wall"
Parlons boutique means to talk shop.

And if you thought you might be able to get a bit off your decorator's bill by paying cash, you might say:

"**Si nous parlions finances**?" (Incidentally, French workmen, like their English counterparts, very often love to receive cash ("les espèces"). Like food, wine, leisure and avoiding paying parking fines, cheating the Inland Revenue (**"le fisc"**), is one of a Frenchman's greatest pleasures. They have taken the practice of working illegally for cash to the level of an art-form:

Il se fait payer au noir means that he gets paid cash in hand. **Travailler au noir,** "on the black" means to work on the side – to "moonlight" so to speak).
Idiomatic parler

I am not for one mimute suggesting that you would murder the French language, "pour l'amour de Dieu!" (for heaven's sake!) but if you come across someone whom you think **is** doing just that, you would be justified in saying:

- **Vous parlez français comme une vache espagnole!** Do not ask me why it has to be a **Spanish** cow!
- **J'en parlerai à mon cheval** means that I do not care what you are talking about.
- **Grand parleur, petit faiseur** is the polite(r) version of our "he is all mouth and trousers!" ie He talks a good game but there is not much action.

And finally, to finish on a more refined note, here is a proverb that comes from La Fontaine, a great French story-teller from way, way back:

- "Il est bon de **parler** et meilleur de **se taire**". This generally translates as "Speech is silver; silence is golden".

Conclusion

So there you have it! **Parler**. Obviously, it is an incredibly important verb (archiimportant?) because all of us have to speak or talk some of the time – and some of us like to speak or talk all of the time! But, I hope you will agree, it is not difficult to find your way around it. It is a regular "…er" verb and is not difficult to conjugate. In use it either has a direct object when you are talking languages and the only prepositions that follow it are **a**, **de**, **pour** and **contre**. Its reflexive role is very limited indeed; and there are few important idiomatic uses you need to know of. Although it is used colloquially quite a lot, these are expressions you can acquire very gradually indeed. So, armed with those comforting thoughts, let us move on to our next "killer" verb, **mettre**. But first, as always, some conversations illustrating **parler** in use.

Parler: Conversation One

One of Cécile's clients is a famous language school in Paris that wants better to understand the needs of French people who either speak or want to speak English. So she begins her research outside the Sorbonne, one of France's greatest universities, located in Paris' 5th arrondissement. She is stopping young students as they go in and out. First, she stops a young man carrying a pile of books.

Cécile:	Excusez-moi mais, dites-moi, est-ce que vous parlez anglais?
Jeune homme:	Anglais? Oh là, là! Je parle un tout petit peu anglais. Je suis très peu doué en langues étrangères.
Cécile:	J'admire votre franchise, jeune homme! Moyennant quoi, je vais vous poser quelques questions très faciles! D'abord, comment dit-on "comment allez-vous?" en anglais?
Jeune homme:	"Comment allez-vous?" Ça se dit "How are you?" je crois
Cécile:	Chapeau! Et si on disait "où allez-vous?" en anglais.
Jeune homme:	Ça c'est "where you are going?" je crois.
Cécile:	Presque: "where are you going" est la bonne réponse! Mais pas mal, pas mal. Et maintenant, parlons sport: "J'aime le foot mais je préfère le rugby". En anglais, c'est quoi au juste?
Jeune homme:	Ah, non, c'est trop, ça. Évidemment je suis presque nul en anglais!
Cécile:	Pas du tout. Mais, dites-moi, est-ce que vous croyez que c'est important de parler anglais de nos jours?
Jeune homme:	Important?! Moi, je dirais plutôt que parler anglais est indispensable de nos jours, archiindispensable, même!
Cécile:	Si vous avez raison, que devez-vous faire pour parler mieux l'anglais?
Jeune homme:	On peut étudier l'anglais, ça c'est sûr. Mais, ça ne fait pas avancer le schmilblick à mon avis. Non. Si l'on veut parler bien l'anglais, même le perfectionner, il faut passer beaucoup de temps en Angleterre, peut-être dans une boite où il faut absolument parler anglais. C'est en forgeant qu'on devient forgeron, vous-savez!
Cécile:	Tout à fait. Et est-ce que vous avez l'intention de passer une période en Angleterre?
Jeune homme:	Mais, oui, aussitôt que mes études se termineront. Je voudrais travailler à Londres.
Cécile:	À Londres? Bravo! Mais le saviez-vous?: Londres est la cinquième ville de France!
Jeune homme:	Franchement, je ne comprends pas.

Cécile:	C'est à dire qu'il y a presque cinq cents mille français et françaises qui habitent Londres en ce moment. Il y a des endroits, paraît-il, comme South Kensington, par exemple, où les habitants sont presque cent pour cent français! Est-ce que vous avez jamais entendu parler du lycée de South Kensington?
Jeune homme:	Vaguement, oui.
Cécile:	Bon, mais maintenant il y en a deux!
Jeune homme:	Oh là, là! Ça veut dire que si je veux parler anglais, je dois aller à…
Cécile:	À Glasgow, peut-être!
Jeune homme:	Glasgow? Où ça? Mais regardez, je dois m'en aller - c'est l'heure de manger. Je ne peux plus parler. Bye-bye!
Cécile:	Bye-bye, jeune homme!

Parler: Conversation Two

If one or two of the students at the Sarbonne are "nul" en anglais, what about some of the teaching staff, "les professeurs de faculté?" Maryse manages to stop one before she leaves for the day.

Maryse:	Vous m'avez dit tout à l'heure que vous êtes prof à la fac. Vous êtes prof de quoi au juste?
La professeur:	J'enseigne l'anglais, madame.
Maryse:	Parfait, parce que je fais une recherche pour un client sur les compétences des étudiants en anglais. Parlons d'abord alors de vos étudiants et de vos étudiantes. Parlent-ils bien l'anglais?
La professeur:	Dans un premier temps, il faut faire la distinction entre la langue parlée et la langue écrite. Ici nous mettons l'accent sur la littérature anglaise et les grands dramaturges comme Shakespeare. Pour nous, parler anglais est moins important que lire l'anglais.
Maryse:	Je comprends. En effet, je parlais tout à l'heure à un étudiant très gentil. Il parle très peu l'anglais mais il comprends l'importance de la langue, ça c'est sûr.
La professeur:	Je ne peux pas parler pour lui personnellement bien sûr <u>mais</u>, oui, les jeunes de nos jours se rendent compte que parler français n'est plus suffisant. Nous vivons dans un monde global où l'anglais est la lingua franca.
Maryse:	Je suis d'accord. Et pourrions-nous parler de vous maintenant? Où, et comment, est-ce que vous avez appris à parler anglais?
La professeur:	Moi? D'abord à l'école, bien-sûr. Après à l'université, et après ça en Angleterre où j'ai vécu pendant dix ans et où je me suis mariée à un anglais, quelle surprise!
Maryse:	Et qu'est-ce que vous parlez à la maison - français ou anglais?
La professeur:	Pour la plupart du temps nous nous parlons anglais chez nous malgré le fait que mon mari parle bien le français. À nos enfants, moi, je parle français et mon mari leur parle en anglais.
Maryse:	Bon. Cela veut dire, alors, qu'ils sont bilingues, vos enfants.
La professeur:	À proprement parler, ils ne sont pas encore bilingues mais ils perfectionnent leur anglais et leur français. Dans quelques années ils seront vraiment bilingues, je crois.
Maryse:	Et dans l'avenir, voudriez-vous qu'ils habitent en Angleterre, comme vous?

La professeur:	On ne sait jamais. Qui sait ce qu'apporte l'avenir. En principe, oui, mais ce que, moi, j'aimais quand je vivais en Angleterre, c'était que les Anglais sont beaucoup plus décontractés que les Français. Par exemple, ils savent mieux que nous comment joindre l'utile à l'agréable. La vie là-bas est moins stressante, je crois.
Maryse:	À la campagne, je partage votre avis à cent pour cent, mais à Londres, mettons, par rapport à Paris?
La professeur:	Oui, je crois. Et Londres, ça bouge, vous savez. Notre capitale est devenue trop conservatrice à mon sens. On se croirait au dix-neuxième siècle!
Maryse:	Vous en rajoutez, madame!
La professeur:	Peut-être. Quelques fois je me mets le doigt dans l'oeil. Mais pourquoi pas? Je ne suis que prof en fin de compte!
Maryse:	J'admire votre franchise, madame! Vous m'avez déjà donné tout ce dont j'ai besoin – plus, même. Merci bien.
La professeur:	Ça m'a fait beaucoup plaisir, madame. Et bonne chance avec votre recherche!
Maryse:	C'est gentil. Merci encore une fois. Au revoir.
La professeur:	Au revoir, madame.

Some words you might not yet know

la franchise -	frankness
moyennant quoi -	in return for which
chapeau! -	well done!
indispensable -	indispensable
perfectionner -	to improve
c'est en forgeant qu'on devient forgeron -	practice makes perfect
se terminer -	to finish
le saviez-vous? -	did you know?
des endroits (m) -	places
enseigner -	to teach
les compétences (f) -	the skills/capabilities
dans un premier temps -	to begin with
faire une distinction entre -	to distinguish between
la langue écrite -	the written language
la langue parlée -	the spoken language
mettre l'accent sur -	to emphasise
un(e) dramaturge -	a playwrite
vivre -	to live
global(e) -	global
la lingua franca -	the lingua franca
se marier à -	to marry
quelle surprise! -	what a surprise!
les gosses (m,f) -	kids
dans l'avenir (m) -	in the future
on ne sait jamais -	one never knows
apporter -	to bring
en principe -	in principle
décontracté(e) -	relaxed/laid back
joindre l'utile à l'agréable -	to mix business with pleasure
stressant(e) -	stressful
partager l'avis de quelqu'un à cent pour cent -	to agree 100% with someone
par rapport à -	compared with
conservateur/trice -	conservative
ça bouge -	there is a lot happening/going on
on se croirait... -	you would think we were...
se mettre le doigt dans l'oeil -	to be entirely mistaken/to kid oneself

Parler: Exercises

Complete the blank spaces:

1.   (   ) parlent anglais.

2.   Il aurait (   ) français.

3.   Il faut que vous (   ) japonnais.

4.   (   ) français quand vous êtes en France.

5.   Ils parlent bien (   ) français.

6.   Ma fille a commencé à (   ) à seize mois.

7.   J'ai (   ) Xavier hier.

8.   J'ai rencontré Simone dans le café hier et nous (   ) de choses et d'autres.

9.   Mon mari a (   ) elle à son prof.

10.   Nous (   ) d'aller à Londres mais c'est trop cher là-bas en ce moment.

11.   Ces patins à roulettes me (   ) de ma jeunesse.

12.   Je ne (   ) jamais contre notre femme de ménage: elle est excellente.

13.   Mon fils m'a dit hier qu'il a vaguement (   ) parler de Victor Hugo.

14.   Quand je suis tout seul je me (   ) souvent.

15.   Ils se (   ) parlés toute la journée.

16.   Tu (   ) d'un culot.

17.   C'est à moi que vous (   )?

18.   Ne m'en (   ) pas.

19.   Si nous (   ) vacances?

225

20. J'en (   ) à mon cheval.

21. Il est bon de (   ) et meilleur de se faire.

Parler: Answers

1. Ils
2. parlé
3. parliez
4. Parlez
5. le
6. parler
7. parle à, parlé de
8. avons parlé
9. parlé d'
10. parlions
11. parlent
12. parle or parlerais
13. entendu
14. parle
15. sont
16. parles
17. parlez
18. parlez
19. parlions
20. parlerai
21. parler

Chapter Eleven
Mettre

Introduction

Basically, **mettre** means **to put** or **to place**. In English, we put things somewhere, and we can put people somewhere. So it is in French with **mettre**: "J'ai mis mes chaussures dans l'armoire" – I put my shoes in the wardrobe. Immediately, you can see that **mettre** is a transitive verb; it is followed by a direct object – shoes, raincoats, butter… and so on. And it is the same with people: "Mum and Dad put granny in a home", for example.

But **mettre**, like "put", is a very general sort of word indeed – and often we can find a more **precise** word. In English this is easy to see. Whilst we could say, "Dad put some wallpaper on the wall", it would be a better English sentence if we said: "Dad hung some paper on the wall". Quite apart from anything else, it would get tedious if we constantly said "put" when more precise words were available.

Very often, French does not work quite like English and one verb often has to perform many different functions. **Mettre** is one such verb. It is a protean work horse, "un cheval de labour". It has to do the job of many English verbs. (Incidentally, in case you are wondering: "protean" means versatile – but I seem to use the word so often in this book, I, too, felt it was time for a change!)

Then there is **se mettre**, another work horse verb; here it is often the change in preposition that gives it some variety.

But it is also a very useful idiomatic verb: "**mettre du beurre dans les épinards**", for example, means to have some very handy extra money. There are lots more like this.

So, "once more unto the breach…" (Henry V!). Let us first conjugate **mettre**.

The Mettre Conjugations

Present Tense		**Future Tense**	
Je mets	Nous mettons	Je mettrai	Nous mettrons
Tu mets	Vous mettez	Tu mettras	Vous mettrez
Il met	Ils mettent	Il mettra	Ils mettront
Elle met	Elles mettent	Elle mettra	Elles mettront

Imperfect Tense

Je mettais	Nous mettions
Tu mettais	Vous mettiez
Il mettait	Ils mettaient
Elle mettait	Elles mettaient

Perfect Tense

J'ai mis	Nous avons mis
Tu as mis	Vous avez mis
Il a mis	Ils ont mis
Elle a mis	Elles ont mis

Future Perfect Tense

J'aurai mis	Nous aurons mis
Tu auras mis	Vous aurez mis
Il aura mis	Ils auront mis
Elle aura mis	Elles auront mis

Pluperfect Tense

J'avais mis	Nous avions mis
Tu avais mis	Vous aviez mis
Il avait mis	Ils avaient mis
Elle avait mis	Elles avaient mis

Present Conditional Tense

Je mettrais	Nous mettrions
Tu mettrais	Vous mettriez
Il mettrait	Ils mettraient
Elle mettrait	Elles mettraient

Past Conditional Tense

J'aurais mis	Nous aurions mis
Tu aurais mis	Vous auriez mis
Il aurait mis	Ils auraient mis
Elle aurait mis	Elles auraient mis

Present Subjunctive Tense

Je mette	Nous mettions
Tu mettes	Vous mettiez
Ils mette	Ils mettent
Elles mette	Elles mettent

Imperative

Mets
Mettons
Mettez

Mettre: The Basics

As we have just noted, basically **mettre** means to put (or to place). So you can use **mettre** to say that you are putting, you have already put or you will put something somewhere:

- "Maman, **je mets** la confiture dans le frigo, d'accord?" ie Mum, I am putting the jam in the fridge, ok?

In the past tense you could say:

- "Maman, **j'ai mis** les oeufs dans le placard: c'est moins froid là-bas" ie Mum, I have put the eggs in the cupboard: it is not so cold there.

In the future tense you could say:

- "Maman, **je mettrai** le journal sur la table dans le salon. Ça va?" ie I will put the newspaper on the table in the lounge. Is that alright?

In other tenses, too, you can just as easily use **mettre**:

- "Maman, **je mettais** le vin dans le garage quand j'ai entendu quelqu'un frappant à la porte" ie Mum, I was putting the wine in the garage when I heard someone knocking on the door.
- "Maman, **je mettrais** les tasses dans le lave-vaisselle mais c'est plein à craquer" ie Mum, I would put the cups in the dishwasher, but it is full to bursting.
- "Maman, **j'aurais** mis ton panier dans la cuisine mais le sol est encore mouillé" ie Mum, I would have put your basket in the kitchen, but the floor is still wet.
- "Maman, **mets** ma canne à pêche dans l'abri, s'il te plaît" ie Mum, put my fishing rod in the shed, please.

But as I said earlier, you can also use **mettre** to talk about putting **someone** somewhere:

- "Papa, je vais **mettre grand-maman** à côté de moi: j'ai eu très peu d'occasion de lui parler" ie Dad, I am going to put (seat) granny next to me: I have had very little chance to talk to her.

Note here that "chance" is translated by "occasion", not by chance. This word is reserved for luck, opportunity… and so on. Remember my fishing example in the **Être** chapter: "… de la chance, monsieur?" Note also, that there are several ways of talking about **sitting down** in French. We will see one in the last section of this chapter that uses **mettre**. One final thought: **grand-maman** is these days a very out of date way of translating "granny". Several of our French friends much prefer "mamie", and "grand-papa" is much more often "pépé".

In this last example, it is clear that in English, another verb can be used instead of "to put" – and often, in fact, we will use another verb. For example, instead of saying: "Put the radio on", we would probably say: "Switch the radio on". Whilst it is exactly the same in French, **mettre** tends to get used in a lot of contexts where we might prefer another verb altogether. Here are just one or two examples:

- "In England, we normally **send** our children to school at five (years of age). This might well be translated in French as:
  "En Angleterre, normalement **nous mettons** nos enfants à l'école à l'âge de cinq ans".

- "I have got nothing to **wear** and we are going out tonight!" This might well be rendered as:
  "Je n'ai rien à **me mettre** – et nous sortons ce soir!"

So often is **mettre** used in such ways that we will look further at such applications in the next section, **Getting Better**.

Summary

From what you have already seen, **mettre** is indeed a protean verb! Use it to:

- talk about putting things somewhere
- talk about putting people somewhere
- talk about sending people somewhere and even
- wearing things.

And if you want to know how else this verb can be used in lots of other similar contexts, read on!

Getting Better

In this section we will certainly examine those ways that **mettre** can be used to say what we might say using other verbs altogether. I say "might" because "put" is one of these incredibly useful words in English, too. A bit like "get", for example, with the addition of a preposition, "put" can mean many different things: to put on, to put off, to put in, to put out, to put over, to put under… and so on. Very often too, "put" plus a preposition can mean something else altogether from place: "I put one over on him", for example. So let us begin by showing how **mettre** can be used in French, where a phrasal verb would be employed in English.

To put in can mean to **install**, or to **build** or to **construct**. In French, **mettre** can do these jobs;

- "**J'ai mis** quelques étagères dans la cuisine pour mon gendre" ie I put some shelves in the kitchen for my son-in-law.

And following the same DIY theme, we might:

Put up:

- "**J'ai mis** un placard sur le mur de la petite chambre" ie I put up a cupboard in the small bedroom. Or…
- "Si vous partagez mon point de vue, **mettez les mains en l'air**" ie If you agree with my point of view, put your hands up.

Put into:

- "Quand mon mari m'a dit que je devrais acheter un nouveau lave-linge, **il m'a mis une idée dans la tête**" ie When my husband said that I should buy a new washing machine, he put an idea into my head.
- "My teacher advised me to put all my verbs into the plural" ie Mon prof m'a conseillé de **mettre tous mes verbes au pluriel**.

Put on:

- "Mon père **a mis** un revêtement assorti sur le mur derrière le bahut" ie My father put a matching wallcovering on the wall behind the sideboard.

- "**Il a mis** de la peinture sur la vieille table dans la cuisine" ie He put a coat of paint on the old table in the kitchen. But:
- "When he has some spare time, he likes to go to the betting shop and put a few pounds **on** the horses" ie "Pendant son temps libre il aime aller jouer au PMU."

The PMU, Pari mutual urbain, is the equivalent of our Tote and the "bureau du PMU" is the nearest thing France has to what we call betting shops. But to put money on horses, you do not have to go to such bureaux: you can place your bets in very many a French café where the PMU will have a very noticeable presence! Here you can place a bet on what they call "le tiercé". It is so-called because you place your bet on three horses, not one. They can win in no particular order or they can come in certain specific orders. Obviously, the odds, as we call them, will be different according to the bet you place. You can win, ie "réussir le tiercé":

- dans l'ordre
- dans le désordre, or
- dans un ordre different.

Now you can see where I spend too much of my time!

Put out:

- "Darling, have you put the cat out, yet?" ie "Chérie, **as-tu mis le chat dehors** encore?"

Put to:

- "Le pianiste m'a dit que je devrais **mettre tous mes vers en musique**" ie The pianist said to me that I should put all my verses to music.

Sorry, but I cannot resist this one here. All languages have **homonyms**, ie words that sound the same but are spelled differently. Here is a famous French example: "Le **ver** de la pomme n'est pas le **vers** de La Fontaine et le **verre** à champagne n'est pas le **vert** de la campagne!" Here, four different words all sound exactly the same: un **ver** is a worm; un **vers** is a verse; un **verre** à champagne is a champagne glass – et le **vert** de la campagne is the green of the countryside! To these one might add the preposition, **vers**, meaning "towards".

Hopefully, I have given you enough examples to illustrate that **mettre** can be used in French where the phrasal verb "to put" would normally be used in English.

However, and as I have already suggested earlier in this second-level section, **mettre** can be used where in English we would probably use an altogether different verb from "to put…" In my very first example, I said that **mettre** could translate install, build or construct. And in the **Basics** section, I showed that **mettre** could be used to translate to switch, to send and to wear. So, how else can **mettre** be deployed?

First, the verb can be used to oblige or to compel someone to do something. For example:

- **"Il m'a mis dans la nécessité** de faire réparer la toiture" ie He made me get the roof repaired.
- **"Je l'ai mis dans l'obligation** de rendre visite à sa mère pendant son séjour à l'hôpital" ie I made him feel obliged to visit his mother during her stay in hospital. (Incidentally, when you are visiting a **place** you must use the verb **visiter**. When you are visiting a **person**, however, you need **rendre visite à**).

Second, mettre can be used to take time for something or someone to do something:

- "À moins d'aller en voiture, le trajet est fatiguant. **Le train met quatre heures à le faire** - parce qu'il y a une attente d'une heure à Limoges" ie Unless you go by car, the journey is tiring. The train takes four hours to get there – because there is an hour's wait at Limoges.

Please note the clause "à moins d'aller". Using the construction "à moins de…" there is no **subject**. In English we would say "unless **you** go…" But in French, the subject is understood. It may become clear in the following clause. For example:

- "À moins de payer 10€, **vous** ne pouvez pas voir l'exposition" ie Unless (you) pay 10€, **you** cannot see the exhibition.

Third, use **mettre** to talk about the care or pain involved in doing something. For example:

- "Il faut **mettre beaucoup de soins** à restaurer cette vieille voiture. Elle vaut une petite fortune" ie You must take great care in restoring this old car. It is worth a small fortune.

Fourth, you can use **mettre** to talk about doing something eagerly:

- "Ma mère **a mis de l'ardeur à acheter** un cadeau pour sa soeur à l'occasion de son anniversaire de mariage" ie My mother eagerly bought a present for her sister's wedding anniversary.

Fifth, it can be used to talk about spending money on something. For example:

- **"J'allais mettre mille euros pour le tableau**, mais ma femme m'a dit que c'était trop cher" ie I was going to spend a thousand euros on the painting, but my wife said that it was too expensive.

Sixth, use it to talk about giving some money to someone or something:

- "Je suis prêt à **mettre cinq cent euros pour mon organisation caritative préferée**" ie I am prepared to give five hundred euros to my favourite charity.

Seventh, **mettre** can be used to talk about paying the price for something. To illustrate:

- "Chérie, je suis d'accord avec toi. Mais si tu veux un beau complet, il faut **y mettre le prix**" ie Darling, I agree with you. But if you want a really nice suit, you really have to pay the price for it.

Eighth (and I use this expression a lot!), if you want to suppose something or other, you can also use **mettre**:

- "**Mettons** qu'il arrive à midi. Aura-t-il le temps de faire tout ce qu'il nous faut?" ie Let us suppose that he arrives at midday. Will he have the time to do everything that we need done?
- "D'accord, j'achèterai du steak haché à la boucherie ce matin **mettons**, mais après?" ie OK. I will buy some minced steak at the butcher's this morning, let's say, but then what?

Let us stop there, shall we?! Again, I feel, you have got plenty of examples which show the versatility of **mettre**. A bit like **faire**, it can be used in so many ways and in so many different contexts.

Now You Are Really Speaking French!

There are two roles for **mettre** at this level. First, there is the pronominal form of **mettre**, **se mettre**, including **se mettre à** and **s'y mettre**. Then there is **mettre**'s role in idiomatic language. This verb has very many idiomatic applications and we will look at these in some detail. So let us kick off this section with **se mettre**.

Se mettre

One of the most common uses of this construction involves putting yourself somewhere. For example:

- "Veux-tu **te mettre** là, Robert, à côté de Céline?" ie Do you want to sit next to Céline, Robert?
- "Où veux-tu que **je me mette** (subjunctive), Valérie – au bout de la table peut-être?" ie Where do you want me, Valérie – at the end of the table, perhaps?
- "Je vais **me mettre** ici, en face de Nathalie – si cela te convient" ie I am going to sit here, opposite Nathalie, if that is ok with you.

When it comes to the business of sitting down, you have quite a choice of words in fact. There is **mettre**, of course, but you have also got **s'assoir** and **s'installer**:

- "Je vais **m'assoir** ici, Jean-Louis" or
- "Je vais **m'installer** ici, Jean-Louis".

I am not aware of any difference between them. It is, therefore, a question of learning **one** of them – and sticking with it!

A **second** use of **se mettre** arises when you want to talk about how you (or someone else) is or should be dressed. For example:

- "Chérie, tu sais que nous sommes invités chez les Dupont demain soir, **Comment je me mets**?" ie Darling, you know that we are invited to the Duponts tomorrow night. What sort of thing should I wear?
- "La dernière fois que j'ai croisé Danielle chez les Dupont, **elle s'était mise** très simplement" ie The last time that I saw Danielle at the Duponts, she was very simply dressed.

Third, use **se mettre** when you want to say that an idea has got into your head. For example:

- "**Je me suis mis cette** idée dans la tête: Jean-François, malgré ses protestations, est fana d'écologie" ie I have got this idea into my head: despite Jean-François' protestations, he is an ecology freak.

Se mettre à

When coupled with the preposition **à**, **se mettre** can have several different meanings. For example, when it is followed by a **verb**, it generally means to start to do something:

- "Ma femme était assise à côté de Jean-Paul quand, tout d'un coup, **il s'est mis à rire** sans aucune raison, paraît-il" ie My wife was sitting next to Jean-Paul when, all of a sudden, he began laughing for no reason, it seems.
- "Il faisait beau tout à l'heure mais **voilà qu'il se met à pleuvoir**!" ie It was fine just now but now it's coming on to rain!

Se mettre à can also be followed by a **noun**. We met the idea of going on a diet in an earlier chapter:

- "J'ai trop mangé, Anna. Je dois vraiment **me mettre au régime**" ie I have eaten too much, Anna. I really must go on a diet.

It can also be used to say that you have taken to something or other. To illustrate:

- "**Je me suis bien mis** au français. Oui, au début, je l'ai trouvé difficile, mais de nos jours je l'adore!" ie I have really taken to French. Yes, in the beginning, I found it difficult, but nowadays I love it!

S'y mettre

In the examples immediately above, **se mettre à** means generally to start doing something. **S'y mettre**, too, has this same general meaning. For example:

- "Qu'est-ce que tu es énervant quand **tu t'y mets**!" ie You can be a real pain once you get started!

Idiomatic mettre

The French language is replete with colloquial and idiomatic uses of **mettre**. Let us begin with some of the more well known colloquial expressions that use this verb. There is no particular order to those that I have listed.

In an earlier chapter we met "on se casse", let us split. Other expressions also mean the same thing:

> **Mettre les voiles** and…
> **Mettre les bouts:**

- "Regarde l'heure: **on met les bouts**?" – Look at the time, shall we split?

Mettre les pouces means to concede or to give in.
Mettre au clou means to pawn something. A pawn-broker is known as "un prêteur sur gages."
We have met this one already: **mettre du beurre dans les épinards** means to give life a bit of a fillip financially.
Se mettre les pieds sous la table means to put one's feet up.
Se mettre le doigt dans l'oeil is another expression you have already met. It means to get something completely wrong, to "bark up the wrong tree."
Mettre quelqu'un en boule means to annoy someone.
Mettre quelqu'un en boîte means to wind someone up.
Mettre la main à la pâte means to give someone a helping hand.
C'est à se mettre à genoux means that something is marvellous.
Mettre les bouchées doubles means to get cracking.
Mettre le paquet means to pull out all the stops:

- "Pour ceux qui vendent les vélos, le Tour de France est l'occasion parfaite pour **mettre le paquet**" ie For those who sell bicycles, the Tour de France is the perfect opportunity to make an all out effort.

Mettre au rencart means to throw things out.
Y mettre son grain de sel means to have one's say, to stick one's nose in something.
Mettre quelqu'un dedans means to trick someone into something.
Earlier in the chapter we talked, literally, about sitting down at the table. But **se mettre à table** colloquially means "to let the cat out of the bag" or to "spill the beans".

In so far as there is much of a distinction between colloquial and idiomatic language, let us now look at some of the more well-known idiomatic uses of **mettre**:

Mettre la charrue avant les boeufs means to "put the cart before the horse". For example:

- "Robert, tu a mis les tomates dans la poêle avant les oignons. **Tu mets la charrue avant les boeufs!**" ie Robert, you have put the tomatoes in the pan before the onions. You are putting the horse before the cart!

Mettre quelque chose sur ses tablettes means to write something on one's jotter pad.
Mettre des bâtons dans les roues de quelqu'un means to put a spoke in someone's wheel.
Mettre la puce à l'oreille de quelqu'un means to get somebody thinking.
Mettre quelqu'un au pied du mur means to trap someone so they cannot easily escape.
En mettre sa main au feu means to stake your life on something:

- "La Deuxième Guerre mondiale a éclaté en 1939: **j'en mettrais ma main au feu!**" ie The Second World War broke out in 1939: I would stake my life on it!

Se mettre dans le bain means to get into the swing of things.
Se mettre sur son trente-et-un is another expression you have already encountered. It means to get dressed up, to "put on your Sunday best".
Se mettre en quatre pour quelqu'un means to bend over backwards to help someone.
Se mettre au pieu means to hit the sack/hay.

Conclusion

Mettre is a verb you will come across every day almost in conversation – if only because it means "to put in" or "to place", something we are likely to say very often in English, too. Beyond that it is used in its pronominal form, **se mettre**, to convey less obvious meanings of "to put", to wear, for example.

Finally, it is a very important idiomatic verb, quite one of the most important in our "killer" list. For all these reasons, get to know it!

Normally here we have the first of two conversations. This time, however, I have got something different for you – a **poem** by **Jacques Prévert**.

Jacques Prévert, who died in 1977, was a much-loved poet and screen-writer ("scénariste"). He wrote highly accessible, realistic poems with huge appeal to school-children in particular. His film credits include "Les Enfants du Paradis" (1945), a landmark film in the history of French cinema.

The poem I have chosen is one of his most famous, "Déjeuner du matin". It is deceptively simple and very easy to memorise. More than that though, he uses **mettre** six times in what is, after all, a fairly short poem!

Déjeuner du matin

Il a mis le café
Dans la tasse
Il a mis le lait
Dans la tasse de café
Il a mis le sucre
Dans le café au lait
Avec la petite cuiller
Il a tourné
Il a bu le café au lait
Et il a reposé la tasse
Sans me parler

Il a allumé
Une cigarette
Il a fait des ronds
Avec la fumée
Il a mis les cendres
Dans le cendrier
Sans me parler
Sans me regarder

Il s'est levé
Il a mis
Son chapeau sur sa tête
Il a mis son manteau de pluie
Parce qu'il pleuvait
Et il est parti
Sous la pluie
Sans une parole
Sans me regarder

Et moi, j'ai pris
Ma tête dans ma main
Et j'ai pleuré.

Mettre: Conversation

Thierry and Corinne have decided it is now high time that they did something to refresh their rather tired-looking kitchen, so they have planned to go to one of Paris' many out-of-town shopping centres where there is a wide choice of stores, materials and fittings. But before they leave the apartment, which is on the ground floor with a large communal garden, they still have one or two things to do.

Corinne:	Thierry, mais tu n'as pas encore débarrassé la table! Mets les assiettes dans le lave-vaisselle et mets les petites casseroles dans l'évier s'il te plaît. On ne peut pas laisser la cuisine dans un tel état!
Thierry:	Oui, chérie...
Corinne:	Et as-tu mis le chat dehors?
Thierry:	Pas encore.
Corinne:	Et qu'est-ce que tu vas te mettre, Thierry? Il fait froid dehors. Tu as besoin d'une écharpe et d'un manteau, tu sais.
Thierry:	Oui, chérie.
Corinne:	Et je n'ai rien à me mettre. J'aurais dû passer au pressing hier chercher mon manteau bleu. Il ne me reste que mon truc rouge et franchement, j'en ai assez.
Thierry:	Tant pis, Corinne. Mais dépêche-toi. Il est presque onze heures. On a très peu de temps si, après, tu veux rendre visite à ta cousine à Neuilly. Franchement, je me passerai bien d'aller chez elle cet aprèm. P.S.G. passe à la télé à seize heures, tu sais.
Corinne:	Vraiment, Thierry, tu es impossible! Allons-y! Je suis prête.
Thierry:	Enfin! Mais comment y aller? En train?
Corinne:	Mais tu sais, Thierry, le train met une bonne heure avec le changement à Étoile. Pourquoi ne pas prendre la voiture? Comme ça, il y aura de la place pour mettre nos achats dans le coffre et sur la banquette arrière si nécessaire.
Thierry:	Tu as raison, Corinne. Attends que j'aille chercher la bagnole. Je n'en ai que pour deux minutes.

Five minutes later, Thierry returns:

	Oh là, là! Corinne! Problème!
Corinne:	Qu'est qu'il se passe, Thierry? Où est la voiture?
Thierry:	Encore au garage, Corinne. Elle ne démarre pas. La batterie est morte.
Corinne:	C'est pas vrai! Tu me mets en boite! Que faire, alors?

Thierry:	Je sais pas, Corinne. Mais maintenant ma priorité est de recharger la batterie. On ne peut aller nulle part avec une batterie morte. Et il se fait tard, Corinne. Je commence à avoir faim.
Corinne:	Moi, aussi.
Thierry:	Donc, je suggère que nous renoncions à notre idée d'aller à Castorama et cetera aujourd'hui. Vaut mieux à mon sens s'y rendre demain et puis rendre visite à ta cousine. Qu'est-ce que tu en penses, Corinne?
Corinne:	Oui, je comprends, Thierry. Et ça veut dire que tu peux voir P.S.G. à la télé cet aprèm, hein?
Thierry:	Quelle excellente idée, Corinne! Moyennant quoi, je vais préparer quelque chose de spécial pour déjeuner - des lasagnes, peut-être.
Corinne:	Thierry, tu me mets déjà l'eau à la bouche!

Some words you might not yet know

- reposer -   to put down
- faire des ronds -   to make circles (with cigarette smoke)
- les cendres (f) -   cigarette ash
- un cendrier -   an ash-tray
- pleurer -   to cry
- tant pis -   too bad
- une bagnole (fam) -   a car
- la banquette arrière -   the back seat
- une batterie -   a (car) battery
- mort(e) -   dead/flat
- nulle part -   anywhere
- P.S.G. -   Paris Saint Germain
- les lasagnes (f) -   lasagne
- se mettre l'eau à la bouche -   to make one's mouth water

Mettre: Exercises

Complete the blank spaces:

1. Papa, je (   ) ton journal sur la table. Ça va?

2. Ils ont (   ) leurs bottes de caoutchouc dans l'appentis.

3. J'aurais (   ) le bois dans le bûcher mais c'était trop mouillé là-bas.

4. Maman, je (   ) les verres dans le bahut mais il y a très peu de place pour eux.

5. Je n'ai rien à me (   ) - et nous sortons ce soir.

    Put one of the three following words in the space below:
6. Papa, je vais (   ) mamie à côté de toi, ca va? (mettre, mis, mettez)

7. Maman, (   ) ma bicyclette au garage, s'il te plaît. (mettes, mets, mettras)

8. En Angleterre, nous (   ) nos enfants à l'école à l'âge de cinq ans. (mettre, mettez, mettons)

9. J'ai (   ) quelques étagères dans la chambre de mon voisin. (mis, mettrais, mettais)

10. Jeremy, as-tu (   ) le chien dehors encore? (mets, mettons, mis)

    Translate the underlined parts of the following French sentences into English:

11. Il m'a mis dans la nécessité de faire réparer la voiture.

12. Le train met une heure à le faire.

13. Il faut mettre beaucoup de soin en faisant le repassage.

14. Je vais mettre mille euros pour ce vieux livre.

15. Mettons qu'elles arrivent cet aprèm.

16. Veux – tu te mettre à côté de moi?

17. Je dois vraiment me mettre au régime.

18. Tu te mets le doigt dans l'oeil, Francis.

Using the verb mettre in some form or another, translate the underlined parts of these English sentences into French:

19. I really am knackered, I think I am going to hit the sack.

20. Have you seen Jacques today? He is dressed up to the nines.

21. I bent over backwards for him but he did not appreciate my efforts.

Mettre: Answers

1. mets
2. mis
3. mis
4. mettrais; j'aurais mis
5. mettre
6. mettre
7. mets
8. mettons
9. mis
10. mis
11. He made me
12. The train takes
13. Take
14. I am going to spend
15. Let us suppose that
16. Do you want to sit
17. I must really go on
18. You are barking up the wrong tree
19. me mettre au pieu
20. Il se met sur son trente-et-un
21. Je me suis mis en quatre pour lui.

Chapter Twelve
Dire

Introduction

Dire has two broad meanings in French: to **say** and to **tell**. To illustrate:

"Qu'est-ce que **tu dis**?" ie What are you saying? and…
"**Dites**-moi, où est mon écharpe?" ie Tell me, where is my scarf?

Immediately you should be able to see how frequently **dire** will be used in conversation, if only in these very basic but very important roles.

But **dire** is also used in quite a large number of fixed expressions. You have already met some of these:

"**Ça va sans dire**" ie That goes without saying and…
"**Qu'est-ce que cela veut dire**?" ie What does that mean?

Dire also has a small number of pronominal applications, so we will look at these.

As for idiomatic uses, it has vey few indeed.

But there are lots of what dictionaries often call "locutions", ie colloquial expressions like "dis donc" which you will hear very frequently and which has all sorts of uses. So we will certainly have a look at a few of these. But, as usual, let us begin with its conjugations.

The Dire Conjugations

Present Tense

Je dis	Nous disons	
Tu dis	Vous dites	
Il dit	Ils disent	
Elle dit	Elles disent	

Future Tense

Je dirai	Nous dirons
Tu diras	Vous direz
Il dira	Ils diront
Elle dira	Elles diront

Imperfect Tense

Je disais	Nous disions
Tu disais	Vous disiez
Il disait	Ils disaient
Elle disait	Elles disaient

Perfect Tense

J'ai dit	Nous avons dit
Tu as dit	Vous avez dit
Il a dit	Ils ont dit
Elle a dit	Elles ont dit

Future Perfect Tense

J'aurai dit	Nous aurons dit
Tu auras dit	Vous aurez dit
Il aura dit	Ils auront dit
Elle aura dit	Elles auront dit

Pluperfect Tense

J'avais dit	Nous avions dit
Tu avais dit	Vous aviez dit
Il avait dit	Ils avaient dit
Elle avait dit	Elles avaient dit

Present Conditional Tense

Je dirais	Nous dirions
Tu dirais	Vous diriez
Il dirait	Ils diraient
Elle dirait	Elles diraient

Past Conditional Tense

J'aurais dit	Nous aurions dit
Tu aurais dit	Vous auriez dit
Il aurait dit	Ils auraient dit
Elle aurait dit	Elles auraient dit

Present Subjunctive Tense

Je dise	Nous disions
Tu dises	Vous disiez
Il dise	Ils disent
Elle dise	Elles disent

Imperative

Dis
Disons
Dites

Dire: The Basics

Basically, **dire** means to say or to tell. Whilst these two ideas are very close, there is some clear blue water between them, perhaps more so in French than in English.

Dire: to say

First, there is **dire**, to say: then there is **dire que**, to say that. Let us look at both. First, **dire**:

- "**Dis** bonjour à papa, Violaine. Il vient de rentrer" ie Say hello to daddy, Violaine. He has just come home.
- "Je ne sais plus quoi **dire**" ie I am at a loss for words.
- "Où va-t-il? **Il ne le dit pas**, paraît-il" ie Where is he going? He is not saying, it seems.
- "Je **n'ai rien à dire**. C'est ma faute. C'est la fin de l'histoire" ie I have nothing to say. It is my fault – and that is the end of the story.
- "Il sait ce **qu'il dit**" ie He knows what he is saying.
- "Comment ça **se dit** en français?" ie How do you say that in French?
- "Comment **dit-on** "comment allez-vous?" en espagnol?" ie How do you say "how are you?" in Spanish?

There you have seven different examples, all in the present tense of **dire**, meaning to say. Now let us consider some examples of **dire que**, to say that...

- "Mon fils **m'a dit qu'**il allait nous écrire quand il serait arrivé a Sydney" ie My son said to me that he was going to write to us the moment that he arrived in Sydney.
- "D'après le mec à la radio ce matin, **il a dit qu'**il pleuvrait plus tard" ie According to the bloke on the radio this morning, he said that it would rain later.
- "**Tu m'as dit que** tu arrêterais de fumer mais qu'est-ce qui me **dit que** c'est vrai?" ie You said to me that you would stop smoking, but how do I know it is the truth?
- "Inutile de vous **dire que** je ne suis pas resté dans l'hôtel pour une deuxième semaine: c'était beaucoup trop bruyant" ie Needless to say that I did not stay in the hotel for a second week: it was much too noisy.
- "Est-ce qu'on peut **dire que** dans les Pyrénées il y a pas mal de neige l'hiver?" ie Can one say that the Pyrenees get lots of snow in winter?
- "**On dit que** les plages de la Côte d'Azur sont plutôt moches au mois d'août. Est-ce que c'est vrai?" ie Rumour has it that the beaches of the south of France are pretty awful in August. Is it true? (Incidentally, another way of saying "rumour has it" is "le bruit court que.")
- "Il va sans **dire que** si on veut devenir chirurgien on ne peut pas avoir horreur du sang!" ie It goes without saying that if you want to become a surgeon, you cannot be afraid of blood!

Dire: to tell

When it is a case of somebody telling someone something, **dire** will also be the appropriate verb to use. For example:

- "J'ai quelque chose à vous **dire**: vous êtes renvoyé!" ie I have got something that I want to tell you: you are fired! (Incidentally, the two reasonably polite words to use when dismissing someone are **renvoyer** and **virer**. However there are other more familiar ways of getting this rather unpleasant message across: **mettre quelqu'un à la porte** is considered ok, but **foutre quelqu'un à la porte** is considered much more vulgar, as you might expect).
- "Mon petit doigt me **dit que** tu es sorti avec Hélène hier soir – et n'essaye pas de le nier!" ie A little birdie told me that you went out with Helen last night – and do not try to deny it!
- "Je vais **te dire** quelque chose qui va te faire rire!" ie I am going to tell you something that is going to make you laugh.

Summary

Dire is an important and useful verb. Use it to:

- say something to somebody
- tell somebody about something.

In practice, there is quite a lot of overlap between "say" and "tell", as there is in English. We can just as easily say "I told her" as we can say "I said to her". So do not get unduly concerned about these, frankly, rather subtle differences.

Getting Better

The main way you can build on the basics of **dire** is to start using **dire** where in English we might use different verbs altogether. The most important ones are to please (**plaire**), to think (**penser**), to assume (**supposer**), to decide (**décider**), to admit (**admettre**), to remind (**évoquer**) and to show (**indiquer**). Here are some examples of all these verb equivalents in use:

Plaire:

- "Tout me **dit** en ce moment" ie I like everything at the moment.
- "Je sais qu'il y a un tiramisu pour le dessert, mais ça **ne me dit pas**: je le trouve trop sucré à mon goût" ie I know that there is a tiramisu to follow, but I do not like it: for my taste, it is too sweet.
- "**Rien ne me dit** ce soir. Je ne pense pas que j'aie faim" ie I do not fancy anything, this evening. I don't think that that I am hungry.

Penser:

- "Qu'est-ce que **tu dis** de mes gants, chérie? Je les ai achetés au marché à Nation" ie What do you think of my gloves, darling? I bought them at the market at Nation. Nation is a very large square ("place") on the east side of Paris. It is one of three great revolutionary places of Paris, the other two being République and Bastille. A little known fact is that far more people were executed at Nation during the French Revolution than at Concorde, the original site of the guillotine. It was moved from Concorde to Nation because the locals complained of the stink!
- "Qu'est-ce que **vous diriez** d'une omelette norvégienne? Je l'adore" ie What would you say to a Norwegian omelette. I love it.
- "C'est quoi au juste, cette viande? **On dirait** de l'agneau" ie What is this meat, exactly? It looks like lamb. **On dirait** is a very useful expression. It can mean it looks like, it smells like, it sounds like… and so on.
- "**Et dire** que j'aurais pu aller à Londres pendant les émeutes!" ie And to think that I might have gone to London during the riots!

Supposer:

- "**On le dit** caché quelque part où la police ne peut pas le trouver" ie He is rumoured to be hidden somewhere where the police cannot find him
Note here that in French, "police" is always singular – "la police" – never plural as it is in English.

Décider:

- "Bon, c'est **dit**" ie That is settled then.
- "**Disons** que vous passez demain, alors. Je préparerai du thé on ne peut plus anglais. **Disons** à quinze heures?" ie Let us say that you drop by tomorrow. I will prepare a typically English tea. Let us say at 3 o'clock? Note here the use of the twenty-four hour clock. This is very common in France. For further thoughts on this subject, see Chapter Twenty-Two, **Venir**.

Admettre:

- "Il faut bien **dire** que je ne suis pas très poisson. Je déteste les arêtes" ie I must admit that I am not very fond of fish. I hate the bones.

Two points to note here:

First, to say you are not fond of something, say, "Je ne suis pas très… followed by what it is you are not fond of. "I am not very fish" sounds bizarre, I agree. But:

"Je suis très chocolat" – I am very fond of chocolate, or…
"Mon mari est très chou-fleur" – My husband is very fond of cauliflower.

Second, "une arête" is a **fish** bone. All other bones are "os". In the singular, the "s" of this word is pronounced; in the plural, it is not.

Évoquer:

- "Tergiverser. Le mot me **dit** quelque chose, mais c'est quoi au juste?" ie Tergiverser (to equivocate, remember?) The word rings a bell, but what does it mean exactly?
- "Ed Miliband? Franchement le nom ne me **dit** pas grand-chose. C'est un homme politique, n'est-ce pas?" ie Ed Miliband? Frankly, the name does not mean much to me. He is a politician, isn't he?

Indiquer:

- "Quelle heure est-il? Ma montre **dit** onze heures – mais je crois qu'elle a cinq minutes d'avance" ie What time is it? According to my watch, eleven o'clock, but I think I am five minutes fast.

You have enough examples here to show just how useful **dire** can be. But that is not the end of the story. It has other important uses, too. We will examine these in the next section.

Now You Are Really Speaking French!

We have already encountered the expression **vouloir dire**, to mean, but there are also **faire dire** and **laisser dire**. Then we also have **c'est pas pour dire** and **il n'y a pas à dire**.

There are also several locutions featuring **dire** – so we will have a look at some of these. Many of them are quite colloquial.

And **dire** is occasionally used in its pronominal form, **se dire**. We will examine this application, too.

Faire dire

Faire dire something to somebody, means to send word of something or somebody. For example:

- "Mon fils m'a **fait dire** sa victoire, hier. Malheureusement, je n'ai pas pu la voir à la télé: en rentrant, ma voiture est tombée en panne!" ie My son sent me word of his win yesterday. Unfortunately, I was not able to see it on the television: returning home, my car broke down.

Laisser dire

This means to let someone talk. You will hear it in remarks such as:

- "**Laisse dire**!" ie Let them talk, never mind what they say!

C'est pas pour dire

You can use this expression when you want to say something along the lines of "Well, it is not for me to say, but…" For example:

- "**C'est pas pour dire** mais j'ai bien réussi ce curry, mon vieux!" ie Perhaps I should not say so, but I have made a pretty good job of this curry, mate!

On the other hand, you can complain using this expression, too:

- "**C'est pas pour dire** mais elle aurait pu me dire qu'elle allait inviter Miriam. Elle sait pertinemment que nous ne nous entendons pas bien" ie It is not for me to say but she could have told me that she was going to invite Miriam. She knows perfectly well that we do not get on with each other.

Il n'y a pas à dire

This expression means that there is "no getting away from" something, that there is no doubt about it. For example:

- "**Il n'y a pas à dire** – la cuisine Londonienne est de nos jours supérieure à la cuisine Parisienne" ie There is no doubt about it - the standard of cooking in London nowadays is better than in Paris.

Locutions featuring dire

Quite the most useful of these, in my view, is **comment dirais-je**? which means "how shall I put it?" Every time you feel you are getting stuck for the right word (indeed any word!), slip in a **comment dirais-je**? It slows things down and gives you a bit of thinking space. Very often, your interlocuteur will take this as an opportunity to provide the word that you are looking for:

- "J'aime beaucoup Jasmine mais elle est parfois, **comment dirais-je**?..."
  "Cancanière?"
  "Cancanière, tout à fait! C'est le mot juste!" ie
  I like Jasmine a lot but sometimes she is a bit, how shall I put it?
  Gossipy?
  Gossipy, absolutely! That is the right word!

Then there is **dis-donc**. This seems to crop up in all sorts of arbitrary contexts but is usefully employed to introduce a question:

- "**Dis-donc**, est-ce qu'on peut trouver un bus dans les parages de Saint Mandé?" ie Tell me, can one find a bus going to Saint Mandé in these parts?

A slightly different application is illustrated in this example which is said with more than a bit of irony:

- "**Dis-donc**, ne te gêne pas!" ie Well, don't mind me!

And here is another example:

- "C'est joli, **dis-donc**!" ie By the way, isn't that pretty!

Here are some other **dire** locutions:

Comme on dit means "as they say" or "so to speak". It works like **pour ainsi dire** that we met earlier – **quoi** even!
C'est moi qui vous le dis means "take my word for it."
C'est vous qui le dites means "that is what **you** say!"
C'est peu dit means "that is an understatement."
À qui le dites-vous! means "don't I know it", or "you're telling me!"
C'est à dire means "that's to say".
C'est le moins qu'on puisse dire is an expression you have already encountered. Note the use of the subjunctive after "le moins". We noted in an earlier chapter that the subjunctive is employed with the **superlative**, ie **the best**. But is also used when talking about the **worst** or the **least**.

Pronominal dire

Se dire can mean to say to **oneself**:

- "**Je me suis dis** que je dois rendre visite à mon oncle. Il est tout seul depuis la disparition de sa femme. Il doit se sentir seul" ie I said to myself that I must visit my uncle. With the death of his wife, he is all alone. He must feel lonely.

(Incidentally, **se sentir** means to feel something emotionally, whereas **sentir** means to feel something physically, eg:

- "J'ai senti une main sur mon épaule" ie I felt a hand on my shoulder)

Se dire can also be used when **claiming** to be someone or something:

- "**Il se dit** le fils d'un aristo mais, franchement il est un peu gâteux!" ie He claims to be the son of an aristocrat but frankly, he is a bit soft in the head! By the way, the French love to abbreviate ("abréger", remember?), especially words that can, therefore, end in an "o" like "aristo". Here are just a few of the many examples that abound:

  un écolo　　　　-　　　an ecologist

un collabo	-	a collaborist (in World War II)
un maso	-	a masochist
un toxico	-	a drug addict
un mégalo	-	a megalomaniac
un intello	-	an intellectual
un facho	-	a facist
un invalo	-	an invalid
le/la proprio	-	the landlord/landlady
un gaucho	-	someone politically left-wing

Se dire can also substitute for **se croire**. For example:

- "Avec ce beau temps, on se dirait en Angleterre, vous savez!" ie With this beautiful weather, you would think we were in England! I often say this to the "marchands de fruits et légumes" ie the fruit and vegetable merchants in the markets.
Say it loudly when there are crowds in the market. I guarantee a very lively response! And finally…

Ça ne se dit pas means "it is not polite to say that", or…
Ça se dit en français? means "is that how you say it in French?" or…
Ça se dit de la même façon en anglais et en français means that it is the same in English and in French.

<u>Conclusion</u>

We have covered more than enough ground in this chapter. **Dire**, to say or to tell, has many useful applications in French. Beyond using it in its most basic form to say something or to say something to somebody, or to tell somebody something, it can be used where we, in English, might use different verbs altogether: to please, to think, to assume, to decide, to admit, to remind and to show were some that we looked at.

But some of its locutions are also very useful indeed to know. **Comment dirais-je** is a stand-out example.

And we also saw that **se dire** can be used in several useful ways.

For these reasons, and more, **dire** is a verb that you must get to know. It is a true "killer" verb. But unlike a lot of them, it has very few idiomatic applications. This should make it just that bit easier to master.

Dire: Conversation One

Maryse is once more in the streets of Paris. This time she is stopping people to ask them what common signs and abbreviations actually mean.

Maryse:	Bonjour, monsieur. Dites-moi, si vous voyez dans une boucherie une pancarte avec les mots "en réclame", qu'est-ce que ça veut dire?
Homme:	Eh bien, c'est simple. Ça veut dire tout simplement que la viande est vendue temporairement moins chère. Par exemple, le prix normal, disons 10 euros du kilo, est exceptionnellement pour la réclame, 8 euros du kilo.
Maryse:	Et si dans un restaurant la note qu'on vous donne se dit TTC, qu'est-ce que cela veut dire?
Homme:	TTC? Ca veut dire Toutes Taxes Comprises. Ça signifie, je crois, corrigez-moi si je me trompe, que le service, et tout ce qui va avec, est compris.
Maryse:	Et si, dans une vitrine, vous voyez "rabais de 20% sur du blanc", qu'est-ce que ça veut dire?
Homme:	Alors, ça veut dire qu'il y a, pour le moment, une remise sur les draps et le linge de maison en général, et tout le monde peut acheter ses blancs à cette période-là à un prix réduit.
Maryse:	Et quand on voit dans les vitrines "sans RDV", qu'est-ce que cela veut dire?
Homme:	Quand on voit "sans RDV", cela veut dire qu'il n'est pas nécessaire d'avoir rendez-vous à une heure précise. Ça arrive de nos jours chez certaines coiffeuses. En effet, parfois on ne peut pas prendre rendez-vous ni chez la coiffeuse, ni chez le dentiste par exemple.
Maryse:	Et ça vous plaît d'y aller sans RDV?
Homme:	Oh! Pas forcément. Ça dépend. Mais si cela veut dire qu'on peut se faire couper les cheveux "sur le champ", pour ainsi dire, tant mieux. D'autre part, s'il faut attendre longtemps c'est pas toujours très agréable, vous savez.
Maryse:	Je comprends, monsieur. Merci bien.
Homme:	De rien, madame. Au revoir.

Dire: Conversation Two

Maryse and François have invited two good friends, Alain and Simone, to dinner at their apartment. The meal has been a huge success and they have now all moved into the lounge for some "digestives".

Simone:	C'était un vrai régal, Maryse. Mais à vrai dire je ne connais pas la façon dont tu as réussi tes jarrets de veau. Est-ce qu'il y a un petit secret, peut-être?
Maryse:	Non, pas forcément, Simone. C'est une recette q'un chef du coin m'a donnée. Mais, François, doucement avec le calva, tu vas être complètement paf!
François:	Arrête de dire des bêtises, Maryse. D'ailleurs, j'aime un petit pousse-café de temps en temps.
Maryse:	D'accord, mais ne bois pas cul sec.
Alain:	C'est pas pour dire, Maryse, mais après un tel repas un verre ou deux de calva est très agréable.
François:	Et que diriez-vous d'un bon armagnac? J'en ai un très vieux dans le bahut.
Alain:	Non, merci, François. J'ai déjà bien bu.
Simone:	Parlons d'autre choses. On dit que le dernier film de Max Delonne est un vrai navet. Tu l'as vu, Maryse?
Maryse:	Non. Franchement je suis pas très Delonne. Je le trouve, comment dirais-je…?
Alain:	Plutôt laid, peut-être?
Simone:	Ça va sans dire qu'il n'est pas beau, je suis d'accord, mais il a un certain charme quand même.
Alain:	Est-ce que tu l'as vu dans "Les Enfants des bidonvilles"
François:	"Les Enfants des bidonvilles?" Ce film me dit quelque chose mais de quoi s'agit-il au juste?
Maryse:	Ah, oui, ce film est passé à la télé récemment. Et dire que j'aurais pu le louper! C'était incroyable, c'est le meilleur film dans lequel j'aie jamais vu Delonne.
Simone:	Oui, tu as raison, Maryse – et ça me fait penser à "La Haine" tu sais.
François:	"La Haine" était un vrai film noir, très sombre, très… comment dirais-je…?
Alain:	Très déprimant, François?
François:	Oui, trop déprimant à mon goût. Moi, je suis très comédie musicale. Quand je sors, quand je vais au cinéma, j'aime m'amuser, j'aime rire.
Maryse:	Il n'y a pas à dire. Le gros problème, c'est qu'il y a très peu de comédies musicales françaises en salle en ce moment.

Simone:	Et "Le Pianiste?"
Maryse:	Oui, mais depuis... quoi? "Le Pianiste" passait il y a quelques années. En ce moment tous les films que, moi, je voudrais voir sont soit américains, soit anglais. Et je n'aime pas trop les films en v.o. J'ai toujours du mal à lire les sous-titres.
Simone:	Oui, je partage ton avis à cent pour cent, Maryse. Et souvent, tu sais, les sous-titres n'ont rien à voir avec la bande sonore. Mais regarde l'heure, Alain. Inutile de te le dire, il se fait tard. Ma montre dit onze heures trente mais je crois qu'elle a cinq minutes de retard. Il ne faut pas que nous loupions le dernier bus, vas-y, Alain!
Alain:	Mais, oui chérie.
Maryse:	Mais que diriez vous d'une soireé cinéma la semaine prochaine? Apparemment, le dernier film de George Clooney va sortir la semaine prochaine.
Simone:	Oh là, là! George Clooney. Même en v.o., qu'est-ce qu'il est beau, lui!

Some words you might not yet know

- une pancarte - a sign
- en réclame - at a reduced price
- temporairement - temporarily
- exceptionnellement - exceptionally
- corrigez-moi si je me trompe - correct me if I am mistaken
- compris(e) - included
- un rabais - a discount
- les blancs (m) - white goods (sheets, etc) for the household
- une remise - a reduction
- le linge - household linen
- précis(e) - precise/exact
- parfois - sometimes
- ni... ni - neither... nor
- sur le champ - on the spot
- doucement - go carefully
- le calva - calvados
- paf (fam) - drunk
- les bêtises (f) - nonsense
- d'ailleurs - besides
- un pousse-café - a mixture of alcohol and coffee taken after a meal
- boire cul sec - to down a drink in one
- le dernier film - the latest film
- laid(e) - ugly
- un bidonville - a shanty town
- noir(e) - black
- sombre - dark
- déprimant(e) - depressing
- une comédie musicale - a musical comedy
- soit... soit - either... or
- et? - (here) and what about?
- v.o. - "version originale" ie a film shown in its original language
- un sous-titre - a sub-title
- une bande sonore - a sound-track
- il se fait tard - it's getting late
- de retard - slow
- louper - to miss

261

Dire: Exercises

Complete the blank spaces:

1.   Qu'est-ce que tu as (   )?

2.   Il faut que je te (   ).

3.   (   ) – moi, où allons-nous?

4.   Je ne sais plus quoi (   ).

5.   Comment ça se (   ) en français?

6.   Il va sans (   ) que Paris est une ville très chère.

7.   Comme on (   ) en Angleterre – cheers!

8.   Il faut bien (   ) que je ne suis pas très chocolat.

9.   Quelle heure est-il? Ma montre (   ) neuf heures.

Choose one of the three words in brackets and put it in the space in each sentence:

10.   Rien ne me (   ) ce soir. Je n'ai pas faim. (disons, dites, dit)

11.   Je n'ai rien à (   ). C'était ma faute. (dire, dit, disais)

12.   Qu'est-ce que cela veut (   )? (dire, dites, aurait dit)

13.   Qu'est-ce que vous (   ) de mes chaussures? (dire, dites, disons)

14.   Boui-boui? Le mot me (   ) quelque chose, mais c'est quoi au juste? (dire, diriez, dit)

15.   Ma fille m'a fait (   ) sa réussite. (dit, dire, dis)

16.   C'est pas pour (   ), mais je ne suis pas mal du tout au tennis. (dire, dise, dit)

Translate the underlined part of each English sentence into French:

17. There is no doubt about it: England are useless at football.

18. I like Bruno a lot but, how shall I put it, he is a bit mean.

19. He is a bit on the fat side, so to speak.

20. He claims to be intelligent, but I am not so sure.

21. She is very beautiful – that is the least one can say.

Dire: Answers

1. dit
2. dise
3. Dis / Dites
4. dire
5. dit
6. dire
7. dit
8. dire
9. dit
10. dit
11. dire
12. dire
13. dites
14. dit
15. dire, dit, dis
16. dire
17. Il n'y a pas à dire
18. comment dirais-je?
19. pour ainsi dire
20. Il se dit
21. C'est le moins qu'on puisse dire.

Chapter Thirteen
Payer

Introduction

Payer, like **passer**, is another of those "tin" verbs: what you see is what you get. It means either **to pay**, as in to pay the price, or **to pay for**, as in to pay for a car, say. It is also a pronominal verb, **se payer**, meaning to pay for oneself. It has relatively few locutions and very few idiomatic uses. So this chapter will be quite short. Short but important. **Payer** is a genuine "killer" verb; you will be able to use it almost every day. So let's begin by seeing how this regular "…er" verb is conjugated.

The Payer Conjugations*

Present Tense

Je paye	Nous payons
Tu payes	Vous payez
Il paye	Ils payent
Elle paye	Elles payent

Future Tense

Je payerai	Nous payerons
Tu payeras	Vous payerez
Il payera	Ils payeront
Elle payera	Elles payeront

Imperfect Tense

Je payais	Nous payions
Tu payais	Vous payiez
Il payait	Ils payaient
Elle payait	Elles payaient

Perfect Tense

J'ai payé	Nous avons payé
Tu as payé	Vous avez payé
Il a payé	Ils ont payé
Elle a payé	Elles ont payé

Future Perfect Tense

J'aurai payé	Nous aurons payé
Tu auras payé	Vous aurez payé
Il aura payé	Ils auront payé
Elle aura payé	Elles auront payé

Pluperfect Tense

J'avais payé	Nous avions payé
Tu avais payé	Vous aviez payé
Il avait payé	Ils avaient payé
Elle avait payé	Elles avaient payé

Present Conditional Tense

Je payerais	Nous payerions
Tu payerais	Vous payeriez
Il payerait	Ils payeraient
Elle payerait	Elles payeraient

Past Conditional Tense

J'aurais payé	Nous aurions payé
Tu aurais payé	Vous auriez payé
Il aurait payé	Ils auraient payé
Elle aurait payé	Elles auraient payé

Present Subjunctive Tense

Je paye	Nous payions
Tu payes	Vous payiez
Il paye	Ils payent
Elle paye	Elles payent

Imperative

Paye
Payons
Payez

*Note that there are two different ways of conjugating this verb. The alternative is "je paie, tu paies…" etc, but I hav not used this conjugation in the chapter.

Payer: The Basics

Basically, **payer** means either **to pay** or **to pay for**.

In its role of "pay", the verb is most frequently used to say how you will pay or settle ("régler") a bill. For instance, you might wish to pay your bill:

payer comptant - to pay cash.
payer en espèces - also to pay by cash.
payer rubis sur l'ongle - to pay cash on the nail ("rubis" is a reference to ruby-coloured wine).
payer en chèque - to pay by cheque.
payer par carte (de crédit) – to pay by credit card.
payer par carte bancaire – to pay using your bank card, ie your debit card.
payer en plusieurs versements – to pay by instalments.
payer en versements mensuels – to pay by monthly instalments.
payer en versements annuels – to pay by annual instalments.
payer en crédit – to pay by credit.
payer en nature – to pay by kind.

When it comes to someone paying you, you might wish to be paid in any of the ways outlined above. Additionally, you might be paid:

à l'heure – by the hour.
à la pièce – by piece work.
pour tes déplacements – to be re-paid your travel expenses.

You might also get paid holidays and many state benefits:

prendre quatre semaines de congés payés – to take four weeks of paid holidays (Incidentally, France was the first country in the world to give workers paid holidays. The "Front Populaire" government led by Léon Blum first gave two weeks paid holidays in 1936).

Now let us turn "to pay for", ie to purchase goods and services. Here it is important to realise that in English we talk about paying **for** something or other:

- "I paid a lot of money for my new car", for example. In French this sentence - is translated as:

"J'ai payé très cher ma nouvelle voiture." Immediately you can see that "for" is not translated in the French sentence, simply because **payer** means to **pay for**. Similarly:

"Ma femme a payé très peu cher sa nouvelle robe" ie My wife paid very little for her new dress.

(Incidentally, very often in English we use the word **new** in one of two ways. We talk about something that is new to us but is, in fact, second-hand. Cars are a good example:

- "I have just bought a new car." This might well be a second-hand car that is **new to me**. In French, this translates as "Je viens d'acheter **une nouvelle voiture**." A second-hand car is **une occasion**. If you want to specify that your new car is actually **brand new**, you will need to say:
- "Je viens d'acheter une voiture **toute neuve**".)

Summary

And that is it really. At this basic level use **payer** to say:

- how you would like to pay for something
- how to be paid for something you might do for somebody, and
- that you are paying for something.

Getting Better

In a bar you might want to offer to buy a round of drinks, say. We can use **payer** here.

You might want to say that you have paid a price for something you have done in the past, say. **Payer** is the verb to use in such circumstances.

You might also want to talk about something you have done having paid off. Again, **payer** is the appropriate verb.

Let us look at each of these situations in turn:

- "The drinks are on me!" Should you want to say something along these lines, use:
  Payer à boire à quelqu'un – for example:
  "Cette fois-ci, je vais **payer à boire à tout le monde**" ie This time, everyone's drinks are on me. Alternatively:

  "C'est moi qui **paye à boire**".

In the second situation, you might want to say that you have paid the price for some impetuosity or imprudence in your past life:

- "Je n'avais que vingt ans quand je me suis marié avec Marie, mais je ne me suis pas rendu compte que **je payerais** cher mon imprudence" ie I was only 20 years old when I married Marie, but I did not realise that I would pay dearly for my impetuosity. Or:
- "Il fumait deux paquets de cigarettes par jour, mais **il l'a payé** de sa santé" ie He used to smoke two packets of cigarettes a day, but he paid for it with his health.

On the other hand, something you are doing or perhaps have done might have paid off:

- "Mon succès au rugby **me paye** de tous mes efforts" ie My success at rugby makes all my hard work worthwhile.

<u>Now You Are Really Speaking French!</u>

Payer has meanings other than those that we have already encountered. For example, you can use it to talk about making sacrifices or to talk about pulling your weight and to say that something does not look very nice. Then there is the pronominal form, **se payer**, which you can use when you want to talk about treating yourself. Here are some examples of each of these uses of **payer** in action.

Making sacrifices / Pulling your weight

- "Notre P.D.G. nous a dit aujourd'hui que pour que notre entreprise devienne une complète réussite il faut que **chacun paye de sa personne**" ie Our Managing Director told us today that if our company is to be completely successful, each and everyone of us must pull our weight.

Not looking nice

- "La maison que tu voudrais acheter: à mon sens **elle ne paye pas de mine**" ie The house that you would like to buy: in my opinion it is not much to look at.
  Or:

- "L'entrée que tu as commandée **ne paye pas de mine**" ie The starter that you have ordered does not really look very appetising.

Se payer

You can use **se payer** when you want to talk about treating yourself. For example:

- "J'ai gagné le gros lot cet-aprèm. **On va se payer** un bon dîner dans un palace parisien ce soir" ie I hit the jack-pot this afternoon. We are going to treat ourselves to a slap up dinner at one of Paris' best restaurants tonight. Paris' great **hotel** restaurants such as The Ritz, Le George V, Le Meurice, Le Crillon and so on are referred to as "palaces", to be distinguished from other 3-star Michelin restaurants such as Ledoyen, Guy Savoy or Pierre Gagnaire, for example.

But there are other uses of **se payer**, too:

Se payer une pinte de bon sang means to have a good laugh.
Se payer la tête de quelqu'un means to make fun of someone.
Se payer une bonne grippe means to catch a bad dose of the flu.
Se payer une crève carabinée means much the same thing.
Se payer un arbre means to wrap your car around a tree.
Se payer une bonne tranche means to have a good time.
Se payer du bon temps means to have a wicked or a mental time.
Se payer quelqu'un means to beat someone up.

Finally, here are a couple of idiomatic expressions that feature **payer**:

Payer en monnaie de singe means to pay someone with beautiful words and facial expressions rather than to pay with real money.

And here is the only proverb I know:

Qui paye ses dettes s'enrichit which means, as you have probably worked out, literally: he who pays his debts enriches himself. However, the enrichment is a psychological rather than pecuniary enrichment. Once one's debts are paid off, one feels altogether more contented.

And that's it!

Conclusion

There is not much to **payer** really. The basics are the most important: how to pay someone and how to get paid by someone; to pay for something, in other words to buy something; and how you might pay a price in a non-monetary sense for something you might do or have done. **Se payer** has a few idiomatic uses but not many. It is an easy verb to conjugate and to use. But like all our "killer" verbs it is a very important and useful one to find your way around. So use it!

Conversation

Maryse and François are considering having their bathroom re-furbished. Currently they have a bath, but they would prefer a shower. They would also like a heated towel rail and new tiles. So they have asked someone around to discuss the possibilities and to ask for an estimate.

François:	Voici la salle de bain dont nous parlions au téléphone la semaine dernière. Comme je vous ai dit, nous voudrions une douche au lieu de la baignoire, un sèche-serviette au mur à côté, et de nouveaux carreaux sur les murs et sur le sol.
L'artisan:	Je comprends. Évidement, je dois commencer avec toutes les dimensions de la salle de bain et puis nous pouvons discuter les autres aspects des travaux.
Maryse:	D'accord. Faites ce qu'il vous faut. Voudriez-vous prendre un café, peut-être?
L'artisan:	C'est génial. Merci bien.

Fifteen minutes later:

	Ça y'est. J'ai pris toutes les mesures de la salle de bain. Je peux donc vous donner un devis pour la main-d'oeuvre. Après, c'est à vous de choisir la douche, le carrelage et cetera.
François:	Et combien de temps estimez – vous pour faire les travaux, grosso modo?
L'artisan:	Je ne peux pas vous donner le temps exact, bien-sûr, mais mettons une semaine si mon fils peut m'aider. Tout seul, deux semaines à peu pres. Je sais qu'il est libre début mars. Nous pourrions la faire mettons la première semaine de mars, si cela vous convient?
Maryse:	Oui, en principe, ça nous convient. Mais ça dépend de votre devis, ça va sans dire!
L'artisan:	Mais bien-sûr, madame.
François:	Bon. Mais puis-je vous parler d'un sujet délicat: comment voudriez vous que nous vous payions? Si vous avez l'intention de nous facturer, il faudra, évidement, que nous payions la T.V.A. Par contre, nous pourrions vous payer comptant, en espèces, quoi.
L'artisan:	Oui, tout à fait. L'idée de payer moins de taxe me plaît énormément, à mon fils aussi! Mais je suis une P.M.E., vous savez, et franchement il serait prudent de passer quelque chose au crédit de mon compte bancaire. Si vous deviez me payer moitié-moitié, c'est à dire cinquante pour cent en chèque, cinquante pour cent en espèces, et puis je pourrais vous offrir une réduction de dix pour cent sur la

main-d'oeuvre. Et si vous me précisez tous les materiaux dont vous avez besoin, je peux les acheter chez Casto en utilisant ma carte de fidélité. Ça va?

François:	Oui, ça va!
L'artisan:	Nous sommes d'accord, alors! Je ferai mes calculs cette semaine et vous pouvez attendre mon devis ce week-end.
Maryse:	Excellent, monsieur...?
L'artisan:	Monsieur Duval. Mais tous mes potes m'appelent Johnny!
François:	C'est Johnny, alors! Nous attendons votre devis avec impatience, Johnny. Et à bientôt.
Johny:	En effet. À bientôt. Et merci pour le café, madame...?
Maryse:	Johnny, je m'appelle, Maryse – ça va? Et mon mari s'appelle François.
Johny:	Nous avons fait des progrés ce soir, n'est-ce pas?
François:	Tout à fait, Johnny. Au revoir et à bientôt!

Some words you might not yet know

• la salle de bain -	the bathroom
• une douche -	a shower
• une baignoire -	a bath
• un sèche-serviette -	a heated towel rail
• les carreaux(m) -	tiles
• le sol -	the floor
• les travaux (m) -	the work(s)
• ça y est -	that's it/that's done
• les mesures (f) -	the measurements
• un devis -	an estimate
• la main d'oeuvre -	the labour
• le carrelage -	(also) the tiles
• facturer -	to bill s.o.
• la T.V.A. -	la taxe sur la valeur ajoutée, ie the VAT
• une P.M.E. -	une petite ou moyenne enterprise (an S.M.E.)
• moitié-moitié -	half-and-half
• les matériaux (m) -	the materials
• une carte de fidélité -	a loyalty card
• attendre quelque chose avec impatience -	to look forward to something

Payer: Exercises

Complete the blank spaces:

1.   Combien avez-vous (   )?

2.   J'ai (   ) ce costume très peu cher.

3.   Il faut que vous me (   ) cette brouette trente euros.

4.   (   ) – moi immédiatement!

Translate into English the underlined parts of the following sentences:

5.   Cette fois-ci, <u>c'est moi qui paie à boire.</u>

6.   Il buvait deux bouteilles de vodka par jour mais <u>il a payé de sa vie.</u>

7.   Son succès à la fac <u>se paie de tous ses efforts.</u>

8.   L'entrecôte que tu as commandée <u>ne paie pas de mine.</u>

9.   <u>Tu vas te payer</u> une jolie robe aujourd'hui, chérie.

10.   Il n'avait pas un sou. Donc, <u>il m'a payé en monnaie de singe.</u>

Payer: Answers

1. payé
2. payé
3. payiez
4. Paye / Payez
5. the drinks are on me
6. he paid with his life
7. makes all his/her success worthwhile
8. does not look very appetising
9. You are going to treat yourself
10. he paid me with beautiful words.

Chapter Fourteen
Penser

Introduction

Penser, to think, is bound to be a very important French verb if only because it is a very important English verb! For example, whenever someone asks us for an opinion, chances are we will begin by saying "Well, I think that…" We all have opinions, lots of them, and this is how we will probably express them. But we also think about people and things without necessarily expressing an opinion: "I was thinking… Shall we go to the cinema tonight?"

So it is in French. When we think about people and things we will use **penser à**; and if we are expressing opinions, we will use **penser de**. But we can also think in the abstract. There is no better example of this in any language, I suspect, than Descartes' famous dictum:

"**Je pense**; **donc je suis**" ie I think; therefore I am. So there are both profound philosophical and practical reasons for getting to know **penser**. So let us begin by conjugating it.

The Penser Conjugations

Present Tense

Je pense	Nous pensons
Tu penses	Vous pensez
Il pense	Ils pensent
Elle pense	Elles pensent

Future Tense

Je penserai	Nous penserons
Tu penseras	Vous penserez
Il pensera	Ils penseront
Elle pensera	Elles penseront

Imperfect Tense

Je pensais	Nous pensions
Tu pensais	Vous pensiez
Il pensait	Ils pensaient
Elle pensait	Elles pensaient

Perfect Tense

J'ai pensé	Nous avons pensé
Tu as pensé	Vous avez pensé
Il a pensé	Ils ont pensé
Elle a pensé	Elles ont pensé

Future Perfect Tense

J'aurai pensé	Nous aurons pensé
Tu auras pensé	Vous aurez pensé
Il aura pensé	Ils auront pensé
Elle aura pensé	Elles auront pensé

Pluperfect Tense

J'avais pensé	Nous avions pensé
Tu avais pensé	Vous aviez pensé
Il avait pensé	Ils avaient pensé
Elle avait pensé	Elles avaient pensé

Present Conditional Tense

Je penserais	Nous penserions
Tu penserais	Vous penseriez
Il penserait	Ils penseraient
Elle penserait	Elles penseraient

Past Conditional Tense

J'aurais pensé	Nous aurions pensé
Tu aurais pensé	Vous auriez pensé
Il aurait pensé	Ils auraient pensé
Elle aurait pensé	Elles auraient pensé

Present Subjunctive Tense

Je pense	Nous pensions
Tu penses	Vous pensiez
Ils pense	Ils pensent
Elles pense	Elles pensent

Imperative

Pense
Pensons
Pensez

Penser: The Basics

Use **penser** to say that you are thinking and **penser à** to say that you are thinking about something or someone. For example:

- "**Tu penses** maman. **À quoi penses-tu**? ie You are thinking, mummy. What are you thinking about?

Whatever your mother is thinking, you might be thinking about, say, your holidays:

- "Moi, **je pense à** nos vacances" But, perhaps you are thinking about others, perhaps those less fortunate than yourself:
- "Tu sais, **je pense à** tout le monde, surtout aux malheureux – les sans-abri par exemple" ie I think about everybody, above all the unhappy – the homeless, for example.

In these three examples you can see that we are using **penser à quelque chose ou à quelqu'un**. Here are some more examples of this construction in action:

- "**Je pensais à** l'anniversaire de ma mère quand le courrier est arrivé?" ie I was thinking about my mother's birthday when the post arrived.
- "Il a vu **à qui je pensais** quand je lui ai donné son cadeau!" ie He saw who I was thinking about when I gave him his present!
- "Si j'avais su qu'elle était malheureuse, **j'aurais pensé à** lui acheter un bouquet de fleurs" ie If I had known that she was unhappy, I would have thought about buying her a bunch of flowers.

And here is an example using the imperative:

- "**Pensez** donc **à** ce que vous dites" ie Think, therefore, about what you are saying.

And do not forget that when you use **penser** in the negative, you may well need the following verb in the subjunctive:

- "**Je ne pense pas** que "belle" **soit** le mot juste" ie I do not think that "beautiful" is the right word.

Use **penser de** to say that you are thinking about ie that you have an opinion about someone or something. For example:

- "Qu'est-ce que **tu penses de** ce costume, chérie? Est-il un peu froissé?" ie What do you think of this suit, darling? Is it a bit crumpled?
- "Qu'est-ce que **vous avez pensé du** film "La Haine?" Était-il trop pessimiste?" ie What did you think of the film "La Haine? Was it too pessimistic?
- "Que **penseriez-vous d**'un week-end à Londres? On dit que l'Eurostar est très raisonnable en ce moment" ie What would you say (think) about a weekend in London? Apparently, the Eurostar is very reasonable at the moment.

However, **penser** need have no indirect object at all. Very often indeed, **penser** might be followed instead by **que**: **je pense que**… Here are some examples:

- "**Je pense que** Stephen Hawking est incroyablement intelligent. Il est l'un des grands libre penseurs de notre âge" ie I think that Stephen Hawking is incredibly intelligent. He is one of the great free thinkers of our age.
- "Quand **je pense qu'il** neigeait quand nous sommes partis d'Edimbourg!" ie And to think that it was snowing when we left Edinburgh!
- "**Pensez qu'**elle est encore si belle à soixante ans!" ie And to think that she is still so beautiful at sixty years of age!
- "Faire ses devoirs? **Il ne pense qu'à** jouer au foot!" ie Do his homework? All he thinks about is playing football!

Sometimes, too, **penser** can be followed by another verb in the **infinitive**. For example:

- "Ma fille et mon gendre, **ils pensent avoir** trouvé un bel appartement à New York" ie My daughter and my son-in-law think they have found a beautiful apartment in New York.

- "Quand j'ai entendu le tremblement de terre, **je pensais mourir**!" ie When I heard the earthquake, I thought I was going to die!

And in these next two examples, **penser** is used in the sense of having the intention to do something:

- "**Ils pensaient partir** la semaine prochaine mais Anne est tombée malade" ie They intended leaving next week but then Anne fell ill.
- "S'il fait beau demain, **elle pense arriver** vers dix-huit heures" ie If it is fine tomorrow, she is hoping to arrive around six o'clock.

Finally (and this really **is** basic!) it is quite possible to follow **penser** with – nothing!:

- "**Qu'est-ce que tu penses**?" or "**Que penses-tu**?" ie What do you think? What do you reckon?

The beguiling simplicity of this construction masks the fact that one cannot think and leave it at that. There has to be an object of one's thoughts, even if it is not stated:

- "Que **penses-tu** (de quelque chose)?"

Summary

Penser is yet another hugely important "killer" verb. Use it to say:

- that you are thinking of someone or something (**penser à**…)
- that you have an opinion about something (**penser de**…)
- use it also when you follow it with "que"; with a verb in the infinitive or indeed with nothing at all!

Getting Better

Because **penser** is often followed by **à** or by **de**, it follows that the clauses beginning with **à** or **de can be replaced by y** or **en**. To illustrate, you will recall in the **Aller** chapter that instead of saying:

- "Je vais **à Londres**" you can say "J'**y** vais" Here, **y** replaces "**à** Londres."

In this following exchange, **en** can substitute for **de**:

- "Je voudrais **de** belles tomates, s'il vous plait"
  "Oui, madame. Combien **en** voulez-vous?" ie
  I would like some nice tomatoes, please.
  Yes, madam. How many (of them) would you like?

The rules apply to **penser**, too. To illustrate; first with **penser à** and **y**:

- "Il a dit "merde" sans **y penser**" ie He said "shit" without thinking (about it).
- "Je sais que tu aimes cette chemise à carreaux, chérie, mais **penses-y** avant de l'acheter" ie I know that you like this checked shirt, darling, but think it over before buying it.
- "Tu m'as engueulé, je sais, mais **n'y pensons plus**" ie I know that you gave me a bit of a dressing down, but let us forget it.
- "Mais **j'y pense** – c'est demain l'anniversaire de ma mère!" ie I have just remembered – tomorrow is my mother's birthday!

Now here are some examples using **en** and **penser de** constructions:

- "Qu'est-ce que **tu penses de** cette soupe aux asperges? Vraiment, **qu'en penses-tu**?" ie What do you think of this asparagus soup? Really, what do you think of it?
- "Le film qu'on a vu ce soir? Franchement, il est difficile de savoir ce que **j'en ai pensé**" ie The film that we saw this evening? Frankly, it is difficult to know what I thought of it.
- "Je ne dis rien, mais **je n'en pense pas** moins!" ie I am not saying anything, but that does not mean that I do not have an opinion (on it)!

Penser also has meanings beyond thinking. You can use it to suppose, to dream, to believe, to expect or to imagine, for example. Here are some illustrations:

- "Roger m'a dit hier qu'il passerait aujourd'hui. **Pensez-vous** qu'il viendra?" ie Roger told me yesterday that he would pass-by today. Do you suppose/believe/expect/imagine that he will come?
- "**Je n'aurais jamais pensé** qu'il dirait cela. Je l'ai toujours pris pour un gentleman" ie I would never have thought/believed/imagined/ dreamt that he would say that. I have always taken him for a gentleman.

And do not forget **faire penser** that you met in an earlier chapter. This construction can mean to remind:

- "La photo de Paul sur le chambranle: est-ce que cela **vous fait penser à** quelque chose?" ie The photograph of Paul on the mantelpiece: does that remind you of something?

Finally here, **penser** can also mean to think something out or through. For example:

- "Ce projet de loi, c'est vraiment bien **pensé**" ie This (parliamentary) bill is really very well thought through.

So you can see from all this that **penser**, like a lot of our other "killer" verbs, is very flexible and versatile. But perhaps of all its related meanings, **penser** is most frequently used where perhaps **croire** or **réfléchir** might be more appropriate.

In practice, **penser** and **croire** are used highly interchangeably, but **croire** is really stronger than **penser**. It means to **believe** (or at least to **assume**):

- "Est-ce qu'il y a une station-service dans cette ville?"
  "**Je ne pense pas** mais **je crois qu**'il y en a à la périphérie" ie
  Is there a petrol station in this town?
  I do not think so, but I believe there is one on the outskirts.

Réfléchir is slightly different again in that it is used when one wants to think **hard** about something ie give something your full consideration:

- "Vous m'avez dit tout à l'heure que vous aimez ce mobile, madame. Voulez-vous que je l'emballe pour vous?"
  "Non, attendez un instant. Il faut que **j'y réfléchisse**" ie
  You told me just now that you like this mobile telephone, madame. Would you like me to wrap it up for you?
  No, wait a moment. I really have to think about it.

Now You Are Really Speaking French!

This section is, of necessity, quite short – simply because **penser** figures very little in the figurative realm of the French language. I know of only one proverb, of a few locutions – and of one or two rather vulgar allusions that depend on **penser**. So first, the proverb:

- **Honni soit qui mal y pense** is a heraldic dictum that dates from the period of Edward III of England. The story goes that his then mistress, the Countess of Salisbury, dropped her garter ("sa jarretière") during a ball at court. When the King went to pick it up to give it back to her, the courtiers expressed vocal surprise. Whereupon he cried out: "Honni soit qui mal y pense!" which, translated, means: "Evil be to him who evil thinks".

Now the locutions:

- "Il vient? **Pensez-vous**!" means "Is he coming? Is he heck as like!"
- "**Il ne pense** qu'à ca!" means "He has got a one-track mind!"
- "**Tu penses** que je vais lui dire!" means "You bet I will tell him!"

And finally the vulgar ones!

- **Ce que je pense** is a euphemism for "crap", "shit", "you know what":
- "Zut alors, j'ai marché dans **ce que je pense**!" ie Dammit, I have just stepped into a load of you know what!
- **Où je pense** is a reference to the anus. In English you might say: "That book of yours – you can shove it where the sun doesn't shine! In French, that is best rendered as:
  "Ton bouquin, tu peux le foutre **où je pense**!"

Conclusion

Another "killer" verb out of the way. Like all the others, **penser** is very important because you will hear it every day and chances are that you will use it every day to say:

- what you think of, think about and just think!
- what you suppose, believe, imaging, dream… and so on.

So that is it! Now for a couple of conversations.

Penser: Conversation One

Today we find Maryse in the streets of Sarlat. Her client wants to know how people who have lived in Paris compare life there with life "en province", in the provinces.

Maryse:	Bonjour, monsieur. Êtes-vous sarladais?
Homme:	Non, je suis parisien. Je suis né à Paris. Mais j'habite Sarlat depuis dix ans.
Maryse:	Et Sarlat vous plaît?
Homme:	Oui, beaucoup.
Maryse:	Pensez-vous que la vie ici est plus agréable qu'à Paris?
Homme:	Oui, je pense que c'est beaucoup plus agréable ici en Dordogne.
Maryse:	Mais est-ce que vous pensez que la vie est moins chère ici?
Homme:	Oui, pour la plupart du temps. Le logement est beaucoup moins cher mais il y a d'autres choses qui sont, je pense, aussi chères qu'à Paris.
Maryse:	Ah bon? Par exemple?
Homme:	Je pense que la nourriture est aussi chère ici, plus chère, même – à cause du manque de grandes surfaces, vous savez. À Paris il y a tellement de concurrence entre les supermarchés, tandis qu'ici, il faut voyager un peu pour trouver les promotions.
Maryse:	Bien sûr. Vous pensez, quand même, qu'il y a des avantages à habiter en province?
Homme:	Tout à fait. Je pense que c'est beaucoup plus facile d'aller voir ses amis, on a beaucoup moins de stress, la campagne est partout et les gens sont plus chaleureux, je pense. Surtout, on a beaucoup moins de possibilités de dépenser son argent!
Maryse:	Oui! Mais une supposition. Si vous deviez choisir la ville idéale où vous pourriez habiter, quelle ville choisiriez-vous?
Homme:	Je pense que je choisirais une petite ville, comme Sarlat, près d'une plus grande ville. Ici, on est pas loin de Bordeaux, étant donné que nous avons six trains directs par jour. Bergerac n'est pas trop loin, non plus – et, bien sûr on a Brive à trente kilomètres. Donc, ma ville idéale est – Sarlat!
Maryse:	Merci bien, monsieur. Au revoir.
Homme:	De rien, madame, au revoir.

Penser: Conversation Two

Corinne is still in Sarlat. This time she stops a man who also says that he, too, has lived in Paris.

Corinne:	Vous m'avez dit toute à l'heure que bien que vous ayez habité Paris, vous préférez votre mode de vie ici en Dordogne.
Homme:	Oui. Quand j'habitais Paris, je pensais qu'elle était la plus belle ville du monde! De nos jours je crois que Sarlat est la plus belle ville du monde!
Corinne:	Vraiment!
Homme:	J'en rajoute peut être. Quand même, je pense que ma vie est beaucoup plus agréable, ici.
Corinne:	Travaillez-vous?
Homme:	Non, je suis retraité, depuis trois ans.
Corinne:	Qu'est-ce que vous faisiez dans la vie?
Homme:	J'étais chauffeur de taxi!
Corinne:	À Paris?
Homme:	À Paris même.
Corinne:	Mais le stress à part, est-ce que Paris vous manque?
Homme:	Oh là, là! Il faut que je réfléchisse… Oui, un tout petit peu. L'architecture de Paris est magnifique, bien sûr, mais Sarlat me fait penser à Paris, vous savez. Le centre de Sarlat est tellement beau.
Corinne:	Quoi d'autre?
Homme:	Oui, le sport me manque aussi. J'allais souvent voir P.S.G., pour le foot mais aussi pour le rugby.
Corinne:	Mais le rugby est excellent dans le sud-ouest de la France, n'est-ce pas?
Homme:	Pas mal. Mais la meilleure équipe de nos jours est Clermont Auvergne – et Clermont est un bout, vous savez?
Corinne:	Oui. Mais ne pensez-vous pas que Sarlat possède une bonne équipe?
Homme:	Pas mal du tout. En effet, j'y vais souvent.
Corinne:	Et la région dans laquelle Sarlat se trouve. Qu'en pensez-vous?
Homme:	La région est époustouflante, vraiment! La vallée de la Dordogne est si belle et le paysage est ravissant. J'adore les petits villages comme La Roque Gageac et la cuisine est sublime. Mais je ne pense pas que le climat soit parfait: l'hiver est triste dans les parages; il pleut beaucoup et souvent il fait très froid. Et presque tout est fermé – les restaurants, les hôtels, les magasins… et cetera. L'hiver on a beaucoup d'opportunité à réfléchir, vous savez!
Corinne:	Je suis d'accord. Quand même, les avantages sont nettement plus importants que les inconvénients, n'est-ce pas?

<u>Homme:</u>	Tout à fait. Et pour les gens comme moi – les retraités par exemple – on peut apprécier la beauté de la région. On a le temps!
<u>Corinne:</u>	Oui, mais le temps passe vite – et il faut en profiter. Quelles sont vos distractions, monsieur?
<u>Homme:</u>	J'aime peindre et j'aime le rugby, bien sûr. Pour le moment ça me suffit. Mais je crois que ma femme n'est pas aussi contente que moi à la campagne. Elle est née à Paris et Paris lui manque beaucoup. Mais nous y montons de temps en temps et nous avons gardé notre petit appartement dans le Marais. Donc, on ne peut pas se plaindre!
<u>Corinne:</u>	Je suis d'accord. Bon. Merci bien, monsieur – et bonne continuation en Dordogne!
<u>Homme:</u>	Merci bien, madame. Au revoir.

Some words you might not yet know

• sarladais(e) -	(here) someone who is born in Sarlat
• le logement -	housing
• la nourriture -	food
• un manque de -	a lack of
• les grandes surfaces (f) -	the large (often out-of-town) supermarkets
• la concurrence -	competition
• tandis que -	whereas
• partout -	everywhere
• chaleureux(se) -	welcoming
• dépenser -	to spend
• une supposition -	a supposition
• choisir -	to choose
• vous ayez habité -	the past subjunctive of habiter
• le mode de vie -	the lifestyle
• Paris même -	Paris itself
• *est-ce que Paris vous manque? -	do you miss Paris?
• époustouflant(e) -	amazing / incredible
• le paysage -	the countryside
• ravissant(e) -	ravishing
• triste -	sad
• les avantages/les inconvénients (m) -	the advantages and the disadvantages
• nettement -	clearly, decidedly
• une distraction -	a hobby/past time
• peindre -	to paint
• garder -	to keep
• un appartement -	an apartment
• se plaindre -	to complain
• bonne continuation! -	carry on enjoying yourself!

*some thoughts on manquer, to miss

Quite honestly, no French verb has ever given me more problems than **manquer** – and I suspect a lot of learners would endorse that view.

Manquer itself, poses few, if any problems. It simply means **to miss**:

- "La gare est à cent mètres: vous ne pouvez pas la **manquer**" ie The station is 100 metres away: you cannot miss it.
- "Jean-Louis est passé. **Je l'ai manqué** de cinq minutes" ie Jean-Louis passed by. I missed him by five minutes.

In these examples, **manquer** is a transitive verb with a direct object. Hence, no problem.

However, difficulties do arise when the verb is **manquer à**, and has an **indirect** object. To illustrate, take the examples I gave you in Conversation Two:

> "**Est-ce que Paris vous manque**? Now at first sight, this seems to translate as: "Does Paris miss you?" (!) Of course not! **You miss Paris**!

I also gave you:

> "**Oui, le sport me manque, aussi**" Again, this seems to mean:
> "Yes, the sport misses me!" In fact it means, **I miss the sport**! It follows that:

> "**La campagne me manque**" does not mean the countryside misses me; rather, "I miss the countryside".

This (to British eyes) illogicality is explained because it is here a question of manquer **à**, not manquer (or even manquer **de**). So if you want to say "I miss my children", you will need to say:

- "**Mes enfants me manquent**".

And if you want to say to someone "I miss you", you will need to say:

- "**Tu me manques**."

In short, you can see from these examples that **manquer à** conjugates like **manquer**.

Here is a fully worked example based on "I miss Paris":

Paris me manque	Paris nous manque
Paris te manque	Paris vous manque
Paris lui manque (m)	Paris leur manque.
Paris lui manque (f)	

This example shows clearly that the **subject** and the **verb** always **agree**; it is the **indirect object pronoun** that **changes**. That is because "I" is not the **subject** of the French sentence, **Paris** is: "I" (me) is the indirect object pronoun. Paris is the third person singular subject. Hence the verb is always **manque** in this example. In the "I miss you" example above, the full conjugation is as follows:

Tu me manques   Tu nous manques
Tu lui manques (m)   Tu leur manques
Tu lui manques (f)

I know, simple isn't it!

Penser: Exercises

Complete the blank spaces:

1. Je (   ) donc je suis.

2. À quoi (   ) – vous, madame.

3. (   ) donc à ce que vous dites.

4. Je ne (   ) pas que froid soit le mot juste.

5. Qu'est-ce que tu penses (   ) ce café, Xavier?

    Choose one of the three words in brackets and place in the space provided in each sentence:

6. Qu'est-ce que vous avez (   ) film "Le Parrain"? (pensé au, pensé de, pensé du)

7. Que penseriez-vous (   ) un weekend à Londres? (à, de, d')

8. Mon fils pense (   ) trouvé une nouvelle voiture. (à, de, avoir)

9. Je pense (   ) elle est belle. (que, qu', d')

10. Il a dit "oui" sans (   ) penser. (en, y, à)

11. Qu'est-ce que vous pensez de cette terrine? Vraiment, qu' (   ) pensez-vous? (y, de, en)

12. Je n'aurais jamais (   ) qu'il dirait cela. (penser, pensé, pensais)

13. Le tableau qu'il a peint: est-ce que cela vous fait (   ) quelque chose? (penser à, penser de, penser)

14. Sa suggestion est vraiment bien (   ). (penser, pensée, pensez)

289

Translate the underlined parts of the following sentences into French:

15.   This dress? <u>I am really going to have to think hard about it.</u>

16.   <u>I do not think</u> that there is a department store in this town.

17.   He is coming? <u>Is he heck as like!</u>

18.   Oh heck. I have just stepped into a lot of <u>you know what!</u>

19.   That friend of Tom <u>has a one track mind!</u>

20.   You know what they say: <u>evil be to him who evil thinks.</u>

21.   Your present? You can shove it <u>where the sun doesn't shine!</u>

Penser: Answers

1. pense
2. pensez
3. Pensez
4. pense
5. de
6. pensé du
7. d'
8. avoir
9. qu'
10. y
11. en
12. pensé
13. penser à
14. pensée
15. Il faut que j'y réfléchisse
16. Je ne pense pas
17. Pensez-vous!
18. ce que je pense!
19. ne pense que ça!
20. Honi soit qui mal y pense
21. où je pense!

Chapter Fifteen
Arriver

Introduction

Arriver is a regular "...er" verb which has **être** in the compound tenses because it is a so-called verb of movement. It basically means – what a surprise – **to arrive** or **to come**; but it also has a second, very important, role to play when you want to say that sometimes you do this or that.

It can also be used in place of several other verbs – notably, **approcher** (to approach), **atteindre** (to reach), **réussir** (to succeed) and **se produire** (to happen). We will look at these applications in this chapter too.

However, the idiomatic uses of **arriver** are very limited indeed. This chapter will, therefore, be relatively short. Let us begin as usual, then, with its conjugations.

The Arriver Conjugations

Present Tense

J'arrive	Nous arrivons		
Tu arrives	Vous arrivez		
Il arrive	Ils arrivent		
Elle arrive	Elles arrivent		

Future Tense

J'arriverai	Nous arriverons
Tu arriveras	Vous arriverez
Il arrivera	Ils arriveront
Elle arrivera	Elles arriveront

Imperfect Tense

J'arrivais	Nous arrivions
Tu arrivais	Vous arriviez
Il arrivait	Ils arrivaient
Elle arrivait	Elles arrivaient

Perfect Tense

Je suis arrivé(e)	Nous sommes arrivé(e)s
Tu es arrivé(e)	Vous êtes arrivé(e)s
Il est arrivé	Ils sont arrivés
Elle est arrivée	Elles sont arrivées

Future Perfect Tense

Je serai arrivé(e)	Nous serons arrivé(e)s
Tu seras arrivé(e)	Vous serez arrivé(e)s
Il sera arrivé	Ils seront arrivés
Elle sera arrivée	Elles seront arrivées

Pluperfect Tense

J'étais arrivé(e)	Nous étions arrivé(e)s
Tu étais arrivé(e)	Vous étiez arrivé(e)s
Il était arrivé	Ils étaient arrivés
Elle était arrivée	Elles étaient arrivées

Present Conditional Tense

J'arriverais	Nous arriverions
Tu arriverais	Vous arriveriez
Il arriverait	Ils arriveraient
Elle arriverait	Elles arriveraient

Past Conditional Tense

Je serais arrivé(e)	Nous serions arrivé(e)s
Tu serais arrivé(e)	Vous seriez arrivé(e)s
Il serait arrivé	Ils seraient arrivés
Elle serait arrivée	Elles seraient arrivées

Present Subjunctive Tense

J'arrive	Nous arrivions
Tu arrives	Vous arriviez
Il arrive	Ils arrivent
Elle arrive	Elles arrivent

Imperative

Arrive
Arrivons
Arrivez

Arriver: The Basics

Basically, use **arriver** to talk about arriving or coming. The simplest use of the verb is to say that you are coming:

- "**J'arrive**!" You would say this when someone asks you if you are ready to go out, for example:
- "Arthur, je suis prêt à sortir. Tu viens?"
- "T'en fais pas, papa. **J'arrive**!"

You can use this expression to talk about buses, trains, cars etc. arriving also:

- "Le train en provenance de Strasbourg **arrive** dans cinq minutes" ie The train coming from Strasbourg will arrive in five minutes.
- "Le bus en provenance de Lyon est **arrivé** à la gare routière il y a dix minutes" ie The coach from Lyon arrived at the coach station ten minutes ago.
- Le train à destination de Toulouse **arrivera** dans trente minutes ie The train bound for Toulouse will arrive in thirty minutes.

(Incidentally, whilst the expressions "en provenance de" and "à destination de" sound a bit excessive, their employment eliminates the ambiguity that exists in French when otherwise talking about a train or bus coming or going).

But it is not just vehicles and people that can arrive. For example:

- "**Ce paquet m'est arrivé** ce matin" ie This package arrived this morning.

- "Sébastien, **l'eau n'arrive plus** à la maison. Je me demande s'il y a une fuite quelque part?" ie Sebastien, the water is not coming to the house. I wonder if there is a leak somewhere?
- **"Le moment arrive** où nous devrions remplacer l'évier, chérie. Il y a une grosse fissure dedans" ie It is time to replace the sink, darling. There is a big crack in it.
- "Attends, attends! Ton tour **arrivera** bientôt" ie Hang on a minute. It will be your turn soon!

And **arriver** can be coupled with **faire** in **faire arriver**:

- "Si nous commencions à manger ça pourrait **faire arriver** mon frère!" ie If we were to begin eating, then that could cause my brother to arrive!
- **"Pour faire arriver** l'électricité à la maison, dans un premier temps il faudra nous mettre en contact avec E.D.F" ie To get electricity to the house, as a first step we will have to get in contact with E.D.F (Électricité de France).

The **second** important use of **arriver** is to say that sometimes you like to do this or that:

- "Est-ce qu'il **vous arrive** d'aller au cinéma?" ie Do you sometimes go to the cinema?
  "Oui, **ça m'arrive**" ie Yes, I do (sometimes).

Here are some more examples of this construction in action:

- "Est-ce que vous écoutez la radio quelque fois?
  Oui, il **m'arrive** d'écouter la radio le soir lorsque je suis seul à la maison" ie
  Do you sometimes listen to the radio?
  Yes, I sometimes listen to the radio when I am alone at home.

- "Est-ce que vous lisez des journaux nationaux?"
  "Non,mais ma femme les lit le matin quand elle prend son petit déjeuner; et **il lui arrive** également de les lire à d'autres moments de la journée, quand elle a un moment pour se détendre" ie
  Do you read any national newspapers?
  No, but my wide reads them in the morning when she has breakfast; and she also reads them sometimes at other times of the day, when she has a moment to relax.
- "C'est vrai que mon fils raconte des bobards de temps en temps, mais **il ne lui arrive pas** souvent de mentir" ie It is true that my son tells "porkies" from time to time, but is it not often that he tells lies.

And that is about as much as you need at this basic level.

Summary

Use **arriver**:

- to talk about people and methods of transport coming and arriving – arriving at and arriving from
- to talk about things arriving – packages and letters, water and electricity, even about time arriving to do this or that
- to talk about getting people and things to arrive using **faire arriver**
- to talk about things you and others might do sometimes using the construction **il arrive de**…

Getting Better

The two main roles for **arriver**, outlined in the previous section, are easily the most important. However, as I said in the introduction, **arriver** can also be used in place of several other verbs – notably, **approcher**, **atteindre**, **réussir** and **se produire**. We will look at these now.

Approcher

We have already seen that we can use **arriver** to talk in particular about vehicles approaching: trains, buses and many other forms of transport. People approach, too, as do things (eg packages and letters). Turns and moments can also approach.

Beyond these examples, seasons and other times can also arrive:

- "Bien qu'il fasse encore chaud en ce moment, l'hiver **arrivera** bientôt" ie Although it is still hot at the moment, winter will arrive shortly.
- "Le moment de passer à l'heure d'été **arrive** ce week-end, je crois" ie It will be time to put the clocks forward to summertime this weekend, I believe.
- "Son heure de gloire **est arrivée**. Il mérite bien sa décoration" ie His hour of glory has arrived. He really deserves his award.

Atteindre

Arriver can also be used to talk about reaching, getting to or achieving this or that. For example:

- "Notre bâtiment donne sur une rue très bruyante. Apparemment le bruit **arrive** même aux apparts au septième étage" ie Our building overlooks a very noisy street. Apparently the noise even reaches those apartments on the seventh floor.
- "La nouvelle de sa victoire **est arrivée** jusqu'à nous la semaine dernière. Nous étions ravis" ie The news of his/her victory arrived last week. We were delighted.

Réussir

Arriver can also be employed to talk about succeeding at something. For example:

- "Je voudrais **arriver** à lui faire comprendre que si l'on veut perdre même quelques kilos, il faut manger moins" ie I would love to get him to understand that even if you only want to lose a few kilos, you have to eat less.

And you can also use **arriver** to talk about getting on in life:

- "Il a beaucoup d'ambition, lui. Il veut vraiment **arriver**" ie He has lots of ambition. He really wants to get on in life.
- "Il **n'arrivera** jamais à rien" ie He will never get anywhere.
- "Il **arrivera** à ses fins: il possède tellement de charme" ie He will get his way: he has so much charm.
- "On **n'arrivera** jamais à rien avec lui" ie We will never get anywhere with him.

And it can also mean to manage:

- "**Je n'y arrive pas**!" ie I cannot do it!
- "**Je n'arrive pas** à réparer ce jouet. C'est bel et bien cassé" ie I cannot repair this toy. It is well and truly broken.

Se produire

Arriver can be used also to talk about things that happen. For example:

- "Ce genre d'erreur **arrive** souvent. De nos jours les gosses n'ont aucune compréhension d'orthographe" ie This type of error happens often. Nowadays, the kids have no understanding of spelling.
- "En essayant d'attraper le bus, il est tombé et il s'est cassé la cheville. Cela peut **arriver** à n'importe qui" ie Trying to catch the bus, he fell and broke his ankle. That can happen to anyone.
- "Tu ne sais pas ce qui m'est **arrivé**!" ie You would never guess what happened to me!
- "Il m'est **arrivé** un drôle de truc en allant au bureau" ie A funny thing happened to me on the way to the office.
- "Malgré son grand âge, **il lui arrive** encore de faire dix kilomètres à pied" ie Despite his age, he sometimes manages to walk ten kilometres.

And here is, perhaps, the simplest use of **arriver** in this context:

- "Qu'est-ce qu'il t'**arrive**?" ie What is happening? What is the matter with you?

Now You Are Really Speaking French!

At this third level, there is very little to add. You should know about **en arriver à**, to come to; and there are several impersonal uses of arriver similar to the **il m'arrive de** construction that we met in the **Basics** section. And there is one proverb and one colloquialism. And that is it!

En arriver à

Use this construction when you want to say something along the lines of "we have not come to that yet, have we?" For example:

- "Divorcent-ils? **On n'en est pas encore arrivé là. On en arrive à** se demander s'ils comprennent les conséquences" ie Are they going to get divorced? They have not come to that yet, surely. One wonders whether they understand the consequences.

Impersonal arriver

Impersonal verbs are invariable: they only ever exist in the "il" form – as in "il fait beau" and all those other weather constructions that you met in the **Faire** chapter. Here you have already met **il m'arrive de**… earlier in the chapter. Other impersonal forms of arriver include:

Il est arrivé un accident: an accident has occurred.
Il leur est arrivé un malheur: something awful has happened to them.
Il m'arrive souvent des choses extraordinaires: extraordinary things sometimes seem to happen to me.
Quoi qu'il arrive: whatever happens.
Comme il arrive souvent: as often happens.

The proverb

Arriver comme les carabiniers means to arrive too late when everything is over.

The colloquialism

Arriver dans un fauteuil, literally to arrive in an armchair, means to romp home:

- "Le Front national **est arrivé dans un fauteuil** aux élections municipales récemment" ie The National Front romped home at the recent municipal elections.

Conclusion

Arriver's basic uses are its most important – in particular to describe arriving and to talk about things that sometimes happen. But it can also be used instead of several other verbs, notably **atteindre**, **réussir** and **se produire**. There are also some other noteworthy impersonal forms of **arriver**. Let us finish with a couple of conversations that showcase **arriver**.

Arriver: Conversation One

Annie is standing outside a cinema in Brive asking people in the queue about their cinema-going habits.

Annie:	Bonjour, mademoiselle, cela vous arrive d'aller au cinéma, évidemment.
La jeune fille:	Oui il m'arrive d'aller au cinéma.
Annie:	Très peu ou souvent?
La jeune fille:	En fait, j'y vais assez souvent.
Annie:	Assez souvent? Qu'est-ce que cela veut dire au juste?
La jeune fille:	Mettons une fois par semaine, environ.
Annie:	C'est à dire régulièrement!
La jeune fille:	Oui, je suppose!
Annie:	Et quel genre de film préférez-vous?
La jeune fille:	En principe je vais voir les films psychologiques – j'adore les films d'Alfred Hitchcock, par exemple.
Annie:	Est-ce que vous avez vu "Psycho", par exemple?
La jeune fille:	"Psycho?" Oh là, là! Oui, une fois. Mais rien que d'y penser j'ai la trouille!
Annie:	Et est-ce qu'il vous arrive d'aller voir les films de science-fiction?
La jeune fille:	Oui, je les adore aussi.
Annie:	Et quel est votre film de science-fiction préféré?
La jeune fille:	Sans aucun doute, "2001 Odyée de l'Espace."
Annie:	Bien sûr. Je l'ai vu aussi. Incroyable! Et quels autres genres de film aimez-vous?
La jeune fille:	Franchement, c'est plus facile de vous signaler les genres de films que j'aime beaucoup moins.
Annie:	Ah bon? Lesquels?
La jeune fille:	Je n'aime pas trop les films comiques, les films d'aventure – et les westerns, je déteste.
Annie:	Et les films policiers?
La jeune fille:	Oui, il m'arrive d'aller voir des films policiers – oh, et les films d'amour aussi. Mais il faut choisir. Il y en a de bons, il y en a de mauvais.
Annie:	Et les films pornographiques?
La jeune fille:	Non, jamais. Ces films sont commerciaux, très mauvais, et n'ont aucun but précis, sans histoire. Et le scénario est très mauvais en général. Ils n'ont pas d'intérêt.
Annie:	Bon, je vous remercie.
La jeune fille:	Je vous en prie, madame.

Arriver: Conversation Two

Corinne and Thierry are at home one night and the conversation turns to their son, Julien and his future. Corinne would like him to go to university after the bac – but Thierry has other ideas.

Thierry: Pour l'instant, je sais que Julien est content au lycée: il a beaucoup de bons copains et il aime les matières qu'il étudie. Et il a beaucoup d'ambition. Il veut vraiment arriver.

Corinne: Oui, mais il n'arrivera jamais à rien s'il ne continue pas ses études, Thierry. Et tu sais qu'il veut trouver un emploi après le bac. Vaut mieux à mon avis qu'il aille à la fac. Moi, je veux qu'il devienne médecin. Je voudrais arriver à lui faire comprendre qu'une carrière médicale peut ouvrir tellement de possibilités. Il pourrait devenir généraliste ou bien…

Thierry: Mais, Corinne, tu te rends parfaitement compte qu'on arrivera jamais à rien avec lui si on continue à lui parler de faire médecine. Il n'est pas très sciences. Il aime les trucs plus créatifs. Tu sais qu'il aime faire la cuisine, par exemple. Il pourrait devenir chef au début et après-qui sait? S'il devait être propriétaire d'un restaurant trois étoiles, tu serais très contente n'est-ce pas? Il pourrait faire fortune. Mais il faut qu'il continue ses études bien sûr, mais dans une école hôtelière plutôt qu'à la fac.

Corinne: Quoi qu'il arrive, donc, il doit travailler sans relâche. Mais à son âge, tant mieux. De nos jours il y a trop de tentations pour les jeunes: la drogue, l'alcool – et les filles, ça va sans dire! Comme il arrive souvent, les jeunes quittent l'école, ils cherchent n'importe quel emploi, ils rencontrent quelqu'un, ils se marient, un enfant arrive et... c'est ça. Leur vie est finie!

Thierry: Tu est trop pessimiste, Corinne! Quel âge avais-tu quand tu t'es mariée?

Corinne: Tu te rends parfaitement compte Thierry que j'avais vingt-huit ans. Est-ce que tu as oublié?

Thierry: Et est-ce que tu es allée à la fac? Non. Et moi, j'avais trente ans quand nous nous sommes mariés et moi – je ne suis jamais allé à la fac non plus. Qu'est-ce que tu conclus alors?

Corinne: Oui, Thierry mais nous parlons d'une période tout à fait différente de celle-ci. De nos jours il y a trois millions de chômeurs, plus peut être, parmi lesquels plus d'un million au-dessous de vingt cinq ans. La comparaison n'est pas juste, Thierry.

Thierry: D'accord, mais combien de ces chômeurs possèdent un diplôme universitaire, je me demande! À en croire les statistiques que j'ai

301

vues récemment, il y a des milliers de jeunes gens sans emploi. Mais pour les apprentis, ceux qui acquièrent des compétences et au bout de quelques années un métier, pour eux leur avenir est très encourageant.

Corinne: Comme il arrive souvent, tu gagnes, Thierry! Je suis d'accord. La prochaine fois que nous parlerons à Julien à ce sujet, je serai plus objective, ça va?

Thierry: Oui, ça va, bien sûr. Et si on allait à notre restaurant préféré du coin, Corinne? J'ai faim, tellement faim!

Some words you might not yet know

- souvent - often
- régulièrement - regularly
- supposer - to suppose
- genre - type
- les films psychologiques - psychological films
- signaler - to indicate
- les films comiques - comedy films
- les films d'amour - romantic films
- un but - an objective / goal
- le scénario - the script
- un copain - a friend
- une matière - a subject
- les études (f) - studies
- une carrière médicale - a medical career
- un(e) généraliste - a general practitioner
- la médecine - medicine
- un restaurant trois étoiles - a 3-star Michelin restaurant
- faire fortune - to make a fortune
- une école hôtelière - a catering school / college
- travailler sans relâche - to work with one's head to the grindstone
- se rendre parfaitement compte - to know full well
- conclure - to conclude
- un chômeur - an unemployed person
- parmi lesquels - amongst whom
- un diplôme universitaire - a university diploma
- un apprenti - an apprentice
- acquérir - to obtain
- une compétence - a skill
- au bout de quelques années - after a few years
- encourageant(e) - encouraging
- gagner - to win

Arriver: Exercises

Complete the blank spaces:

1.   Tu viens, Charlotte? T'en fais pas, maman, (   ).

2.   Le car en provenance de Strasbourg (   ) dans deux minutes.

3.   Un colis lui est (   ) ce matin.

4.   Le moment (   ) où je devrais sortir.

5.   Si nous devions faire semblant de partir, ça pourrait faire (   ) ma tante.

6.   Est-ce qu'il vous (   ) d'aller au théatre?

7.   Il (   ) arrive de regarder la télé quand je suis seul à la maison.

8.   Elle est (   ) hier.

9.   Je voudrais (   ) à lui faire comprendre que minuit est trop tard pour se coucher.

10.   Il n'(   ) jamais à rien.

11.   J'ai essayé, maman mais je (   ) pas.

Choose one of the three words in brackets and place in the space provided in each sentence:

12.   T'en fais pas, Alexandre. Ça peut (   ) à n'importe qui. (arrivez, arriver, arrivais)

13.   Il m'(   ) un drôle de truc en allant à l'école, ce matin. (a arrivé, est arrivé, est arrivait)

14.   Qu'est-ce qui vous (   )? (arrive, arrivez, arriver)

Put the underlined English words into French:

15. Are they going to get divorced? <u>They have not yet come to that</u>, surely.

16. They are over three hours late. <u>Something awful has happened to them.</u>

17. <u>Whatever happens,</u> I am going to bed at eleven o'clock.

18. <u>As often happens,</u> I could not get to sleep.

19. U.K.I.P. <u>romped home</u> at the recent local elections.

20. <u>An accident has occurred</u>. Call an ambulance quickly.

21. As usual, <u>he arrived too late when everything was over.</u>

Arriver: Answers

1. j'arrive
2. arrive
3. arrivé
4. arrive
5. arriver
6. arrive
7. m'
8. arrivée
9. arriver
10. arrivera
11. n'y arrive
12. arriver
13. est arrivé
14. arrive
15. On n'est pas encore arrivé là
16. Il leur est arrivé un malheur
17. Quoi qu'il arrive
18. Comme il arrive souvent
19. est arrivé dans un fauteuil
20. Il est arrivé un accident
21. Il est arrivé comme les carabiniers.

Chapter Sixteen
Partir

Introduction

You have already met **partir** several times; you know it means **to leave**. Or **to go away**, on holiday, for example. You also know that as a verb of movement, it is conjugated with **être** in compound tenses. You've already met it in its subjunctive form. So you already know it quite well. The other good news is that it has very few important idiomatic uses; it figures in a couple of proverbs – and that's about it. It is not a reflexive or pronominal verb.

However, it has one or two important **locutions**, notably **à partir de**. And **repartir**, to go back again, is also important.

But it is a true "killer" verb, like so many that we have met so far, because it occurs so frequently in every day speech. So let us begin with its conjugations.

The Partir Conjugations

Present Tense

		Future Tense	
Je pars	Nous partons	Je partirai	Nous partirons
Tu pars	Vous partez	Tu partiras	Vous partirez
Il part	Ils partent	Il partira	Ils partiront
Elle part	Elles partent	Elle partira	Elles partiront

Imperfect Tense

		Perfect tense	
Je partais	Nous partions	Je suis parti(e)	Nous sommes parti(e)
Tu partais	Vous partiez	Tu es parti(e)	Vous êtes parti(e)s
Il partait	Ils partaient	Il est parti	Ils sont partis
Elle partait	Elles partaient	Elle est partie	Elles sont parties

Future Perfect Tense

		Pluperfect Tense	
Je serai parti(e)	Nous serons parti(e)s	J'étais parti(e)	Nous étions parti(e)s
Tu seras parti(e)	Vous serez parti(e)s	Tu étais parti(e)	Vouz étiez parti(e)s
Il sera parti	Ils seront partis	Il était parti	Ils étaient partis
Elle sera partie	Elles seront parties	Elle était partie	Elles étaient parties

Present Conditional Tense

Je partirais	Nous partirions
Tu partirais	Vous partiriez
Il partirait	Ils partiraient
Elle partirait	Elles partiraient

Past Conditional Tense

Je serai parti(e)	Nous serions parti(e)s
Tu serais parti(e)	Vous seriez parti(e)s
Il serait parti	Ils seraient partis
Elle serait partie	Elles seraient parties

Present Subjunctive Tense

Je parte	Nous partions
Tu partes	Vous partiez
Il parte	Ils partent
Elle parte	Elles partent

Imperative

Pars
Partons
Partez

Partir: The Basics

Partir means to leave or to go away. As such it is an intransitive verb – it never has an object. If you **do** want to talk about leaving a person or a place you'll need **quitter** or **laisser** ("on vous laisse", I will have to leave you now, is a very common expression), not **partir**; and if it is a question of leaving something somewhere you will also need **laisser**. This makes life much easier!

So, let us begin with some simple uses of **partir**, first in the present tense:

- "**Je pars**. Sinon, je serai en retard" ie I am leaving. If not, I will be late. Or:
- "Est-ce que **tu pars** avant midi? C'est dommage, parce que j'ai préparé un tourain pour déjeuner" ie, Are you leaving before mid-day? What a shame, because I have made a tourain for lunch. Tourain is a garlic soup made with little more than duck fat, onions, flour, water, eggs, vinegar – and of course, garlic – lots of it! It is a speciality of south-west France.
- "**Partez-vous** en vacances cette année? J'espère, parce que vous avez besoin d'un repos bien mérité." I hope so, because you need a well-deserved rest.

Now here are some examples of **partir** in use in some other tenses:

- "Si tu pouvais t'occuper de notre chien, **nous partirions** au Portugal" ie If you were able to look after our dog, we would leave for Portugal. Or:
- "Si **vous étiez parti** avant midi, vous auriez pu attraper le dernier train en partance pour Londres" ie If you had left before mid-day, you could have caught the last train bound for London. Or:

- "**Il faudra que vous partiez**: ce que vous venez de dire est tout à fait inacceptable" ie You will have to leave: what you just said is totally unacceptable.

And it goes without saying that **partir** can be employed in the infinitive, too:

- "Je dois **partir**: il se fait tard et je dois me lever de bonne heure demain." ie I must leave: it is getting late and I have to get up early tomorrow.

And you have already met **partir** in the interrogative expression "où partir?"

Partir in the infinitive is also employed in expressions such as:

Partir à la chasse, to go hunting.
Partir en voyage, to go on a trip.
Partir à la pêche, to go fishing.
Partir à la guerre, to go to war.
Partir en voiture, to go by car.
Partir en avion, to go by plane.
Partir en courant, to run off.
Partir à pied, to go off on foot…and many more.

In these examples in particular, **partir** is a very close substitute indeed for **aller**, although you rarely hear anyone say "je **vais** en **vacances**". However, partir has several other related meanings. These include **démarrer** (to start), **être lancé** (to go off), **commencer** (to begin) and **disparaître** (to disappear). We shall have a look at these in the next section.

Summary

Use **partir** to say:

- that you want or need to leave or go away, but not to say that you want to leave a place, a person or a thing
- that you plan to go off hunting, fishing, walking…and so on.

Partir can substitute for several other verbs, notably **aller**, **démarrer**, **être lancé**, **commencer** and **disparaître**. We will also look at the expression **à partir de** in this section.

Aller

You might assume that **partir** is only used to describe going off somewhere relatively far away. But you can also use it for much shorter journeys!:

- "Où est Jean-Luc, je me demande? Je crois qu'**il est parti** dans sa chambre" ie Where is Jean-Luc, I wonder? I think he has gone to his bedroom. Or:
- "Marie-Claude m'a dit tout à l'heure quelle avait besoin de **partir** acheter du dentifrice en ville" ie Marie-Claude told me just now that she needed to go into town to buy some toothpaste. Or:
- "Il me faut **partir** faire mes courses. Nous n'avons plus ni pain ni farine" ie I will have to go shopping. We have no more bread or flour.

Démarrer

This verb is often used to describe cars starting and planes taking off. For example, using **partir** you might say:

- "Ma voiture **est partie** immédiatement, malgré les ennuis que j'ai eu avec elle hier." ie My car started straight away, despite the problems that I had with it yesterday. Or:
- "C'était vraiment triste de dire au revoir à Bernard, mais j'étais heureuse que son vol **soit parti** à l'heure" ie It was really sad to say goodbye to Bernard, but I was pleased that his flight took off on time.

Être lancé

Use this expression when you want to say that something has gone off, like a champagne cork or a gun, for example:

- "Je n'ai pas secoué la bouteille mais le bouchon **est parti** quand même au plafond" ie I did not shake the bottle but the cork hit the ceiling nonetheless. Or:
- "André m'a dit que c'était un accident: le coup **est parti** tout seul" ie André told me that it was an accident: the gun went off on its own.

Commencer
Partir can be used instead when you want to talk about something starting from somewhere, for example:

- "Le voyage **part** de Paris mais vous pouvez **partir** aussi de Lyon si vous voulez" ie The journey starts in Paris but you can also start from Lyon if you wish. Or
- "Vous y allez en voiture? La bonne nouvelle est qu'il y a une autoroute qui **part** de Stasbourg – mais elle est à péage" ie You're going there by car? The good news is that there is a motorway which starts at Strasbourg – but it is a toll road.

But you can also use **partir** to talk about more abstract departures. For example:

- "Vous parliez de vos problèmes de gestion financière. Notre analyse **part** de la constatation que vous avez des difficultés de trésorerie" ie You were talking about your financial management problems. Our analysis starts from the observation that you have cash flow difficulties.

Disparaître
Imagine you have some spots or marks on your clothes. You can use **partir** to talk about getting them out:

- "La tache **est partie** au lavage. Malheureusement, la couleur **est partie** aussi!" ie The stain came out in the wash. Unfortunately, the colour came out, too! Or:
- " C'est dommage que ta chemise blanche ait (subjunctive) ces taches. T'en fais pas, ce produit que je viens d'acheter **les fera partir**" ie It is a shame that your white shirt has these marks. Never mind, this product that I have just bought will get them out.

À partir de can be used when you want to say, for example, that the film will be showing at the cinema **from**, say, Monday next:

- "Je voudrais voir le dernier film de Thomas Villepin. Apparemment, ça passe au cinema **à partir de** lundi prochain" ie I would like to see Thomas Villepin's latest film. Apparently it is on at the cinema from next Monday. Or:
- "J'ai vu dans les vitrines de mon magasin préféré que leurs pulls en cashmere commencent **à partir de** 50€" ie I saw in the windows of my favourite shop that cashmere pullovers start from 50€.

Now You're Really Speaking French

There is relatively little more to know about **partir** at this level. It is not a reflexive or pronominal verb, there are very few locutions – and the idiomatic use of **partir** is very limited. So, here is what you might get to know at this final level.

Partir ventre à terre is an idiomatic expression that means to go off at great haste:

- "Tout d'un coup, je me suis rendu compte que mon train partait à neuf heures plutôt qu'à dix heures. Inutile de dire que **je suis parti ventre à terre!**" ie Suddenly I realised that my train left at nine-o-clock rather than ten-o-clock. Needless to say, I was off in a flash!

Avoir maille à partir avec quelqu'un means to get into trouble with someone or to have a brush with someone:

- "Du début, nous ne nous entendions pas. Quand il a refusé net de me payer ce qu'il me devait **j'ai eu maille à partir avec lui**" ie From the beginning we did not get on with each other. When he refused point blank to pay me what he owed me, I had quite an argument with him.

Partir à Tataouine means metaphorically to go to the ends of the earth. Tataouine was a penal colony in Tunisia at the beginning of the twentieth century, incidentally. If you saw the film "Star Wars" you may remember the planet "Tatooine". This name derives from Tataouine. Well I never!

C'est parti is a locution you may well hear coming from your waiter in a restaurant, for example. It broadly means "it will be coming soon", "things are rolling".

Partir en couille is a mildly vulgar expression broadly meaning to "go down the tubes" or to "go down the chute". For example:

- "Avec le mauvais temps, le spectacle **est parti en couille**" ie Because of the bad weather the whole show went down the tubes ("les couilles", incidentally, are testicles!)

Conclusion

Partir is a very important "killer" verb. Use it to say:

- that you went or will go away, on holiday, for example
- that you plan going off doing something – hunting or fishing, for example
- that you're leaving to go shopping
- that your train or plane has left or is leaving
- that you've managed to get stains out of your clothes…and much more

Finally, let's have a look at some conversations that illustrate **partir** in action.

Partir: Conversation One

Annie has a young daughter, Carla. She has a pen-friend ("une correspondante") in England whom she would like to visit. She and Annie are talking it over.

Carla: Maman, je viens de recevoir une lettre de Natasha à Londres. Elle voudrait me voir cet été, paraît-il. Tu sais qu'elle est ma correspondante depuis très longtemps et je voudrais lui rendre visite, vraiment. Qu'en penses-tu, maman?

Annie: En principe, c'est une excellente idée Carla. Je sais qu'elle est ta correspondante depuis quelques années et que tu voudrais lui rendre visite à Londres. Mais cet été? Je ne suis pas sûre, Carla. Quand partirais-tu? Tu sais que nous partons en Tunisie début août pour deux semaines et que tu dois repartir de nouveau fin août rendre visite à Maurice en Bretagne. Peut-être que tu pourrais partir en Angleterre fin juillet, alors – si la mère de Natasha n'y voit pas d'inconvénient.

Carla: Je ne pense pas, maman. Elle dit dans sa lettre que ses parents seraient ravis de m'inviter chez eux à partir de mi-juillet jusqu'à début septembre.

Annie: Ah bon? Dans ce cas, sors ton agenda, Carla – et examinons les possibilités ensemble. Mais n'oublie pas qu'il y a d'autres considérations. Par exemple, comment partirais-tu, en train ou en avion? Si tu prends le train, Natasha peut te rejoindre à la gare, St. Pancras je crois. Mais si tu pars en avion, il s'agit de Gatwick ou Heathrow, je suppose. À mon avis, le train est beaucoup plus commode pour toi et pour elle. Et cela veut dire que tu pourrais partir de Brive – la gare la plus commode pour moi.

Carla: Nous sommes d'accord, alors, maman?

Annie: Carla, qu'est-ce que je t'ai dit toute à l'heure? En principe, oui. Mais nous devons discuter de ton voyage avec papa, tu sais. Mais je suis sûre qu'il sera d'accord. Il faut saisir l'occasion. Mais avant que tu partes, tu auras besoin d'un passeport, n'oublie pas. Tu n'es jamais partie à l'étranger toute seule auparavant – et tu n'as que quatorze ans. Oh là, là! Rien que d'y penser j'ai la trouille!

Carla: Maman, vraiment! Quel âge as-tu?!

Partir: Conversation Two

Maryse and François have gone out to a local restaurant with two friends, Éloïse and Bernard. They have just finished ordering their meals.

Serveuse:	C'est parti. Vos entrées devraient arriver bientôt.
François:	Merci bien. Alors, quoi de neuf? Êtes-vous déjà partis en vacances cette année?
Maryse:	François, vraiment! As-tu oublié qu'Éloïse et Bernard sont allés aux États-Unis au mois de mai et qu'ils sont partis en Chine au mois de juin? Je suis désolée mais parfois François a la tête comme une passoire!
Éloïse:	C'est pas la peine, Maryse. Bernard a le même problème. Tu sais qu'il a oublié notre anniversaire de mariage cette année. Qu'est-ce que je l'ai engueulé!
François:	Mais c'est tout à fait naturel, Éloïse. L'avenir de son affaire le préoccupe, n'est-ce pas, Bernard?
Bernard:	Loin de moi le désir de gâter le plaisir de notre soirée mais oui, tu as raison, François. Même quand nous sommes partis en Chine, nous y sommes allés pour affaires. Éloïse s'est bien amusée, je crois, mais pour moi… franchement je ne veux plus en parler.
Maryse:	Mais vous êtes partis aux États-Unis en vacances, n'est-ce pas?
Éloïse:	Oui, mais même là-bas Bernard était obligé de rencontrer quelques collègues américains à New York.
François:	Je ne suis jamais allé à New York. On dit que c'est une ville qui ne dort jamais. C'est vrai?
Bernard:	Oui, c'est vrai – ça bouge, New York. Mais je préfère Chicago – les clubs de jazz y sont incroyables!
Éloïse:	C'est vrai. Mais si c'est le jazz que vous cherchez, il faut que vous partiez à la Nouvelle-Orléans. Bourbon Street est extraordinaire!
Maryse:	Et n'oublions pas que la Nouvelle-Orléans faisait partie de la colonie française dans le temps. L'influence française y est très évidente, même de nos jours
Éloïse:	Ah bon? Tu connais la Nouvelle-Orléans alors?
Maryse:	J'y suis allée une fois mais il y a longemps. J'avais une amie qui était partie aux États-Unis à la fin des années quatre-vingt-dix et elle y a passé quelques années. Mais, regardez nos entrées arrivent.
Serveur:	Les escargots sont pour qui?
François:	Pour moi, s'il vous plait.
Serveur:	Et les écrevisses pour les dames?
Maryse:	Oui.
Serveur:	Et les cuisses de grenouilles pour monsieur. Voilà.

Bernard:	Merci bien.
François:	Ça sent bon, Bernard. Ça me met l'eau à la bouche!
Maryse:	Espèce de glouton, François! Tu as tes escargots! Bon appétit tout le monde.
All together:	Bon appétit.
Éloïse:	Oh là, là! Je partirais à Tataouine pour ces écrevisses: ells sont divines, vraiment!
Maryse:	Mais attention, François. Tu as dèjà fait tomber du beurre sur ta chemise. Les tâches ne partiront jamais au lavage, tu sais.
François:	Désolé, Maryse.
Éloïse:	T'en fais pas Maryse. J'ai trouvé un produit qui fait partir même les tâches de graisse. C'est vraiment très efficace.
Maryse:	Une bonne nouvelle, Éloïse. Où est-ce que tu l'as trouvé?
Éloïse:	Malheureusement, je l'ai acheté à New York!
Maryse:	Dans ce cas, François, je crois que nous devrions partir aux États-Unis. En fait nous devrions y partir ventre à terre!
François:	Oui, chérie. Est-ce que demain c'est trop tard?!

Some words you might not yet know

• recevoir -	to receive
• en principe -	in principle
• repartir -	to go back again
• n'y voir pas d'inconvénient -	to have no objections
• un agenda -	a diary
• examiner -	to examine
• ensemble -	together
• les considérations (f) -	considerations
• soupçonner -	to suspect
• commode -	convenient
• un passeport -	a passport
• seul(e) -	alone
• auparavant -	before
• les États-Unis -	the United States
• la Chine -	China
• avoir une tête comme une passoire -	to have a memory like a sieve
• un anniversaire de mariage -	a wedding anniversary
• une affaire -	a business
• préoccuper -	to preoccupy
• gâter	to spoil
• dormir -	to sleep
• un club de jazz -	a jazz club
• incroyable -	incredible
• extraordinaire -	extraordinary
• une colonie française -	a French colony
• l'influence (f) -	influence
• les années quatre-vingt-dix -	the nineties
• les escargots (m) -	snails
• les écrevisses (f) -	crayfish
• les cuisses de grenouilles (f) -	frogs' legs
• sentir -	to smell
• un glouton -	a glutton
• divin(e) -	divine/heavenly
• laisser tomber -	to drop
• le beurre -	butter
• la graisse -	(animal) fat
• efficace -	effective

Partir: Exercises

Fill in the blank spaces:

1.   Je vais (   ) cet après-midi.

2.   Tu (   )? Dépéche-toi, alors.

3.   Elles sont (   ) hier.

4.   Si tu devais m'accompagner je (   ) aussi tôt que possible.

5.   Je (   ) demain matin.

6.   Si tu pouvais t'occuper de notre perroquet nous (   ) en Espagne.

7.   Il faudra que vous (   ). Vous n'êtes pas catholique.

8.   Où (   )? Moi, j'aimerais aller en Angleterre.

9.   Est-ce que vous (   ) en vacances cette année?

10. Jean-Luc n'est pas là. Il est (   ) à la chasse.

11. Le film passe en salle (   ) lundi prochain.

Translate the underlined parts of the following English sentences into French:

12. Suddenly I realised that my plane was due to depart at eleven o'clock. Needless to say <u>I was off in a flash.</u>

13. Because of the bad weather, the garden party <u>went down the tubes.</u>

14. When he refused point blank to pay me, I <u>had quite an argument with him.</u>

15. <u>You have never been</u> to England alone before.

318

Partir: Answers

1. partir
2. pars
3. parties
4. partirais
5. partirai
6. partirions
7. partiez
8. partir
9. partez
10. parti
11. à partir de
12. je suis parti(e) ventre à terre
13. est parti en couille
14. j'ai eu maille à partir avec lui
15. Tu n'es jamais parti(e).

Chapter Seventeen
Servir

Introduction

In its most basic transitive form, **servir** means to **serve something**: "**Servez** le café maintenant s'il vous plait", Serve the coffee now please.

But it is often used to describe serving **someone**: "**On vous sert**, madame?", Is someone serving you, madam?

Perhaps more often, though, you'll want or need to employ **servir à**, which means to be of use in some way or another: "Ça **sert à** ouvrir une bouteille de bière, monsieur" That is used to open a bottle of beer, sir.

Servir de is generally used to describe someone acting in some role or other: "**Elle sert de** guide aux touristes" She works as a tourist guide.

Then there's the pronominal form, **se servir**, which has broadly two meanings: to help oneself, at the table, for example; and to make use of something – your car, for example.

Finally, there is a limited passive role for **se servir**: "Ce foie gras **se sert** assez frais", This foie gras is best served quite cool.

But there are few idiomatic uses for the verb. This helps to make life a lot easier!

The Servir Conjugations

Present Tense

Je sers	Nous servons		
Tu sers	Vous servez		
Il sert	Ils servent		
Elle sert	Elles servent		

Future Tense

Je servirai	Nous servirons
Tu serviras	Vous servirez
Il servira	Ils serviront
Elle servira	Elles serviront

Imperfect Tense

Je servais	Nous servions
Tu servais	Vous serviez
Il servait	Ils servaient
Elle servait	Elles servaient

Perfect Tense

J'ai servi	Nous avons servi
Tu as servi	Vous avez servi
Il a servi	Ils ont servi
Elle a servi	Elles ont servi

Future Perfect Tense

J'aurai servi	Nous aurons servi
Tu auras servi	Vous aurez servi
Il aura servi	Ils auront servi
Elle aura servi	Elles auront servi

Pluperfect Tense

J'avais servi	Nous avions servi
Tu avais servi	Vous aviez servi
Il avait servi	Il avaient servi
Elle avait servi	Elles avaient servi

Present Conditional Tense

Je servirais	Nous servirions
Tu servirais	Vous serviriez
Il servirait	Ils serviraient
Elle servirait	Elles serviraient

Past Conditional Tense

J'aurais servi	Nous aurions servi
Tu aurais servi	Vous auriez servi
Il aurait servi	Ils auraient servi
Elle aurait servi	Elles auraient servi

Present Subjuntive Tense

Je serve	Nous servions
Tu serves	Vous serviez
Il serve	Ils servent
Elle serve	Elles servent

Imperative

Sers
Servons
Servez

Servir: The Basics

Use **servir** first of all to ask someone to serve you something, in a restaurant or at home:

- "Vous pouvez **servir** le vin blanc maintenant, s'il est frais" ie You can serve the white wine now, if it is chilled.
- "Bruno, je voudrais que **tu serves** le fromage après le dessert: n'oublie pas que nos invités ce soir sont on ne peut plus anglais!" ie Bruno, I would like you to serve the cheese after the dessert: do not forget that our guests this evening could not be more English!

Use it also, say in a shop, to get someone to serve you:

- "Est-ce qu'il y a quelqu'un qui peut nous **servir**, s'il vous plaît? Franchement, on n'arrive pas à **se faire servir** ici" ie Is there someone who can serve us? Frankly, it is not easy to get served here.

And perhaps at someone's house, the hostess may say to you:

- "Passons à table, **c'est servi**!" ie Come and sit down at the table now, it is ready!

But perhaps the most practical use of **servir** arises when you go into a shop not knowing the name of what it is you want. I cannot tell you how many times over the years I have been into a shop needing to buy something but not knowing the name for it in French. Typically this is what I say:

- "Bonjour, monsieur. Je cherche un truc qui **sert à** (faire quelque chose)… mais je ne sais pas comment ça s'appelle" ie Good morning. I am looking for a gadget which is used to (do whatever)…but I do not know what it is called (in French).

So when you want to say that you're looking for something that is used to…use **servir à**. For example:

- "Je cherche quelque chose qui **sert à** aiguiser mes couteaux et à la fois quelque chose qui **sert à** tailler mes crayons. Pouvez-vous m'aider s'il vous plaît?
  Bien sûr, monsieur. Pour vos couteaux vous avez besoin d'un aiguiseur et pour vos crayons un taille-crayon" ie:
  I am looking for something which will sharpen my knives and at the same time something that will sharpen my pencils. Of course, sir. For your knives you need an "aiguiseur" and for your pencils you need a "taille-crayon."

Perhaps, now, you go into a shop that sells lots of different glasses for the household. You are struck by the bewildering variety of shapes, sizes, colours and materials – but you are particularly attracted to one particular glass. So you call over the lady sales-assistant:

Vous: "Bonjour madame. Pourriez-vous m'aider s'il vous plaît. Je trouve ce verre-ci très joli: j'aime la forme et la couleur. Mais dites-moi, **à quoi ça sert** au juste?" ie Good morning, madam. Could you help me please. This glass is very pretty: I like the shape and the colour, but tell me, what is it used for exactly?

La vendeuse: "Ce verre-ci est un verre à vin, monsieur, et la forme, c'est à dire une flûte, suggère que **ça sert à** contenir le champagne Et c'est une flûte en cristal. C'est très joli, je suis d'accord" ie This glass is a wine glass, sir, and its shape, in the form of a flute, suggests that it is used to hold champagne. And it is made of crystal. It is very pretty, I agree.

Note carefully that the sales-assistant calls the glass "un verre **à** vin" rather than "un verre **de** vin". The distinction is very important: get it wrong and you will seriously confuse people! So here are the rules:

À is used with double-barrelled nouns to describe what things are **used for**. So:

Un **verre à vin** means a wine-glass.
Un **couteau à pain** means a bread-knife.
Une **tasse à café** means a coffee-cup.
Une **brosse à dents** means a tooth-brush.
Une **machine à laver** means a washing-machine.
Un **fer à repasser** means an iron.
Une **boîte aux lettres** means a letter-box…and so on.

So, if instead of asking for "un verre **à** vin", you asked for un "verre **de** vin", you would be asking for a glass **full** of wine! Basically you will use **de** rather than **à** to say that containers are full of something, where things come from ("un vin **de** Bordeaux, for example) or even what something is made from, although "en" is often used for this purpose.

But **servir à** has many more applications some of which have little to do with what something is used for. For example:

* "Cela ne **sert à rien**" ie It is useless.

But, it may not literally be useless. Perhaps there's simply no point in doing something:

* "**Ça ne sert à rien** de pleurer, Marise. Ta poupée est cassée et je ne sais pas comment la réparer" ie There's no point in crying, Marise: you doll is broken and I do not know how to repair it.

Or, perhaps something you have bought at a shop has broken – but you bought it a while ago, you don't have a guarantee and you've no proof of purchase!:

* "**À quoi servirait** de réclamer, Jean-François? Ça fait longtemps que tu l'as acheté et tu as perdu le reçu. Achètes-en un autre" ie What is the point of complaining, Jean-François. You bought it a long time ago and you've lost the receipt. Buy another one.

Now, let's have a brief look at **servir de**. As I said earlier, use **servir de** when you want to describe the role that someone or something plays. For example:

- "Sa connaissance de langues étrangères est excellente et **elle sert d**'interprète à l'O.N.U à New York" ie Her knowledge of foreign languages is excellent and she works as an interpreter at the United Nations in New York. Or
- "Nous avons rénové l'ancienne grange attenante et de nos jours **ça sert de** maison d'amis" ie We have renovated the adjoining former barn and nowadays we use it to put up friends.

Summary

Servir is a really useful verb. Use it to:

- ask to be served in a restaurant, say
- get someone to serve you in, say, a shop
- ask someone to say what something might be used for
- say that there's really no point in doing this or that, and…
- say what role someone or something plays.

Getting Better

At this level of knowledge, the pronominal form of **servir**, **se servir**, is very useful indeed to know. Above all, use it to say that you want to **serve yourself**, at the table or in a shop, for example:

- "Puis-je **me servir** d'haricots verts, Sophie?" Ils sont vraiment délicieux!" ie Can I help myself to the green beans, Sophie? They are really delicious! Or
- "Est-ce que'on peut **se servir** dans ce magasin, madame?" "Oui, c'est bien un magasin libre-service, monsieur" ie Can I help myself in this shop, madam? Yes, it is indeed a self-service shop, sir.

But you can also use **se servir** to talk about making use of this or that. For example:

- "Je voudrais acheter cet outil-ci, monsieur mais, franchement, je ne sais pas bien **m'en servir**" ie I would like to buy this tool here but, frankly, I do not really know how to use it. Or
- "Je t'ai déjà dit qu'il a le bras long - **il se sert** aux maximum de toutes ses relations" ie, I have already told you that he has influence in high places – he makes full use of all his acquaintances.

Se servir can also be employed in the passive. Here are a couple of examples of this construction in use:

- "Ce vin blanc est délicieux, monsieur, mais pour mieux apprécier ses qualités le vin devrait **se servir** frais, mettons à huit degrés". This wine is delicious but to really appreciate its qualities, you should serve it cool – let's say at eight degrees. Or
- "D'après le mec qui me l'a vendu, le fromage **se sert** idéalement, assez fait" ie According to the guy who sold it to me, this cheese is best served quite ripe.

Now You're Really Speaking French

Servir and **se servir** have no idiomatic uses at all to my knowledge – no proverbs, no locutions, not even any slang. So I have only two further points to make about the verb. First, when you want to say "well done!" to someone, never say "bien fait!", well done's literal translation because "bien fait!" means:

Que cela vous serve (subjunctive**) de leçon**! ie "Serves you right!"

If you do want to say "well done!" say "bravo!"

And should you want to describe someone as self-seeking or self-serving (ie selfish) you need the adjective "égoïste"**.** This has nothing to do in any way with **se servir**.

Conclusion

Servir, **servir à**, **servir de** and **se servir** are all really useful verbs. Like all our other "killer" verbs, you will find them in virtually daily use!

At this point, instead of a conversation highlighting the verb **servir**, I had hoped to give you the lyrics to a song, "Ça Sert à Quoi, Tout Ça?" by Maxime Le Forestier. Unfortunately, permission to include the song in this book had not been given when we went to press.

However, I recommend that you listen to this and many other songs by Maxime Le Forestier. His music is thoughtful, contemplative and often beautiful. He sings very clearly and you will find him relatively easy to understand. Moreover, he is several notches above the standard of typical modern French pop music.

Servir: Conversation

Since their arrival in Dordogne, Maryse, François and their two children have been renting an apartment in Brive, but their intention is to buy an old house for renovation in the Sarlat area. They have been viewing several possibilities and today we find them with a local estate-agent viewing a property only a few kilometres from the medieval town.

L'agent immobilier:	Nous revoilà devant la maison que vous avez vue il y a quelques jours. Vous savez déjà qu'elle a été construite en 1873, et qu'elle servait de ferme jusqu'à 1997, c'est à dire jusqu'à la disparition de M. Delprat. Elle est inoccupée depuis cette date et, évidemment, il y a des travaux à faire. Mais c'est une affaire à 150,000€ et elle ferait une belle demeure pour vous et votre famille. Et il y a plusieurs dépendances pour restaurer.
François:	Oui, et celle-ci à votre gauche, monsieur – dans le temps, à quoi elle servait?
L'agent:	Ça servait de grange pour l'âne, parce qu'avant l'arrivée du premier tracteur en 1955, la charrue était tirée par des ânes, vous savez.
Maryse:	Oh là, là! Il n'y avait pas de cheveaux à la ferme, alors?
L'agent:	Pas du tout. À l'époque, le cheval était un animal trés prisé et pour la plupart il servait de moyen de transport. L'âne faisait le labourage.
Maryse:	Et le petit bâtiment à côté - ça servait à quoi?
L'agent:	Ç'était une porcherie. Le fermier aurait élevé quelques cochons, qu'il aurait tués au mois de février – et l'appentis au-dessous de la porcherie servait de "cuisine," entre guillemets, c'était où la fermière préparait toutes ses charcuteries – le boudin noir, les rillettes et cetera.
François:	Mais Maryse, ça me servirait d'atelier. Je pourrait y garder tous mes outils de jardinage.
Maryse:	Ou bien ça servirait de deuxième cuisine. Nous pourrions y stocker notre barbecue, nos grosses casseroles et bien d'autres bidules encore.
L'agent:	Bon, passons maintenant à l'intérieur. Il nous reste tellement de curiosités à voir!
François:	Y compris ce placard dans le vestibule. Ça servait à quoi, je me demande?
L'agent:	Ça ne servait pas à grand-chose, je soupçonne. Mais le vestibule lui-même est incroyable n'est-ce pas? Quand je l'ai

vu pour la première fois, j'ai failli tomber dans les pommes, tellement il-était énorme.

Maryse:	Et la cuisine est à côté, n'est-ce pas?
L'agent:	Allons-y. Mais attention à la marche.

But despite the warning, François trips over the step and falls down:

François:	Oh là, là! Maryse – ça m'a fait mal, tu sais.
Maryse:	Que cela te serve de leçon, François! Tu sais que ses vieilles maisons sont dangereuses. Il faut faire gaffe!
L'agent:	Votre femme a raison, monsieur. Et attention au plafond aussi. Dans la cuisine il y des crochets de boucher qui, dans le temps, servaient à suspendre les jambons. Ils n'ont aucune utilisation de nos jour mais ils nous font penser quand-même au bon vieux temps.
Maryse:	Oui, c'était le bon temps!
L'agent:	Maintenant, passons aux autres pièces.

Half an hour later:

	Et nous revoilà devant la façade de la maison. Qu'est-ce que vous en pensez cette fois-ci. Pas mal, hein!
François:	Pas mal du tout, à mon avis.
Maryse:	Oui, je suis d'accord, François. Mais, restaurer cette vieille ferme – ça va nous coûter cher, François.
L'agent:	Peut-être, mais vous pourriez le faire au fur et à mesure, vous savez. Quelques pièces sont déjà habitables, la cuisine fonctionne bien, il y une salle de bain à l'étage qui fonctionne bien, aussi – et il y a tellement de potentiel, tellement de possibilités. Et à ce prix de vente, franchement c'est donné! Quelques Anglais on déjà vu la propriété – et vous connaissez les Anglais! Et n'oubliez pas que nous ne sommes pas exactement hors des sentiers battus ici: Sarlat n'est qu'à dix minutes en voiture. Je n'essaie pas de vous baratiner mais je voudrais que vous l'achetiez. Vous y seriez très contents, j'en suis sûr.
François:	Je ne peux pas nier que la maison est fort tentante, monsieur. Il faut que nous réfléchissions – mais pas pour longtemps! En voiture, Simone!

Some words you might not yet know

• nous revoilà -	here we are again
• construit(e) -	built
• la disparition	the death
• une affaire -	a bargain
• une demeure -	a home
• les dépendances (f) -	the out-buildings
• la restauration -	the restoration
• un âne -	a donkey
• un tracteur -	a tractor
• une charrue -	a plough
• prisé(e) -	prized
• un moyen de transport -	a means of transport
• le labourage -	the ploughing
• un bâtiment -	a building
• un cochon -	a pig
• entre guillemets -	in inverted commas
• le boudin noir -	black-pudding
• les rillettes (f) -	a coarse, fatty pâté
• les outils de jardinage (m) -	garden tools
• une barbecue -	a barbecue
• le vestibule -	the hall
• faillir -	to almost (do something)
• tomber dans les pommes -	to faint
• énorme -	enormous
• le plafond -	the ceiling
• un crochet de boucher -	a meat-hook
• dans le temps -	in the old days
• suspendre -	to hang
• un jambon -	a leg of ham
• le bon vieux temps -	the good old days
• habitable -	habitable
• fonctionner -	to work
• le potentiel -	potential
• le prix de demande -	the asking price
• hors des sentiers battus -	off the beaten track
• *en voiture, Simone! -	allons-y/let's go!

*En voiture, Simone! is an expression that dates back to the days of Simone Louise de Pinet de Borde des Forest, who, in 1929, passed her driving test and became a rally-driver, retiring from the sport in 1957. She was the subject of much admiration, including that of Juan Fangio, the Italian world-champion racing driver.

But her name entered French vocabulary when in 1962, Guy Lux created what became a very successful T.V. game-show, "Intervilles" (known as "It's a Knockout" in Britain), in which different towns competed. Lux often got a game started with his famous war-cry "en voiture, Simone!" – even though many suspect that the "Simone" in question was Simone Garnier, his female co-presenter. Nonetheless, because of the programme, the expression passed into "le langage populaire".

Servir: Exercises

Fill in the blank spaces:

1.   (   ) l'omelette maintenant, s'il vous plait.

2.   Ce machin? À quoi ça (   )?

3.   Qu'est-ce qu'elle fait, dans la vie? Elle (   ) de récéptionniste dans un hôtel.

4.   (   ) – toi.

5.   Passons à table. C'est (   ).

Translate the underlined parts of the following English sentences into French:

6.   I am looking for something which can be used to clean my car.

7.   This chair is very comfortable, but what is it used for exactly?

8.   This glass is used to hold red wine.

9.   It is useless. It is going into the dustbin.

10.   What is the point of complaining? It is too late now.

11.   Can I help myself to the vegetables, Janine?

12.   Serves you right! You really should not have gone to the betting shop.

Servir: Answers

1. Servez
2. sert
3. sert
4. Sers
5. servi
6. qui sert à
7. à quoi ça sert au juste?
8. sert
9. Cela ne sert à rien
10. À quoi servirait de?
11. Puis-je me servir
12. Que cela vous serve de leçon!

Chapter Eighteen
Connaître

Introduction

Connaître basically means to know **a person** or to know **a place**. It is the companion verb to **savoir**, to know a fact. It is easy to confuse the two although they do have quite separate meanings. But we shall examine **savoir** in the next chapter.

However, **connaître** has meanings beyond knowing people and places; you can use it to talk of knowing languages and science, for example; and you can use it to talk about experiencing emotions. You can also use it to talk about enjoying success at something or other; and **faire connaître** can be employed to make known something or other.

Se connaître and **s'y connaître en quelque chose** can also be employed. But the idiomatic role of **connaître** is very limited indeed.

The Connaître Conjugations

Present Tense		**Future Tense**	
Je connais	Nous connaissons	Je connaîtrai	Nous connaîtrons
Tu connais	Vous connaissez	Tu connaîtras	Vous connaîtrez
Il connaît	Ils connaissent	Il connaîtra	Ils connaîtront
Elle connaît	Elles connaissent	Elle connaîtra	Elles connaîtront

Imperfect Tense		**Perfect Tense**	
Je connaissais	Nous connaissions	J'ai connu	Nous avons connu
Tu connaissais	Vous connaissiez	Tu as connu	Vous avez connu
Il connaissait	Ils connaissaient	Il a connu	Ils ont connu
Elle connaissait	Elles connaissaient	Elle a connu	Elles ont connu

Future Perfect Tense		**Pluperfect Tense**	
J'aurai connu	Nous aurons connu	J'avais connu	Nous avions connu
Tu auras connu	Vous aurez connu	Tu avais connu	Vous aviez connu
Il aura connu	Ils auront connu	Il avait connu	Ils avaient connu
Elle aura connu	Elles auront connu	Elle avait connu	Elles avaient connu

Present Conditional Tense

Je connaîtrais	Nous connaîtrions
Tu connaîtrais	Vous connaîtriez
Il connaîtrait	Ils connaîtraient
Elle connaîtrait	Elles connaîtraient

Past Conditional Tense

J'aurais connu	Nous aurions connu
Tu aurais connu	Vous auriez connu
Il aurait connu	Ils auraient connu
Elle aurait connu	Elles auraient connu

Present Subjunctive Tense

Je connaisse	Nous connaissions
Tu connaisses	Vous connaissiez
Il connaisse	Ils connaissent
Elle connaisse	Elles connaissent

Imperative

Connais
Connaissons
Connaissez

Connaître: The Basics

Use **connaître** when you want to say that you know someone or that someone knows you. For example:

- "**Je connais** Philippe Duclos: c'était un camarade de classe au lycée il y a quelques années" ie I know Philippe Duclos: he was a class-mate at school several years ago.

  (Incidentally, you can see that the noun "lycée" is masculine despite the fact that it ends with two "e"s. The vast majority of French nouns ending this way are feminine, but a small group of 29 French nouns are masculine. The majority of these come from Greek words, are very technical and are little known. But some of them are everyday words, notably "lycée" and "musée"; and others get an airing from time to time. The ones you are most likely to encounter include:
  - un athée – an atheist
  - un trophée – a trophy
  - un scarabée – (a type of) beetle
  - l'apogée – the peak of something).

- "Et **je connais** Louise Caulnes de vue. Elle habitait au sixième étage quand nous habitions 231 Rue du Dragon" ie And I know Louise Caulnes by sight. She lived on the sixth floor when we lived at 231 Rue du Dragon.
- "**J'ai connu** Albert Henry quand nous travaillions ensemble à ma dernière agence de publicité" ie I knew Albert Henry when we were working together at my last advertising agency.

- "Mon prof **me connaît** assez bien parce que j'ai l'habitude de lui poser des questions à la fin de ses leçons" ie My teacher knows me quite well because I am in the habit of asking him questions at the end of his lessons.
- Ma mère a **connu** mon père quand ils étaient étudiants à la fac à Nancy" ie My mother knew my father when they were university students at Nancy.
  In this example **connu** could be translated as "met".

Connaître also means to know a place. For example:

- "Oui, **je connais** le quartier de Londres dont tu parles: j'y ai passé beaucoup de temps dans ma jeunesse" ie Yes, I know that part of London you are talking about: I spent a lot of time there when I was young.
- **Connaissez-vous** le Musée d'Orsay? On dit que c'est une ancienne gare" ie Do you know the Musée d'Orsay? It is said to be a former railway station.
- "**Je ne connais pas** Montpellier mais je crois que c'est une ville universitaire pas loin de la frontière espagnole" ie I do not know Montpellier but I believe that it is a university town not far from the Spanish border.

But you can also employ **connaître** when you want to say that you are acquainted or familiar with something or other ie when you know about something (or someone). For example:

- "J'ai rencontré Amélie dans la rue hier et je lui ai dit: **connais-tu** la dernière nouvelle? – ma soeur est enceinte!" ie I met Amélie in the street yesterday and I said to her: have you heard the latest news? – my sister is pregnant!
- "**Connaissez-vous** un bon médecin dans les parages – le mien est franchement nul" ie Do you know of a good doctor in these parts – frankly, mine is useless.
- Oui **je connais** quelqu'un de bonne réputation – le docteur Phillipon – mais c'est un médecin non-conventionné. Cela vous va?" ie Yes, I know someone by reputation – Doctor Phillipon – but he is private. Is that ok?
  In France, General Practitioners can either be "conventionné(e)" or "non-conventionné(e)". The former are linked to the state health-care system. Consequently their consultation charge (as I write, 23€) is fixed by the government. The latter are not linked in this way and can consequently charge whatever they see fit, usually about 50% more per consultation (more again on Saturdays). The fees of both types are subject to a "remboursement" ie a reimbursement, but not for the full amount. Consequently, most French people have an insurance policy ("un contrat d'assurance") which, when claimed, makes up the difference. But the premiums are often viewed as expensive and the French can sometimes be heard grumbling about the cost of health-care in France,. However, although their system is not perfect, it is generally judged by observers to be one of the best, if not the best, in the world.

There is a lot more that I could say here with regard to **connaître** and knowing about this or that. But I think you have got enough to be getting on with.

Summary

- Above all, use **connaître** when you want to talk about knowing someone, someone knowing you and knowing places. These are quite the most important basic uses of **connaître**
- Also use it when you want to say that you know about someone or something.

Getting Better

You can make further ground with **connaître** by becoming more familiar with its role in knowing about someone or something.

Then there is **connaître**'s role in describing your experiences and how you feel.

Connaître can also be used to express enjoying, notably success.

Faire connaître means to announce or to make known, so we will have a look at this too.

Knowing about

It is not about knowing facts that we are talking here (that is **savoir**'s job) but rather knowing about or having heard about methods in particular. For example:

- "J'ai rencontré une étudiante brésilienne ce matin et je lui ai demandé si **elle connaissait** bien les coutumes françaises" ie I met a Brazilian student this morning and I asked her if she knew French customs very well.
- "Je tousse en ce moment. Donc, j'ai demandé à la pharmacienne si elle pouvait me conseiller quelque chose. Elle a posé beaucoup de questions et puis elle m'a donné ce médicament-ci. **Qu'est-ce qu'elle connaît** son affaire!" ie I am coughing at the moment, So I asked the pharmacist whether she could suggest something. She asked me so many questions, then she gave me this medicine here. Wow! Does she know what she is talking about!
- (Incidentally, if you do go into a French chemist for such a reason, the pharmacist will almost certainly ask you whether you have "une toux sèche", a dry cough, or "une toux grasse", a chesty cough. You might be surprised by how technical the pharmacist's knowledge can be – and by how many different remedies are available. Our experience is that French pharmacies are, for the most part, noticeably superior to their British counterparts; the staff are better trained and more knowledgeable and the range of solutions on offer is wider. Oh, and their premises look better organised, too!)
- "Mon appareil photo est foutu, paraît-il. Donc, je l'ai ramené au magasin. Mais le mec qui me l'a vendu, **il n'y a rien connu**" ie My camera no longer works, it seems. So I took it back to the shop. But the guy who sold it to me did not know anything about it.

Connaître and your experiences

The experiences I am talking about here are your life experiences rather than your experiences with a product, for example. So:

- "J'ai vu un sans-abri cet aprèm. Le pauvre! Il m'a parlé brièvement de ses expériences. **Il a connu** des temps meilleurs, ça c'est certain" ie I saw a homeless person this afternoon. Poor thing! He talked to me briefly about his experiences. He has seen better times, that's for sure.

But you can also use **connaître** to talk about, say, the experiences of your country – its economy, for example:

- "Où en est la Grande Bretagne de nos jours?" "Àlors, c'est vrai que le pays **a connu** une crise économique grave comme tous les pays occidentaux bien-sûr, mais en ce moment (je touche du bois!) il existe des signes que nous sommes sur la voie de la reprise" ie What is the current state of Great Britain? Well, it is true that the country has experienced a very serious economic crisis like all countries in the western world but, at the moment (touching wood!), there are signs that we are on the road to recovery.

Connaître and success

Avoir and **être** are verbs that are frequently used when talking about someone or something being successful, but **connaître** can also be used in such contexts. To illustrate:

- "**Il a connu** un succès d'estime avec son dernier roman" ie He has enjoyed critical success with his latest novel.
- "Il n'est pas beau, je suis d'accord, mais il a **connu** du succès auprès des femmes" ie He is not handsome, I agree, but he has enjoyed considerable success with women.
- "Serge Dupin? Il ne me dit rien franchement. Quand même, **il a connu** un boeuf avec son dernier tube" ie Serge Dupin? I am not at all keen on him, frankly. Nonetheless he enjoyed a monster with his latest hit.

Faire connaître

This means, as you would expect given the presence of **faire**, "to make known". For example, use it to introduce somebody to someone, as in this example:

- "Hier était une très grande réussite: **j'ai fait connaître** ma cousine au chef d'orchestre du Birmingham Symphony Orchestra. Étant donné son expérience, il lui a dit qu'il pourrait l'auditionner" ie Last night was a great success. I introduced my cousin to the leader of the Birmingham Symphony Orchestra and he said, given her experience, that he could offer her an audition.
- "Mon oncle **m'a fait connaître** les joies des échecs et cette année pour mon anniversaire il m'acheté un nouveau échiquier en ivoire" ie My uncle introduced me to the joys of chess and this year, for my birthday, he bought me a new ivory chessboard.
- "Ce morceau de musique **a fait connaître** le musicien américain Jacob Bechstein aux audiences françaises pour la première fois" ie This piece of music brought the American musician Jacob Bechstein to French audiences for the first time.

Now You Are Really Speaking French!

At this level you should become familiar with the pronominal form of **connaître**, **se connaître** and also with **s'y connaître en quelque chose**. The former means **to know oneself** and the latter **to know a lot about something**. There are also one or two locutions worth knowing, several idiomatic expressions and one proverb. So "vas-y!"

Se connaître

- **Connais-toi toi-même** means "know thyself". But note also this application:
- "Ce matin mon père a fait une réclamation au garage. Le mécanicien lui a dit que sa voiture n'était rien qu'un tas de ferraille. **Il ne se connaissait plus**" ie This morning my father made a complaint at the garage. The mechanic told him that his car was nothing more than a pile of metal. He was beside himself with rage.

S'y connaître en quelque chose

- "Quelle surprise que mon père soit si en colère au garage ce matin. **Il s'y connaît** en voitures. Mais à vrai dire, quand il s'agit d'embêter les autres, **il s'y connaît!**" ie What a surprise that my father was angry at the garage this morning. He knows all there is to know about cars. But to be honest, when it comes to annoying people, he is an expert!

Idiomatic connaître

There are not really many idioms. Here are the ones you are most likely to hear:

Connaître la musique means to know the score.
Connaître les ficelles means to know the ropes.
En connaître un bout means to know a thing or two – as does
En connaître un rayon.

The one **proverb** that features our verb is:

À l'oeuvre on reconnaît l'artisan which means "you can tell an artist by his handiwork".

Locutions

Ça me connaît! means "I know all about it!"
Je ne connaîs que ça! means "Don't I know it!"
Un bon digestif après le dîner, je ne connais que ça means there is nothing like a good digestive after dinner.
Je ne le connais ni d'Eve ni d'Adam means "I do not know him from Adam".
Je te connais comme si je t'avais fait means "I know you like the back of my hand".

Conclusion

Use **connaître:**

- when you want to talk about knowing people and places
- when you want to talk about knowing something about someone or something
- to talk about experiences you have had in your life (especially the bad ones!)
- to talk about the success you have or expect to enjoy
- to talk about making someone or something known to someone.

Also:

- use **se connaître** and **s'y connaître en quelque chose**
- Finally, familiarise yourself with one or two of the idioms and locutions that employ **connaître**.

But do not forget that, although some of these refinements are useful, it is in its basic role, to know a person and know a place, that you will find **connaître** yet another very useful "killer" verb in everyday conversation.

Connaître: Conversation One

Maryse is in the streets of Sarlat to find out how well French people know their important historical figures, places and dates. She stops people and shows them photographs. Her first interviewee is a woman.

Maryse:	Bonjour madame. Connaissez-vous votre histoire de France?
Femme:	Oh là, là! Quelle question! Oui, je crois que je connais quelques dates importantes, celles que j'ai apprises à l'école, bien-sûr.
Maryse:	D'accord. Commençons, alors, avec la date de la Révolution française
Femme:	Ah, ça c'est simple comme bonjour. Mille sept cent quatre-vingt-neuf
Maryse:	Bravo, madame. Et est-ce que vous connaissez la date de la fin de la guerre d'Algérie?
Femme:	C'est plus difficile, ça. Quand même, je crois que c'était en 1962, non?
Maryse:	Tout à fait, madame. Chapeau! Et finalement les élections présidentielles de 1981: est-ce que vous connaissez le nom du président élu?
Femme:	1981? C'était François Mitterand n'est-ce pas?
Maryse:	Vraiment, madame, votre connaissance de l'histoire française est étonnante! Mais maintenant je vais vous montrer des photos de quelques sites emblématiques de la France, ça va? D'abord, celle-ci.
Femme:	Mais c'est la Tour Eiffel. Tout le monde la connaît!
Maryse:	Bien-sûr. Mais celle-ci?
Femme:	Ça, c'est le Musée d'Orsay, je crois.
Maryse:	Absolument, et celle-ci?
Femme:	C'est une cathédrale, évidemment, mais je ne sais pas si c'est la cathédrale de Reims ou la cathédrale de Rouen. Je crois que c'est celle de Reims.
Maryse:	Encore une fois – la bonne réponse! Félicitations, madame. Mais dites-moi, comment ça se fait que vous êtes aussi cultivée?
Femme:	Peut-être à cause de mon métier, madame.
Maryse:	Ah bon? Qu'est-ce que vous faites dans la vie, au juste?
Femme:	Moi, je suis historienne, madame!

François, Maryse and their two friends, Alain and Simone, have been to the cinema in Sarlat where they have watched a live broadcast of a performance by the London Symphony Orchestra at the Royal Albert Hall in London. They are now in a local bar and are discussing what they have just seen.

François:	Est-ce que cela vous a plu?
Simone:	Ah oui, personnellement tout était merveilleux, surtout le concerto pour piano de Mozart, le vingt-septième, je crois. Le pianiste, dont je ne connais pas le nom, était vraiment à la hauteur.
Maryse:	Tout à fait, Simone. À propos, il s'appelle Vladamir Kubeck et j'ai entendu parler de lui. Il est à son apogée en ce moment, me semble-t-il.
Alain:	Peut-être. Mais pour moi, l'orchestre n'était pas convaincant pendant les passages très mélodiques. Les cuivres et les cordes étaient trop forts et je me demande si le premier violon connaît son affaire.
Simone:	Non, je ne suis pas de tout d'accord avec toi, Alain. Vraiment tu coupes les cheveux en quatre!
François:	Mais passons au morceau du compositeur anglais, Edward Elgar, la deuxième symphonie. Je ne la connais pas du tout mais je l'ai trouvée étonnante, époustouflante même. Le dernier mouvement était sublime à mon avis.
Maryse:	Je suis tout à fait d'accord avec toi, François. Et le chef d'orchestre en connaît un bout, ça c'est sûr! À la fin du dernier mouvement ces gestes étaient aussi inspirants que la musique. En fait il m'a emballé dès la première note de la symphonie. Et à la fin j'ai failli crier "Bis!"
Alain:	Tu t'es laissée emporter: c'était un beau mec, Maryse!
Simone:	Vraiment, Alain, tu sais bel et bien que Maryse est une mélomane aussi exigeante que toi. Elle a raison, le chef d'orchestre, dont je ne connais pas non plus le nom, était formidable. Je suis sûr qu'il va connaître un succès d'estime avec cette représentation-là.
Alain:	Je plaisantais, Simone. Cette émission devrait faire connaître la musique d'Elgar à une audience française plus large, je crois. Je voudrais entendre son concerto pour violoncelle. D'après certains, c'est aussi formidable que sa deuxième symphonie.
François:	J'ai une idée. L'Opéra à Bordeaux n'est pas très proche, pour ainsi dire mais il y a un train direct six fois par jour. Si on y allait, mettons pour le week-end? Nous pourrions partir samedi matin et nous pourrions revenir dimanche après-midi.
Simone:	Quelle excellente idée, François. Bien que je connaisse Bordeaux assez bien, c'est une belle ville et l'Opéra y est magnifique.

Alain:	Je ne le connais pas, mais je suis pour.
Maryse:	Moi aussi. D'accord tout le monde? Dans ce cas, je vais me renseigner auprès de l'Office de Tourisme de Sarlat. S'il y a quelque chose d'intéressant nous pourrions y aller le week-end prochain peut-être?
François:	Pourquoi pas? Il faut saisir l'occasion. Les soldes commencent la semaine prochaine, n'est-ce pas? Et j'ai encore besoin d'un imper chic à un prix raisonnable!
Maryse:	Tais-toi, François. Ça suffit!

Some words you might not yet know

- un concerto -   a concerto
- être à la hauteur -   to be on top form
- à propos -   by the way (at the beginning of a sentence)
- me semble-t-il -   it seems to me
- l'orchestre (m) -   the orchestra
- convaincant(e) -   convincing
- un passage (musicale) -   a musical passage
- mélodique -   melodic
- les cuivres (m) -   the brass section
- les cordes (f) -   the string section
- couper les cheveux en quatre -   to split hairs
- un morceau -   a musical piece
- un compositeur -   a composer
- une symphonie. -   a symphony
- étonnant(e) -   astonishing
- époustouflant(e) -   staggering / amazing
- sublime -   sublime
- un mouvement (musicale) -   a movement
- le chef d'orchestre -   the conductor
- les gestes (m) -   hand / arm movements
- inspirant(e) -   inspiring
- emballer -   to love
- "Bis!" -   "Encore!" or "More!"
- se laisser emporter -   to get carried away
- un beau mec (fam) -   a good-looking guy
- bel et bien -   well and truly
- un(e) mélomane -   a music lover
- exigeant(e) -   demanding
- une représentation -   a performance
- une violoncelle -   a cello
- d'après certains -   according to some
- auprès de -   at
- saisir l'occasion -   to seize the opportunity
- se taire -   to be quiet

Connaître: Exercises

Fill in the blank spaces:

1.   Je (   ) Philippe Durand. C'est un ami à moi.

2.   Est-ce que tu (   ) ma soeur? Elle est allée au même lycée, je crois.

3.   Dans le temps, je (   ) Paris. Mais ça fait longtemps que je n'y suis pas allé.

4.   (   )-vous le Musée Jacqmart-André? On dit que c'est vraiment intéressant.

Translate the underlined parts of the following English sentences into French:

5.   I saw a new doctor today. Oh boy, <u>does she know what she is talking about</u>!

6.   My computer has broken down so I took it back to the shop I bought it from. But the guy who sold it to me, <u>he did not know anything about it.</u>

7.   The poor tramp I saw in the street today – boy, <u>has he seen better times</u>!

8.   <u>He had a critical success</u> with his latest album.

9.   Yesterday <u>I introduced my brother to</u> a good friend of mine.

10.   This play <u>has really brought the author to</u> a much bigger audience.

345

Translate the underlined French sentences into English:

11.   <u>Il ne se connaissait plus</u> quand je lui ai dit qu'il était ignorant.

12.   <u>Il s'y connait en</u> vieux timbres. Sa collection est énorme.

Connaître: Answers

1. connais
2. connais
3. connaissais
4. Connaissez
5. Qu'est-ce qu'elle connaît son affaire!
6. il n'y a rien connu
7. il a connu des temps meilleurs
8. Il a connu un succès d'estime
9. j'ai fait connaître mon frère à
10. a fait connaître l'auteur à
11. He was beside himself with rage
12. He knows all there is to know about / he is an expert on.

Chapter Nineteen
Savoir

Introduction

In the last chapter I called **savoir** the "companion" verb to **connaître**. And so it is. It, too, means **to know**, but now the emphasis is knowing facts rather than people or places. It is important to emphasize, though, that while this distinction is fairly clear at the basic level there are possible overlaps as we climb **savoir**'s greasy pole.

Beyond facts of course, we have already seen that this verb can be used to talk about knowing how to do things – swimming, for example (remember the **Pouvoir** chapter?) So we will look at its role in this context, too.

It can also be used instead of **se rendre compte** ie to realise.

You will also find savoir employed in the subjunctive.

But there is no pronominal form of **savoir**, no locutions, very few idiomatic expressions and scarcely any proverbs! Not bad, eh? So let us get down to the conjugations of **savoir**.

The Savoir Conjugations

Present Tense

Je sais	Nous savons
Tu sais	Vous savez
Il sait	Ils savent
Elle sait	Elles savent

Future Tense

Je saurai	Nous saurons
Tu sauras	Vous saurez
Il saura	Ils sauront
Elle saura	Elles sauront

Imperfect Tense

Je savais	Nous savions
Tu savais	Vous saviez
Il savait	Ils savaient
Elle savait	Elles savaient

Perfect Tense

J'ai su	Nous avons su
Tu as su	Vous avez su
Il a su	Ils ont su
Elle a su	Elles ont su

Future Perfect Tense

J'aurai su	Nous aurons su
Tu auras su	Vous aurez su
Il aura su	Ils auront su
Elle aura su	Elles auront su

Pluperfect Tense

J'avais su	Nous avions su
Tu avais su	Vous aviez su
Il avait su	Ils avaient su
Elle avait su	Elles avaient su

Present Conditional Tense

Je saurais	Nous saurions
Tu saurais	Vous sauriez
Il saurait	Ils sauraient
Elle saurait	Elles sauraient

Past Conditional Tense

J'aurais su	Nous aurions su
Tu aurais su	Vous auriez su
Il aurait su	Ils auraient su
Elle aurait su	Elles auraient su

Present Subjunctive Tense

Je sache	Nous sachions
Tu saches	Vous sachiez
Il sache	Ils sachent
Elle sache	Elles sachent

Imperative

Sache
Sachons
Sachez

Savoir: The Basics

Savoir means to know something and at this level should be immediately distinguishable from **connaître**

- "Je connais David Dunce et **je sais qu'il est con**!" ie I know David Dunce and I know that he is stupid!
- "**Je sais que** Paris est la capitale de la France; **et je sais aussi que** Londres est la capitale de l'Angleterre" ie I know that Paris is the capital of France; and I also know that London is the capital of England.

But what about Scotland, Wales and Ireland? Do you know their capitals?

- "Oui. **Je sais qu**'Edimbourg est la capitale de l'Écosse, que Cardiff est la capitale du Pays de Galles et que Dublin est la capitale de l'Irlande."
  "Chapeau!"
  "Et je sais que les Champs Élysées est la plus belle avenue du monde!"
  "Ah, bon?"

Which only goes to show that a fact does not necessarily have to be a fact to use **savoir**! One of my university professors of economics wrote in the foreward to his economics text book that "facts seldom speak for themselves and rarely, if ever, with one voice". How true!

Savoir also works in many other tenses, notably in the imperfect and pluperfect tenses. For example:

- "Si je **savais**, je lui rendrais visite à l'hôpital" ie If I knew for sure, I would go and visit him/her at the hospital.

And do you remember this example in an earlier chapter?:

- "Si **j'avais su**, je l'aurais fait moi-même" ie If I had known, I would have done it myself.

Nor do you need the **if** clause necessarily:

- **"Il ne savait pas où** se mettre" ie He did not know where to put himself.

But now can you see that we have strayed from the straight and narrow world of facts. You can always tell when this is happening because when it is a question of knowing **something**, **savoir** is normally followed by **que**:

- **"Je sais que** tu as raison!" ie I know that you are right!

But **savoir** can be followed by many other parts of speech. Here are some examples:

- **Je sais ce que je sais** means I know what I know.
- **Il ne sait pas ce qu'il dit** means He does not know what he is saying.
- **Je ne sais quoi faire** means I do not know what to do.
- **Savez-vous quand il vient?** means Do you know when he will come?
- **Savez-vous la nouvelle?** means Have you heard the news?
- **Je n'en sais rien** means I do not know anything about it.

En often precedes **savoir**. One expression you will hear (or see) frequently is:

- **Pour en savoir plus sur...** which means For more information about......
- **J'aimerais en savoir plus sur**... which means I would like to know more about...
- **Qu'en sais-tu?** which means What do you know about it?

However, we have also seen in the **Pouvoir** chapter that when **savoir** is followed by another verb in the infinitive, it means to know how to do something:

- **Tu sais** nager? – Can you swim?
- **Mon grand-père sait** parler aux enfants – My grandfather is good at talking to children.
- **Il sait plaire à sa femme** – He knows how to please his wife.

All these examples use the **present** tense, of course. But you will often find **savoir** employed in the **conditional** tense (without an **if** clause). For example:

- "Je sais que vous voudriez savoir s'il y a une épicerie dans le prochain village mais **je ne saurais pas** vous répondre" ie I know that you would like to know whether there is a grocer's shop in the next village but I am afraid I cannot answer you.

- Le Maire de Saint Cyprien a le bras long. **Il saurait** frapper à toutes les bonnes portes même auprès du Ministre ie The mayor of Saint Cyprien would be able to knock on all the right doors. He has influence, even with the Minister.

Often, too, you will find savoir used in the perfect tense:

- "Mon frère **a toujours su** y faire" ie My brother has always known how to go about things in the right way.
- "J'ai toujours cru qu'on peut acheter n'importe quoi sur Internet sans risque mais ma femme – **je n'ai jamais su** la convaincre" ie I have always believed that it is safe to buy anything on the Internet but my wife – I have never been able to convince her.

One final point in this **Basics** section. **Savoir** can also be used when you want to say that you **realise** this or that. Normally, you would use **se rendre compte** but as these following examples show, **savoir** works perfectly well instead:

- "**Sans le savoir** ma mère a mis deux cuillères à café de sucre dans mon thé – mais **elle sait** que je déteste le sucre" ie Without realising it my mother put two teaspoons of sugar in my tea – but she knows that I hate sugar.
  A small culinary aside here: in recipes, a teaspoon of whatever is almost always referred to as a "cuillère à café" ie a coffee spoon.
- "Ma grand-mère a presque cent ans. Franchement, **elle ne sait plus** ce qu'elle dit" ie My grandmother is nearly a hundred. Frankly, she no longer realises what she is saying.

Summary

Savoir is very frequently encountered at this basic level. Use it:

- to say that you know something that can be considered a fact, even if it is not true! Here, use **je sais que**…
- to express ideas in tenses other than the present, notably the conditional, the perfect and the pluperfect tenses
- when you want to talk about something: here you will often precede it with **en** – **je n'en sais rien** for example
- very importantly, when you want to say that you know how to do something: **je sais nager**, for example.

These uses alone make **savoir** a very important and genuine "killer" verb at this **Basics** level.

Savoir is used in a wide array of expressions which are quite difficult to classify in any structured way. We shall have a look at these.

And it is occasionally followed by **falloir**. Some examples will make this use clear.

Savoir is also often used in the subjunctive – so we will have a look at some of these, too.

Finally, you will often hear it in its imperative form.

Some expressions using savoir:

Quite the most basic and easiest of these is **qui sait**? ie who knows?:

- "Est-ce qu'il va pleuvoir demain? **Qui sait**?" ie Is it going to rain tomorrow? Who knows?

Then there is **je sais bien, mais…** ie I know, but…

- "Je vais vous emmener **je ne sais où**" ie I am going to take you goodness knows where.
- "**Je ne sais pas qui** de ses amis m'a, dit que…" ie One of his friends, whose name I have forgotten, told me that…
- "**Je ne sais pas depuis combien de temps** il ne l'a pas vue" ie It has been I do not know how long since he last saw her.
- "Ce jardin **a je ne sais quoi** d'italien" ie This garden has something Italian about it.
- "Ma fille était tellement triste que **je ne savais quoi** faire pour la consoler" ie My daughter was so sad I was at a loss to know how to console her.

Here is a phrase you will hear very often:

On ne sait jamais ie You never know.

And sometimes you will hear **savoir** followed by **falloir**, as in these examples:

- "Veux-tu l'écharpe rouge ou l'écharpe rose?: **faudrait savoir**!" ie Do you want the red scarf or the pink scarf?: make up your mind!
- "Est-ce que la propriétaire va renouveler notre bail?: **faudrait savoir**!" ie Is the landlady going to renew our lease (or not)?: we ought to know!

With regard to **savoir** and the subjunctive, here are some examples:

- "Pour autant que **je sache**, les prévisions pour le week-end sont bonnes" ie As far as I know, the weather looks set fair for the weekend.
- "Va-t-il pleuvoir demain? Pas que **je sache**" ie Is it going to rain tomorrow? Not as far as I know.
- "Pascal est venu à notre réunion, mais pour autant que **je ne sache**, je ne l'ai pas invités!" ie Pascal came to our get-together but I am not aware that I invited him!

You will also hear **savoir** used in its imperative form. Here are some examples:

- "**Sachez** que je n'achèterais jamais une bouteille de vin à un tel prix" ie I will have you know that I would never buy a bottle of wine at such a price.
- "**Sachons**-le bien: s'il fait froid demain, je ne vais pas à la plage" ie Let us be quite clear: if it is cold tomorrow, I am not going to the beach. An alternative way of rendering "sachons-le bien" is "soyons clairs là-dessus". You will hear this expression quite frequently.

One final thought here. We have spoken elsewhere about the sloppiness of much conversational French, notably the habit of omitting letters or words – the **ne** in the double negative **ne pas** for example. So it is with **savoir**. Instead of **je ne sais pas** you will often hear what sounds like **j'ai pas**. The **e** of **je**, the **ne** and the **s** of **sais** are omitted and the whole construction is elided. Personally, I find it ugly, but you will hear it quite frequently, I am afraid.

Now You Are Really Speaking French!

This section is very short because, to repeat what I said in the introduction, there is no pronominal form of **savoir** – and the idiomatic applications are very few in number. Here are those that use this verb:

Être payé pour le savoir means to know it to one's cost.
Si jeunesse savait, si vieillesse pouvait, a proverb, means that youth is wasted on the young.
Savoir où le bât blesse means to know the secret hurts of someone. A "bât" is a donkey's saddle and if a donkey is required to carry or pull too much then it can suffer pain and injury. Obviously this will be hidden by the saddle itself.
Bon sang ne saurait mentir means that children inherit the good qualities and the faults of their parents.

Savoir and Connaître: a post script

At the basic level of knowing people, places and facts, **savoir** and **connaître** are clearly distinguishable: they are different verbs. However, beyond these basic meanings, overlaps start to occur. To illustrate, in the **Connaître** chapter I used the example of going to the pharmacist with a cough: "Qu'est-ce qu'elle connaît son affaire!" Does she know what she is talking about! Clearly we are not talking here about the pharmacist's knowledge of people and places but about, if you like, the science of pharmacology. She knows about pharmacology. But to be able to give good advice, she must know the facts underpinning the science of pharmacology. Here, therefore, the basic distinction is quite blurred. So, how do we separate out theses two verbs when there is much potential overlap?

Consider this example:

- "**Je connais** les règles de football" ie I know the rules of football.

But you can also say:

- "**Je sais** quelles sont les règles de football" ie I know what are the rules of football or what the rules of football are.

Similarly:

- "**Je connais** la date de naissance de Napoléan" or
- "**Je sais** quelle est la date de naissance de Napoléan" or

- "**Il connaît** mon adresse e-mail" or
- "**Il sait** quelle est mon adresse e-mail"

But if you wish, you can leave out the "what is/what are" parts of the **savoir** sentences. Then the **connaître** and **savoir** sentences are identical.

Conclusion

Savoir is a verb you will probably use several times in a typical day. **Je sais** and **je ne sais pas** slip from the lips with great ease. So, look out for it – and use it, particularly when you want to talk about what you or someone else seem to know. Here are a couple of conversations that show the verb in action.

Savoir: Conversation One

Julien has an unexpected day without school because of a teacher strike, but it is fairly obvious to Monique that he is at a bit of a loose end.

Monique: Qu'est-ce qu'il y a, Julien. Tu as l'air ennuyé.
Julien: Oui, maman. Je ne sais quoi faire aujourd'hui et c'est barbant à la maison.
Monique: Et tes devoirs?
Julien: Je les ai finis hier soir, maman. J'ai essayé de me mettre en contact avec Arnaud mais il n'a pas répondu. Je ne sais pas où il est.
Monique: Et Christophe?
Julien: Sa mère m'a dit qu'il est sorti et elle ne sait pas quand il rentre.
Monique: François alors?
Julien: La même chose. Il n'est pas là.
Monique: Que faire, alors? J'ai une idée, Julien. Tu pourrais m'aider. J'ai un tas de papiers que je dois trier.
Julien: Mais, maman, vraiment! Ce que tu fais – je n'en sais rien!
Monique: Mais, je peux te montrer. Et c'est pas difficile, vraiment.
Julien: Peut-être. J'aimerais en savoir plus sur ton travail, c'est sûr.
Monique: Excellent. Donc, commençons avec ce tas-là: les réponses écrites aux interviews que j'ai faites la semaine dernière. Trie – les selon leurs réponses à la première question: "Travaillez-vous ou non?". Tu auras deux tas, alors: "Oui" et "Non."
Julien: Et après?
Monique: Avec ceux qui disent "Oui," passe à la quatrième question où je demande s'ils sont contents de leur travail – encore une fois "Oui" ou "Non."
Julien: Mais, maman, c'est pas très intéressant-ça. D'ailleurs...

The telephone rings. Julien answers:

Salut, Christophe, qu'est-ce que tu fabriques aujourd'hui?... Ah bon?... Ah bon?... Ah bon?... À toute à l'heure, alors. Salut!

He puts the phone down:

Monique: Qu'est-ce qu'il se passe? C'était Christophe, non?
Julien: Tout à fait. Mais sais-tu la nouvelle?
Monique: Quoi?

Julien:	C'était son anniversaire avant hier et son papa lui a acheté une motocyclette. Mais il l'avait à peine sorti qu'il a eu un accident. Il vient de rentrer de l'hôpital bredouille – apparemment, sa motocyclette est bonne pour la casse.
Monique:	Le pauvre! Tu vas le voir immédiatement, j'imagine?
Julien:	Mais bien sûr. C'est dommage que je ne puisse pas t'aider maman!
Monique:	Ah bon?!

Savoir: Conversation Two

François' boss, his company's Marketing Director, has called a meeting of all the product managers to discuss progress to date.

Le Chef de marketing:	Vous savez que l'année se passe assez bien malgré les problèmes que l'on a connus au mois de janvier. Mais je crois que nous pourrions augmenter notre part de marché pendant les six prochains mois. L'économie commence à repartir: c'est l'occasion rêvée pour mettre le paquet. Qu'est-ce que tu en penses, Vincent?
Vincent:	Oui, vous avez raison. À en croire les derniers chiffres, nos clients devraient avoir un peu plus d'argent dans leurs poches – et je crois, aussi, que le marché n'est pas encore à saturation. Pour autant que je sache, notre gouvernement n'a pas l'intention de changer de cap, nous non plus. Mais bien qu'il y ait des créneaux à occuper, je ne pense pas que notre stratégie publicitaire soit adéquate. En ce moment, la concurrence est acharnée et nos détaillants ont besoin de notre aide.
François:	Je suis d'accord avec Vincent. Sachons-le bien: nous sommes numéro deux sur le marché et nous devrions faire le forcing où nos produits seront menacés par les nouveautés venant des nouvelles entreprises numériques.
Le Chef de marketing:	Tu as raison, François. Donc, qu'est-ce que tu préconises?
François:	Tout le monde autour de cette table sait que notre image de marque, due largement à nos efforts à la télé, est vraiment forte. Mais la plupart de nos clients croient que nous sommes relativement chers.
Vincent:	Peut-être, François mais il y en a qui croient que nos produits proposent un bon rapport qualité-prix.
François:	Malheureusement, de moins en moins, Vincent. Voilà donc je préconise les actions suivantes: D'abord une nouvelle étude sur la qualité de nos produits et leurs prix. Ça fait longtemps qu'on ne l'a pas fait. Mais ce genre d'analyse est très spécialisé et je doute que nous puissions faire cette expertise en interne. Je connais un consultant en études de marché

– et je sais qu'il est très expérimenté. Je voudrais lui en parler.

Deuxième action. Nous devrions soutenir nos détaillants, en leur donnant une remise sur nos prix catalogue de dix pour cent.

Le Chef de marketing: Mais ça devrait réduire notre marge bénéficiaire.

François: D'autre part, nos revendeurs seraient plus motivés pour stocker et pour vendre nos marques, plutôt que les marques de nos concurrents. Je crois que cette stratégie serait très éfficace.

Finalement je crois que notre site web n'est pas adéquat. Nos pages web sont difficiles d'accés parce que notre navigateur ne vaut pas grand-chose et aussi parce que le responsable n'est plus à la hauteur. Je sais qu'il est enthousiaste mais ce n'est plus suffisant. On a besoin de quelqu'un qui connaît bien les développements récents – surtout la tendance importante de s'éloigner de l'ordinateur et d'aller dans la direction des mobiles et des tablettes. Ça, c'est l'avenir, vous savez, pour tout le monde et pour notre enterprise.

Le Chef de marketing: François, je partage ton avis à cent pour cent. En effet c'est le bon moment pour saisir l'occasion. Étant donné que tes idées sont très pertinentes, François, je veux que tu prépares un rapport indiquant les grandes lignes de tes stratégies – mettons pour la prochaine réunion de ce groupe, dans un mois. Ça va?

François: Mais bien sûr. Ça me fera plaisir.

Le Chef de marketing: Merci bien tout le monde. À la prochaine fois.

Some words you might not yet know

- ennuyé(e) - bored
- barbant(e) - boring
- se mettre en contact avec quelqu'un - to get in touch with someone
- répondre (à) - to reply
- un tas - a pile
- trier - to sort
- d'ailleurs - besides
- salut - hello / goodbye
- une motocyclette - a motorcycle (not a motorbike)
- rentrer bredouille - to come home empty- handed
- être bon pour la casse - a write-off
- augmenter - to increase
- la part de marché - market share
- l'occasion rêvée. - the perfect opportunity
- repartir - to grow again
- à en croire les derniers chiffres - according to the latest statistics
- être à saturation - to be saturated
- le cap - the strategy / the direction
- un créneau - a gap
- une stratégie publicitaire - an advertising strategy
- adéquate(e) - adequate
- la concurrence - the competition
- acharné(e) - fierce
- un détaillant - a retailer
- faire le forcing - to go for the hard sell
- menacé(e) - threatened
- une nouveauté - something new
- numérique - digital
- préconiser - to recommend
- l'image (f) de marque - brand image
- proposer - to offer
- un bon rapport qualité-prix - good value for money
- de moins en moins - less and less
- une action - an action
- une étude - a study
- en interne - in-house
- un consultant en études de marché - a market-research consultant
- les prix catalogue - list prices
- la marge bénéficiaire - the profit margin
- d'autre part - on the other hand
- un revendeur - a re-seller
- une marque - a brand
- un site web - a website

- une page web -   a webpage
- un navigateur -   a web browser
- un responsable -   a manager
- éloigner -   to move away from
- un ordinateur -   a computer
- un mobile -   a mobile telephone
- une tablette -   a tablet computer
- pertinent(e) -   relevant
- un rapport -   a report
- les grandes lignes -   the major aspects
- à la prochaine fois -   until the next time

Savoir: Exercises

Put one of the three words in brackets in the spaces below:

1.   (Je, Ils, Vous) (   ) savez que j'ai raison.

2.   Il (avait, avaient, avions) (   ) su de n'y pas aller.

3.   Si j'(ai, avais, avait) (   ) su, je l'aurais fait moi-même.

4.   (Sache, Sachez, Sachons) (   ) vos verbes!

5.   Il faut que je (sache, sais, sait) (   ) mon code de la route si je veux passer mon examen du permis de conduire.

6.   Il ne (su, sache, savait) (   ) pas où se mettre.

7.   Je sais ce que je (sait, sais, saurai) (   ).

Translate the following English sentences into French:

8.   Can you swim?

9.   I know how to please my son.

10.   I know that you would like to go to South Africa.

11.   My friend would be able to knock on all the right doors.

12.   My wife always knows how to go about things in the right way.

13. Without realising it, I switched on the television.

14. This garden has something French about it.

15. You never know. It could rain today.

16. As far as I know, the train arrives at eleven o'clock.

17. I know what the rules of football are.

18. He knows what his e-mail address is.

19. I do not know what to do today.

20. Everyone around this table knows that I am right.

21. I know that my son's teacher is enthusiastic – but this is not enough.

Savoir: Answers

1. Vous
2. avait
3. avais
4. Sachez
5. sache
6. savait
7. sais
8. Savez-vous nager?
9. Je sais plaire à mon fils
10. Je sais que vous voudriez aller en Afrique du Sud
11. Mon ami(e) saurait frapper à toutes les bonnes portes
12. Ma femme a toujours su y faire
13. Sans le savoir j'ai branché la télé
14. Ce jardin a je ne sais quoi de français
15. On ne sait jamais. Il pourrait pleuvoir aujourd'hui
16. Pour autant que je sache, le train arrive à onze heures
17. Je sais quelles sont les règles de football
18. Il connaît son adresse e-mail
19. Je ne sais quoi faire aujourd'hui
20. Tout le monde autour de cette table sait que j'ai raison
21. Je sais que le prof de mon fils est enthousiaste – mais ce n'est pas suffisant.

Chapter Twenty
Rendre

Introduction

You have already encountered **rendre** several times: **rendre visite** à quelqu'un, **se rendre compte** and **rendre de la monnaie**, for example. These uses of **rendre** are enough to show how important and useful **rendre** actually is. In this chapter devoted to the verb we will certainly reprise what you already know about it. But we will also have a look at it in action, particularly in place of **aller**, to talk about going somewhere or other. But is has other meanings, too. (It can even mean to vomit!)

As you know it is also employed in its pronominal form **se rendre**, meaning to go, for example. It also has one or two uses in locutions. So there is plenty to get on with. Let us begin with its conjugations.

The Rendre Conjugations

Present Tense

Je rends	Nous rendons		
Tu rends	Vous rendez		
Il rend	Ils rendent		
Elle rend	Elles rendent		

Future Tense

Je rendrai	Nous rendrons
Tu rendras	Vous rendrez
Il rendra	Ils rendront
Elle rendra	Elles rendront

Imperfect Tense

Je rendais	Nous rendions
Tu rendais	Vous rendiez
Il rendait	Ils rendaient
Elle rendait	Elles rendaient

Perfect Tense

J'ai rendu	Nous avons rendu
Tu as rendu	Vous avez rendu
Il a rendu	Ils ont rendu
Elle a rendu	Elles ont rendu

Future Perfect Tense

J'aurai rendu	Nous aurons rendu
Tu auras rendu	Vous aurez rendu
Il aura rendu	Ils auront rendu
Elle aura rendu	Elles auront rendu

Pluperfect Tense

J'avais rendu	Nous avions rendu
Tu avais rendu	Vous aviez rendu
Il avait rendu	Ils avaient rendu
Elle avait rendu	Elles avaient rendu

Present Conditional Tense

Je rendrais	Nous rendrions
Tu rendrais	Vous rendriez
Il rendrait	Ils rendraient
Elle rendrait	Elles rendraient

Past Conditional Tense

J'aurais rendu	Nous aurions rendu
Tu aurais rendu	Vous auriez rendu
Il aurait rendu	Ils auraient rendu
Elle aurait rendu	Elles auraient rendu

Present Subjunctive Tense

Je rende	Nous rendions
Tu rendes	Vous rendiez
Il rende	Ils rendent
Elle rende	Elles rendent

Imperative

Rends
Rendons
Rendez

Rendre: The Basics

We met quite the most basic role for **rendre** in the **Être** chapter. Remember this?:

- "Si la caissière, au lieu de vous **rendre** la monnaie sur 10€, vous **rend** sur la monnaie de 20€, seriez vous...?" In this example, **rendre** means to give back (or to take back) something or other.

Here are a couple more examples:

- "Mon médecin était incroyable. J'étais vraiment malade mais **il m'a rendu** la santé. En effet, **il m'a rendu** la vie" ie My doctor was incredible. I was really ill but he restored my health. Indeed, he saved my life.
- "Cette lessive **rendrait** l'éclat du neuf à votre linge. C'est un produit miraculeux!" ie This detergent will make your washing as good as new. It is a miracle product!

Beyond notions of giving something back, **rendre** can be used to talk about repaying this or that. To illustrate:

- "Quand je me suis cassé la jambe, Cécile a été vraiment gentille. Après, j'ai voulu lui **rendre** la politesse. Donc, je lui ai acheté quelque chose de spécial – un bracelet en or" ie When I broke my leg, Cecile was really kind. Afterwards I wanted to return her kindness so I bought her something special – a gold bracelet.

One can even use **rendre** to talk about giving back someone's freedom:

- "La décision du gouvernement de l'Afrique du Sud de **rendre** la liberté à Nelson Mandela était courageuse mais opportune" ie The South African government's decision to free Nelson Mandela was courageous but timely.

Beyond giving back and repaying, **rendre** can also be used where we in English might use the verb to make, as in "to make someone happy". For example:

- "Quand ma fille m'a dit qu'elle m'accomagnerait à la Nouvelle-Zélande, elle m'a **rendu** vraiment heureuse" ie When my daughter told me that she would come with me to New Zealand, she made me really happy.

On the other hand, **rendre** can be used to say that something is driving you mad!:

- "J'ai ce problème avec la boîte de vitesse depuis le jour où j'ai acheté la voiture. C'est à vous **rendre** fou!" ie I have had this problem with the gearbox since the day I bought the car. It is enough to drive you mad!

Rendre can also be used to say that something is producing or rendering something – a liquid, for example. In the kitchen you might put some salt on your aubergines, say, to get some of the juice out:

- "Pour **rendre** l'eau de vos aubergines, coupez-les en lamelles et saupoudrez – les avec une couche très fine de sel. Au bout d'une demi-heure, lavez – les et séchez – les avec un torchon sec" ie To get the liquid out of your aubergines cut them into slices and cover them with a fine coating of salt. After half an hour, wash them and dry them with a dry tea towel. (You can do the same with cucumbers, incidentally!)

Trees, too, can yield their fruit:

- "Cette année mes noyers **ont bien rendu,** et les noix elles – même sont délicieuses" ie This year my walnut trees have given a good crop – and the walnuts themselves are delicious.

You can also use **rendre** to talk about something producing an effect. For example:

- "Le bureau **rend bien** dans le vestibule, mais, à mon sens, **il rendrait mieux au salon**" ie The desk looks good in the hall but in my opinion, it would look better in the lounge.

On a much less pleasant note, **rendre** can also mean to vomit!:

- "Je n'aurais pas dû manger deux barbes à papa, maman. Maintenant j'ai envie de **rendre**" ie I should not have eaten two candy-floss, mummy. Now I feel sick!

Penultimately in this section, please note that **rendre** can be used to talk about surrender:

- "A la fin de la bataille de Waterloo, les soldats français **ont rendu** leurs armes. Les troupes britanniques avait gagné une victoire remarquable" ie At the end of the Battle of Waterloo, the French soldiers laid down their arms. The British troops had won a remarkable victory.

Finally, let us briefly reprise **rendre visite à quelqu'un**, an expression which is often used to talk about, say, visiting a friend:

- "Je dois **rendre visite à Juliette** ce weekend. Je sais qu'elle est en bonne voie de guérison et qu'elle apprécierait de la compagnie" ie I must pay Juliette a visit this weekend. I know that she is well on the way to recovery and that she would appreciate some company.

Summary

Use **rendre** when you want to:

- say that you are expecting something back – change in the supermarket, for example
- talk about repaying this or that – someone's kindness, for example
- talk about making someone happy (or sad!)
- talk about things yielding something – liquids, fruit trees, etc.
- talk about something producing an effect – hopefully a desired effect!
- say that you feel sick
- say that someone is surrendering.

Getting Better

If you want to talk abut going somewhere you already know to use **aller**. However, in many cases you could just as easily use **se rendre**, the pronominal form of **rendre**. In this section we will look at **se rendre** in some detail, beginning with its uses in place of **aller**, meaning to go. Here are some examples:

- "Cet aprèm je **me rends** aux grands magasins au centre ville. J'espère y acheter une table anglaise et même des tables gigognes pour le séjour. Qui sait, je pourrais même trouver une table de chevet pour la petite chambre" ie This afternoon I am going to the department stores in the centre of town. I hope to buy (there) a gate-legged table and a nest of tables for the living room. Who knows, I might even find a bed-side table for the small bedroom. Or
- "Mon fils **s'est rendu** au terrain de golf hier avec ses crosses de golf. Malheureusement il n'était pas autorisé à jouer à cause de son âge" ie My son went to the golf course yesterday with his golf clubs. Unfortunately, he was not allowed to play because of his age. Or
- "**S'ils s'étaient rendus** à la plage ce matin ils auraient pu se baigner mais à partir de midi les vagues étaient trop fortes. Le revers de la médaille était qu'ils pouvaient **se rendre** a la pêche" ie If they had gone to the beach this morning they could have swum, but from midday the waves were too strong. The other side of the coin was that they could go fishing.

When **se rendre** is followed by an adjective, however, it can mean to make oneself this or that. For example:

- "Si tu continues à manger comme ça, Jean-Luc, tu vas **te rendre** malade" ie If you continue eating like that, Jean-Luc, you are going to make yourself ill. Or
- "S'il continue à s'habiller comme l'as de pique, il va **se rendre** ridicule!" ie If he continues to dress like the ace of spaces, he is going to make himself look ridiculous! Or
- "Je sais ce qu'elle fabrique. Si elle continue à vous aider toute la journée, toutes les semaines, elle croit qu'elle va **se rendre** indispensable" ie I know what she is up to. If she carries on helping you all day, throughout the weeks, she believes that she it going to make herself indispensible.

Now You Are Really Speaking French!

Se rendre is used in expressions such as **se rendre compte que** – to realise. This is a use of the verb that you are already familiar with. Beyond that, it is used in several locutions and in one idiomatic expression that I know of. And that is it!

- **"Je me suis rendu compte que** j'aurais dû quitter ma boîte il y a plusieurs années mais elle manquait toujours de personnel et j'avais, donc, l'impression que mes compétences étaient vraiment bien prisées" ie I realised that I should have left my company several years ago but they were always short-staffed and I thought, therefore, that my skills were really highly valued. Or
- **Elle s'est rendu compte** presque dès le premier jour **que** la comptabilité n'était pas son truc. Au bout d'un an elle s'est dit "ça suffit, j'en ai assez. Je m'en vais" ie She realised almost from the first day that accounting was not for her. After a year she said "that's enough, I am fed up. I'm off."

Now for those **locutions**:

Rendre le dernier souper means to give up the ghost.
Rendre l'âme means the same thing:

- "Enfin ma tondeuse a **rendu l'âme**" ie My lawnmower has given up the ghost at last.

Rendre gloire à means to pay homage.
Rendre grâce à quelqu'un means to give thanks for someone.

And here, finally, is the only idiomatic expressions featuring **se rendre**, to my knowledge at least:

Rendre son tablier, a bit like "to throw in the towel", means to quit one's job or "démissionner":

- "Étant donné ce que vous avez fait dans cet atelier, j'ai parfaitement le droit de procéder à un licenciement pur et simple. Vaut mieux à mon sens que je vous persuade de **rendre votre tablier**. Comme ça vous aurez plus d'opportunité de trouver un autre emploi" ie Given what you did in the work-shop, I am perfectly in my rights to fire you. In my view it would be better if I could persuade you to resign. That way you will have more chance of finding another job.

Conclusion

Rendre is a word likely to be in fairly regular use whenever you need to talk about giving (or taking) back, about going somewhere, about realising – and much more. In particular, use it just for a change instead of **aller**: it is a good idea to introduce some freshness into your conversations wherever possible.

And now for a couple of conversations.

Rendre: Conversation One

Maryse recently bought a pair of shoes in a shop in Sarlat but she is not happy with them. The first time that she wore them the soles began to detach themselves from the uppers. Naturally, she decided to take them back to the shop.

Le serveur:	Bonjour madame. Qu'est-ce qu'il fait beau! Que puis - je faire pour vous, aujourd'hui?
Maryse:	Vous vous souvenez de moi, peut-être. Vous m'avez servie quand j'ai acheté ces chaussures il y a quelques jours.
Serveur:	Mais bien sûr, madame. J'espère que vous en êtes contente?
Maryse:	Franchement, non. À vrai dire les semelles ont commencé à se détacher la première fois que je les ai mises. C'est pour ça que je suis revenue. Je voudrais les rendre.
Serveur:	Je suis vraiment désolé, madame. Cela ne m'est jamais arrivé auparavant. Je suis navré de vous avoir dérangée. Mais laissez-moi les voir...
	Oui, vous avez raison. Alors, que voulez-vous que je fasse? Je peux vous rendre les mêmes chaussures si vous voulez. Sinon, vous pouvez choisir autre chose. Et cela va sans dire que je peux vous rendre l'argent si vous voulez. Comment est-ce que vous avez payé – en espèces, par chéque ou avec une carte bancaire?
Maryse:	J'ai payé en espèces. Et souvenez-vous qu'au lieu de me rendre la monnaie sur 50€ vous m'avez rendu la monnaie sur 100€?
Serveur:	Oh là, là! Vous avez raison, madame. Je me rappelle, maintenant. C'était mardi dernier que vous les avez achetées, n'est ce pas? Nous étions débordés ce jour-là. Normalement je fais très peu d'erreurs, mais...
Maryse:	Ne vous inquiétez pas, monsieur. Ça m'arrive aussi de temps en temps.
Serveur:	Vous êtes très gentille, madame. Mais revenons à nos moutons! Comme je disais tout à l'heure, vous pouvez reprendre le même modèle ou bien vous pouvez choisir autre chose. Si vous voulez je peux vous donner un avoir. Si vous choississez quelque chose ce matin, étant donné votre gêne, je serais ravi de vous proposer une remise de 20% sur n'importe quel modèle de votre choix.
Maryse:	Ma foi! Comme quoi!
Serveur:	Quoi, madame!
Maryse:	Que les meilleurs magasins ne sont pas forcément les plus chers. J'ai payé trois fois rien ces chaussures et quand je suis revenue les rendre, je n'attendais pas grand-chose.
Serveur:	En effet, comme quoi, madame!

| Maryse: | Dans ce cas, je choisirai le modèle le plus cher que vous me proposez. Avec une remise de 20% ça sera une affaire quelque soit le prix! Allons-y. |
| Serveur: | Allons-y, madame! |

Rendre: Conversation Two

Corinne and Thierry have bought that old farmhouse and are now in the middle of making it look and feel a bit more habitable!

Corinne:	Que penses-tu, Thierry? Devrions – nous mettre la vieille armoire dans notre chambre? Elle rendrait bien je crois. Puis nous pourrions mettre le canapé–lit dans la chambres d'à côté – il y aurait de la place, puis la chaise berçante ça irait dans le séjour, puis nous...
Thierry:	Attends un instant, Corinne! Tu sautes du coq à l'âne! Revenons à nos moutons: que faire avec le bahut? Je crois que ça rendrait bien dans la salle à manger. Qu'en penses-tu?
Corinne:	Désolée, Thierry. Je suis tellement excitée, c'est tout. Oui, tu as raison. Le bahut rendrait bien dans la salle à manger. En tout cas, le bahut sert à contenir nos couverts en argent et la vaisselle. C'est logiquement là qu'il faut le poser. Mais les rideaux qu'on avait dans l'appart. Ils sont assez sales et décolorés – mais ma lessive devrait leur rendre l'éclat du neuf. Je crois que nous pourrions les accrocher aux fenêtres dans la salle à manger. Je ne veux pas les remplacer. De nos jours, les rideaux coûtent les yeux de la tête!
Thierry:	Si tu me dis que les rideaux coûtent les yeux de la tête, je veux bien te croire, Corinne! Mais passons à autre chose. Qu'est-ce que tu penses de la couleur des murs dans le séjour? Devrais – je leur donner un coup de peinture? Ils rendraient mieux, je pense.
Corinne:	Ça, c'est sûr, Thierry. En ce moment la couleur est trop foncée: quelque chose de plus clair serait une excellente idée à mon avis – rose pâle peut-être?
Thierry:	On voit cette couleur partout de nos jours. Quand même, ça servirait à éclaircir la pièce, je suis sûr. D'accord, je le ferai, la semaine prochaine peut-être. En attendant nous pouvons la tolérer telle qu'elle.
Corinne:	Et l'entrée, qu'en penses – tu Thierry? J'aime moins bien le papier peint. C'est sale et abimé. Nous pourrions l'enlever et si les murs derrière sont en bon état nous pourrions leur donner un coup de peinture aussi. Cela me rendrait vraiment heureuse. En fin de compte,

l'entrée est la première chose qu'on voit quand on entre dans une maison. C'est la première impression qui compte.

Thierry: D'accord. On pourrait commencer demain. Après tout, c'est un jour férié et Bricomarché est ouvert toute la journée. Mais nous devrions nous y rendre de bonne heure, avant que la foule arrive.

Corinne: Et si nous nous y rendions de bonne heure nous aurions largement le temps pour aller aux Meubles Céleguin et puis rentrer à midi, mettons. Ça veut dire que nous pourrions passer le reste de la journée dans l'entrée.

Thierry: D'accord, mais dans un premier temps je dois vérifier que j'ai tous les outils dont nous avons besoin, y compris le machin qui sert à brûler la vieille peinture – comment ça s'appelle, déjà?

Corinne: Le chalumeau?

Thierry: Le chalumeau!

Corinne: Et tes pinceaux? Tu en as assez?

Thierry: Je crois, mais peut-être je devrais me rendre à Tout Pour la Maison. Ils ont une excellente gamme de pinceaux, et le rapport qualité – prix est excellent aussi.

Corinne: Mais d'abord pourrions – nous essayer de réparer la gazinière? Tu sais que je dois l'allumer chaque fois avec une allumette, et les allumettes sont toutes mouillées à cause de l'humidité dans la cuisine. Vraiment c'est à vous rendre fou!

Thierry: Je comprends, Corinne. Mais avec tout ce qu'on doit faire demain il nous faudra nous lever à cinq heures du matin. Ça va?

Corinne: Thierry, j'espère que tu plaisantes. Franchement, je suis déjà crevée. Je souhaite que nous n'ayons pas acheté cette maison. Elle me tuera!

Thierry: Pas encore, j'espère Corinne. Il nous reste encore six pièces à décorer! Vivement les vacances!

Some words you might not yet know

- se souvenir de quelqu'un - to remember somebody
- à vrai dire - to be honest
- se détacher - to come apart
- navré(e) - sorry
- se rappeler - to recall
- débordé(e) - snowed under
- modèle (m) - style, design
- un avoir - a credit note
- la gêne - trouble, bother
- n'importe quel(le) - any
- ma foi! - well!
- comme quoi! - it just goes to show!
- trois fois rien - next to nothing
- attendre - to expect
- quelque soit - whatever
- une armoire - a wardrobe
- une chaise berçante - a rocking-chair
- sauter du coq à l'âne - to jump from one subject to another
- revenons à nos moutons - let us get back to the subject
- la salle à manger - the dining room
- les couverts (m) en argent - the silver cutlery
- la vaisselle - the crockery
- les rideaux (m) - the curtains
- décoloré(e) - discoloured
- la lessive - washing powder
- accrocher - to hang
- les fenêtres (f) - windows
- remplacer - to replace
- coûter les yeux de la tête - to cost the earth
- les murs (m) - the walls
- donner un coup de peintre - to give a lick of paint
- foncé(e) - dark
- clair(e) - light
- rose pâle - magnolia
- éclaircir - to lighten
- la pièce - the room
- tolérer - to put up with
- tel(le) quel(le) - as it is
- l'entrée (f) - the hallway
- papier peint (m) - wallpaper
- c'est la première impression qui compte - first impressions count
- un jour férié - a bank holiday
- les foules (f) - the crowds
- les outils (m) - tools

- brûler -   to burn
- la peinture -   paintwork
- un chalumeau -   a blow torch
- les pinceaux (m) -   paintbrushes
- tenir -   to stock
- une gamme -   a range
- la gazinière -   the gas cooker
- allumer -   to light
- une allumette -   a match
- mouillé(e) -   damp
- l'humidité (f) -   dampness
- creve(é) -   tired / exhausted
- décorer -   to decorate

Rendre: Exercises

Choose one of the three words in brackets for the spaces below:

1.   (rend, rendra, rendu) Elle m'a (   ) la monnaie sur 50€.

2.   (rendrai, rendre, rendu) Cette lessive va (   ) l'éclat de neuf à mon linge.

3.   (rendais, rendra, rendu) Mon mari m'a (   ) vraiment heureuse quand il a acheté ce beau diamante.

4.   (rendre, rends, rendrait) C'est à vous (   ) fou, ce machin.

5.   (rendez, rendra, rendre) Cette année je crois que mes figuiers vont bien (   ).

6.   (rendu, rendaient, rendent) La Deuxième Guerre mondiale s'est terminée quand les soldats allemands ont (   ) leur armes.

Translate into French the underlined parts of these English sentences:

7.   I must pay my mother a visit this weekend.

8.   This morning I went to the market in town.

9.   If we had gone to the sales yesterday we would have been very disappointed.

10.   If you carry on drinking like this you are going to make yourself sick.

11.   She is trying to make herself indispensable.

12.   <u>I realise that</u> I cannot keep on working like this.

13.   <u>He realised</u> that he would not get promoted without a professional
       qualification.

       Translate the underlined parts of the following French sentences into English:
14.   Enfin ma machine à coudre <u>a rendu l'âme.</u>

15.   À mon avis, vous devriez <u>rendre votre tablier</u>. Franchement, vous êtes nul!

Rendre: Answers

1.   rendu
2.   rendre
3.   rendu
4.   rendre
5.   rendre
6.   rendu
7.   Je dois rendre visite à ma mère
8.   je me suis rendu(e)
9.   Si nous nous étions rendu(e)s
10. tu vas te rendre malade
11. se rendre
12. Je me rends compte que
13. Il s'est rendu compte
14. has given up the ghost
15. resign, quit your job.

Chapter Twenty-One
Prendre

Introduction

Prendre means **to take** as in "I will take a bath now" or "I will take these pink socks, please." But it has many more applications when you use it to render English phrasal verbs such as to take out, to take on, to take in, to take up etc – and we will look at lots of these in this chapter. Very often, too, it is used where we might use "to have" in English – "I will have the roast beef, please." Indeed, **prendre** can be used interchangeably in these dual meanings, to take and to have.

But **prendre** also has a pronominal form, **se prendre**, which is often used when you want to say, for example, "who does he think he is?" Variants on **se prendre** are **se prendre à**, **s'en prendre à** and **s'y prendre**.

The verb also has lots of idiomatic uses. So let us begin, as always, with its conjugations.

The Prendre Conjugations

Present Tense

Je prends	Nous prenons
Tu prends	Vous prenez
Il prend	Ils prennent
Elle prend	Elles prennent

Future Tense

Je prendrai	Nous prendrons
Tu prendras	Vous prendrez
Il prendra	Ils prendront
Elle prendra	Elles prendront

Imperfect Tense

Je prenais	Nous prenions
Tu prenais	Vous preniez
Il prenait	Ils prenaient
Elle prenait	Elles prenaient

Perfect Tense

J'ai pris	Nous avons pris
Tu as pris	Vous avez pris
Il a pris	Ils ont pris
Elle a pris	Elles ont pris

Future Perfect Tense

J'aurai pris	Nous aurons pris
Tu auras pris	Vous aurez pris
Il aura pris	Ils auront pris
Elle aura pris	Elles auront pris

Pluperfect Tense

J'avais pris	Nous avions pris
Tu avais pris	Vous aviez pris
Il avait pris	Ils avaient pris
Elle avait pris	Elles avaient pris

Present Conditional Tense

Je prendrais	Nous prendrions
Tu prendrais	Vous prendriez
Il prendrait	Ils prendraient
Elle prendrait	Elles prendraient

Past Conditional Tense

J'aurais pris	Nous aurions pris
Tu aurais pris	Vous auriez pris
Il aurait pris	Ils auraient pris
Elle aurait pris	Elles auraient pris

Present Subjunctive Tense

Je prenne	Nous prenions
Tu prennes	Vous preniez
Il prenne	Ils prennent
Elle prenne	Elles prennent

Imperative

Prends
Prenons
Prenez

Prendre: The Basics

Prendre basically means to take. But it has several take applications. Already you know that in a restaurant you will use **prendre** to order your meal: "**Je prends** les escargots s'il vous plaît." Here, **prendre** really means "to have", ie I will have the snails, please. And in the boulangerie you might say: "**Je prends** deux baguettes, s'il vous plaît", I will have two baguettes please.

But **prendre** has many more uses and can be a substitute for many other verbs: **Prendre un bain de soleil** means to sunbathe, for example.

There are so many different uses of **prendre** that I shall make no attempt to list them here in these introductory paragraphs. Instead I will simply give you lots of examples of **prendre** in use:

- "Tu devrais **prendre** ta douche ce matin, Janine. Le plombier arrive cet après-midi pour couper l'eau dans la salle de bain" ie You should take your shower this morning, Janine. The plumber is coming to cut the water off in the bathroom this afternoon.
- "Le photographe **a pris** des photos de nos enfants dans le jardin mais franchement j'ai été déçue. Celles sur la balançoire étaient plutôt floues"ie The photographer took some pictures of our children in the garden but frankly, I was disappointed with them. Those of them on the swing were rather fuzzy.
- "Nous avons plusieurs livres au sujet de la Seconde Guerre mondiale, monsieur. Lesquels **prenez-vous**?" ie We have several books on the subject of the Second World War, sir. Which ones will you take?
- "Si tu sors ce matin, Jean-François, **prends** ton parapluie. Il pleut à grosses gouttes et la gare est assez loin des magasins" ie If you go out this morning, take your umbrella, Jean-François. It is raining heavily and the station is quite a long way from the shops.

- "Voudrais-tu une tasse de café, Hélène?"
  "Oui, merci"
  "Bon et rappelle-moi, est-ce que **tu prends** du sucre?" ie
  Would you like a cup of coffee, Hélène?
  Yes, please.
  Good. Remind me, do you take sugar?
- "Si vous allez à Lille ce weekend, **prenez** le train. C'est beaucoup plus commode" ie If you go to Lille this weekend, take the train. It is much more convenient.
- "Bien que ce soit une exellente idée, je préfère **prendre** ma voiture – elle est beaucoup plus confortable que le train" ie Although it is a good idea, I prefer to take my car. It is much more comfortable than the train.
- "Vous voulez aller au Printemps? Dans ce cas, **prenez** la rue Saint Honoré. C'est un peu moins direct mais la rue est vraiment belle avec ses illuminations à Noël?" ie You want to go to Printemps? In that case, take the Rue Saint Honoré. It is a bit less direct but it is really beautiful with its illuminations at Christmas.
- "Quelle est votre pointure, madame?"
  "Normalement en chaussures **je prends** du 38" ie
  What is your shoe size, madame?
  Normally I take a 38.
- "J'ai beau faire, le feu ne veut pas **prendre**. Je crois que le bois est encore mouillé" ie Whatever I do, the fire won't start. I think that the wood is still damp.
- "Au feu rouge, **prenez** à gauche. La pharmacie ne se trouve qu'à cent mètres" ie At the traffic lights, bear left. The chemist is only one hundred metres away.
- "J'ai bossé sans relâche cette année mais à Noël je vais **prendre** quelques jours de congé" ie I have worked ceaselessly this year but at Christmas I am going to take a few days off.
- "Mes gosses sont fabuleux et je les adore – mais **ils me prennent** tout mon temps" ie My kids are fabulous and I adore them but they take up all my time.
- "Je ne comprends pas. J'ai ajouté trois feuilles de gélatine au mélange mais, **il ne prend pas**" ie I do not understand. I added three gelatine leaves to the mixture but, nontheless, it is not setting.
- "Le vendeur a essayé de me convaincre que je devrais acheter une nouvelle voiture mais, franchement, avec moi, **ça ne prends pas**!" ie The salesman tried to convince me to buy a new car but, frankly, with me that does not wash!

- "Cette maison va me tuer – il y a trop de boulot. Je vais **prendre** une femme de ménage" ie This house is going to kill me – there is too much work. I am going to take on a cleaning lady.
- "Je suis désolé, madame mais aujourd'hui le train à destination de Bordeaux **ne prend pas** de voyageurs à Bergerac à cause des travaux sur la ligne" ie I am sorry madam, but today, the Bordeaux train is not taking on any passengers at Bergerac because of work on the line.
- "Parce que vous n'avez pas de renseignements imprimés, pourriez-vous me donner du papier et un stylo pour que je puisse **prendre** des notes, s'il vous plaît?" ie Because you have no printed information, could you give me some paper and a pen so that I can take down some notes, please?
- "Je crois que **je prends** l'entrecôte, s'il vous plaît – et **je la prends** saignante" ie I think I will have the entrecôte steak, please – and I will have it rare.
  A small grammatical note here. When you want to indicate an action that is about to take place and which expresses personal intentions, use either the present tense of the verb **aller** plus the infinitive, or the present tense of **prendre**. So you can say "**je vais prendre** l'entrecôte" but never use the future of **prendre** to say that you will have this or that. So never say "**je prendrai**." Either say "**je prends**" or "**je vais prendre**".
- "Tu peux **prendre** le beurre dans le frigo, Alain, s'il te plaît. Je veux l'ajouter à ma sauce" ie You can take the butter out of the fridge, please Alain. I want to add it to my sauce.
- "Je suis allé à la retoucherie ce matin chercher mon pantalon mais **il m'a pris** 15€ pour le racourcir. C'est du vol, ça!" ie I went to the clothes repair shop this morning to pick up my trousers but he charged me 15€ to shorten them. That is daylight robbery!
- "Je suis allé chez le prêteur sur gages hier. Tu sais, **il prend** une commission de 30% sur le prêt. C'est exorbitant, je crois" ie I went to the pawnbroker's yesterday. Do you know, he charges 30% commission on the loan. It is too much, I think.
- "Ma soeur à cassé un vase tout à l'heure mais c'est à moi que maman l'a reproché. C'est toujours moi qui **prend** pour ma soeur!" ie My sister broke a vase just now but my mother blamed me. I always get blamed for what my sister does!
- "Il a reçu la nouvelle de la disparition de son oncle la semaine dernière. **Il l'a mal pris**" ie He received the news that his uncle died last week. He took it rather badly.
- "Je sais qu'il a un comportement bizarre en ce moment mais il y a plusieurs façons de **prendre** le problème" ie I know that he is behaving strangely at the moment, but there are several ways of tackling the problem.

Summary

Prendre has many applications. Most of them mean to take or to have in many different contexts. Occasionally as you have seen though, **prendre** can be used to render other English verbs – to start, to bear, to let, to charge, to blame and to tackle.

Getting Better

You can build on your basic knowledge of **prendre** by getting to know the verb in its **pronominal** form. We will begin with **se prendre**, then go to **se prendre à**, then to **s'en prendre à** and finally to **s'y prendre**.

Se prendre

Use **se prendre** when you want to say, for example, that someone takes himself for this or that:

- "Franchement je ne crois pas que Jacques soit très intelligent mais **il se prend pour un intellectuel**" ie Frankly, I do not think that Jacques is very intelligent but he likes to think he is an intellectual.
- "Hier, Jean-Luc m'a dit qu'il a fait les recherches pour son doctorat en philosphie à la Sorbonne. Pour qui **se prend-il**? Je ne peux pas le prendre au sérieux!" ie Yesteday, Jean-Luc told me that he did research for his PhD at the Sorbonne. Who does he think he is? I cannot take him seriously!
- "Chaque fois que je met le tapis oriental sur le plancher, il bouge et **on se prend les pieds dedans**" ie Every time that I put the oriental rug on the floor it moves and one trips oneself up.
- "Mon chien est adorable mais coquin. Presque chaque fois qu'il sort, **il se prend** la patte dans un piège!" ie My dog is adorable but mischievous. Almost every time that he goes out he gets his paw stuck in a trap!

Se prendre à

Se prendre à means to start to do something. For example:

- "Chaque fois que mon mari **se prend à faire la vaisselle**, j'ai peur parce que je sais qu'il va casser quelque chose" ie Each time that my husband begins to do the washing-up I am afraid because I know that he is going to break something.
- "Au moment où **je me suis pris à** examiner mon relevé de compte bancaire, je me suis rendu compte que j'étais à decouvert de 500€" ie The moment I began examining my bank statement, I realised that I was 500€ overdrawn.

S'en prendre à

S'en prendre à quelqu'un means to attack somebody or to lay into somebody, even to take it out on somebody. For example:

- "Inutile de me blâmer. Si tu as un problème tu devrais **t'en prendre à** ton chef de service. En fin de compte c'est de sa faute à mon avis" ie It is no good blaming me. If you have a problem you should take it out on your head of department. It is his fault in my opinion.
- "**Il s'en est pris à moi** parce que j'avais laissé ouverte la porte de secours, mais ce n'était pas ma faute – la serrure était cassée" ie He laid into me because I had left the security door open, but it was not my fault – the lock was broken.

S'y prendre

S'y prendre means to get or to go about something. For example:

- "Mon chef d'atelier m'a demandé de réparer la direction assistée mais **je ne savais pas m'y prendre**" ie My foreman asked me to repair the power – assisted steering, but I did not know how to go about it.
- "Je ne peux pas le faire tout seul, chérie. Si tu veux mettre la machine à laver dans le garage, il faut **s'y prendre à deux**" ie I cannot do it all alone, darling. If you want to put the washing-machine in the garage, it will take the two of us.

And if you want to say to someone, "how do you do/manage to do that?!" – say in admiration – you need:

- "Comment **tu t'y prends**?!" or "Je ne sais pas comment **tu t'y prends**!"

Now You Are Really Speaking French!

At this third level it is really all about locutions and idioms. First, the locutions;

Prendre quelqu'un ou quelque chose pour means to take someone for something or another or to take something as a pretext for something or other. Here are some examples:

- "Vous voulez 50€ pour un kilo de foie de veau? **Vous me prenez pour un imbécile** ou quoi? Le prix normal c'est 30€ le kilo, grosso modo" ie You are asking 50€ for a kilo of calves liver? Do you take me for an imbecile or what? The normal price is 30€ a kilo, more or less.
- "Je n'aime pas **qu'on me prenne pour** un radin. J'apprécie le bon rapport qualite-prix, c'est tout!" ie I do not like being taken for a cheap-skate. I appreciate value for money, that is all!
- **Ne prenez pas** cette opportunité pour prétexte. Vous ne pouvez pas augmenter le prix comme bon vous semble" ie Do not take this opportunity as a pretext. You cannot raise the price as you see fit.

Prendre sur soi means to grin and bear it or to take it upon oneself to do something. For example:

- "J'etais très décu de ne pas être invité au mariage de mon neveu. J'ai dû **prendre sur moi**" ie I was really disappointed not to be invited to my nephew's wedding. I just had to grin and bear it.
- "Quand je me suis rendu compte que la maison d'à côté avait été cambriolée, **j'ai pris sur moi** de m'adresser au commissariat de police" ie When I realised that the house next door had been burgled, I took it upon myself to go to the police station.

Idiomatic prendre

Prendre un bain de foule means to mingle with the crowd.
Reprendre ses billes means to renege on a deal.
Se laisser prendre au baratin de quelqu'un means to be taken in by someone's smooth talking.
Prendre quelque chose / quelqu'un en main means to take charge of something or someone.

Prendre quelque chose à coeur means to take a passionate interest in something.

Reprendre du poil de la bête means to be on the mend again.

Prendre la mouche means to go into a huff.

Prendre des vessies pour les lanternes means to be taken in, to have the wool pulled over one's eyes.

Se prendre pour le nombril du monde ("le nombril" is your belly-button) means to think you are the centre of the universe.

Prendre ses jambes à son cou means to make a dash for it.

Prendre le large (the open sea) means to clear off.

Prendre la poudre d'escampette means to run off.

Prendre une biture means to get blind drunk.

Il ne faut pas prendre les enfants du bon Dieu pour des canards sauvages means that one should not take people for idiots.

Prendre un canard means to suck on a lump of sugar soaked in some drink or another.

Prendre ses cliques et ses claques means to get hold of all your possessions and run for it, quickly.

Prendre au mot means to accept something said by someone who is talking nonsense.

Prendre le train de onze heures means to walk.

Se faire prendre pour un pigeon means to get taken in.

N'être pas à prendre avec des pincettes means to be repulsive.

Prendre la tangente means to escape.

Prendre le taureau par les cornes is the exact equivalent of the English idiom "to take the bull by the horns".

Prendre une veste means to experience a failure.

Finally, here are some **argotic** meanings of **prendre**:

Prendre son pied means to have an orgasm and
Prendre son pied avec quelqu'un means to "have it off" with someone.

Prendre can mean to "cop a bollocking":

- "Qu'est-ce qu'il a pris!" ie He got a right old bollocking!

En prendre plein la gueule means to get one's balls chewed off or to get beaten up.

Prendre un coup / un gnon / une avoine or **une beigne** means to get a clout or a bang, or to take the rap / carry the can.

Prendre le max means to get the book thrown at you.

Prendre la tête à quelqu'un means to annoy someone, "to get on their wick/tit", "to do someone's head in":

- "Les langues étrangères, **ça me prend la tête**" ie Foreign languages really freak me out.

Se prendre can mean to crash into something:

- "**Il s'est pris** le poteau en pleine gueule" ie He walked slap-bank into the post.

This expression also means to make life difficult for oneself or to worry:

- "**Tu ne vas pas te prendre** la tête pour un PV" ie Do not get into a state over a lousy parking ticket. Un PV is short for "procès-verbal" meaning a fine.

Finally, never render "he is going to take me to the cinema" with "**il va me prendre** au cinéma." That would mean that he is going to "have it off" with you in the cinema!

Conclusion

Prendre is a very useful verb because it has so many different applications – many of them literal but also many which are figurative. You will hear it every day, reason enough to get to know it really well.

And now for a couple of conversations that feature **prendre**.

Prendre: Conversation One

Jacques is in Sarlat and he is asking people about how they travel from place to place in France. First, he stops a young woman.

Jacques:	Dites-moi, madame, quand vous voyagez en France, comment voyagez-vous?
Jeune femme:	Ça dépend. Pour les trajets relativement courts normalement je prends ma voiture mais s'il s'agit d'un voyage plus long, à Paris, mettons, je prends le train. Le service Brive-Paris est excellent.
Jacques:	Et si vous avez beaucoup de bagages?
Jeune femme:	Je prends ma voiture.
Jacques:	À part Paris, est-ce qu'il vous arrive d'aller ailleurs en France?
Jeune femme:	Mais bien sûr. Je vais assez souvent a Montpellier où j'ai une soeur.
Jacques:	Et vous y allez en voiture ou en train?
Jeune femme:	Normalement je prends le train mais de temps en temps je prends ma voiture.
Jacques:	Et pour d'autres voyages est-ce qu'il vous arrive de prendre l'avion?
Jeune femme:	Pas très souvent mais je suis allée en Bretagne en avion une fois.
Jacques:	Et comment l'avez-vous trouvé?
Jeune femme:	Pas très commode. À l'époque, il fallait prendre l'avion de Bordeaux mais de nos jours nous avons un aéroport à Brive, bien sûr. Et même quand on arrive à sa destination il faut prendre soit le bus soit le train pour aller au centre ville. Non, je n'aime pas trop prendre l'avion.
Jacques:	Et est-ce que vous allez à Clermont de temps en temps, parce que là vous pouvez prendre le tramway qui est très commode à mon avis?
Jeune femme:	Oui, je sais. J'y suis allée plusieurs fois et j'ai trouvé le tramway tres agréable.
Jacques:	Alors, merci bien madame. Et bon voyage!
Jeune femme:	Il n'y a pas de quoi, monsieur. Au revoir.

Prendre: Conversation Two

Maryse really is not happy with the gas cooker in the kitchen: it constantly fails to light and she hates the oven, which never seems to reach the desired temperature. So she and François have gone to a kitchen and bathroom shop just outside Brive. They are immediately impressed by the choice of models.

Maryse: Oh là, là!, François, il y a tellement de fourneaux à gaz! Comment choisir?

François: Mais en principe nous avons une bonne idée de ce que nous cherchons. Nous avons les dimensions de la vieille cuisinière. Nous voulons évidemment un modèle de la même taille mais nous sommes d'accord sur le fait que nous voudrions six brûleurs et deux fours, tout en fonte et surtout quelque chose qui est équipé pour le gaz en bouteille. Je peux déjà voir quelques modèles qui pourraient nous convenir.

Maryse: Mais si tu me dis qu'il y a plusieurs modèles possibles, encore une fois, François, comment choisir?!

François: Il y a plusieurs façons de prendre le problème, Maryse. Je suggère que nous commencions en prenant des notes. Tu as apporté ton bloc – notes, n'est-ce pas?

Maryse: Bien sûr. Commençons donc avec ce modèle-ci.

Two or three minutes later:

            Maintenant ce modèle-ci.

Two or three minutes later:

            Et puis ce modèle-ci. Et c'est tout je crois, François. On a déjà tellement d'information! Et on n'a pas encore surfé sur Internet! Je crois que nous devrions parler à un vendeur, François.

François: Je suis d'accord. Je vais chercher quelqu'un.

Five minutes later François returns with a sales assistant:

            Je vous ai déjà expliqué ce dont nous avons besoin. Pourriez-vous nous aider à prendre une décision?

Vendeur: D'abord combien voulez-vous dépenser? Les trois modèles que vous aimez se vendent à des prix différents. Ce modèle-ci est le moins cher, celui-ci est le plus cher – et celui-ci est entre les deux.

Maryse:	La chose la plus importante est le rapport qualité-prix à mon sens.
Vendeur:	Je comprends. Bon, si vous deviez prendre le modèle le moins cher, vous auriez une excellente gazinière, il n'y a aucun doute. C'est soldé en ce moment et c'est une affaire. Elle a toute la fonctionnalité dont vous avez besoin. Mais le revers de la médaille est la qualité - qui n'est que moyenne, disons.
	Par contre, la qualité du modèle le plus cher est superbe. En fin de compte le problème se réduit à une question de budget: plus la gazinière est chère, plus elle est performante.
François:	Le monsieur a raison, Maryse. Je crois que nous ne devrions pas prendre une décision aujourd'hui. Il faut y réfléchir un peu. Question de fric, Maryse!
Maryse:	Je suis d'accord, François.
François:	Mais si nous devions prendre le modèle le plus cher, comment pourrions nous payer: à crédit?
Vendeur:	Mais bien sûr, monsieur!
François:	Et la livraison? Vous l'avez en stock, j'imagine.
Vendeur:	Attendez que je vérifie...
	Oui, nous ne sommes pas encore en rupture de stock – et nous pourrions la livrer sur-le-champ. Dites-moi, où habitez-vous?
Maryse:	Sarlat, monsieur.
Vendeur:	Bon, nous livrons à Sarlat le mardi et le vendredi.
Maryse:	C'est fort tentant de la prendre immédiatement, François. Tu sais combien je déteste la gazinière que nous avons en ce moment.
François:	Je comprends, Maryse. Alors, si nous devions régler en espèces, pourriez-vous nous faire un prix?
Vendeur:	Si vous deviez régler en espèces, je pourrais vous offrir une remise de dix pour cent, monsieur.
Maryse:	Dix pour cent, François. Pas mal, hein!
François:	D'accord. On la prend. Livraison vendredi, n'est-ce pas?
Vendeur:	Oui monsieur, vendredi.
Maryse:	Avec une nouvelle gazinière, je serai aux anges! François, je t'adore!

Some words you might not yet know

• ça dépend -	it all depends
• les bagages (m) -	luggage
• comment l'avez vous trouvé(e)? -	how was it?
• le tramway -	the tramway
• un fourneau -	a stove
• un brûleur -	a gas burner
• un four -	an oven
• en fonte -	made of cast-iron
• le gaz en bouteille -	bottled gas
• un bloc-notes -	a notepad
• surfer sur Internet -	to surf the internet
• la foncionnalité -	functionality
• question de fric -	it is a question of money
• la livraison -	the delivery
• être en rupture de stock -	to be out of stock
• livrer -	to deliver
• faire un prix -	to offer something at a reduced price

Prendre: Exercises

Choose one of the three words in brackets for the spaces below:

1. (prends, prendre, pris) Je devrais (   ) ma douche maintenant.

2. (prenez, prendrai, prendre) Est-ce que vous (   ) du sucre, madame?

3. (prends, prenez, prend) Si vous allez à Londres demain, (   ) le train, c'est plus commode.

4. (prendre, prenez, pris) J'ai beau faire, le feu ne veut pas (   ).

5. (prennent, prends, pris) J'adore mes enfants mais ils me (   ) tout mon temps.

6. (prends, prenez, prendre) Le vendeur a essayé de me baratiner mais franchement, avec moi ça ne (   ) pas.

7. (prenais, prends, prendre) J'adore le ris de veau mais je vais (   ) l'entrecôte, s'il vous plaît.

8. (pris, prendra, prenne) Il a mal (   ) la nouvelle.

Translate into French the underlined parts of the following English sentences:

9. To me he is rather stupid but <u>he likes to think</u> he is rather clever.

10. The last time my dog went into my neighbours field <u>he got his paw stuck</u> in a trap.

11. As soon as <u>he started</u> examining his car, he realised that the battery was flat.

12. I do not know <u>how you do it</u>, darling!

13.   <u>Do not take me</u> for an idiot!

14.   My daughter was very disappointed not to be invited to the party. <u>She just had</u> <u>to grin and bear it.</u>

Translate the following underlined parts of these French sentences into English:

15.   Il y avait tellement de monde que <u>j'ai pris un bain de foule!</u>

16.   Je lui ai dit qu'il était con et <u>il a pris la mouche.</u>

17.   Il était d'accord avec moi: le problème était très grave, mais <u>il a pris le</u> <u>taureau par les cornes.</u>

18.   Quand je suis tombé dans la rivière, <u>qu'est-ce que j'ai pris par ma mère!</u>

19.   <u>Tu vas pas te prendre la tête</u> pour un PV.

20.   Tu sais, <u>il se prend pour le nombril du monde.</u>

21.   J'ai essayé d'apprendre le chinois mais <u>ça me prend la tête.</u>

Prendre: Answers

1. prendre
2. prenez
3. prenez
4. prendre
5. prennent
6. prend
7. prendre
8. pris
9. il se prend
10. il s'est pris la patte
11. il s'est pris
12. comment tu t'y prends
13. Ne me prenez pas
14. Elle a dû prendre sur elle
15. I mingled with the crowd
16. he went off in a huff
17. he took the bull by the horns
18. my mother really gave me a bollocking
19. Do not get into a state
20. he thinks he is the centre of the universe
21. that really freaks me out.

Chapter Twenty-Two
Venir

Introduction

Venir is a very important verb of movement. Basically it means **to come**, although it has several related meanings, as we will see shortly. It is only ever used intransitively. In other words it is never followed by an object, be it direct or indirect.

Often it is followed by the prepositions **à** or **de**. It can also be preceded by **faire** (you met **faire venir** in the **Faire** chapter).

It can be employed impersonally (**il vient**, etc). And it also has some limited pronominal applications, **s'en venir**.

Finally it is widely encountered in locutions, idioms and even proverbs.

Here is how it is conjugated.

The Venir Conjugations

Present Tense

Je viens	Nous venons
Tu viens	Vous venez
Il vient	Ils viennent
Elle vient	Elles viennent

Future Tense

Je viendrai	Nous viendrons
Tu viendras	Vous viendrez
Il viendra	Ils viendront
Elle viendra	Elles viendront

Imperfect Tense

Je venais	Nous venions
Tu venais	Vous veniez
Il venait	Ils venaient
Elle venait	Elles venaient

Perfect Tense

Je suis venu(e)	Nous sommes venu(e)s
Tu es venu(e)	Vous êtes venu(e)s
Il est venu	Ils sont venus
Elle est venu(e)	Elles sont venues

Future Perfect Tense

Je serai venu(e)	Nous serons venu(e)s
Tu seras venu(e)	Vous serez venu(e)s
Il sera venu	Ils seront venus
Elle sera venu	Elles seront venues

Pluperfect Tense

J'étais venu(e)	Nous étions venu(e)s
Tu étais venu(e)	Vous étiez venu(e)s
Il était venu	Ils étaient venus
Elle était venue	Elles étaient venues

Present Conditional Tense

Je viendrais	Nous viendrions
Tu viendrais	Vous viendriez
Il viendrait	Ils viendraient
Elle viendrait	Elles viendraient

Past Conditional Tense

Je serais venu(e)	Nous serions venu(e)s
Tu serais venu(e)	Vous seriez venu(e)s
Il serait venu	Ils seraient venus
Elle serait venue	Elles seraient venues

Present Subjunctive Tense

Je vienne	Nous venions
Tu viennes	Vous veniez
Il vienne	Ils viennent
Elle vienne	Elles viennent

Imperative

Viens
Venons
Venez

Venir: The Basics

Above all, use **venir** when you want to say that you are coming (you already know that you can also use **arriver** for such purposes):

- "Dépêche-toi, André. Tu sais que nous sommes en retard".
  "T'en fais pas, maman, je viens!" ie
  Hurry up, André. You know that we are late.
  Don't worry, mum, I'm coming!

Use it also when you want to know when someone is coming, how someone is coming and where someone comes from. For example:

- "Mon mari m'a dit qu'**il viendrait** à midi, mais il m'a téléphoné tout à l'heure pour me dire **qu'il viendra** plus tard" ie My husband told me that he would come at midday, but he telephoned me just now to tell me that he will be coming a bit later.
- "Je crois que ma nièce **viendra** en train ce qui veut dire qu'elle ne peut pas arriver pour le thé de cinq heures" ie I think that my niece will come by train which means that she cannot arrive for afternoon tea.
- "Vous avez un accent légèrement anglais, monsieur. **D'où venez-vous** exactement?" ie You have a slight English accent. Where do you come from exactly?
- "Je soupçonne que **ce vin vienne** d'Espagne. D'autre part, **ça pourrait venir** du Maroc" ie I suspect that this wine comes from Spain. On the other hand, it could come from Morocco.

Often **venir** will be followed by another verb in the infinitive, as this example illustrates:

- "Je sais que vous n'aimez pas tellement les immigrants mais vous devez vous rendre compte que, pour la plupart du temps **ils sont venus travailler**" ie I know you do not much like immigrants, but you must realise that for the most part, they have come to work.

And **venir de** can also be followed by an infinitive. Here are two different illustrations of this very useful construction:

- "Il a dit qu'il arriverait à cinq heures. Mais, regarde, il n'est pas ecore quatre heures **et il vient d'arriver**!"ie He said that he would arrive at five o'clock. But, look, it is only four o'clock and he has just arrived!
(Incidentally, in an earlier chapter I suggested that the French love the 24-hour clock. True. But they also use the 12-hour clock. From your point of view it is "kif-kif" – it makes no odds, remember! **However**, after midday the half-hour intervals **always** employ "trente", never "midi". So, for example, you can say **either** "huit heures et demie" **or** "huit heures trente". However, you can **never** say "midi et demie" – it **has** to be "midi trente". And the same is true for all the hours that follow: "seize heures trente", "vingt heures trente" etc. It is also true for the quarter-hour intervals. So, yes, you can say "huit heures et quart" or "dix heures moins quart", but you can **never** say "treize heures et quart" or "seize heures moins quart" – it **must** be "treize heures quinze" or "seize heures moins quinze", for example).

This use of **venir**, to say that something has just happened, is very common indeed and should be mastered. It employs **venir** in the **present tense** and can be used in all its conjugations. For example:

- "**Nous venons d'arriver** à Paris et il pleut déjà!" ie We have just arrived in Paris and already it is raining!

Alternatively, **venir** can be employed in the **imperfect tense**, as this second example illustrates:

- "**Elle venait de** se lever quand le facteur a frappé à la porte. Quelle chance, parce qu'il avait apporté un colis très important" ie She had just got up when the postman knocked on the door. What luck, because he had brought a very important package.

In this example, **elle venait de se lever** means that she had just got up. Again, this is a very important construction to describe what had just happened.

But **venir à** can also be followed by an infinitive. In such cases it tends to mean "if something or other were to happen." Here are a few examples:

- "Mon père est vraiment malade et il a quatre-vingt-cinq ans. **S'il venait à mourir**, je serais inconsolable malgré son âge" ie My father is really ill and he is eighty five years old. Were he to die, I would be inconsolable, despite his age.
  Here, **s'il venait à**... means "if he were to..." This construction is another version of **s'il devait**..., "if he were to", that you met in an earlier chapter.
- "Maurice pourrait venir cet aprèm. **S'il venait à passer**, pourrais-tu lui donner cette paire de gants qu'il a laissée la dernière fois?" ie Maurice might come this afternoon. **If he were to pass by**, could you give him this pair of gloves that he left behind last time?
- "**Si le temps vient à** s'éclaircir ce soir, nous pourrions nous promener le long de la promenade" ie Were it to brighten up this evening, we could go for a walk along the promenade.

Summary

Already you can see how useful **venir** is. Use it to:

- say that you (or someone else) is coming, was coming, came, will come, would come and so on
- say where someone or something comes or came from
- to say that something has just happened
- to say that something had just happened
- to say that something might happen or if it were to happen...

Getting Better

You can build on this solid foundation using **venir** in place of other French verbs, notably **atteindre**, to come up to, **se détacher**, to come off and **survenir**, to take place.

You can also use it in expressions such as "the time will come when" and "the time has come". Then there is the noun, **le va-et-vient**, which means the comings and goings of someone or something.

Venir and atteindre

Here are some examples:

- "Les inondations de cet hiver étaient à la fois effrayantes et dévastatrices. **L'eau nous est venue** aux genoux" ie The floods this winter were both frightening and devastating. The water came up to our knees.
- "À marée haute, **la mer vient jusqu'aux falaises**. Souvent le chemin est submergé" ie At high-tide, the sea comes right up to the cliffs. Often the pathway is submerged.

Venir and se détacher

Again, here are a couple of examples:

- "Si tu éclabousses le papier peint avec beaucoup d'eau, **ça vient** tout seul, ou presque" ie If you splash the wallpaper with lots of water, it comes off all on its own, almost.
- "J'ai dévissé la vis avec mon tourne-vis quelques fois et le tasseau **est venu** facilement" ie I turned the screw with my screwdriver a few times and the shelf support came off easily.

Venir and survenir

Once more, some examples:

- "Il m'a fallu rendre une rédaction sur la Révolution française, mais j'étais à court d'idées et **l'inspiration me venait** très lentement jusqu'au moment où j'ai téléphoné à mon camarade de classe, Ahmed. Il m'a donné tellement de tuyaux!" ie I had to write an essay on the French Revolution but I was short of ideas and the inspiration was coming very slowly until the moment I telephoned my classmate, Ahmed. He gave me so many tips!
- "Bertrand était nul au foot quand il était jeune mais, de nos jours, il est fantastique. Qu'est-ce qui s'est passé? Comment **est-il venu à** ce niveau aussi rapidement?" ie Bertrand was useless at football when he was young, but nowadays he is fantastic. What happened? How did he get to this level so quickly?

Now for the expressions dealing with time:

- "L'attitude française envers les musulmans est en ce moment méfiante, franchement. Mais à mon avis **le moment viendra où** tout cela changera et nous vivrons ensemble en bonne harmonie" ie French attitudes towards Muslims are at the moment distrustful, frankly. But in my opinion, the time will come when all that will change and we will live together harmoniously.
- "Dans les années **à venir**, nous reviendrons sur le passé de plus en plus. Pourquoi? Parce que l'avenir sera pire que le présent" ie In years to come, we will look back on the past more and more. Why? Because the future will be worse than the present.

Finally in this section, that noun **le va-et-vient** of someone or something:

- "Je n'aime pas trop ce café. Je me sens déboussolé. Il y a trop de monde. Je ne supporte pas ce **va-et-vient**" ie I do not like this café very much. I feel disorientated. There are too many people. I cannot stand all these comings and goings.
- "Mon manuscrit a fait **le va-et-vient** d'une maison d'édition à l'autre. J'en ai assez. Je vais le publier moi-même" ie My manuscript has gone from one publisher to another. I have had enough. I am going to publish it myself.

Now You Are Really Speaking French!

At this highest level all that remains is **venir** in its very limited pronominal form, **s'en venir**, its locutions, its idioms and its proverbs.

S'en venir means to **approach:**

- "La voiture **s'en venait** lentement, paraît-il. Mais tout d'un coup, elle a commencé à accélérer et elle m'a forcé à me jeter sur le trottoir. Heureusement, je n'étais pas blessé" ie The car was approaching slowly, it seems. But suddenly it began to accelerate and it forced me to throw myself on to the pavement. Luckily I was not hurt.

The locutions

There are two important ones – **en venir à** and **y venir**:

- "Comment les choses **en sont – elles venues là**? Je croyais que leur mariage était solide comme un roc" ie How come things got into this state? I thought that their marriage was rock-solid.
- "C'est tragique qu'elle ait perdu son mari. Mais elle a très peu de choix. Il faudra bien qu'**elle y vienne**" ie It is tragic that she has lost her husband. But she has not got much choice. She will just have to get used to it.

The idioms

Venez voir mes estampes japonaises means come on up and see my etchings!
Voir venir quelqu'un means to see what someone is getting at:

- "**Je te voyais venir** avec tes gros sabots" ie I could see exactly what you were driving at. Or
- "**J'ai vu venir** le coup gros comme une maison" ie I saw the whole thing coming a while off.

Je viens! means "I'm coming!" (sexually)
Revenons à nous moutons means "Let us get back to the subject". (You have already met this one).

À beau mentir qui vient de loin means that it is easy to tell lies when no-on can check up on the truth.

The proverbs

Tout vient à temps à qui sait attendre means "Everything comes to he who waits".
L'appétit vient en mangeant means "The more you have, the more you want".

Conclusion

Venir, to come, may not be in quite the same league as **aller**, to go, but it is a very important verb indeed. The constructions **je viens de**… and **je venais de**… are particularly useful. Let us end this chapter with a couple of conversations that showcase the verb.

Venir: Conversation One

Annie needs to go out to do some shopping and Carla wants to come with her but, as usual, she is not quite ready!

Annie:	Carla, j'ai débarrassé la table et je viens de faire la vaisselle. Je suis prête à partir. Es-tu prête aussi?
Carla:	Presque, maman. Je dois ranger ma chambre et puis je viens.
Annie:	Bon, mais dépêche-toi Carla. Tu sais que j'ai très peu de temps ce matin. Il faut que je revienne à midi. L'électricien vient cet aprèm et je dois faire mes courses avant qu'il arrive.
Carla:	Je sais, je sais, maman. T'en fais pas – je viens!

Five minutes later:

Annie:	Qu'est-ce que tu fabriques dans ta chambre! Allons-y!
Carla:	Je viens, maman, vraiment je viens!

She emerges from her room:

Annie:	Enfin!
Carla:	Désolée, maman, mais ma chambre était un vrai bordel
Annie:	Carla, vraiment! Tu sais que ce mot-là n'est pas poli – et ça, c'est le moins qu'on puisse dire!
Carla:	Désolée, maman... une pagaille, alors, ça va?
Annie:	C'est mieux, disons. Mais sortons. Je suis vraiment pressée, maintenant. Et regarde l'heure. Il est presque onze heures déjà. Carla, tu peux être tellement frustrante de temps en temps.
Carla:	Je sais maman, mais tu m'aimes vraiment!
Annie:	Oui, je t'aime – mais j'aime faire mes courses aussi, Carla! Allons-y!

They leave at last. About two hours later they return. There is a note on the mat:

Carla:	C'est quoi ça, maman?
Annie:	C'est l'électricien qui venait installer quelques nouvelles prises dans la cuisine. Il est venu il y a quinze minutes. Nous venons de le louper. Merde!
Carla:	Maman, tu sais que c'est pas poli, ce mot merde!
Annie:	Ça c'est envoyé, Carla!

Venir: Conversation Two

Corinne and Thierry are expecting someone to call them about the garden. It is too big for them to do alone – they feel they need some help.

Thierry: Le jardinier aurait dû venir à onze heures, Corinne. Il est presque midi et il n'est pas encore venu. Qu'est-ce qu'il fabrique, lui?

Corinne: Je ne sais pas. Sois patient, Thierry, il viendra bientôt, j'en suis sûre.

Thierry: Tu as raison, Corinne. Mais tu sais que je connais rien au jardinage, et j'ai besoin de quelqu'un. Il est très bon jardinier, apparemment. J'espère qu'il viendra bientôt. Nous avons dit que nous irions à la jardinerie cet aprèm, et il y a tellement de trucs que je voudrais acheter.

Corinne: Par exemple?

Thierry: Bon, je voudrais acheter un tuyau d'arrosage, des cisailles de jardinier, un banc de jardin, d'autres outils de jardinage – sans parler d'une biche Bambi, un puits miniature, quelques lutins, un nichoir et une vasque pour oiseaux!

Corinne: Thierry, vraiment, maintenant tu te moques de moi. Nous voulons un jardin, pas un champ de foire!

Thierry: Je plaisante, Corinne, je te taquine!

Corinne: Je m'en doutais mais je ne suis jamais certaine – tu peux être un clown, parfois.

Thierry: Je sais, mais prends-moi au sérieux pour un instant. Tu sais que je viens de bêcher le lopin de terre derrière la porcherie et je voudrais y créer un potager. J'apprécierais son avis. Quels sont les meilleurs légumes à y planter, je me demande?

Corinne: C'est pas petit, ce lopin de terre dont tu parles. Nous pourrions y avoir des pommes de terre, des carrottes, des rutabagas, des navets, des panais, des poireaux, des oignons, des salades, des tomates, des choux de Bruxelles, des haricots vert, des blettes – même des poivrons rouges. Oh là, là!

Thierry: Tu as oublié les petits-pois Corinne! Mais, sérieusement, tu as raison. Mais je voudrais un beau potager plein de beaux légumes. Mais je ne peux pas le faire moi-même. J'ai besoin d'un jardinier – et il n'est pas encore venu!

Corinne: J'ai une idée. Pourquoi ne pas manger maintenant. S'il vient pendant que nous déjeunons, tant pis. S'il ne vient pas, mettons, à quatorze heures, je suggère que nous sortions. On peut lui laisser un message sur la porte. Peut-être pourrait-il revenir ce soir. La nuit tombe assez tard au mois de mai!

Thierry:	C'est possible. Mais, je serais plus content s'il venait à arriver dans la journée – demain peut-être.
Corinne:	On verra. Mais mangeons. Je viens de préparer une belle soupe pleine de bons légumes – des pommes de terre, des carrottes, des rutabagas, des navets, des panais, des poireaux, des...
Thierry:	Arrête, Corinne. C'est à ton tour de me taquiner maintenant!

Some words you might not yet know

• un bordel -	literally, a brothel, here a mess
• une pagaille -	a mess / shambles
• frustrant(e) -	frustrating
• une prise -	an electric socket
• louper -	to miss
• ça c'est envoyé! -	nice one!
• un jardinier -	a gardener
• le jardinage -	gardening
• la jardinerie -	the garden centre
• un tuyau d'arrosage -	a garden hosepipe
• les cisailles (f) de jardinage -	garden shears
• une biche -	a deer
• un puits miniature -	a miniature well
• un lutin -	a gnome
• un nichoir -	a nesting box
• une vasque -	a drinking bowl (for birds)
• un champ de foire -	a fairground
• taquiner -	to tease
• un clown -	a clown
• bêcher -	to dig
• un lopin de terre -	a piece of ground
• un potager -	a vegetable garden
• planter -	to plant
• les panais (m) -	parsnips
• une salade -	a lettuce
• des blettes (f) -	Swiss chard
• les poivrons (m) rouges -	red peppers
• les petits-pois (m) -	peas
• le jour tombe -	it gets dark
• la journée -	the day(time)
• un tour -	a turn

Venir: Exercises

Fill in the blank spaces:

1.   (   ) venons en Espagne cette année.

2.   Nous (   ) venus l'année dernière.

3.   (   ) viendraient si elles avaient le temps.

4.   Ils (   ) venus s'ils avaient eu les moyens.

5.   Il faut que tu (   ) avec moi.

6.   (   ). Il se fait tard.

7.   Je crois que mon oncle (   ) en train, ce qui veut dire qu'il ne peut pas arriver avant seize heures.

8.   Mon ami espagnol est (   ) travailler en France.

Translate the underlined parts of the following French sentences into English:

9.   Elle a dit qu'elle arriverait à seize heures et, regarde, <u>elle vient d'arriver.</u>

10.   <u>Nous venions de nous installer</u> quand le dîner est arrive.

11.   <u>S'il venait à pleuvoir</u> cet aprèm, nous pourrions aller au cinema.

12.   À marée basse, <u>la mer vient</u> jusqu'aux rochers là-bas.

408

13. Mon prof m'a demandé d'écrire un poème, mais l'inspiration m'est venue très lentement.

14. À mon avis le moment viendra où nous vivrons ensemble.

15. Comment les choses en sont-elles venues là? Ils semblaient très heureux ensemble.

Translate these French sentences into English:

16. Venez voir mes estampes japonaises!

17. Il a vu venir le coup gros comme une maison.

18. Elle a perdu son permis de conduire pour deux ans. Il faudra bien qu'elle y vienne.

19. J'en ai assez de cette discussion. Revenons à nos moutons.

20. Il a été gâté par ses parents mais l'appétit vient en mangeant.

21. Il est très impatient, lui, mais tout vient à temps à qui sait attendre.

Venir: Answers

1. Nous
2. sommes
3. Elles
4. seraient
5. viennes
6. Viens or Venez
7. viendra
8. venu
9. she has just arrived
10. We had just sat down
11. Were it to rain
12. the sea comes
13. the inspiration came to me very slowly
14. the time will come when
15. How come things have got into this state?
16. Come up and see my etchings!
17. He saw the whole thing coming a while off
18. She has lost her driving licence for two years. She will just have to get used to it
19. I have had enough of this discussion. Let's get back to the subject
20. He has been spoilt by his parents but the more you have, the more you want
21. He is very impatient but everything comes to he who waits.

Chapter Twenty-Three
And One For Luck!

Introduction

Have you guessed what it is? Well, it is MANGER! Is there a more appropriate verb on which to finish than **manger**? You know what the French say (actually, Molière said it first): "Les autres peuples mangent pour vivre mais les Français vivent pour manger!" And I am certainly not going to translate that for you!

It is not an exaggeration to say that whilst the French like to drink, they are obsessed with eating. We were at a dinner-party not so long ago. We were there for a good four hours. After the initial small talk (**"papotage"**) we talked about nothing but food. For a full hour or more we talked about nothing but foie gras: how and where to buy it, how to prepare it, how best to eat it and, of course, what best to drink with it. Wonderful!

So how are we to approach this almost mythical verb? First we will see how it is used in everyday conversation. Then we will examine some of its idiomatic uses. And we will finish with some conversations.

The Manger Conjugations

Present Tense

Je mange	Nous mangeons		
Tu manges	Vous mangez		
Il mange	Ils mangent		
Elle mange	Elles mangent		

Future Tense

Je mangerai	Nous mangerons
Tu mangeras	Vous mangerez
Il mangera	Ils mangeront
Elle mangera	Elles mangeront

Imperfect Tense

Je mangeais	Nous mangions
Tu mangeais	vous mangiez
Il mangeait	Ils mangeaient
Elle mangeait	Elles mangeaient

Perfect Tense

J'ai mangé	Nous avons mangé
Tu as mangé	Vous avez mangé
Il a mangé	Ils ont mangé
Elle a mangé	Elles ont mangé

Future Perfect Tense

J'aurai mangé	Nous aurons mangé
Tu auras mangé	Vous aurez mangé
Il aura mangé	Ils auront mangé
Elle aura mangé	Elles auront mangé

Pluperfect Tense

J'avais mangé	Nous avions mangé
Tu avais mangé	Vous aviez mangé
Il avait mangé	Ils avaient mangé
Elle avait mangé	Elles avaient mangé

Present Conditional Tense		Past Conditional Tense	
Je mangerais	Nous mangerions	J'aurais mangé	Nous aurions mangé
Tu mangerais	Vous mangeriez	Tu aurais mangé	Vous auriez mangé
Il mangerait	Ils mangeraient	Il aurait mangé	Ils auraient mangé
Elle mangerait	Elles mangeraient	Elle aurait mangé	Elles auraient mangé

Present Subjunctive Tense		Imperative
Je mange	Nous mangions	Mange
Tu manges	Vous mangiez	Mangeons
Il mange	Ils mangent	Mangez
Elle mange	Elles mangent	

Manger: The Basics

Manger means **to eat** – literally and metaphorically, as we will see shortly. So use **manger** when you want to talk about eating. For example:

- "J'ai faim. Je dois **manger**" ie I am hungy. I must eat.
- "J'ai tellement faim. Est-ce qu'il y a de quoi **manger**?" ie I am so hungry. Is there anything to eat?
- "Mon mari, **il mange** comme quatre" ie My husband eats like a horse
- "Par contre, ma fille **mange** très peu, comme un moineau" ie On the other hand, my daughter eats very little, like a bird (or like a sparrow, "un moineau").
- **Il a mangé** tout ce qui restait dans le frigo. Il devait avoir faim" ie He ate all that was left in the fridge. He must have been hungry.
- "**Je n'ai mangé qu'**un sandwich à midi. Ce n'était pas suffisant. Maintenant je crève de faim!" ie I only ate a sandwich at lunchtime. It was not enough. Now I am starving!
- "Si **je n'avais pas mangé** si peu à midi, je n'aurais pas pu **manger** autant ce soir" ie If I had not eaten so little at midday, I would not have been able to eat so much this evening.
- "Si tu veux perdre du poids, il faut que **tu manges** un peu moins" ie If you want to lose some weight, you must eat less.

These, of course, are all examples of **manger** employed in its literal sense to eat food. (Incidentally, in English we often talk about **drinking** soup. The French prefer **eating** soup). But **manger** has several figurative meanings, too. Here are some examples:

- "Je me suis fâchée hier. J'étais avec Pierre dans un resto et il y avait une jolie jeune fille d'en face. **Il l'a mangée** des yeux pendant le repas" ie I was angry yesterday. I was with Pierre in a restaurant and there was this pretty young girl opposite. He devoured her with his eyes throughout the meal.
- "Ma femme a tellement d'activités **qui mangent** son temps. Je voudrais qu'elle en fasse moins. En ce moment je la vois très peu " ie My wife does so many things that eat up her time. I would like her to do less. At the moment, I see very little of her.
- "Il a fondé son affaire il y a quelques années. Au début tout s'est bien passé mais de nos jours **il mange** de l'argent. À vrai dire, il est presque au bord de la faillite" ie He established his business several yeas ago. In the beginning everything went well, but nowadays it is eating up money. To be honest, he is on the edge of bankruptcy.
- "Je ne l'ai pas reconnu mais je peux vous dire sans hésitation qu'une barbe touffue **lui mangeait** le visage" ie I did not recognise him but I can tell you without hesitation that his face was half hidden under a bushy beard.

Now back to food! Very often you will hear people using the pronominal form of **manger**, **se manger**, as these examples illustrate:

- "C'est quoi ça? **Cela se mange**?" ie What is that? Can you eat it?
- "Ce fromage **se mange** coulant" ie This cheese **is best eaten** runny.
- "À mon avis, les haricots verts **se mangent** mieux croquants" ie In my opinion, green beans are best eaten when they are crunchy.

Summary

For such an important verb there is relatively little more to say about it at this basic level. It is a very straight-forward verb and one that is used every day. Use it to say what you like to eat, where you like to eat, when you like to eat and how you like to eat. Start asking other people about their eating habits and you will make friends for life!

Now You Are Really Speaking French!

Unusually, this last chapter cuts straight to the chase! There is no **Getting Better** because you are almost there already. So let us see how French people **really** use **manger**! The applications that follow are almost all figurative, often idiomatic, sometimes proverbial and occasionally vulgar! So here we go:

Manger avec les chevaux de bois means to have eaten nothing, to have fasted. The reference is to wooden horses, those that you will find on a carousel at a fairground. Needless to say, they eat nothing!

Se laisser manger means to get exploited or used without defending yourself.

Manger le morceau means to confess, to "spill the beans". The reference here is to people in the 19th century who had been held by the police for questioning, had confessed – and were consequently given some scraps of food by way of recompense.

Manger son pain blanc en premier means to go from a state of happiness to one which is much less so.

Manger sur le pouce is a very frequently heard expression and means to eat something in a hurry, often on the move – and sometimes from a fast-food joint. "Le pouce" is a reference to your thumb.

Manger à tous les râteliers means to exploit all opportunities for personal benefit. "Un râtelier" is a wall-hung vessel containing food for animals – horses, cows and sheep.

Manger de la vache enragée literally means to eat a rabid cow, in short, to live a pretty miserable life.

Ça ne mange pas de pain means that something does not cost very much.

Avoir mangé du lion means to have lots of energy (you have met this one already).

Manger les pissenlits par la racine literally to eat dandelions by the roots, means to have passed away, to be pushing up the daisies, so to speak.

Manger la consigne means to forget one's instructions.

En manger means to have a hard time:

- "**Il en a mangé** dans sa vie" ie He has certainly been through tough times in his life.

Finally in this chapter, I thought that you might like to have in your possession a rather more argotic handle on the issue of the French and their food. None of what follows actually uses **manger**. It is good vocabulary nonetheless but be a little bit careful where you use it!

You already know that **bouffer** is a more familiar form of **manger**: "Oh là-là!, qu'est-ce que j'ai bien **bouffé**!" Another verb is **grailler** but you hear this far less often. From **bouffer** we get "la bouffe", grub, and "la malbouffe", junk-food.

If you want simply to snack, you can use **casser le croûte** and to ask for a snack use **le casse-croûte**. If, on the other hand, you really want to stuff yourself, then **bouffer à la pelle** is a useful expression.

If you are really hungry you can use **avoir la fringale** or **avoir une creux**. **Crever de faim** means that you are dying of hunger.

If you really want to say that you have a healthy appetite, use **avoir un bon coup de fourchette**.

If you feel really full after a meal you can say **J'ai bien bouffé** or **Je suis calé**.

If guests call unexpectedly and you are required to feed them, you can say **J'en ai assez pour un régiment** – enough to feed an army.

If you are lousy at carving the roast use **charcuter le rôti** and ask someone else to do it for you!

That is by no means the end of the story and it can get quite a lot more vulgar. But nothing I have said here will ever get you thrown out of a "boui-boui!"

Now for some conversations.

Manger: Conversation One

Annie is in Sarlat asking people about their eating habits. She begins by stopping a man who, judging by his size, is fond of his food.

Annie:	Bonjour monsieur. Serait-il impoli de vous demander si vous aimez manger?
L'homme:	Quelle question! Que pensez-vous?
Annie:	La réponse est "oui", alors!
L'homme:	Mais bien sûr, madame.
Annie:	D'abord, qu'est-ce que vous aimez manger: de la viande, du poisson, des légumes, des fruits, du fromage?
L'homme:	J'aime tout madame et je mange tout. Mais je dois admettre que je mange pas mal de viande. Oui, je suis très viande.
Annie:	Et quelle est votre viande préférée, monsieur?
L'homme:	Je mange beaucoup d'agneau, y compris ses abats et j'aime beaucoup le veau. Un bon ris de veau est sublime à mon sens.
Annie:	Et préférez-vous manger à la maison ou au restaurant?
L'homme:	Je mangé dans des restos de temps en temps, comme tout le monde, j'imagine. Mais ma femme fait la popote chez nous et elle est une excellente cuisinière.
Annie:	Et quand vous sortez, où allez-vous, dans les fast-foods ou dans les petits restaurants chics?
L'homme:	Les fast-foods? Jamais! J'ai horreur de la malbouffe. Je préférerais manger dans un boui-boui, franchement. Souvent on y mange bien. J'aime les petits bistros qui proposent des plats régionaux et des plats du bon vieux temps – le navarin de mouton et la blanquette à l'ancienne, par exemple. Il y en à Sarlat, vous savez.
Annie:	Oui, je sais. Mais ici les plats classiques de la région sont partout. Ici en peut manger du confit de canard n'importe où et à toute heure. Souvent les gens du coin se plaignent: pour eux il y a très peu de variété a Sarlat.
L'homme:	Ils ont raison, je crois. Mais à deux pas de Sarlat, à la campagne, il y a tellement de bons restos à prix modérés. Ici, le problème, ce sont les touristes. Ils savent à quoi s'attendre et ils sont contents avec. C'est notre patrimoine culturel ici en Dordogne, le foie gras, et tout le bataclan vraiment.
Annie:	Vous avez raison. Nous avons de la chance d'avoir une telle cuisine dans ces parages. Ici on mange bien et la cuisine périgourdine continue à faire courir les foules, heureusement pour nous. Merci bien, monsieur, et bon appetit!
L'homme:	Je vous en prie, madame. Au revoir.

Manger: Conversation Two

Thierry arrives home from the office – and he is starving.

Thierry:	J'ai mangé avec les chevaux de bois, aujourd'hui, Corinne. Je crève de faim.
Corinne:	Mais tu n'as pas mangé à la cantine à midi comme d'habitude?
Thierry:	J'y suis allé casser la croûte mais presque rien ne restait. J'aurais pu sortir manger sur le pouce mais j'étais tellement occupé que je ne pouvais pas trouver même cinq minutes.
Corinne:	Mais ne fais pas ça trop souvent, Thierry, tu auras des problèmes avec ton estomac. C'est pas bon ni de rien manger, ni de manger trop vite. Mon père a fait ça toute sa vie et il a fini avec un ulcère – qui est très douloureux, tu peux m'en croire!
Thierry:	Je sais, Corinne, mais arrête de dire des bêtises. Ton père avait soixante ans quand il a commencé à souffrir de son ulcère.
Corinne:	Je sais. Quand même...
Thierry:	Étant donné que nous parlons bouffe, y a-t-il de quoi manger ou dois-je attendre un tout petit peu? Il y a du fromage dans le frigo, n'est-ce pas?
Corinne:	Tu te rends parfaitement compte qu'il y a toujours un plat prêt à manger quand tu rentres le soir. Pour ce soir j'ai préparé un bourguignon avec le jarret de boeuf que j'ai acheté hier.
Thierry:	Oui, ça sent bon Corinne. Ça me met déjà l'eau à la bouche. Et avec ça?
Corinne:	Il y a des pommes de terre vapeur, des carottes et du choux.
Thierry:	Oh là, là! Dans combien de temps?
Corinne:	Dans cinq minutes. Peux-tu attendre?
Thierry:	D'accord

Five minutes later Corinne brings everything to the table:

Corinne:	Passe à table alors mais attention, tout est chaud.
Thierry:	Alors, on attaque?
Corinne:	Bien sûr. Voici la louche pour le bourguignon. Et mange beaucoup de légumes avec, Thierry. Si tu veux rester en bonne santé tu dois manger beaucoup de légumes, tu sais. Oh, et n'oublie pas Thierry, qu'une pomme de terre n'est pas un légume – c'est un féculent! Donc, mange beaucoup de carrottes et de choux. Je veux que tu vives longtemps, pas du tout comme mon père.

Thierry:	Ta mère a vécu jusqu'à quatre-vingt-dix ans, Corinne, et elle mangeait comme un moineau. Elle mangeait très peu de légumes, pas de fruits mais beaucoup de foie gras, de confit de canard et de charcuterie. Elle adorait la graisse. Vraiment son régime n'etait pas sain du tout!
Corinne:	Comment ça se fait qu'elle a vécu si longtemps alors?!
Thierry:	Parce qu'elle ne se surmenait pas, elle faisait une sieste chaque jour, elle se couchait assez tôt, elle ne s'inquiétait jamais – et elle croyait en Dieu! Est-ce que ça suffit?! Et elle fumait!
Corinne:	Pas trop, Thierry. Elle aimait un petit cigare après son dîner, c'est tout vraiment…
Thierry:	Et elle buvait!
Corinne:	T'en rajoutes, Thierry. Un verre de pastis avant le repas, un verre de rouge avec et peut-être un digestif après, parfois. C'est tout. Et son médecin lui disait toujours qu'un verre ou deux par jour fait du bien.
Thierry:	Dans ce cas, verse un peu de cet excellent rouge dans mon verre, Corinne.
Corinne:	Attention, Thierry, tu as déjà sifflé presque toute la bouteille. Tu auras la gueule de bois demain matin et tu dois bosser, tu sais. Ça suffit, je crois.
Thierry:	Mais j'ai bien mangé ce soir, Corinne. Pas de problème.
Corinne:	Quand même. Je vais remettre le bouchon. Tu peux la finir demain soir.
Thierry:	Vivement demain alors!

Some words you might not yet know

- admettre - to admit
- les abats (m) - offal
- le ris de veau - veal sweet breads
- faire la popote (fam) - to do the cooking
- une cuisinière (fam) - a cook
- les fast-foods (m) - the fast-foods restaurants
- un navarin de mouton - a mutton stew
- la blanquette à l'ancienne - a veal stew
- le confit de canard - preserved duck
- à toute heure - at any time
- savoir à quoi s'attendre - to know what to expect
- le patrimoine - heritage
- le bataclan - the lot, the whole kit and caboodle
- la cantine - the restaurant at work
- l'estomac (m) - the stomach
- un ulcère - an ulcer
- douloureux (se) - painful
- tu peux m'en croire! - believe you me!
- un bourguignon - boeuf bourguignon, a stew made with beef and red wine
- pommes de terre (f) (à la) vapeur - boiled potatoes
- le choux - cabbage
- alors, on attaque? - can we start?
- rester en bonne santé - to stay in good health
- vivre - to live
- se surmener - to over-work
- une sieste - a nap
- croire en Dieu - to believe in God
- un cigare - a cigar
- le pastis - an aniseed-based alcoholic drink
- verser - to pour
- siffler (fam) - to drink
- avoir la gueule de bois - to have a hangover
- remettre - to put back

Manger: Exercises

Complete the blank spaces in the French sentences below:

1. Il a faim. Il doit (   ).

2. Je (   ) le poulet demain.

3. Elle a (   ) tout ce qu'il y avait dans le frigo.

4. J'aurais (   ) l'omelette mais j'avais déjà bien (   ) à midi.

5. Il faut que tu ( ) beaucoup ce matin, Marcel; il n'y aura pas de quoi
   (   ) cet aprèm.

6. (   ) tes légumes, Thierry. Ça te fera du bien.

7. Mon mari a tellement d'activités qui (   ) son temps.

8. C'est quoi, ça? Cela se (   )?

Translate the underlined parts of the following French sentences into English:

9. T'en fait pas. J'ai mangé quelque chose sur le pouce à midi.

10. Je ne pouvais pas garder son secret. Quand j'ai vu sa femme, j'ai mangé le
    morceau.

11. Pierre Martin? Le pauvre! Il mange les pissenlits par les racines!

12. Elle en a mangé dans sa vie. Elle a l'air assez vieille de nos jours.

Translate the underlined parts of these English sentences into French:

13. If you want to lose weight do not go to Jane's house. <u>She always has enough to feed an army</u>!

14. <u>I have had nothing to eat</u> all day. I'm starving!

15. Mutton stew? <u>That does not cost very much</u>.

Manger: Answers

1. manger
2. mangerai
3. mangé
4. mangé, mangé
5. manges; manger
6. Mange
7. mangent
8. mange
9. I had a quick bite of something
10. I spilled the beans / I let the cat out of the bag
11. He is dead!
12. She has been through tough times in her life
13. Elle en a toujours assez pour un régiment
14. J'ai mangé avec les chevaux de bois
15. Ça ne mange pas de pain.

Twenty-Four
Putting It All Together

Introduction

You should by now realise why I have adopted a **structural** approach to learning French, not a **contextual** one. Yes, the verbs you have learned to use all have contexts, but they are the servants not the masters in this journey through the French language. It is a bit like a house with a garden, I guess. The garden, or rather the land that the house is built on, is the context; but you live in the house, not the garden. The house must be well built to stand up and do its job. If not, it will fall down.

But gardens matter; so too, does the road and wider neighbourhood that locates the house. And you are not likely to live in a house forever if you do not like its location. That is why this final chapter, **Putting It All Together**, self-consciously offers you the contexts that, chances are, matter. But I cannot second-guess them all. So I have tried to pick some obvious ones – ones that are relevant to you, hopefully.

In The Beginning

Chances are your first visits to France will have been or will be on holiday. Perhaps you will be staying at a camping site; perhaps in a gîte; perhaps even in a hotel. You may need to fend for yourself. You will probably need to buy food; you will probably want to eat out occasionally – and you will probably want to visit local places of interest. You will probably need to travel around a bit, too – by bus, coach, car, train (or even plane).

So how do you handle these typical situations? Here are a few dialogues to help you in some of these contexts, using as much vocabulary as it likely to be necessary.

Context 1:
You have seen on the internet a gîte for rent in August and you want to know more about it. You decide to telephone the owner.

You: Bonjour, madame. Je crois que vous avez un gîte à louer près de Carcassonne en août l'année prochaine. Je voudrais en savoir plus, s'il vous plaît.

The owner: Mais oui, monsieur, bien sûr. Vous savez déjà que le gîte se trouve à trois kilomètres de Carcassonne, une ville médiévale complètement entourée de murs fortifiés avec une histoire qui remonte aux Cathares.

423

	Le gîte lui-même a trois chambres, chacune avec un grand lit, un salon, une salle à manger, une salle de bain avec douche, une cuisine bien équipée, y compris une gazinière et tout ce dont vous avez besoin, un garage pour deux voitures et un petit, mais joli, jardin. Dans le jardin il y a une balançoire pour enfants. Tout est en excellent état et le gîte est disponible les deux premières semaines d'août pour 500€ la semaine.
You:	Et si je veux le louer, comment devrais – je vous payer, par chèque, j'imagine.
The owner:	Oui, monsieur, par chèque. Je n'accepte ni les cartes de crédit, ni les cartes bancaire. Si vous voulez le réserver, envoyez-moi votre chèque de cent euros aussitôt que possible. Vous pouvez régler le reste sur place. Et si vous voulez avoir plus de renseignements, n'hésitez pas à me contacter sur Internet ou par téléphone. Au moment où je reçois votre chèque de réservation, je vous enverrai un contrat à signer. Ça va?
You:	Parfait, madame. Votre gîte m'intéresse beaucoup. Je vais en parler à ma femme ce soir et je vous téléphonerai demain matin, si cela vous convient.
The owner:	Ça me convient parfaitement, monsieur. À propos, comment vous appelez-vous?
You:	Je m'appelle Monsieur Thompson, madame, David Thompson et ma femme s'appelle Jane.
The owner:	Merci bien M. Thompson. À demain matin, alors.
You:	À demain. Au revoir.

Context 2

This time you fancy a few days in Paris and you have seen a hotel that looks suitable. Again, you would like to know a bit more about it, particularly about the area in which the hotel is situated.

You:	Bonjour, madame. Nous voudrions passer le week-end prochain à Paris et je voudrais en savoir plus sur votre hôtel, particulièrement le quartier dans lequel votre hôtel se trouve.
The receptionist:	Bien sûr, monsieur. D'abord nous nous trouvons dans le huitième arrondissement de Paris, c'est à dire en plein centre de la capitale. Nous sommes à deux pas du métro Étoile, mais dans une petite rue très près des Champs Élysées mais qui est très peu bruyante quand même. Autour de nous, nous avons tellement de choses: d'excellents restaurants pas forcément

chers, des cinémas sur "la plus belle avenue de monde" pour ainsi dire!, et les musées sont proches aussi, y compris le Louvre dont le métro est Louvre-Rivoli.

Je pourrais continuer, monsieur, mais je peux vous dire sans hésitation que notre situation est très convenable, surtout si vous voulez ne passer qu'un week-end et que vous aimeriez voir et faire autant de choses que possible.

You:	Génial! Et vous avez une chambre pour ce week-end?
Receptionist:	Attendez que je vérifie notre disponibilité… Oui, nous avons une chambre avec grand lit, douche et qui donne sur la rue calme dont je parlais tout à l'heure.
You:	Et le tarif?
Receptionist:	Si vous devriez rester trois nuits je pourrais vous proposer un forfait, 400€ toutes taxes comprises. Le petit déjeuner est supplémentaire à 10€ par personne et par jour. Pour deux jours notre tarif est 180€ par jour, toutes taxes comprises.
You:	Nous ne voulons que deux nuits, vendredi le cinq et samedi le six mai. Ça va?
Receptionist:	Parfait, monsieur. Et à quel nom?
You:	Monsieur Thompson
Receptionist:	M. Thompson. C'est noté, monsieur. Et est-ce que vous avez un numéro de téléphone, monsieur?
You:	Oui, c'est zéro-zéro, quarante-quatre, zéro-sept, zéro-huit, cinquante-deux, soixante-quatre, deux cent trente-huit.
Receptionist:	Parfait, Monsieur Thompson. À vendredi prochain alors.
You:	Merci bien, monsieur
Receptionist:	Je vous en prie. Au revoir.

Context 3

You have arrived in Paris and have just located your hotel. You are at the reception desk.

You:	Bonjour, monsieur. Nous avons une réservation pour deux nuits, ce soir et demain soir.
The receptionist:	Oui, monsieur, à quel nom s'il vous plaît?
You:	Monsieur et Madame Thompson
Receptionist:	Bien sûr. Je me souviens de vous. Je vous ai parlé au téléphone la semaine dernière. Voici la clé. Votre chambre se trouve au troisième étage. Il y a un ascenseur là-bas. Le petit déjeuner est servi à partir de sept heures jusqu'à dix heures dans la

| | salle à manger. Il y a un mini-bar dans votre chambre mais si vous désirez autre chose vous n'avez qu'à nous demander, monsieur. Passez un bon week-end à Paris. |
| You: | Merci bien, monsieur. A bientôt. |

Context 4

The following morning after breakfast, you are at the reception desk asking about places to visit.

You:	Bonjour, monsieur
Receptionist:	Bonjour Monsieur et Madame Thompson. Que puis – je faire pour vous?
You:	Pourriez-vous nous suggérer quelques sites à visiter ce matin, préférablement pas trop loin de l'hôtel? Nous voudrions un peu explorer ce quartier.
Receptionist:	Est-ce que vous aimez visiter les musées?
Jane:	Oui. Est-ce que le Louvre est loin d'ici?
Receptionist:	Pas du tout. Mais le Louvre n'est pas très agréable en ce moment avec tous les touristes qui seront là aujourd'hui. À votre place, moi, je visiterais le Musée Jacquemart –André, Boulevard Haussemann. C'est plus petit que le Louvre, et il y aura moins de monde. Et franchement c'est plus intéressant à mon sens. C'est encore dans le huitième et vous pouvez y aller à pied. Cela vaut bien un effort.
Jane:	Merci, monsieur, c'est gentil. Et après, où pourrions – nous déjeuner dans le coin?
Receptionist:	Il y a une petite brasserie presque à côté qui s'appelle Brasserie d'Antan. Vous pouvez y manger pour trois fois rien par rapport aux restaurants sur les Champs Élysées – et la cuisine y est excellente, vraiment.
You:	Merci bien, monsieur. Ça suffit pour l'instant, je crois!
Receptionist:	De rien, et amusez – vous bien aujourd'hui.

Context 5

You have visited the Musée Jacquemart-André and now you are in the Brasserie d'Antan.

Waitress:	Bonjour, monsieur, bonjour, madame. Est-ce que vous avez choisi?
You:	Oui, on prend la formule à quinze euros.
Jane:	En tant qu'entrée, je prends le saumon fumé, ensuite la salade de gésiers et je ne pense pas que je prenne de dessert.
Waitress:	Et pour monsieur?
You:	Moi, je prends d'abord les oeufs en gelée, puis l'entrecôte saignante et pour dessert la crème brûlée, s'il vous plaît.
Waitress:	C'est parti.

Thirty minutes later:

	Ça a été?
You:	Excellent, merci. Mais, dites-nous. Nous venons de manger dans une brasserie. C'est quoi au juste, une brasserie?
Waitress:	Pour moi une brasserie est à moitié restaurant, moitié café.
Jane:	Qu'est-ce que cela veut dire exactement?
Waitress:	Ça veut dire que l'on peut boire comme dans un café et manger comme dans un restaurant.
You:	Alors, quelle est la différence entre une brasserie et un restaurant?
Waitress:	Dans un restaurant le service est à heures fixes mais dans une brasserie on peut manger à n'importe quelle heure.
Jane:	Mais les plats, sont-ils différents?
Waitress:	Nous proposons des plats simples et rapides et nous avons toujours un plat du jour.
You:	Et c'est moins cher qu'au restaurant?
Waitress:	Normalement, oui. La formule est plus simple, donc moins chère.
You:	Et vos heures d'ouverture?
Waitress:	Nous ouvrons très tôt le matin, et nous fermons vers deux heures du matin, suivant la clientèle.
Jane:	Bon, merci bien, madame. L'addition, s'il vous plaît.
Waitress:	Bien sûr. Je reviens tout de suite.

Context 6

After your blow-out lunch, you decide to take a stroll through the Tuileries Gardens, le Jardin des Tuileries, and you sit down on a bench by the side of the garden's small lake. There is someone else sitting on the bench.

You:	Excusez-moi, madame ça ne vous gêne pas si nous nous mettons à côté de vous?
The woman:	Au contraire, monsieur. Asseyez-vous. Il fait beau aujourd'hui. Il faut en profiter, n'est-ce pas?
Jane:	Tout à fait, madame
The woman:	Vous êtes anglais, non?
You:	Si, est-ce si évident?!
The woman:	Pas vraiment. Vous parlez français d'un accent légèrement anglais mais c'est plutôt la façon dont vous êtes habillés. Vos vêtements sont on ne peut plus anglais! D'où venez-vous au juste?
You:	Nous habitons Londres, mais d'origine je suis de Manchester…
Jane:	Et je suis née à Bristol. Mais n'êtes-vous vous jamais allée à Londres?
The woman:	Oui, plusieurs fois. J'ai une soeur qui habite à South Kensington – et je lui rends visite de temps en temps. L'Eurostar est vraiment très commode.
You:	Vous avez raison, madame. Mais êtes-vous parisienne?
The woman:	Non, je suis née à Dijon mais ça fait longtemps que j'habite Paris.
Jane:	Vous connaissez très bien Paris, alors. Dites-nous, nous n'avons que deux jours à Paris. Où devrions-nous aller demain, à votre avis?
The woman:	La Tour Eiffel est un "must" bien sûr. Et si vous ne connaissez pas bien Paris, vous devriez prendre les bateaux-mouches.
You:	C'est quoi, ça?
The woman:	Ce sont de longs bateaux touristiques, conçus pour des promenades sur la Seine. Vous aurez un point de vue inattendu sur Paris et vous verrez les grands monuments de la ville, y compris Notre-Dame, le Louvre, la Maison de la Radio, la Tour Montparnasse, les tours de La Défense, la Tour Eiffel bien sûr – et vous passerez sous les fameux ponts de Paris. S'il fait beau, c'est fabuleux, vraiment.
You:	Quelle excellente idée, madame. Et où devrions-nous nous adresser?
The woman:	Allez au Pont Neuf, monsieur. Là vous les trouverez.
Jane:	Merci bien, madame
The woman:	Je vous en prie, madame. Et bon séjour à Paris!

Context 7

Before taking a "bateau-mouche", Jane decided she would like to take home a bottle of real French perfume. She pops into a likely-looking perfumerie on the Champs Élysées.

Saleswoman:	Bonjour madame. Vous désirez quelque chose?
Jane:	Oui, je voudrais acheter un parfum pour moi, s'il vous plaît?
Saleswoman:	Oui. Aimez-vous les choses assez fraîches, assez discrètes, ou quelque chose d'un peu plus capiteux?
Jane:	Dites-moi, qu'est-ce que vous me conseillez?
Saleswoman:	Quelque chose d'assez frais. Vous travaillez en collectivité?
Jane:	Je suis professeur
Saleswoman:	Alors, il vaudrait mieux quelque chose d'assez frais – quelque chose d'assez capiteux risque d'indisposer vos élèves. Voilà, je vais vous faire sentir "L" de Lubin. C'est un parfum assez léger, fleuri, il sent très bon et il tient bien.
Jane:	Oui, ça sent bon. Vous l'avez en eau de toilette et en parfum?
Saleswoman:	Ça existe en eau de toilette et en parfum, madame. L'eau de toilette est à partir de 30€ mais vous avez le double de contenance à 50€. Vous avez le parfum qui tient mieux. Vous avez le premier modèle à 45€ et le double de contenance à 80€.
Jane:	Bon, je prends l'eau de toilette à 50€, s'il vous plaît.
Saleswoman:	Bien sûr, madame. C'est tout?
Jane:	Pour l'instant, c'est tout. Merci, bien
Saleswoman:	De rien madame. Au revoir.
Jane:	Au revoir.

Context 8

The "bateau-mouche" along the Seine was really enjoyable. Sadly, it is now time to go home. You decide to take a taxi to the Gare du Nord. The taxi-driver is very chatty and is obviously not originally from France.

Taxi-driver:	Vous repartez en Angleterre?
Jane:	Oui, malheureusement.
Taxi-driver:	Vous vous êtes bien amusés à Paris, j'espère, Paris vous plaît?
You:	Beaucoup. Paris est beau et il y a tellement de choses à faire et à voir. Un week-end n'est qu'un apéro, quoi! Êtes-vous parisien, monsieur?
Taxi-driver:	Non, je suis né en Guinée, en Afrique occidentale.
Jane:	Ça fait longtemps que vous habitez en France?

Taxi-driver:	Je suis venu en France en 1997, madame.
Jane:	Et pourquoi êtes-vous venu en France plutôt que dans un autre pays?
Taxi-driver:	Parce qui je parlais déjà la langue française.
You:	Le français est votre langue maternelle?
Taxi-driver:	Non, ça, c'est le peul.
You:	Le peul?
Taxi-driver:	Oui, ça se parle presqu'un peu dans toute l'Afrique noir. Mais j'ai appris le français à l'école en Guinée.
Jane:	Et la France vous semblait très différente quand vous êtes arrivé, j'imagine.
Taxi-driver:	Tout à fait, madame. En France on ne prend pas beaucoup de temps. On est trop pressé du matin au soir. Tandis qu'en Guinée ils prennent le temps de vivre. C'est à dire, on se lève le matin presque quand on a envie de se lever, on mange quand on a faim et on se promène tranquillement dans la rue. On n'est jamais bousculé. Mais regardez, on est arrivé a la Gare du Nord.
You:	Et combien je vous dois, monsieur?
Taxi-driver:	Ça fait 18€ avec les valises, monsieur.
You:	Voici 20€. Gardez la monnaie.
Taxi-driver:	C'est gentil, monsieur. Merci. Et bon retour en Angleterre.
Jane:	Merci monsieur. Au revoir.

Context 9

You have now arrived at your gîte, near Carcassonne. You are immediately struck by just how much wine-growing there seems to be in the region. You decide to go off exploring the vineyards in the area. You are now in the cave of a local "vigneron" (wine-grower).

You:	Bonjour, monsieur, je voudrais déguster votre vin. Mais d'abord pourriez-vous m'expliquer votre méthode de production?
Wine-grower:	Bien sûr, monsieur. Tout d'abord, il s'agit de terroir. Ici les ceps sont plus productifs sur un terroir arride et pierreux. Ça veut dire que la vigne peut plonger ses racines jusqu'à une remarquable profondeur pour puiser l'eau qui lui est nécessaire.
You:	Y a-t-il d'autres aspects à ce terroir dont vous parlez parce que le mot me dit quelque chose mais je ne sais pas exactement ce que c'est.
Wine-grower:	Je comprends, monsieur. Bon, après vous avez l'orientation du vignoble. Ici mes vignes sont orientées vers le sud, ce qui veut dire

qu'elles reçoivent beaucoup de soleil. Mais elles ont besoin de pluie, aussi, surtout au printemps. Mais la vigne reste une plante assez frileuse, très sensible aux intempéries. Il arrive que la grêle ou le vent fassent des ravages dans les vignobles, détruisant les grappes ou arrachant des plantes entières.

You:	Ah bon? Et le cépage est très important aussi, n'est-ce pas?
Wine-grower:	Incontestablement, monsieur. Ici nous ne produisons que les rouges. Ça veut dire que nous n'avons que le Cabernet Sauvignon et le Merlot. Ailleurs en France vous trouverez d'autres cépages, bien sûr. Mais les vins produits par ces différents cépages sont très différents selon les régions.
You:	Et avant de servir un vin rouge, qu'est-ce que l'on doit faire?
Wine-grower:	Alors, pour des vins rouges, il faut respecter une certaine température. Pour nos vins il faut quinze degrés.
You:	Et quel verre devrait-on utiliser?
Wine-grower:	De préférence, un verre ballon.
You:	Pourquoi?
Wine-grower:	Pour la concentration des arômes, parce qu'on goûte aussi le vin avec le nez.
You:	Bon, puis – je maintenant goûter un échantillon de vos vins, monsieur?
Wine-grower:	Ça me ferait plaisir, monsieur. Commençons avec celui-ci. C'est très fruité et assez léger. Goûtez-le!

Thirty minutes later…!

You:	Oh là, là! Qu'est-ce que j'ai bien bu!
Wine-grower:	Et lequel préférez-vous monsieur?
You:	Je pense que je préfère le premier que j'ai goûté – et je voudrais en acheter une douzaine de bouteilles, s'il vous plaît.
Wine-grower:	Bien sûr, monsieur. Je les mets dans le coffre de votre voiture, ça va?
You:	Bien sûr. Et combien je vous dois, monsieur?
Wine-grower:	Ce vin – ci se vend normalement pour cinq euros la bouteille dans les grandes surfaces, mais ici pour trois euros.
You:	C'est donné! J'en prends deux cartons.
Wine-grower:	Avec plaisir, monsieur. Vous restez dans la région?
You:	Oui, nous avons loué un gîte à deux pas d'ici et nous restons quinze jours, ce qui veut dire que je reviens! Pour l'instant merci et à bientôt!
Wine-grower:	À bientôt, monsieur.

Context 10

The gîte that you have rented is very close indeed to Carcassonne. One of the first things you do there is to take a guided tour of the city with a group of tourists.

Guide:	Carcassonne est connue dans le monde entier pour sa cité médiévale. Le nom de la ville remonte à l'époque de Charlemagne qui a été couronné le jour de Noël, en l'an 800. Il faut se remettre dans le contexte.
	La cité est assiégée par les armées de Charlemagne, et il n'y a plus grand-chose à manger. Mais il reste quand même une princesse qui s'appelle Dame Carcas et elle a un petit cochon. Elle décide d'engraisser ce petit porcelet et, une fois qu'il est bien gras, elle le relâche devant les remparts, vers les armées qui assiègent la ville. Et voyant ce petit cochon bien dodu, bien gras ils se disent: "ben, à l'intérieur ils ont vraiment de quoi manger. On ne va pas poursuivre plus longtemps ce siège vu comment ça se passe". Donc, l'armée s'en va. À ce moment – là Dame Carcas fait sonner les cloches qui sonnent à tout berzingue. C'est pour ça que la ville s'appelle Carcassonne – Carcas sonne!
A tourist:	Quelle jolie histoire! Mais c'est vrai?
Guide:	Soi – disant! Mais après la visite je ne pouvais vous parler d'une autre auberge que celle de Dame Carcas, bien sûr, où l'on vous servira un cochon de lait grillé au miel de Corbières dans un cadre rustique et une ambiance éminemment sympathique. Et peut-être vous laisserez-vous aussi tenter par un cassoulet: confit d'oie, jarret de porc, saucisses, le tout cuit dans une cassole traditionnelle, et le tour de main du chef fera de ce plat un des grands moments de votre périple!
Jane:	Oh là, là! David. Ça me met déjà l'eau à la bouche! Oublions le reste de la visite. Allons-y tout de suite!
You:	Tout à fait. En voiture, Simone!

Getting To Know You

Context 11

Of course, visit a region of France often enough, get to know it and like it – and you might be tempted to buy a holiday home there. That is what we did nearly thirty years ago. Admittedly, prices were rock-bottom in those days – but you can still find plenty of interesting, cheap property off the beaten track. (Do you remember how to say **that** in French?) Even on the Mediterranean coast there are some relatively reasonable, very beautiful locations. One such is Sète. You have only been there once before – but you have already fallen head over heels in love with it. So you decide to learn more about it. You are now in the office of a Sète estate agent.

Estate agent:	Vous connaissez assez bien Sète déjà, j'imagine.
Jane:	Pas vraiment. En effet c'est notre deuxième visite! Mais cette ville a l'air tellement charmante et belle que nous pensons acheter quelque chose ici, mais nous nous demandons si Sète est dans nos possibilités?
Estate agent:	Ça dépend, évidemment, mais si vous commencez avec quelque chose de modeste, vous pouvez toujours monter plus haut plus tard. Laissez-moi vous donner plus de renseignements. Après, si vous voulez que je vous montre quelques possibilités...
You:	Excellente idée, monsieur. Commençons à zéro.
Estate agent:	Bon. Sète est un ancien village de pêcheurs qui a été construit sur le Mont Saint-Clair. C'est une île singulière entre la mer et l'étang de Thau et qui a été reliée par une lagune et un lido. Donc, c'est la Venise du Languedoc avec en plus les canaux qui ont été créés quand le port de Sète a été contruit à côté du village, à l'époque où le canal du Midi a été construit. Alors on vient à Sète pour le charme du port et des canaux, pour la plage de la corniche, pour les musées, et pour tellement de trésors cachés. Et la cuisine sétoise n'est pas la plus mauvaise qui soit!
You:	On peut parler d'une cuisine sétoise, alors?
Estate agent:	Je vous ai déjà expliqué que Sète est un village de pêcheurs. Est-ce que vous êtes très poisson?
Jane:	Oui, nous adorons presque toutes les variétés de poisson.
Estate agent:	La cuisine sétoise est assez proche de celle du sud de l'Italie et le plat le plus typique de Sète, c'est la macaronade.
You:	La macaronade? Le mot me dit quelque chose, mais c'est quoi au juste?
Estate agent:	Ce sont des pâtes avec de la sauce tomate et un fond de sauce qui est à base de fruits de mer et d'encornets farcis.

Jane:	Oui, je m'en souviens, maintenant. Quelqu'un à côté de nous dans le restaurant hier soir prenait ce plat. L'odeur était délicieuse, vraiment!
Estate agent:	C'est marrant, mais même les anglais en vacances ne parle que bouffe!
You:	Mais parlons, maintenant, des maisons, même des appartements, que vous avez à vendre. Sont-ils tous chers?
Estate agent:	En principe, les appartements sont moins chers que les maisons. On peut acheter un studio à partir des 80,000€ et un appartements de deux pièces à partir de 100,000€. Les apparts de trois pièces sont disponibles à partir de 120,000€. On en a quelques-uns à vous montrer à deux pas d'ici sur les canaux, et qui sont très jolis et très pratiques. On peut les fermer à clé et les oublier, jusqu'à votre prochaine visite. À mon avis c'est par là vous devriez commencer votre recherche.
You:	Vous avez raison, monsieur. Commençons avec des appartements de deux pièces. Est-ce que vous pouvez nous en montrer?
Estate agent:	J'ai celui-ci à 90,000€, celui-ci à 100,000€ et celui-ci à 110,000€. Mais, vous savez, en France le prix de n'importe quoi est à débattre. Trop souvent, malheureusement, les vendeurs sont trop avides. Leurs prix de demande sont trop élévés et au bout d'un certain temps ils sont obligés de les réduire.
Jane:	Alors, en principe, il faudrait payer combien pour les appartements qui sont disponibles en ce moment?
Estate agent:	Je connais le propriétaire de l'appartement à 100,000€ et il doit bouger très bientôt. Bon, je suis convaincu qu'il accepterait 80,000€ parce que son appartement est à vendre depuis deux ans. Voudriez-vous le voir.
You:	Oui, je pense. Mais quand?
Estate agent:	Cet après-midi si vous voulez. Il n'est pas là en ce moment. C'est l'occasion parfaite de le voir.
You:	D'accord, mettons à quinze heures, alors. Ça va?
Estate agent:	Oui, ça me convient parfaitement. Je n'ai plus de rendez-vous cet après-midi. Je vais vous rejoindre ici à quinze heures, alors.
You:	Bon. À quinze heures. Au revoir, monsieur.
Estate agent:	Au revoir, Monsieur et Madame Thompson.

Context 12

For some, of course, the dream is to retire to France. Here is a couple who have done just that. For nearly ten years, they have lived in the Corrèze in Turenne, officially recognized as one of France's most beautiful villages. A French reporter has come to interview them for her magazine: she wants to know what retired Brits think of life in deepest, rural France.

Interviewer:	Bonjour Monsieur et Madame Cameron. Ça fait combien de temps que vous habitez en Corrèze?
Mrs Cameron:	Nous habitons en Corrèze depuis presque dix ans.
Interviewer:	Et est-ce que la Corrèze vous plaît?
Mr Cameron:	Oui, énormément. Nous y sommes venus pour la première fois il y a quinze ans, nous sommes tombés amoureux de la région presque immédiatement et nous avons décidé de passer notre retraite ici à Turenne, "l'un des plus beaux villages de France" vous savez.
Interviewer:	Oui, je sais et je suis d'accord – le village est vraiment beau. Est-ce que c'était difficile quand vous êtes arrivés au début? Est-ce que vous parliez français à l'époque?
Mrs Cameron:	Très peu vraiment. Mon mari avait appris le français à l'école – moi aussi – mais c'était pas suffisant. Mais, vous savez, on apprend assez vite quand on vit en France. Il faut! Et les gens du coin sont vraiment sympas. Ils nous aidaient beaucoup au début et ils ignoraient nos erreurs. Maintenant nous parlons assez-bien le français.
Interviewer:	Plus que ça, madame! Vous parlez couramment le français. Franchement, si mon anglais était aussi bon que votre français, je serais vraiment très contente! Et dites-moi, que pensez-vous de la région dans laquelle vous vous trouvez?
Mr Cameron:	Oh, c'est génial. Mais c'est très varié. J'ai bien étudié l'histoire de la Corrèze, qui est impressionante. La Corrèze est devenue un pays pendant la période révolutionnaire. À l'époque elle était composée d'une partie de l'Auvergne, une partie du Limousin, une partie du Quercy et une partie du Périgord. Mais tout cela s'est mélangé et de nos jours tout le monde se sent Corrèzien, du nord au sud. Mais le pays reste divers: vous avez le pays de Treignac, vous avez le pays de Tulle et vous avez le pays de Brive, tous très différents les uns des autres. Mais où que vous soyez, le paysage est tellement beau – et calme!

Et notre village a une histoire incroyable, vous savez. C'était la patrie de Henri de la Tour d'Auvergne, maréchal de France, allié de Louis XIV. C'était l'un des plus grands fiefs du Royaume au XIV siècle, frappant monnaie, levants impôts et jouissant d'une autonomie complète vis-à-vis du pouvoir royal. |

Interviewer:	Et que pensez-vous des habitants du coin?
Mrs Cameron:	Ils sont souriants, acceuillants et conviviaux, les Corrèziens. Nous nous sommes fait beaucoup d'amis dans le village et dans les parages.
Interviewer:	Et comment passez-vous votre temps libre ici en Corrèze?
Mrs Cameron:	Nous continuons à explorer la région. Même après dix ans il y a tellement de choses à voir et à faire. Nous aimons lire, mon mari continue à faire son jardin, surtout son potager. Moi, je cultive mes fleurs. Et nous aimons recevoir nos amis autour d'un verre, quoi. Et, moi, je dois faire tout ce qu'il faut à la maison: mes courses, le ménage, la cuisine etc.
Interviewer:	Et avez-vous des enfants?
Mrs Cameron:	Oui, on en a deux. Ils passent de temps à autre. Nous avons quatre petits-enfants et ils adorent passer leurs vacances scolaires avec nous.
Interviewer:	Et l'hiver, c'est comment ici à Turenne?
Mr Cameron:	C'est calme, ça c'est le moins qu'on puisse dire! Mais nous avons la télé et nous pouvons recevoir les émissions anglaises. Et il y a notre musique: je continue à jouer du piano, ma femme aussi. C'est calme, oui, mais nous y sommes très contents quand même.
Interviewer:	Et un jour dans l'avenir, voudriez-vous repartir en Angleterre?
Mrs Cameron:	Pas forcément. Ça dépend. Mais nous repartons en Angleterre au moins deux fois par an rendre visite à nos gosses et nos petits-enfants. Mais, franchement, nous nous sentons très français de nos jours. L'Angleterre ne nous manque pas du tout!
Interviewer:	Bon, et merci infiniment.
Mrs Cameron:	Il n'y a pas de quoi, madame. Et avant de partir, voudriez vous prendre une tasse de thé et un morceau de Victoria sponge?
Interviewer:	Oh là, là! Ça fait tellement anglais. Ça me ferait très grand plaisir!
Mrs Cameron:	Excellent, et comment prenez-vous votre thé: avec du lait et du sucre?
Interviewer:	Parfait. Vous êtes très gentille, madame.
Mrs Cameron:	C'est à moi, madame. Et en attendant, faites comme chez vous. Nous avons The Daily Telegraph, si vous voudriez lire quelque chose.
Interviewer:	Malheureusement, je ne sais pas lire l'anglais. Mais après cette visite, qui sait!

Context 13

In this final context, we meet a young couple, Steve and Amanda. They have recently come to work in Paris. He is an English teacher in a "lycée" in the Rue Diderot and she is an accountant working for Alstom, the French engineering company that manufactures the TGV (le Train à Grand Vitesse). Her office is in Levallois-Perret in the north west of Paris. They are in their favourite Irish bar in the Rue Montreuil and they are with two French friends, Pascal and Evelyne.

Steve:	Qu'est-ce que vous prenez? C'est mon tour. C'est moi qui paie à boire.
Evelyne:	Merci, Steve, je prends un whisky avec une goutte de soda, s'il te plaît.
Amanda:	Je prends un verre de Sauvignon Blanc, Steve.
Pascal:	Et pour mois une pinte de Guinness, Steve, s'il te plaît.
Steve:	D'accord, whisky, vin blanc et Guinness. Je reviens tout de suite. Et quelque chose à grignoter peut-être?
Amanda:	Des chips peut-être, Steve. C'est tout. Nous sortons plus tard manger dans la Rue Paul Bert.

Steve returns a few minutes later:

Pascal:	Alors, tchin-tchin, tout le monde.
All together:	Tchin-tchin!
Pascal:	Alors, quoi de neuf Steve et Amanda? La dernière fois, vous veniez de trouver un nouvel appart à louer. Tout s'est bien passé?
Amanda:	Oui et non!
Evelyne:	Oui et non? Qu'est-ce que ça veut dire au juste?
Amanda:	L'appart est parfait – pas loin du métro avec une belle chambre et un salon qui sert aussi de salle à manger. La cuisine est une cuisine américaine mais ça marche bien quand même. Et elle est bien équipée. Nous sommes au quatrième étage mais nous avons un ascenseur. Nous ne sommes pas trop loin non plus d'une excellente épicerie et un Dia qui est très peu cher.
Evelyne:	Mais…?
Steve:	Mais le propriétaire nous a déjà dit qu'à la fin de l'année il a l'intention d'augmenter le loyer. Je me suis rendu à la Mairie où je me suis entretenue du problème avec un expert.
Pascal:	Et qu'est-ce qu'il vous a dit, ce type?
Amanda:	Il nous a dit que notre propriétaire a le droit de majorer notre loyer comme bon lui semble. Si c'est le cas, nous serons obligés d'aller ailleurs. C'est dommage mais c'est la vie.

Evelyne:	Mais à mon avis, Amanda, c'est l'occasion rêvée de trouver un appart plus proche de ton boulot. C'est un bout, ton trajet, n'est-ce pas?
Amanda:	Tout à fait. Le matin il me faut au moins une heure et le soir plus, même. Mais si nous devions trouver un appart plus proche de mon bureau, ça veut dire que Steve serait moins proche de son école.
Evelyne:	Tant pis pour lui!
Steve:	Vraiment, Evelyne. Évidemment il faut faire un compromis. On verra. Nous avons au moins six mois pour trouver quelque chose. En attendons, profitons de l'appart qu'on a en ce moment. Maintenant, passons à autre chose. Est-ce que tu as vu le match à la télé hier soir, Pascal? PSG était nul à mon sens.
Pascal:	Oui, mais c'est kif-kif, Lyon était pire même. Quand même, match nul, c'est pas mal pour les lyonnais. Parlons d'autres choses. Êtes-vous jamais allés à Lyon? C'est pas mal là – bas et on y mange bien!
Steve:	La capitale gastronomique de France, d'après certains. Nous devrions y aller. Nous pourrions y passer un week-end. Le TGV passe par Lyon. C'est très rapide – une heure et demie apparemment.
Evelyne:	Quelle excellente idée, Steve. J'y suis allée une fois avec mes parents. On a mangé dans un bouchon. C'était vraiment extra! J'aimerais y retourner.
Pascal:	Et on pourrait y aller dans la journée.
Steve:	Moi, je préférerais un week-end, Pascal. Il y a au moins vingt bouchons à Lyon, paraît-il!
Amanda:	Espèce de glouton! Moi, je voudrais acheter quelques fringues. Les magasins sont excellents, d'après un collègue à moi.
Evelyne:	Moi aussi, Amanda. J'ai besoin de nouvelle lingerie, qui est bonne à Lyon, apparement.
Steve:	Et très sexy, j'espère, Evelyne!
Amanda:	Steve, vraiment, tu ne penses qu'à ça! Il y a d'autres choses dans la vie, tu sais.
Steve:	Oui, le foot – n'est-ce pas, Pascal!
Amanda:	Steve, tu est incorrigible!
Pascal:	Mais tu as oublié la bouffe, Steve. Tu es malade ou quoi?!
Evelyne:	Prenons nos plans au sérieux. Nous pourrions descendre à Lyon le week-end prochain, peut-être?
Amanda:	Pourquoi pas, Evelyne. Mais il y a un problème.
Evelyne:	Quoi?
Amanda:	Je n'ai rien à me mettre!
All together:	Amanda!

One final thought

In preparing this final chapter I searched for something that would sum up as much as possible of this book in one single page. It did not take long to find it – the blood-curdling words to France's national anthem, the Marseillaise. This one piece of French history contains no fewer than **eight** of my "killer" verbs!

But that is not the only reason I have included it. A few years ago a Welsh friend and I were in a Paris bar following the France-Wales rugby international at the Stade Français. We were wearing our colours and were quietly celebrating a rare Welsh win in Paris when in burst a group of French supporters. On seeing us they immediately congratulated us on our win and promptly demanded that we give a rendering of our national anthem, "Mae Hen Wlad Fy' nhadau" which, they insisted was infinitely superior to theirs. Our reward would be not just one drink, but an evening of drinks – on them! So, we duly obliged, but only on one condition: that they would then sing the Marseillaise and allow us to return the vineous compliment. They agreed. So we sang our anthem, to tumultuous applause.

Now it was their turn. But can you imagine their astonishment when, from the very first bar, I joined in and sang it with them right to the end? With that bravura performance, the deal was off. No! We would not be allowed to buy another drink. The drinks were on them! (Can you remember how to say that in French?)

It turned out to be a very long night indeed; and much of the rest of Sunday passed under the shadow of one of the most monumental hangovers I have ever experienced!

The moral of the story is plain to see: for the daddy of all "gueules de bois" sing the Marseillaise in a Paris bar with some very merry Frenchmen. Your studies will be complete!

La Marseillaise
(Chant de geurre de l'armee du Rhin)
dédié au Maréchal Luckner (Rouget de l'Isle, 1792)

Allons enfants de la patrie
Le jour de gloire **est arrivé**
Contre nous, de la tyrannie
L'étendard sanglant est levé (bis)
Entendez-vous dans nos campagnes
Mugir ces féroces soldats
Ils viennent jusque dans nos bras
Egorger vos fils, vos compagnes

Aux armes citoyens
Formez vos bataillons
Marchons, marchons
Qu'un sang impur
Abreuve nos sillons

Que **veut** cette horde d'esclaves
De traîtres, de rois conjurés?
Pour qui ces ignobles entraves
Ces fers dès longtemps préparés (bis)
Français! Pour nous, ah quel outrage
Quels transports **il doit** exciter
Qu'**est-ce** qu'on ose méditer
De **rendre** à l'antique esclavage

Quoi ces cohortes étrangères
Feraient la loi dans nos foyers!
Quoi ces phalanges mercenaires
Terrasseraient nos fiers guerriers (bis)
Grands Dieux! …Par des mains enchaînées
Nos fronts sous le jong ploieraient
Des vils despotes deviendraient
Les maîtres de nos destinées!...

<u>Conclusion</u>

That is it. Twenty-two killer verbs under your belt. Believe me, if you master these verbs and most of what is in this book to boot, you really will be able to speak amazing French. But remember:

C'est en forgeant qu'on devient forgeron.

Practice makes perfect! Good luck – and stay seated on that three-legged stool (remember?)

Some words you might not yet know

- médiéval(e) -   medieval
- entouré(e) -   surrounded
- fortifié(e) -   fortified
- les Cathares -   a people who inhabited the Carcassonne region in medieval times

- disponible -   available
- un contrat -   a contract
- la disponibilité -   availability
- un forfait -   a package
- supplémentaire -   in addition
- le tarif -   the room price
- la clé -   the key
- suggérer -   to suggest
- les sites (m) -   sights
- préférablement -   preferably
- explorer -   to explore
- à votre place -   if I were you
- cela vaut bien un effort -   it is worth the effort
- les oeufs (m) en gelée -   eggs in aspic
- le plat du jour -   the dish of the day
- les heures d'ouverture (f) -   opening hours
- les bateaux-mouches (m) -   river boats
- inattendu(e) -   unexpected
- un séjour -   a stay
- une parfumerie -   a perfume shop
- un parfum -   a perfume
- capiteux -   heady
- travailler en collectivité -   to work with others
- indisposer -   to upset
- les élèves (m) -   pupils
- tenir -   to last
- le double de contenance -   twice the size
- l'Afrique (f) occidentale -   West Africa
- une langue maternelle -   a mother-tongue
- bousculé(e) -   upset / disturbed
- les valises (f) -   suitcases
- garder la monnaie -   to keep the change
- déguster -   to taste
- les ceps (m) -   vines
- arride -   very dry
- pierreux(se) -   stony
- les racines (f) -   the roots
- la profondeur -   the depth
- puiser -   to draw
- l'orientation (f) -   the direction in which the vineyard points

- un vignoble -   a vineyard
- recevoir -   to receive / to get
- au printemps -   in the Spring

- frileux(se) - sensitive
- sensible - (also) sensitive
- les intempéries (f) - bad weather
- les ravages (f) - damage
- détruire - to destroy
- les grappes (f) - the (bunches of) grapes
- le cépage - the grape variety
- ailleurs - elsewhere
- respecter - to observe
- un verre ballon - a balloon glass
- la concentration des arômes - the concentration of aromas
- un échantillon - a sample
- une douzaine - a dozen
- un carton - a case
- remonter - to go back to
- l'époque (f) - the period
- couronné(e) - crowned
- assiegé(e) - under siege
- engraisser - to fatten
- un porcelet - a piglet
- les remparts (m) - the fortified walls
- dodu(e) - plump / chubby
- poursuivre - to continue / to follow
- à ce moment-là - at that moment
- sonner - to ring
- les cloches (f) - the bells
- à tout berzingue - flat out
- soi-disant - allegedly, ostensibly
- une auberge - an inn
- un cochon de lait - a milk-fed pig
- le miel - honey
- un cadre rustique - a rustic setting
- éminemment - eminently
- un cassoulet - a bean stew with meats
- une cassole - a dish specially designed for cassoulet
- le tour de main - the skill
- un périple - a journey
- être dans ses possibilités - to be possible
- modeste - modest
- commencer à zéro - to begin from scratch
- les pêcheurs - fishermen
- un étang - a (small) lake
- relier - to link
- une lagune - a lagoon
- un lido - a lido
- un canal - a canal
- créer - to create
- une corniche - a cliff
- les trésors (m) cachés - hidden treasures
- la cuisine sétoise - the cuisine of Sète
- un fond - a base
- les encornets (m) - squid

- farci(e) - stuffed
- marrant(e) - funny
- pratique - practical
- la recherche - research
- n'importe quoi - anything
- à débattre - up for discussion / to be debated
- avide - greedy
- au bout d'un certain temps - after a while
- bouger - to move
- très bientôt - very soon
- tomber amoureux(se) - to fall in love
- varié(e) - varied
- se mélanger - to mix up
- divers(e) - diverse
- les uns des autres - one from another
- la patrie - the homeland
- un maréchal - a marshal / field marshal
- allié(e) de - allied to
- un fief - a stronghold
- le Royaume - the kingdom
- frappant monnaie - striking coins
- levant impôts - raising taxes
- vis-à-vis - in relation to
- souriant(e) - smiling
- accueillant(e) - welcoming
- convivial(e) - convivial
- les vacances scolaires (f) - school holidays
- en attendant - in the meantime
- les chips (m) - crisps
- une cuisine américaine - a kitchen open to the living room
- s'entretenir de quelque chose - to talk over something
- un bout (fam) - a long journey
- compromettre - to compromise
- quelque part - somewhere
- pire - worse
- un match nul - a drawn game
- parlant de quoi - talking of which
- un bouchon - (here) a traditional Lyon restaurant which serves classic Lyon food

- la lingerie - women's underwear
- l'étendard (m) - the standard / flag
- sanglant(e) - bloody
- mugir - to roar / bellow
- égorger - to cut (throats etc.)
- abreuver - to drench
- un sillon - a ploughed field
- un(e) esclave - a slave
- les traîtres (m/f) - traitors
- un(e) conjuré(e) - a conspirator
- une entrave - a constraint
- un fer - a sword

- oser -   to dare
- l'esclavage (m) -   slavery
- un foyer -   a home
- une phalange -   an army
- terrasser -   to bring / strike down
- un guerrier -   a warrior
- ployer -   to yield
- vil(e) -   vile
- les despotes (m) -   tyrants
- les maîtres (m/f) -   masters
- la destinée -   fate

Postscript

I used several methods to generate candidate verbs for inclusion in this book. I then employed several evaluative criteria to reduce the list to twenty-one.

One of my methods was to ask a lot of French friends and acquaintances for **their** list of twenty-one verbs. These generated thirty more verbs that those that make the cut. But many were only cited once. Those that got two or more mentions but still not enough to qualify were:

- acheter (to buy)
- aimer (to love)
- appeler / s'appeler (to call)
- boire (to drink)
- croire (to believe)
- devenir (to become)
- espérer (to hope)
- s'occuper (to look after)
- regarder (to look)
- sentir / se sentir (to feel)
- vivre (to live)
- voir (to see)

But all of these verbs crop up in the book anyway! However, if you are still thirsty for knowledge, maybe this is where you might go next. Who knows? These may even be the subject matter of my next book!

Index

This vocabulary list shows only words and expressions used in the conversations at the end of each verb chapter and in Chapter Twenty-Four.

a memory like a sieve

B

les bagages (m) *luggage*
une bagnole (fam) *a car*
un bahut *a sideboard*
une baignoire *a bath*
une bande sonore *a sound-track*
la banquette arrière *the back seat*
barbant(e) *boring*
une barbecue *a barbecue*
le bataclan *the lot; the whole kit and caboodle*
les bateaux-mouches *river boats*
un bâtiment *a building*
un bâton *a stick*
une batterie *a (car) battery*
un beau mec (fam) *a good-looking guy*
bêcher *to dig*
bel et bien *well and truly*
de belles éclaircies *bright periods*
les bêtises (f) *nonsense*
beurre (m) *butter*
beurre doux *unsalted butter*
une biche *a deer*
un bidonville *a shanty town*
le bienvenu *the welcome*
un bilan de santé *a health check-up*
"Bis!" *"Encore!" or "More!"*
les blancs *white goods (sheets, etc) for the household*
la blanquette à l'ancienne *a veal stew*
des blettes *Swiss chard*
un bloc-notes *a notepad*
boire *to drink*
boire cul sec *to down a drink in one*
une boîte *a company*
bon appétit! *enjoy your food!*
le bonheur *happiness*
un bon rapport qualité-prix *good value for money*
le bon vieux temps *in the old days*
bonne continuation! *carry on enjoying yourself!*

la bonne taille *the right size*
bonnes fêtes *happy holidays*
un bordel *literally, a brothel, also a mess*
une boucherie-charcuterie *a shop that sells both raw meat and cured pork products*
un bouchon *a traditional Lyon restaurant which serves classic Lyon food*
le boudin noir *black-pudding*
bouger *to move*
un boui-boui (fam) *a grubby little restaurant*
le boulot (fam) *work*
un bourgignon *boeuf bourgignon, a stew made with beef and red wine*
bousculé(e) *upset / disturbed*
un bout (fam) *a long journey*
une boutique *a small shop*
un bras *an arm*
Bravo! *Well done!*
la Bretagne *Brittany*
brûler *to burn*
un brûleur *a gas burner*
un but *an objective / goal*

C

ça bouge *there is a lot happening/going on*
ça c'est envoyé! *nice one!*
ça dépend *it all depends*
ça fait longtemps? *is it a long time?*
ça marche? *that works?*
ça va sans dire *that goes without saying*
ça y est *that's it/that's done*
une cabine d'essayage *a changing room*
caché(e) *hidden*
un cadre rustique *a rustic setting*
un calcul *a calculation*
le calva *calvados*
un canal *a canal*
un canapé *a sofa*
la cantine *the restaurant at work*
le cap *the strategy / the direction*
capiteux *heady*
les carreaux(m) *tiles*
le carrelage *(also) tiles*

une carrière médicale *a medical career*
une carte de fidélité *a loyalty card*
un carton *a case*
une casserole *a saucepan*
une cassole *a dish specially designed for cassoulet*
un cassoulet *a bean stew with meats*
les Cathares *a people who inhabited the Carcassonne region in medieval times*
cela veut dire que *that means that*
les cendres (f) *cigarette ash*
un cendrier *an ash-tray*
le cépage *the grape variety*
les ceps *vines*
c'est à moi *it's my pleasure / it's for me…*
c'est dommage *its a shame*
c'est en forgeant qu'on devient forgeron *practice makes perfect*
c'est la première impression qui compte *first impressions count*
c'est pas la peine *it doesn't matter*
c'est plutôt bon signe *it is rather a good sign*
ça vaut l'effort *it is worth the effort*
une chaise berçante *a rocking-chair*
chaleureux(se) *welcoming*
un chalumeau *a blow torch*
un champ de foire *a fairground*
Chapeau! *Well done!*
une charrue *a plough*
les chaussures (f) *shoes*
le chef d'orchestre *the conductor*
une chemise *a shirt*
la Chine *China*
les chips *crisps*
choisir *to choose*
un chômeur *an unemployed person*
le choux *cabbage*
un cigare *a cigar*
les cisailles (f) de jardinage *garden shears*
clair(e) *light*
la clé *the key*
les cloches (f) *the bells*
un clown *a clown*
un club de jazz *a jazz club*

un cochon *a pig*
un cochon de lait *a milk-fed pig*
une cocotte *a casserole dish*
une colonie française *a French colony*
une comédie musicale *a musical comedy*
une commande *an order*
comme quoi! *it just goes to show*
commencer à zéro *to begin from scratch*
comment l'avez vous trouvez? *how was it?*
commode *convenient*
les compétences (f) *the skills/capabilities*
un compositeur *a composer*
comprehensif (ve) *understanding*
la compréhension *understanding*
les comprimés (m) *tablets*
compris(e) *included*
compromettre *to compromise*
la concentration des arômes *the concentration of aromas*
un concerto *a concerto*
conclure *to conclude*
la concurrence *competition*
le confit de canard *preserved duck*
congé(m) maladie *sick leave*
un(e) conjuré(e) *a consiprator*
un copain *a friend*
une copine *a girlfriend*
conservateur/trice *conservative*
les considérations (f) *considerations*
construit(e) *built*
un consultant en études de marché *a market-research consultant*
un contrat *a contract*
convaincant(e) *convincing*
convenir *to suit*
convivial *convivial*
les cordes (f) *the string section*
corrigez-moi si je me trompe *correct me if I am mistaken*
la corniche *the cliff*
la Corse *Corsica*
un costume *a suit*
couper les cheveux en quatre *to split hairs*
couronné(e) *crowned*
une cousine *a cousin*

coûter les yeux de la tête *to cost the earth*
les couverts en argent *the silver cutlery*
couvrir *to cover*
une cravate *a tie*
un créneau *a gap*
creve(é) *tired / exhausted*
crever de faim *to be starving / famished*
une crise cardiaque *a heart attack*
croire en Dieu *to believe in God*
un crochet de boucher *a meat-hook*
une cuisine américaine *a kitchen open to the living room*
la cuisine sétoise *the cuisine of Sète*
les cuisses (f) de grenouilles *frogs' legs*
les cuivres (m) *the brass section*

D

d'abord *first of all*
d'accord *OK*
dans l'avenir *in the future*
dans le temps *in the old days*
dans un premier temps *to begin with*
dans une certaine mesure *to some extent*
d'après certains *according to some*
d'autre part *on the other hand*
débordé(e) *snowed under*
décoloré(e) *discoloured*
décontracté(e) *relaxed / laid back*
décorer *to decorate*
déguster *to taste*
dehors *outside*
une demeure *a home*
les dépendances *the out-buildings*
dépenser *to spend*
déprimant(e) *depressing*
déranger *to disturb someone*
le dernier film *the latest film*
dès que *as soon as*
la destinée *fate*
un détaillant *a retailer*
détruire *to destroy*
devenir *to become*
un devis *an estimate*
un diplôme universitaire *a university diploma*

la disparition *death*
la disponibilité *availability*
disponible *available*
une distraction *a hobby / past time / relaxation*
divers(e) *diverse / various*
divin(e) *divine / heavenly*
dodu(e) *plump / chubby*
donner *to give*
donner l'exemple *to set an example*
donner un coup de peinture *to give a lick of paint*
dont *of which / about which*
dorloté(e) *pampered*
dormir *to sleep*
le double de contenance *twice the size*
doucement *carefully*
une douche *a shower*
douloureux (se) *painful*
une douzaine *a dozen*
un(e) dramaturge *a playwrite*

E

l'eau (f) bouillante *boiling water*
un échantillon *a sample*
éclaircir *to lighten*
une école hôtelière *a catering school / college*
écraser (une cigarette) *to stub out*
les écrevisses (f) *crayfish*
en effet *indeed*
efficace *effective*
égorger *to cut (throats)*
les élèves (m) *pupils*
éloigner *to move away from*
emballer *to love*
l'embarras du choix *so much to choose from*
éminemment *eminently*
en attaque? *can we start?*
en attendant *in the meantime*
encore *still*
les encornets (m) *squid*

encourageant(e) *encouraging*
les endroits (m) *places*
l'engrais (m) *fertiliser*
engraisser *to fatten*
une entrave *a constraint*
les ennuis (m) *problems*
ennuyé(e) *bored*
énorme *enormous*
enseigner *to teach*
ensemble *together*
ensuite *next*
entendu *of course/understood*
enthousiaste *enthusiastic*
entouré(e) *surrounded*
l'entrée (f) *the hallway*
entre guillemets *in inverted commas*
envelopper *to wrap up*
éplucher *to peel*
l'époque (f) *the period*
époustouflant(e) *amazing; incredible; staggering*
un escalator *an escalator*
les escargots (m) *snails*
un(e) esclave – *a slave*
l'esclavage (m) *slavery*
espèce de…! *you…!*
l'estomac (m) *the stomach*
et? *and what about?*
un étang *a (small) lake*
les États-Unis *the United States*
l'étendard (m) *the standard / flag*
étonnant(e) *astonishing*
être à la hauteur *to be on top form*
être à saturation *to be saturated*
être bon pour la casse *a write-off*
être dans ses possibilités *to be possible*
être en bonne voie de guérison *to be well on the road to recovery*
être enrhumé(e) *to have a cold*
être en rupture de stock *to be out of stock*
être mal garé(e) sur le parking *to be badly parked*
être sorti *to have come out of*
les études (f) *studies*
évidemment *obviously*

éviter *to avoid*
examiner *to examine*
exceptionnellement *exceptionally*
exigeant(e) *demanding*
les exigences (f) *demands*
explorer *to explore*
extraordinaire *extraordinary*

F

facturer *to bill someone*
un faible *a weakness*
faillir *to almost (do something)*
faire des ronds *to make circles (with cigarette smoke)*
faire dorer *to brown*
faire du lèche-vitrines *to go window shopping*
faire fortune *to make a fortune*
faire la popote (fam) *to do the cooking*
faire le forcing *to go for the hard sell*
faire revenir *to turn colour*
faire un prix *to offer something at a reduced price*
faire une distinction entre *to distinguish between*
faire comme chez soi *to make oneself at home*
farci(e) *stuffed*
les fast-foods (m) *the fast-foods restaurants*
les féculents (m) *starchy foods*
félicitations! *congratulations!*
les fenêtres (f) *windows*
un fer *a sword*
fermer *to close*
la ferraille *metallic change*
les fêtes de fin d'année *end of year celebrations*
un fief *a stronghold*
les films comiques *comedy films*
les films d'amour *romantic films*
les films de science-fiction *science fiction films*
les films pornographiques *pornographic films*

les films psychologiques *psychological films*
un flan *a slice of custard tart*
foncé(e) *dark*
la fonctionnalité *functionality*
fonctionner *to work*
un fond *a base*
fondre *to melt*
en fonte *made of cast-iron*
un forfait *a package*
les formules déjeuner *fixed-price lunch menus*
fortifié(e) *fortified*
fou (folle) *mad / crazy*
les foules (f) *the crowds*
un four *an oven*
un fourneau *a stove*
un foyer *a home*
les framboises (f) *raspberries*
franchement *frankly*
la franchise *frankness*
frappant monnaie *striking coins*
frileux(se) *sensitive*
froissé(e) *crumpled*
la frontière *the border*
frustrant(e) *frustrating*

G
gagner *to win*
une gamme *a range*
un garçon de café *waiter (in a coffee bar)*
garder *to keep*
garde la monnaie *to keep the change*
gâter *to spoil*
le gaz en bouteille *bottled gas*
la gazinière *a gas cooker*
la gêne *trouble; bother*
gêner *to embarrass someone*
un(e) généraliste *a general practitioner*
genre *type*
gentil(le) *kind*
les gestes (m) *hand / arm movements*
un gigot (d'agneau) *a leg of lamb*
global(e) *global*

un glouton *a glutton*
les gosses (m, f) *kids*
une gousse d'ail en chemise *a clove of garlic with its skin*
la graisse *(animal) fat*
le grand manitou *the big boss*
les grandes lignes *the major aspects*
les grandes surfaces *the large (often out-of-town) supermarkets*
les grappes (f) *(bunches of) grapes*
grossir *to put on weight*
un guerrier *a warrior*
une guitare accoustique *an acoustic guitar*

H
habitable *habitable*
haut-de-gamme *top of the range*
la Haute Savoie *the most northerly department in the French Alps*
l'Hébreu *the Hebrew language*
hélas *unfortunately*
les heures (f) d'ouverture *opening hours*
histoire de *just to*
hors des sentiers battus *off the beaten track*
hors saison *out of season*
l'humidité (f) *dampness*

I
il se fait tard *it is getting late*
l'image (f) de marque *brand image*
un imper(méable) *a raincoat*
inattendu(e) *unexpected*
incompatible *incompatible*
incontestablement *without doubt*
incorrigible *incorrigible*
incroyable *incredible*
indispensable *indispensable*
indisposer *to upset*
l'influence (f) *influence*
inspirant(e) *inspiring*
les intempéries (f) *bad weather*
en interne *in-house*

J

un jambon *a leg of ham*
le jardinage *gardening*
la jardinerie *a garden centre*
un jardinier *a gardener*
la jeunesse *youth*
je vous en prie *you're welcome*
la journée *the day(time)*
joindre l'utile à l'agréable *to mix business
    with pleasure*
jouer *to play*
un jour férié *a bank holiday*
le jour tombe *it gets dark*

L

le labourage *ploughing*
lâcher *to let go/release*
une lagune *a lagoon*
laid(e) *ugly*
laisser tomber *to drop*
les lames(m) *blades*
la langue écrite *the written language*
la langue maternelle *the mother-tongue*
la langue parlée *the spoken language*
les lasagnes (f) *lasagne*
un légume *a vegetable*
lesquels(m) *which ones*
la lessive *washing powder*
une lettre *a letter*
levant impôts *raising taxes*
un lido *a lido*
le linge *household linen*
la lingerie *women's underwear*
la lingua franca *the lingua franca*
la livraison *delivery*
livrer *to deliver*
le logement *housing*
un lopin de terre *a piece of ground*
une louche *a ladle*
louper *to miss*
un lutin *a gnome*

M

ma foi! *well!*
maigrir *to lose weight*
la main d'oeuvre *the labour*
la maison familiale *the family home*
un maître (m/f) *a master*
manger d'une façon saine *to eat in a
    healthy way*
la malbouffe *junk food*
un manque de *a lack of*
un maréchal *a marshal / field marshal*
marcher *to walk*
la marge bénéficiaire *the profit margin*
une marque *a brand*
marrant(e) *funny*
un match nul *a drawn game*
les matériaux (m) *materials*
une matière *a subject*
la matière grasse *fat*
mécontent(e) *unhappy*
un médicament *a medicine*
la médecine *medicine*
médiéval(e) *medieval*
mélodique *melodic*
un(e) mélomane *a music lover*
menacé(e) *threatened*
merci infiniment *thanks a million*
me semble-t-il *it seems to me*
les mesures (f) *the measurements*
mettre q.ch.en marche *to start*
mettre l'accent sur *to emphasise*
un meurtre *a murder*
le Midi *the South of France*
le miel *honey*
le / la mien/mienne *mine*
mijoter *to simmer*
mince! *drat / blast it!*
un mobile *a mobile telephone*
le mode d'emploi *the usage instructions*
le mode de vie *the lifestyle*
un modèle *a style, design*
modeste *modest*
modifier *to modify*
(de) moins en moins *less and less*
moitié-moitié *half-and-half*

montrer *to show*

un morceau *a musical piece*

mort(e) *dead/flat*

une motocyclette *a motorcycle*

mouillé(e) *damp*

un mouvement (musicale) *a movement*

un moyen de transport *a means of transport*

moyennant quoi *in return for which*

mugir *to roar / bellow*

les murs (m) *the walls*

N

navré(e) *sorry*

nettement *clearly; decidedly*

ni... ni *neither... nor*

n'importe quel(le) *any*

n'importe quoi *anything*

noir(e) *black*

noircir *to blacken*

la note de frais *the expense account*

une note salée *a stiff bill*

la nourriture *food*

nous revoilà *here we are again*

une nouveauté *something new*

nul part *nowhere*

nulle part *anywhere*

numérique *digital*

n'y voir pas d'inconvénient *to have no objections*

O

l'occasion (f) revée. *the perfect opportunity*

occupé(e) *busy*

les oeufs (m) en gelée *eggs in aspic*

on ne sait jamais *one never knows*

on se croirait...*you would think we were...*

un orchestre *an orchestra*

un ordinateur *a computer*

une ordonnance *a prescription*

l'orientation (f) *the direction in which something points*

oser *to dare*

oublier *to forget*

les outils (m) *tools*

les outils de jardinage *garden tools*

P

paf *drunk*

une pagaille *a mess / shambles*

une page web *a webpage*

les panais (m) *parsnips*

une pancarte *a sign*

papier peint (m) *wallpaper*

un parfum *a perfume*

une parfumerie *a perfume shop*

par hasard *by chance*

par rapport à *compared with*

parfois *sometimes*

Paris même *Paris itself*

parlant de quoi *talking of which*

parmi lesquels *amongst whom/which*

la part de marché *market share*

partager l'avis de quelqu'un à cent pour cent *to agree 100% with someone*

partout *everywhere*

pas forcément *not necessarily*

un passage (musicale) *a musical passage*

un passeport *a passport*

passer *to pass*

le pastis *an aniseed-based alcoholic drink*

la pâte *pasta*

une pâtisserie *a cake shop and a cake*

la patrie *the homeland*

le patron *the boss*

pauvre de toi! *poor you!*

un pays *a country*

le paysage *the countryside*

les pêcheurs (m) *fishermen*

peindre *to paint*

la peinture *paintwork*

perfectionner *to improve*

un périple *a journey*

pertinent(e) *relevant*

peser *to weigh*

la petite monnaie *small change*

les petits-pois (m) *peas*

une phalange *an army*

un phallocrate *a male chauvinist pig (m.c.p.)*
la pièce *each one; the room*
pierreux(se) *stony*
les pinceaux (m) *paintbrushes*
pire *worse*
le plafond *the ceiling*
planter *to plant*
le plat du jour *the dish of the day*
le plâtre *plaster*
pleurer *to cry*
ployer *to yield*
plus ou moins *more or less*
une P.M.E. *une petite ou moyenne enterprise (an S.M.E.)*
un poireau *a leek*
les poivrons (m) rouges *red peppers*
pommes de terre (f) à la vapeur *boiled potatoes*
un porcelet *a piglet*
un potager *a vegetable garden*
potelé(e) *chubby*
le potentiel *potential*
pour l'instant *for the moment*
poursuivre *to continue / to follow*
un pousse-café *a mixture of alcohol and coffee taken after a meal*
pratique *practical*
précis(e) *precise/exact*
préconiser *to recommend*
préférablement *preferably*
prendre *to take*
préoccuper *to preoccupy*
en principe *in principle*
prisé(e) *prized*
une prise *an electric socket*
les prix (m) catalogue *list prices*
le prix de demande *the asking price*
prix massacrés *knock-down prices*
les prodigalités (f) *extravagances*
la profondeur *the depth*
proposer *to offer*
un prospectus *a brochure*
prudent(e) *sensible*
P.S.G. *Paris Saint Germain*

puis *then*
puiser *to draw*
un puits miniature *a miniature well*
pulluler *to swarm*

Q

quand même *all the same*
que puis – je faire? *what can I do?*
quelle surprise! *what a surprise!*
quelque part *somewhere*
quelque soit *whatever*
question (f) de fric *it is a question of money*
quoi d'autre? *what else?*
quoi de neuf? *what is new?*

R

un rabais *a discount*
les racines (f) *the roots*
raconter *to tell*
un(e) radin(e) *a cheapskate*
la radio (graphie) *an x-ray*
un rapport *a report*
les ravages (f) *damage*
ravissant(e) *ravishing*
recevoir *to receive; to get*
la recherche *research*
en réclame *at a reduced price*
régaler *to treat*
regarder *to look*
un régime *a diet*
régulièrement *regularly*
remettre *to put back*
une remise *a reduction*
remonter *to go back to*
les remparts *fortified walls*
remplacer *to replace*
remplir *to fill*
rentrer bredouille *to come home empty-handed*
réparer *to repair*
repartir *to go back again; to grow again*
répondre (à) *to reply to*
reposer *to put down*

une représentation *a performance*
le réservoir *the tank*
respecter *to observe*
un responsable *a manager*
la restauration *the restoration*
un restaurant trois étoiles *a 3-star Michelin restaurant*
rester en bonne santé *to stay in good health*
un resto (fam) *a restaurant*
de retard *slow*
réussir *to make a success of*
un revendeur *a re-seller*
revenons à nos moutons *let us get back to the subject*
revoir *to see again*
le rez-de-chaussée *the ground floor*
les rideaux (m) *the curtains*
rien de sérieux *nothing serious*
rigoler *to laugh/to joke*
les rillettes (f) *a coarse, fatty pâté*
rimer *to go with*
rincer *to rinse*
le ris de veau *veal sweet breads*
une robe décolletée *a dress with a low neckline*
rose pâle *magnolia*
le royaume *the kingdom*
un rutabaga *a swede*

S

sain(e) *healthy*
saisir l'occasion *to seize the opportunity*
une salade *a lettuce*
la salle à manger *the dining room*
la salle de bain *the bathroom*
salut *hello / goodbye*
s'amuser *to enjoy oneself*
sanglant(e) *bloody*
les sans abri *homeless people*
la santé *health*
un(e) sarladais(e) *someone born in Sarlat*
s'arracher *to fight over*
sauter du coq à l'âne *to jump from one subject to another*

le saviez-vous? *did you know?*
savoir à quoi s'attendre *to know what to expect*
le scénario *the script*
se baigner *to bathe*
se casser la jambe *to break a leg*
un sèche-serviette *a heated towel rail*
s'éloigner de *to stray from*
s'embraser *to blaze/flare up*
s'entretenir de quelque chose *to talk over something*
s'évaporer *to evaporate*
s'impatienter *to become impatient*
s'inquiéter *to worry*
s'installer *to sit down*
se dégager *to clear*
se dépêcher *to hurry up*
se détacher *to come apart*
se droguer *to take drugs*
se faire une bouffe *to have a bite to eat*
un séjour *a stay*
se laisser emporter *to get carried away*
se libérer *to become available*
se marier à *to marry*
se mélanger *to mix up*
les semelles (f) *the soles (of shoes)*
se mettre en contact avec quelqu'un *to get in touch with someone*
se mettre l'eau à la bouche *to make one's mouth water*
se mettre le doigt dans l'oeil *to be entirely mistaken/to kid oneself*
se plaindre *to complain*
se présenter *to present oneself*
se rappeler *to recall*
se rendre compte *to realise*
se rendre parfaitement compte *to know full well*
se sentir *to feel*
se souvenir de *to remember*
se souvenir de quelqu'un *to remember somebody*
se surmener *to over work*
se taire *to be quiet*
se terminer *to finish*

sensible *sensitive*
sentir *to smell*
seul(e) *alone*
un siècle *a century*
une sieste *a nap*
siffler (fam) *to drink*
signaler *to indicate*
un sillon *a ploughed field*
les sites (m) *sights*
les sites religieux *religious sites*
un site web *a website*
le ski nautique *water skiing*
soi-disant *allegedly; ostensibly*
soit... soit *either... or*
le sol *the floor*
soldé(e) *in the sales*
sombre *dark*
sonner *to ring*
souffrir *to suffer*
soupçonner *to suspect*
souriant(e) *smiling*
un sous-titre *a sub-title*
souvent *often*
un strapontin *a folding seat*
une stratégie publicitaire *an advertising strategy*
stressant(e) *stressful*
sublime *sublime*
suggérer *to suggest*
suivre un régime *to be on a diet*
supplémentaire *in addition*
en supposant que *assuming that*
supposer *to suppose*
sur le champ *on the spot*
surfer sur Internet *to surf the internet*
une supposition *a supposition*
suspendre *to hang*
une symphonie *a symphony*

T

une tablette *a tablet computer*
tandis que *whereas*
tant pis *too bad*
taquiner *to tease*

un tas *a pile*
le tarif *the room price*
tel(le) quel(le) *as it is*
tellement *so much*
temporairement *temporarily*
de temps à autre *from time to time*
une tendance *a tendency / a trend*
tenir *to have/hold; to last; to stock*
tentant(e) *tempting*
terminer *to finish*
terrasser *to bring / strike down*
tolérer *to put up with*
tomber *to fall*
tomber amoureux(se) *to fall in love*
tomber dans les pommes *to faint*
un torchon *a tea towel*
un toubib (fam) *a doctor*
un tour *a turn*
une tour *a tower*
le tour de main *the skill*
un tournevis *a screwdriver*
tout à fait *exactly; absolutely*
tout d'abord *first of all*
de toute façon *all the same*
un tracteur *a tractor*
le train-train quotidien *the daily grind*
le tramway *the tramway*
les traîtres (m/f) *traitors*
travailler en collectivité *to work with others*
travailler sans relâche *to work with one's head to the grindstone*
les travaux (m) *the work(s)*
trébucher *to trip*
très bientôt *very soon*
les trésors (m) cachés *hidden treasures*
trier *to sort*
triste *sad*
trois fois rien *next to nothing*
trouver *to find*
trucs (m) salés *savoury things*
trucs sucrés *sweet things*
tu peux m'en croire! *believe you me!*
tu seras un ange *be an angel*
un tuyau d'arrosage *a garden hosepipe*

la T.V.A. *la taxe sur la valeur ajoutée, ie the VAT*

le type *the chap / bloke*

U

un ulcère *an ulcer*

les uns des autres *one from another*

V

les vacances (f) scolaires *school holidays*

les valises (f) *suitcases*

varié(e) *varied*

la vaisselle *crockery*

une vasque *a drinking bowl (for birds)*

va te faire cuire un oeuf! *get stuffed!*

un verre ballon *a balloon glass*

verser *to pour*

le vestibule *the hall*

la viande *meat*

la vigne *the vine plant*

vignoble *a vineyard*

vil(e) *vile*

une violoncelle *a cello*

une vis *a screw*

vis-à-vis *in relation to*

vivement les vacances! *roll on the holidays!*

vivre *to live*

v.o. *"version (f) originale" ie a film shown in its original language*

en voiture, Simone! *allons-y/let's go!*

le / la vôtre *yours*